WEDDING PROGRAM

Janet Lynn Gaines
and
John Paul DeMyer

~~~

So they are no longer two,
but one.
- Matthew 19:6 -

That nations, hearts, and homes may learn
that love does not so much mean to give
oneself to another
as for both lovers to give themselves
to that Passionless Passion,
Which is God.
- Fulton J. Sheen, 1951 -

~~~

Sunday, October 11, 1998
Five o' clock
The Shoreham Hotel
Washington, District of Columbia

A very special thank you from Janet and Paul
to both of our parents.
Somewhere in our youth or childhood,
we must have learned from you
how to do something good.

PRELUDE:

Canon in D   Pachelbel
Air on the G String   Bach
Simple Gifts   Traditional
Lasia Ch'io Pianga   Handel

ENTRANCE OF MOTHERS/LIGHTING OF CANDLES
Jesu, Joy of Man's Desiring   Bach

ENTRANCE OF MATRON OF HONOR/RING BEARER/FLOWER GIRL
Water Music - Air   Handel

PROCESSIONAL:

Trumpet Voluntary (Prince of Denmark's March)   Clarke

RITE OF MARRIAGE:

Opening Prayer   Father Dan Piekarski
Veil and Cord
First Reading - John 15:9-16   Laura Williamson
Second Reading - Ephesians 3:14-19   William J.F. DeMyer
Third Reading - Kahlil Gibran   Clare Marsch
Lighting of the Unity Candle
Exchange of Vows
Blessing and Exchange of Rings
Declaration of Marriage

This kind of certainty
comes but once in a lifetime.
- Robert J. Waller -

RECESSIONAL:

Spring - Four Seasons   Vivaldi

Let us love not in word or speech but in deed and truth.
- 1 John 3:18 -

WEDDING PARTY:

Matron of Honor Jacqueline Metzger Sister of the Bride
Best Men Thomas Mueller & Frederick Chin Friends of the Groom

USHERS:

Mark Metzger Brother in law of the Bride
Patrick Marsch Brother in law of the Groom
Stephen Williamson Brother in law of the Groom
Timothy Hodkiewicz Brother in law of the Groom

FLOWER GIRL:

Marissa Metzger Niece of the Bride

RING BEARER:

Andrew Williamson Nephew of the Groom

PARENTS:

Mr. and Mrs. Richard Bennett Gaines
Mr. and Mrs. William Francis DeMyer

VEIL AND CORD SPONSORS:

Dr. and Mrs. Robert W. Greenwood Uncle and Aunt of the Bride

CELEBRANT:

Father Daniel Piekarski

MUSIC:

Chamber Music - Con Brio
World Rhythms/Dance - Imani

~~~

And in the sweetness of friendship let there be laughter,
and sharing of pleasures.
For in the dew of little things the heart finds its morning
and is refreshed.
- Kahlil Gibran -
~~~

Give Us This Day

Gospel Reflections

Joseph V. Landy, S.J.

Tahanan Books

MANILA

All scripture quotations are from the
Catholic Book Company's edition of
The New American Bible (revised New Testament),
copyright 1970 and 1986, by the
Confraternity of Christian Doctrine, Washington, D.C.

First published in the Philippines by Tahanan Books
A division of Tahanan Pacific, Inc.
P.O. Box 9079
MCS Mailing Center
1299 Makati, Metro Manila
Philippines

Cover photograph by Jose Ma. Lorenzo Tan
Cover design by Reggie Arambulo
Printed in the Philippines by Island Graphics
1 3 5 4 2

National Library of the Philippines Cataloging-in-Publication Data

Recommended entry:

Landy, Joseph V.

Give us this day : gospel
reflections / by Joseph V. Landy.
- [Makati], Metro Manila : Tahanan
Books, c1994. -
392 p.

1. Bible - Liturgical lessons,
English. I. Title.

BS491.5 226.05'9921 1991 P942000016
ISBN 971-630-044-1

Contents

Foreword by James F. Donelan, S.J xi

The Gospel Reflections:

ADVENT SEASON

1st Sunday
A: "Stay Awake" 1
B: The Lord Is Coming 3
C: Daring to Think About Death. 5

2nd Sunday
A: The Advance Man 7
B: Mark's News Makes Good News 9
C: A Wash in the Waters of the Jordan 11

3rd Sunday
A: Is There a Semite in the House? 13
B: Identity Check 15
C: Simple Justice 17

4th Sunday
A: What's in a Name? 19
B: The Young Lady Who Out-Starred the Stars 21
C: A World Too Good to Be True? 23

CHRISTMAS SEASON

ABC: Vigil of Christmas
A Man Rightly Called Righteous 25

ABC: Christmas
Eve: The Night God Crashed into History 27
Dawn: Shepherds Far from Angelic 29
Day: A Prologue Worth Pondering 31

Sunday in Octave of Christmas: Holy Family
A: An Ordinary Family in a Humdrum Town 33
B: One Big Family 35
C: Growing Pains 37

ABC: Octave of Christmas: Solemnity of Mary
A Scandalous Title? 39

ABC: Epiphany
I: What the Magi Knew 41
II: They Came from the East 43
Baptism of the Lord
A: What Unholy Company He Kept! 45
B: When Ceremonies Count 47
C: "A Voice Came from Heaven" 49

ORDINARY TIME

2nd Sunday
A: A Lamb Led to Slaughter 51
B: Meeting the Man Who Will Change Their Lives 53
C: "The Beginning of His Signs" 55
3rd Sunday
A: An Ordinary Foursome 57
B: It All Started with Fish 59
C: All Eyes on the Pulpit 61
4th Sunday
A: Must a Christian Be a Wimp? 63
B: Spellbinder of Capernaum 65
C: A Near Lynching 67
5th Sunday
A: A Pinch of Salt, a Ray of Sunshine 69
B: A Night of Many Marvels 71
C: Peter's Mighty Catch 73
6th Sunday
A: The Bombshell He Dropped on the Mount 75
B: He Touches Us Too 77
C: Blessings No Money Can Buy 79
7th Sunday
A: How to Handle Scamps and Slobs 81
B: "He Is Blaspheming" 83
C: Turning the World's Wisdom Upside-Down 85
8th Sunday
A: What's the Use of Worrying? 87
B: Second Thoughts About Fasting 89
C: A Few Beads on a String 91
9th Sunday
A: The Lesson of Ruby Towers 93
B: Keeping the Sabbath Holy 95
C: The Good Roman Soldier 97

LENT SEASON

1st Sunday
A: Satan's Wily Traps 99
B: Refreshment in the Desert 101
C: Who's *Not* Afraid of the Big Bad Imp? 103
2nd Sunday
A: Are We Listening? 105
B: "It Is Good that We Are Here!" 107
C: Words Overheard on the Mountain 109
3rd Sunday
A: He Just Asked for a Drink of Water 111
B: Cracking the Whip in the Temple 113
C: "If You Do Not Repent..." 115
4th Sunday
A: Washing in the Pool of Siloam 117
B: The Faith that Brings Eternal Life 119
C: Who Gets Top Billing? 121
5th Sunday
A: Jesus Wept 123
B: "If It Dies, It Produces Much Fruit" 125
C: When Mercy and Misery Met 127
Palm Sunday:
A: Conduct Wildly Out of Character 129
B: A Wilful Act of Defiance 131
C: A Victim in Command to the End 133

EASTER SEASON

Easter Vigil
A: Strange Doings at Daybreak 135
B: A Morning Chock-full of Surprises 137
C: The Empty Tomb 139
ABC: Easter
Morning:
I: Foot-Race at Dawn 141
II: A Morning to Remember 143
Afternoon:
Disillusionment at Emmaus 145
ABC: 2 Easter
I: No Wonder He Had His Doubts 147
II: The Peace that Comes with a Price 149

3 Easter
A: Jesus Conducts a Bible Class 151
B: Why He Rose from the Dead 153
C: Light Brunch for Eight by the Lakeside 155
4 Easter
A: The Enemies at Our Gate 157
B: What Every Pastor Should Know 159
C: One with His Father 161
5 Easter
A: The Monstrous Claim Jesus Made 163
B: Keeping in Touch 165
C: "See How They Love One Another!" 167
6 Easter
A: The Advocate 169
B: Friends of the Lord 171
C: God Is Not Silent 173
Ascension
A: A Quiet Leave-Taking 175
B: "Taken Up into Heaven" 177
C: Great Joy After Losing Their Lord 179
7 Easter
A: A Priest's Brief Prayer After Dinner 181
B: The Winning Side 183
C: Staying Together 185
ABC: Pentecost: Vigil Mass
Living Water, Real Spirit 187
ABC: Pentecost
I: We're All on Stage for Act Three 189
II: The Breath that Turned into a Tornado 191

ORDINARY TIME

Trinity
A: More Real than the Air We Breathe 193
B: "Until the End of the Age" 195
C: The Relevance of the Irrelevant 197
Corpus Christi
A: A Congregation in Uproar 199
B: Words that Do What They Say 201
C: Pilgrims Hungry for the Lord 203
10 Ordinary
A: Party-Poopers 205
B: "He Is Out of His Mind" 207
C: A Mother's Tears 209

11 Ordinary
A: Fields Still Ready for Harvest 211
B: Two Basic Lessons in Agriculture 213
C: The Party-Crasher 215
12 Ordinary
A: The Smile on the Face of the Martyrs 217
B: "Mayday!" 219
C: The Price His Followers Must Pay 221
13 Ordinary
A: What Is Different in the Demands of Jesus 223
B: "She Should Be Given Something to Eat" 225
C: A Rebuke for Two of His Finest 227
14 Ordinary
A: What the Wise and Learned Never Learned 229
B: The Harm Our Tongues Can Do 231
C: Lambs Among Wolves 233
15 Ordinary
A: The Sower and His Soil 235
B: Baggage Check 237
C: Only the Samaritan Stopped 239
16 Ordinary
A: "Let Them Grow Together Until Harvest" 241
B: A Holiday Wrecked 243
C: The Hostess Who Missed the Point 245
17 Ordinary
A: The Treasure, the Pearl, and the Net 247
B: Picnic to Remember 249
C: Our Daddy? 251
18 Ordinary
A: A Very Banal Miracle 253
B: The Bread of Life 255
C: How Rich Fools Die 257
19 Ordinary
A: "Tossed About by the Waves" 259
B: "Stop Murmuring" 261
C: The Man at the Door 263
20 Ordinary
A: The Woman Who Wouldn't Take No 265
B: He Will Raise Us on the Last Day 267
C: Peace at Any Price? 269
21 Ordinary
A: The Rock 271
B: "Such a Silly Religion!" 273
C: The Narrow Gate 275

22 Ordinary
A: Peter Puts Jesus Straight 277
B: Lip Service 279
C: Dining Out with Pharisees 281
23 Ordinary
A: When Christian Offends Christian 283
B: Why All this Rigmarole? 285
C: A Very Christian Kind of Hatred 287
24 Ordinary
A: How Often Forgive? 289
B: The Meaning of "Messiah" 291
C: "This Man Welcomes Sinners" 293
25 Ordinary
A: Unfair! 295
B: Who Is the Greatest? 297
C: Serving Two Masters 299
26 Ordinary
A: Two Very Different Sons 301
B: Jesus Speaks Out on Tolerance 303
C: A Lazarus at Our Door? 305
27 Ordinary
A: Long Shot 307
B: Marriage the Way God Made It 309
C: The Mustard Seed 311
28 Ordinary
A: Fuss Over a Wedding Garment 313
B: Meet the Man Who Has Everything 315
C: Saying Thanks to God 317
29 Ordinary
A: Dual Citizenship 319
B: Who's on First? 321
C: "Pray Always" 323
30 Ordinary
A: The Love of God Comes First 325
B: He Called Him "Rabboni" 327
C: A Flawed Prayer 329
31 Ordinary
A: "But Do Not Follow Their Example" 331
B: Love God and Do as You Please 333
C: Jesus Invites Himself to the House of a Sinner 335
32 Ordinary
A: Waiting for the Groom 337
B: Woe for the Scribes, Praise for the Widow 339
C: All Are Alive to God 341

33 Ordinary
A: God Wants a Return on His Investment 343
B: The Christian View of History 345
C: "They Will Persecute You" 347
Christ the King
A: The Last Surprise 349
B: In Pilate's Chambers 351
C: Acting Like a King 353
February 2: Presentation
A Light to the Gentiles 355
February 19: Saint Joseph
The Guardian 357
March 15: The Annunciation
She Started It All 359
March 24: The Birth of John the Baptist
"John Is His Name" 361
June 29: Peter and Paul
An Odd Couple 363
August 15: The Assumption
We Are All Called to Share Her Glory 365
September 14: Triumph of the Cross
A Triumph? 367
November 1: All Saints
The Whole Crowd of Them 369
November 2: All Souls
Where "Foul Crimes...Are Burnt and Purged Away" 371
November 9: Dedication of John Lateran
God's House Is Our House 373
December 8: Immaculate Conception
Our Solitary Boast 375

Foreword

I first met Joe Landy on June 21st, 1941, at a seminary of the Jesuits called St. Andrew, located along the Old Coast Road going from New York to Boston. Joe walked through the door that day and we volunteered to enter the Society of Jesus together. We met by accident. We both happened to turn up that hour. I think I was late. I was trying to stay in the world as long as I could.

From the beginning Joe was someone who would attract your attention. He was about three years younger than I, which would have made him about seventeen years old. A very young age to enter the Society of Jesus. His total character was that of a holy person, prepared to dedicate his life completely to the work of God. He always had the air of a man on a mission.

These impressions of Joe Landy are derived from close personal contact over the last forty years. In conversation with him you would discover rather quickly that he has very definite opinions which he is not afraid to proclaim loud and strong. His mind acts so quickly. One of his tutors at Oxford once said that Joe has a mind like a steel trap. That's what makes him difficult, in a way, because he suffers fools not happily. But he isn't intellectually arrogant.

Joe's book *Give Us This Day* is a collection of reflections on the Sunday gospels. The book includes selections from A,B, and C liturgical years covering an entire year. In fact, these reflections are a compilation of Joe's homilies. When we were together in Oxford and at the Ateneo de Manila I would make it a point to be in the church or chapel if he was preaching. I remember that his voice was always strong; his argument even stronger. He was a hit with the US troops in the air force bases of England when he served as temporary chaplain. The experience brought him into close contact with the troops. I still enjoy reading his homilies, which would be an indication of how successful they are. I've read *many* homilies, but I still like to take time out to read Joe's.

If it were possible to write a book that would appear in Catholic homes throughout the nation, 52 times in the year, this is the book you are looking for. Here you have a man who can bring into those 52 Sundays such a varied experience, more than many other people whose books I have read. Joe brings a reservoir of experiences and he puts these across in plain language. People who have read the book normally remark on its clarity. I agree. In this book you will find good, clear, and well-structured writing. Joe is very logical and writes with a certain simplicity that you might not expect to find in a book of this kind.

The appeal of this book is very wide. It is not an esoteric religious book. It's really downright, basic stuff. Not much for the mysteries. It will help people out there to understand what God and the Holy Spirit is trying to teach. He is the instrument of the Spirit. Joe's rhetoric is intellectually and emotionally compelling. The reader will gain knowledge, inspiration, and answers to their questions.

I also think that if every rectory in the country had a copy of Joe Landy's book, on the common room desk, it would have wide influence. It would do a lot of good. It might even provide a welcome break for those in search of new material for their worn-out sermons. Normally, in the old days the homily was, strictly speaking, a sort of biographical sketch of some holy person. That's what *homily* means in Greek; it's a reflection on somebody. But today, the homily gives the priest the opportunity to comment on the gospel. It's his job to make the man and woman in the pew understand what Christ is saying in the same aspect. That's the function of the homily and if it does that, then it has succeeded. And if the priest wants to know if he has a good homily, he only has to look at the people to know whether or not he's caught them.

One would be hard-pressed to find a better description of Father Joseph Landy that that of Geoffrey Chaucer's model of the Oxford Don: "Gladly would he learn and gladly would he teach."

If I had to choose someone to be my champion, Joe Landy would be up there. He is a kind fellow. Whenever I needed any help I knew that I could count on Joe. Perhaps through this book, you will learn to count on him.

—**James F. Donelan, S.J.**
Manila, Philippines

Give Us This Day

"Stay Awake"

First Sunday of Advent.
A: Mt. 24: 37-44.

An old fable describes how three apprentice devils prepared for their first journey to earth. Each spent long hours trying to concoct a lie big enough to trap human beings into joining their cause. Finally they presented themselves to Satan, prince of devils and father of lies, to get approval for their schemes.

"I will tell them there is no sin," said the first. "That will not work," chided Satan. "Their TV and tabloids carry little else but murder, mayhem, and rape. Their consciences speak louder than you can. They know in their hearts these are sins."

"I will tell them there is no punishment for sin," said the second. "You may trick a few with that," conceded Satan. "But not all humans are fools. Most realize that a law without teeth is no law at all. Why would a just God prepare the same hereafter for the evil as for the good?"

"I will tell them there is no hurry," said the third. "Splendid!" cried the Great Deceiver. "Keep them putting off the day of reform and you've caught them in our net. As long as they remain napping and unprepared, they are ours."

It is only a fable, but a wise one. It makes the same point Jesus makes at the close of this gospel, when he implores us to stay awake. We are always in danger of falling asleep, telling ourselves not to hurry, that there will always be a tomorrow.

Will there? Death can come suddenly, without a whisper of warning. Jesus recalls those who lived in the time of Noah, little suspecting a storm was approaching. Right up to the day the torrents began, they carried on business as usual.

We have no need to hark back to Noah's time to know how suddenly natural calamities can strike. Our own days have had their share of flash floods, tornadoes, and earthquakes. We have man-made disasters as well, just as lethal and unpredictable. Think of the random and mindless violence that kills every day in our most "civilized" cities, the carnage caused by ethnic cleansing and tribal strife. Few of their victims have warning.

Death can be capricious, too. Jesus reminds us how it can strike one worker and spare the partner standing alongside. The wrecks on our highways often carry the same message. Out of a smashed car a lone survivor may emerge unscathed, while the fellow passengers remain inside, fatally crushed.

The gospel passage is from Matthew's account of the last discourse of Jesus, where his primary concern is not our individual deaths, but the death of the visible universe. When that day comes Jesus will pass judgment on the whole of human history. That he will do so is a key truth of our Christian faith. Jesus spoke of it often. Our Creed declares, "He will come again in glory to judge the living and the dead." When exactly he will come and doomsday dawn, however, Jesus did not reveal, saying only that "no one knows" that day and hour *(Mt. 24:36)*. That is why we must always be prepared.

The lesson we should derive from thinking about the second coming of Jesus is extremely personal. On the last day he will pronounce judgment, not just on the collective history of humanity, but on every individual who ever lived. In another passage of Matthew Jesus paints an imaginative picture of how he will separate the sheep from the goats, placing those destined for bliss on the right, those for damnation on the left. In doing so he will make public the verdicts he has already passed on individuals in the instant after their death. Our entire life on earth, evil deeds as well as good, will supply the script for that final separation.

You may wonder why the Church chooses this gospel for the first Sunday of Advent. Is not Advent supposed to be a joyous season, a time when we prepare to celebrate the first coming of Jesus? Being reminded of his second coming and final judgment hardly seems a good way to get in the Christmas mood.

But it is. The prospect of Jesus returning to judge the world ought not provoke fits of panic. The saints have always looked forward to his Second Coming with longing. The final action of Jesus will be to welcome huge armies of the just into eternal life. That will be the final scene in the drama of Christianity, the goal for which he was born in a manger.

Imagine learning that the Christmas we are approaching will be the actual day of the Second Coming, that before it is over we will hear Jesus pronounce judgment on the world and on ourselves. Think of how earnestly we would prepare for the day, how carefully try to scrape away our least attachment to evil. If we spend the days between now and Christmas doing just that, we will be in the perfect mood to celebrate Christmas.

THE LORD IS COMING

First Sunday of Advent.
B: Mk. 13: 33-37.

❖❖❖

Long before anyone decorated a Christmas tree or heard about Santa Claus, the Church had the season of Advent. From at least the fifth century, the weeks before Christmas have been a time for special prayers and Scripture readings at Mass, all pointing to the birth of the Christ Child at Bethlehem. Like the overture of an opera or the parade that opens a circus, this season aims to put us in the right mood.

Four weeks may seem like a lot of time to spend generating the right mood for a single holy day. It is less time, however, than some merchants spend stirring up enthusiasm for the holiday they still call Christmas. And that is all Christmas means to many people today—a holiday of giving and getting, fun and feasting. It has no more religious significance than the mid-winter revels celebrated by the pagans of ancient Rome.

Precisely because the pagans of today are so loud in their preparations for the biggest spending splurge of the year, many of us find it hard to concentrate on what actually happened at Bethlehem. How can we drown out the hoopla of a commercialized Christmas and fix our attention on its original meaning?

Advent is the Church's way of helping us do that. "Put Christ back in Christmas" is a slogan we have heard so often it sounds trite. But it expresses more succinctly than most Sunday homilies on the subject the purpose of Advent. We want to restore the word *holiday* to its original meaning of *holy day*. Without forfeiting an ounce of its traditional merriment (remember that holiness and merriment are not enemies, but old allies), Christmas should be one of the holiest days of the year. To make sure it will be just that, four weeks of putting ourselves into the mood are hardly too many.

This reading, however, raises a serious question. Granted that the purpose of Advent is to prepare us to commemorate the birth of Jesus, the most joyful event in history, why does the Church select for the gospel a passage that seems wildly out of tune with that purpose? Here we have words Jesus spoke to his apostles shortly before he died. Instead of cheer, they contain a stern warning. How can so grim a gospel get us in the mood for Christmas? What kind of an overture is this?

The servants in the parable are cautioned about the awful consequences if they are caught napping. Their master may return at any hour of the day or night. The thrust of the parable is clear. None of us knows when the world will end or when we ourselves will breathe our last. Jesus may come at any time. We must always be on guard; we may face judgment tomorrow.

The reason the Church chooses this reading for this first Sunday of Advent can be found in the word "Advent" itself. It means a coming, an arrival, an entry. When we speak of the coming of Jesus we are usually referring to his coming as an infant in the manger, the event we celebrate on Christmas. But actually we can speak of three comings of Christ. Like Scrooge's Christmas ghosts, they are past, present, and future.

Jesus Christ *came* into the world when he was born at Bethlehem; he still *comes,* especially through the sacraments, to those who are willing to open their souls to him; and he *will come* on the last day to pass judgment on all human history. Today's reading reminds us that we will not be ready to celebrate his past coming at Bethlehem or to welcome his present coming into our souls through prayer and the sacraments unless we are ready to face his final judgment. Christmas day will be the holy day it should be only if we prepare for it as we would if we knew it was to be our last day on earth.

In other words, let us not sentimentalize Christmas. I have said the purpose of the season is to put us in the right mood. But the right mood is not just the warm feeling we get when we listen to Crosby croon about a white Christmas or hear carols tell how Jesus was born a homeless infant in a cave. The only proper way to celebrate the birth of Jesus into this world is by welcoming the reality of Jesus into our souls.

Attending Mass on Christmas without receiving the Eucharist is like going to the best restaurant in town on Christmas and munching on a toothpick while watching others down a hearty meal. All Catholics should try to receive the Eucharist on Christmas. The weeks of Advent should be spent getting ready.

We will be truly ready to meet Jesus in the Eucharist only if we are ready to face his judgment. Today's gospel asks us to give some thought to that judgment. To put Christ back into Christmas we must put some soul-searching, best done through the sacrament of Penance, into Advent. Only then will the biggest holiday of the year be the holy day it was meant to be.

DARING TO THINK ABOUT DEATH

First Sunday of Advent.
C: Lk. 21: 25-28; 34-36.

At first sight this passage from Luke seems wildly inappropriate for the season. Most people would expect a message of joy, preparing us for what we will celebrate four weeks from now, the good news of the birth of Jesus at Bethlehem. Instead we are told of the panic and confusion that will grip mankind at the end of time and how we must watch and pray if we hope to escape destruction. Jesus gave this warning near the close of his own life, during words he spoke to his disciples shortly before his capture and execution. It looks like a good text for us to ponder at the opening of Lent. Why does the Church choose it for consideration on the first Sunday of Advent?

Here Jesus predicts a cosmic upheaval on the last day, but the details he gives are vague. All we are told is that the sun, moon, and stars will be disturbed and the ocean turned into a roaring chaos. He has no need to paint a more detailed picture, for his purpose is not to terrify his followers. Others may go shrieking through the streets and die of fright when the universe starts falling apart, but Jesus wants his people to be made of sterner stuff. When the trumpet sounds for judgment day, they are to stand erect and raise their heads.

Why? Because their "redemption is at hand." The last stroke of time will be the first stroke of eternity. At the same instant that the flags of nations become obsolete, the flag of Christ's kingdom will be hoisted over all creation. Then mankind "will see the Son of Man coming in a cloud with power and great glory."

Although for some this will be a day of horror, for others it will be the consummation towards which all history has been moving. Here is how the author of *Revelation* describes it: "Then I saw a new heaven and a new earth.... I heard a loud voice from the throne saying, 'Behold, God's dwelling is with the human race.... He will wipe every tear from their eyes, and there shall be no more death or mourning, wailing or pain, for the old order has passed away' " *(21: 1-4).*

What we have in this passage, then, is the Christian view of history. Years do not follow years or centuries follow centuries in an aimless sequence, like leaves swirling through windy forests. Mankind has a goal, which will be reached only when the new heaven and the new earth are born. The march of human history will not come to a halt when our solar clock stops ticking. Our collective destiny is beyond the grave and eternal.

These are words worth pondering as we prepare for Christmas, for we miss the whole point of the coming of Jesus at Bethlehem if we fail to see it as a prelude to his coming on the last day to inaugurate his heavenly kingdom. The angel who visited Mary at Bethlehem saw the connection, telling her that the child soon to be born of her was destined to rule over a kingdom that would last forever *(Lk. 1: 23)*. Thinking about his second coming, then, is a way of getting ready to celebrate his first.

That there will be a last day and a final judgment on all mankind is certain. Every time we recite the Creed we say, "He will come again in glory to judge the living and the dead." And one of the proclamations after the consecration at Mass is "Christ has died, Christ has risen, *Christ will come again.*" Despite these clear affirmations, however, one feels that the second coming of Jesus does not loom high in the consciousness of the average Catholic today. In this respect we differ markedly from our medieval ancestors. Their literature reveals them as people who were constantly aware of their brittle humanity and the inevitability of a final reckoning.

No one knows when the reckoning will come, the day or hour. We all get a laugh from cartoons that depict bearded prophets parading through our streets with banners proclaiming the imminent end of our world. Perhaps we forget that except for their claim to know exactly when doomsday will dawn, these zealots have a point, the same point Jesus makes in this passage. Assuredly there will be a last judgment. We will all be present as active participators. It behooves us always to be ready.

Jesus minces no words in telling us how to be ready. His words are small comfort to those who are "drowsy from carousing and drunkenness and the anxieties of daily life." But for all of us, saints as well as sinners, his prescription is the same: "Be vigilant at all times and pray." This is a good slogan for Advent. The best way of preparing ourselves to celebrate the first coming of Jesus is by rehearsing for his second.

On Christmas, just as on the day of the second coming of Jesus, we want to stand erect and raise our heads. The child born in a manger will one day come again. He is the Lord of history, who will lead his people to "a new heaven and a new earth."

THE ADVANCE MAN

Second Sunday of Advent.
A: Mt. 3: 1-12.

Saints are not always polished people. We honor them for holiness, not manners or apparel. If heaven were to empty out and all its inhabitants return to earth today, many would probably be denied admittance to any country club worth its annual fee. Some might be out of place at a parish social.

The earliest and most notorious instance of sainthood in rags is the central figure of this gospel passage, John the Baptist. Since he is now one of the most revered saints in the Christian calendar, we easily forget how disreputable he must have appeared to his contemporaries. After leaving his home at an early age, he settled in the sweltering expanse of the Palestinian desert. There, far from the commerce of the towns and the carousings of worldlings, he gave his full attention to God. That he possibly cut an odd and unsavory figure in the eyes of fellow Israelites was of no concern to him.

His food was whatever meager nourishment the wasteland offered, such desert delicacies as locusts and wild honey. His wardrobe was of camel's hair, apparel fit for a savage. We ought not sanitize John. See him as he was: an unwashed recluse, neighbor to wolves and hyenas, bedfellow of desert rats.

After reaching manhood, John turned to preaching. Once he did, he was a firebrand. Had he not been overshadowed by Jesus, history would probably record him as the most powerful religious force in first century Palestine. "Jerusalem, all Judea, and the whole region around the Jordan" flocked to him. He had left his home and gone to the desert to listen to God. Now others left their business and swarmed to the desert to listen to him.

John was no diplomat. This we see in his manner of rebuking some Pharisees and Sadducees among his listeners. These would soon be venting their fury against the preaching of Jesus. Here we learn that they had at least as much reason to feel offended by John. One wonders why they were there at all, among the peasants lining up to be washed clean of their sins by John's baptism. Probably their only purpose was to scout this freelance preacher, get some idea of how great a threat he posed to their own positions as religious leaders in Israel.

What they actually got was a tongue-lashing they would never forget. John could have interpreted their presence among his listeners as evidence that important people were at last taking his warnings seriously. Here was his chance to forge an alliance with the religious establishment in Israel. That would have been diplomacy, but John would have none of it. Instead, he lambasted them, fumed that they were a "brood of vipers." Such words were an unpardonable insult to men accustomed to deference from people they considered their inferiors.

The grounds for John's outrage were clear. First, he was incensed at the hypocrisy of the Pharisees and Sadducees. Their presence among penitents at the Jordan was a sham, for in their hearts they felt sure they had nothing to repent of. John wanted proof. "Produce good fruit as evidence of your repentance."

Next, John chided them for their complacency, their presuming that because they were children of Abraham, the God of Abraham must be on their side. Their very genes, they thought, guaranteed their salvation. John flatly disagreed. "Do not presume to say yourselves, 'We have Abraham as our father.' "

Finally, he exposed the sterility of their religious spirit, comparing them to barren trees. Despite their professed piety, the Israelites were not brought closer to God by their presence. John warned of divine retribution. "Every tree that does not bear good fruit will be cut down and thrown into the fire."

This is a disturbing gospel. Genuine prophets make it their business to disturb, puncturing the pretense of those who settle for a merely comfortable religion. In contrast to the austere prophet of the desert, the Pharisees and Sadducees lived in comfort. They had lived that way for so long they were unaware of how far they had drifted from God.

Why does the Church give us this gospel on the second Sunday of Advent? Possibly because it wants to disturb us the way John did the Pharisees. As we prepare to celebrate the birth of Jesus, we recall how John prepared his listeners for the Messiah, making straight the Messiah's path by disturbing the comfortable.

We can put some disturbing questions to ourselves. Do we delude ourselves with the notion that we have no need for reform? Do we flatter ourselves that because we are baptized our salvation is assured? How much good fruit do we produce? How much more Christian are our surroundings because of our presence?

Lord, help us to listen to this ragged man of the desert. Disturb us. Preserve us from being merely comfortable Christians.

MARK'S NEWS MAKES GOOD NEWS

Second Sunday of Advent.
B: Mk. 1: 1-8.

The best guess of biblical scholars is that Mark composed his account of the doings of Jesus some three decades after Jesus ascended to his Father. If so, although always placed second among the four gospels, Mark's was actually the first to exist in its present form. It is also the shortest, the least polished in style, the most loaded with incidental details. Despite—or perhaps because of—these "primitive" traits, many find Mark's gospel their favorite. It is fresher than the other three, discernibly closer to the events it describes.

As a boy growing up in Jerusalem Mark may well have caught glimpses of Jesus, but he was too young ever to have been one of his disciples. Thus he probably never saw Jesus place his healing hands on the sick, never sat at his feet to listen as he unfolded the secrets of God's kingdom. No other gospel, however, has a stronger "eyewitness" flavor. Mark has the knack of the seasoned journalist. He writes as one who has been there.

The reason is that Mark learned most of what he knew about Jesus from the apostle Peter, whose disciple he was. Some have even suggested that Mark's gospel could as well be called the gospel according to Peter. This overstates the case, but not by much. In some passages we can almost detect Peter's voice.

This reading contains the first eight verses of Mark's first chapter. Unlike John, he does not treat us to an elaborate and theologically rich prologue. And unlike Matthew and Luke, he is stone silent about the birth and infancy of Jesus.

Instead, he starts abruptly at the banks of the Jordan, near the edge of the desert. A preacher named John dwells there, the first authentic prophet to appear in Israel for five hundred years. Gathered around him, awaiting his baptism, is a crowd of pilgrims from all over Palestine. From the fourth gospel we know that Peter is part of that crowd, along with some fellow fishermen from Galilee. Present also, although Mark does not tell us so yet, is a carpenter from Nazareth named Jesus.

These eight opening verses are the nearest thing Mark has to a prologue. Brief though they are, they do a prologue's job. In them are hints of the two great themes his gospel will develop, that Jesus is good news and that Jesus means change.

In his very first sentence Mark calls his work a "gospel," a word meaning good news. As the story of Jesus unfolds, much will happen to him that will strike the reader as far from good. The custodians of the Jewish religion will greet him, first with indifference, then suspicion, and finally outright hostility. Still, Mark never forgets that the news he is telling is good. The reason this is so he also states in his first sentence, where he identifies Jesus as the Son of God.

This is the first of only two places in Mark where Jesus is given this title. The second occurs near the end, when the centurion in charge of his execution, seeing Jesus breathe his last, exclaims, "Truly this man was the Son of God!" *(15: 39)*.

Thus at the opening and close of his gospel Mark tells why his news is good. Peter did not follow a man who made a noise for a while as a doer of good and then failed. The man he followed was the Son of God who came into the world to save the world and by his death succeeded. What news could be better?

But this good news, the rest of the prologue makes clear, is not necessarily pleasing news. John, the man sent by God to straighten the path for the coming of Jesus, made sure his listeners knew that. They were to prepare for the Messiah, the one "mightier than I," by submitting to John's baptism. And this baptism was not just an innocuous ceremonial bath. John called it a baptism of repentance *(metanoia)*, a word meaning internal change. And such change is not always pleasing.

True *metanoia* demands more than just regret for the past. Anyone who wakes up with a hangover or languishes in prison can wish the past undone. *Metanoia* means doing something about the past, making as sure as possible it is not repeated. What John looks for in those who seek his baptism are signs of such conversion, a genuine resolve to change. That means abandoning long-festering pagan attitudes, launching an all-out assault on old habits of selfishness, sensuality, pride, and greed.

The point Mark's gospel makes is not just that we are all candidates for change. We have need of Mark to tell us that. The point is rather that change is possible. It is so because, as John says, Jesus cleanses us, not just with water, but with his holy Spirit. And his Spirit bestows power to change.

The good news is that Jesus, Son of God, came into the world. As we approach the celebration of his coming, we should open our souls to him. Cleansed with his Spirit, we can change.

A Wash in the Waters of the Jordan

Second Sunday of Advent.
C: Lk. 3: 1-6.

❖ ❖ ❖

John the Baptist's mission in life was determined even before he was born. In the first chapter of his gospel Luke tells us that an angel appeared one day to John's father and told him his wife would soon give birth to a son whose task would be to "prepare a people fit for the Lord" *(17)*. John's training for this role began early. Unlike Jesus, who had a normal upbringing at Nazareth, John left home while still a youth and went off to be a hermit in the desert. Only after reaching manhood did he hear the call of God and begin to preach.

Luke is at pains to tell who the civil and religious leaders were when John launched his career. On the basis of the names he gives, historians place the year at 27 or 28. These names tell a lot about the moral climate of the times. Herod Antipas was the corrupt son of Herod the Great, himself famed for the slaughter of the Holy Innocents soon after Jesus was born. Herod Antipas was to imprison and then behead John, whose denunciations of sin struck too close to home. It was also this Herod and his court who ridiculed Jesus a few hours before the crucifixion.

The name of Pontius Pilate is inscribed forever in history's hall of infamy as the man who pronounced Jesus guiltless of any crime and in almost the same breath sentenced him to death. Annas and Caiaphas, high priests in Jerusalem, were among those who handed Jesus over to Pilate. In short, this was an age of godless rulers. No age has ever been kind to those who preach reform, but John and Jesus lived in a particularly unkind age.

What of the people to whom John preached? Many Jews of the time were firm in the certitude that the Messiah would come soon. Mostly, however, they expected him to be a political leader who would turn their dreams of national glory into reality, creating an Israel that would lord it over its neighbors. Amid this atmosphere, many false Messiahs emerged, stirred up the masses for a while, then swiftly sank back into oblivion.

One of them set fire to Herod's palace and declared himself king; another plundered an armory in Galilee and staged a brief insurrection; a third actually established a short-lived rebel government; and there were more. None preached a genuine reform of morals or tried to restore a true sense of religion.

None, that is, until John, and he did not claim himself to be the Messiah but the one whose mission was to "prepare the way of the Lord, make straight his paths." His words made no strong impact on Herod and most of the religious leaders, but on the ordinary people of Palestine his effect was electric.

The gatherings John addressed in the wilderness must have had much in common with the revival meetings that were once popular in rural England and America. Crowds converged from every corner of Palestine to listen to John's blistering words and to make public confession of their sins. As a sign of their sincerity John had them undergo a ritual cleansing in the waters of the Jordan.

This ceremony Luke calls a "baptism of repentance," and it was John's trademark. The Greek word Luke uses for repentance is *metanoia*, and its precise nuance is important. Beating one's breast and shouting "I have sinned" is not enough. *Metanoia* is internal, producing new attitudes, new ways of thinking. For people whose religion had in many quarters degenerated into a fastidious attention to externals—ritual washings, rote prayers—John's *metanoia* was revolutionary, involving a total turn-around of one's interior. In no way more than this was he forerunner of the arch-revolutionary, Jesus Christ.

The repentance demanded by both John and Jesus dug into the deepest recesses of the heart, scorching away the residues of pride and pretense, leaving room only for the genuine service of God. Scripture and history provide many graphic instances of *metanoia*. Think of people like Matthew, Zacchaeus, Paul, Francis of Assisi, Ignatius Loyola—to mention just a few.

How much of our own religion is external, how much truly internalized? This is a good question to ponder in the weeks before Christmas. This is probably why the Church selects this reading for Advent, the season that prepares us for Christmas.

Christmas is the season of giving to others. But what do we feel interiorly about others? It is not enough to refrain from unkind speech and give to charities. Kind speech and generous giving can be merely the facade of proper manners, the conventions of good breeding. A Christian must learn to *think* kindly of others, to acknowledge interiorly that, as the passage John quotes from Isaiah says, the salvation of Jesus is meant for "*all* flesh," that is, for all mankind.

IS THERE A SEMITE IN THE HOUSE?

Third Sunday of Advent.
A: Mt. 11: 2-11.

❖❖❖

Some years ago I stood stranded on a roadside near the sea of Galilee, waiting for a bus that never came. A British lady, also touring Israel, soon joined me, and we began exchanging impressions of the land and its people.

"They actually believe they are God's chosen people," she confided, with a blend of astonishment and indignation.

"Well, I guess I am inclined to agree with them there."

"Oh, are you a Jew, or what?" She regarded me curiously.

"A Christian. Christians believe God chose the Jews."

Our theological dialogue was cut short by a jeep that stopped to give us a lift. I can still see her surprise on hearing my words. Many people would share that surprise. They forget, if they ever knew, how Christianity got its start; that as a Pope once put it, spiritually we Christians are all Semites.

The story of Christianity began some twenty centuries before the birth of Christ, with God's promise to make Abraham the source of blessings for "all the communities of the earth" *(Gen. 12:3)*. This was the first of many promises to Abraham and his posterity. Through Moses God told the Jews he had singled them out as his own people; to David he pledged a kingdom that would endure forever; and from among David's offspring the prophets declared that a Messiah would come and bring glory to Israel.

The hope of the Jews for the Messiah never wavered. In the centuries immediately before Christ it burned stronger than ever. Now a conquered people, many Israelites expected the Messiah to use military force to deliver them from foreign control and restore the throne of David. Instead of looking back to a Golden Age, as other nations did, the Jews looked ahead to a golden tomorrow. The Messiah who would usher in this age of peace and prosperity they called "the one who is to come."

That is the phrase John the Baptist uses in this gospel. John, who had once joyfully heralded Jesus as Messiah, was now languishing in Herod's prison. Immobilized, he awaited news of Jesus. John knew better than most how poorly the Israelites were living up to their calling—their rulers subservient to Rome, their morals corrupted by Pharisees, their worship defiled by Sadducees. John had expected Jesus to strike a mortal blow against these faithless children of Abraham. By this time, he had hoped, Jesus would be preparing to ascend David's throne.

But word reached him that Jesus was doing nothing of the sort. The works he performed were not the kind to topple tyrants like Herod. His followers were mostly powerless peasants. So John sent disciples to Jesus for an explanation. Was Jesus in fact "the one who is to come"? Must they look further?

The printed page leaves the tone of this interrogation uncertain. Some think John had actually revised his judgment about Jesus and now doubted his identity as Messiah. More probably the query does not express outright disbelief as much as impatience and frustration. If Jesus was the Messiah, why didn't he start acting like one? When will he get a move on? We have been waiting all these years. Must we wait longer?

To the modern reader the reply of Jesus seems strange, as though he were ducking the question. But to John and his disciples, who knew their Scripture, the meaning was unmistakable. Jesus was loosely quoting some Messianic passages from Isaiah *(26:19; 29:18-19; 35:5-6; 61:1).* And these describe exactly what Jesus had been doing throughout Galilee—restoring sight to the blind; healing the lame, the lepers, the deaf; raising the dead; above all, preaching to God's poor.

In other words, Jesus was the Messiah, but not the kind John had expected. His weapons were not swords and clubs. He would win his throne through compassion, healing, and love.

This gospel is a good selection for Advent. That her son was to be the Messiah God had revealed to Mary before Jesus was born when the angel told her that her child would sit on the throne of David and that his rule would last forever. But Mary soon saw how different his kingdom would be from what the Jews expected. His birth was not in a palace, but in a stable.

Simeon, who beheld the infant Jesus in the temple, mentioned another difference. Jesus fulfilled God's promise in a way no Israelite had dreamed. He came, not just for them, but for mankind, a "light for revelation to the Gentiles" *(Lk. 2: 32).*

God keeps his promises, often in ways we least expect; more wonderful ways, in fact. That explains the reply Jesus sent to John. Preaching the good news to the poor is far better than routing enemy armies. It also explains why we Christians call ourselves the people of God. *We* are the fulfillment of God's promise to the Israelites. Spiritually, we are all Semites.

IDENTITY CHECK

Third Sunday of Advent.
B: Jn. 1: 6-8; 19-28.

❖❖❖

If Jesus were alive today, would we recognize him? I do not mean the historical Jesus, the one who once walked the roads of Palestine and wore the flowing robes of biblical times. But if the eternal Word of God had become man only 30 years ago and now lived in our neighborhood, would we realize who he was?

Picture him as a young man, hale and in the prime of life. He is from a modest but decent home, attends church regularly, works with his father in a local shop. We exchange hellos when we pass on the street or meet in the supermarket, chat together at neighbors' parties. Would we recognize him as the Son of God or at least as a special emissary from the Almighty?

Certainly not. We have no sharper perception than had the people who lived with the historical Jesus at Nazareth or who were baptized with him at the Jordan, and they failed to recognize who he was. In this gospel John the Baptist remarks on this failure. "There is one among you whom you do not recognize."

Centuries earlier God promised to send the Jews a Messiah. In the decades before Christ several claimants to the title came forth, deluded zealots who waged brief uprisings against Rome, then swiftly faded into obscurity. But the hopes of the Jews remained alive, and the search for the Messiah went on. In this passage some religious leaders have come from Jerusalem to see if John the Baptist might be the genuine fulfillment of Jewish dreams. John replies emphatically that he is not.

But, he adds, the Messiah has come, in fact is already here, and no one has recognized him. Jesus has in fact lived with his identity undetected for some 30 years. Even now, as John is talking, he is mingling with the crowd that has come to the Jordan for John's baptism. But so far only John, to whom the Spirit has revealed the truth, truth, knows his identity.

Imagine now that the God-Man were living anonymously in our neighborhood and that we, like John, were in on the secret. Think of the deference we would show him, how promptly we would jump to his help. John thought himself unworthy to untie the straps on the sandals of Jesus. We would consider ourselves unworthy to help him change a tire or mow a lawn. What a generous response we would give if he rang our doorbell and asked us to support some charity or volunteer for some community project!

Now stop for a moment and reflect on this: those who take the words of Jesus seriously will treat *all* other human beings exactly as they would treat Jesus if they recognized him as their neighbor. We will never have the opportunity to show how we would have acted towards Jesus if we had lived alongside him in ancient Palestine. But we do not need it. God knows how we should have acted, for he sees how we treat the actual neighbors we do have. We must learn to recognize Jesus in them.

Seeing Jesus in our neighbor is no make-believe. Whatever we do to our neighbor he will count as done to himself. He told us so. Remember how he described the last judgment *(Mt. 25:31-46)?* Remember him saying he would consider the good or evil we do to others as done to himself?

But how hard it is to recognize Jesus in some people! What about the incorrigible criminals, wasted by drugs and hardened by vice? What about the politicians who line their pockets with money that belongs to the poor? What about the people whose eyes sparkle with delight when they learn some fellow human has been sentenced to life imprisonment or death by execution? The improvident drifters who ruin our cities and drain or public funds? The impossible boss we once had? Is it God's will that we treat these wrecks of humanity as we would Jesus Christ?

Yes. Precisely. Remember that when we try to treat people as we think Jesus would have treated them, we are possibly the nearest thing to Jesus ever to touch their lives. By our mercy and generosity we reflect what Jesus was to the sinners who flocked around him, what he has always been to ourselves.

When God joined the human race he became a blood relative of every member of our race. When Jesus died, he died to help all humans find their way to the Father. We should treat everyone as we would treat Christ because everyone belongs to Christ. We are all family.

During this season of Advent we prepare to celebrate Christ's coming into the world at Bethlehem. But that is an event of the past. We would all like to have been with the shepherds in the cave or among the neighbors of Jesus at Nazareth or part of the crowd at the River Jordan. We would like to have had the chance to behold the historical Jesus in the flesh. But we cannot turn the clock back. All we can do is look at our neighbors today. Do we recognize Jesus in them?

SIMPLE JUSTICE

Third Sunday of Advent.
C: Lk. 3: 10-18.

❖❖❖

Test your response to the following propositions:

1. A man should regard his lawful possessions not merely as his own but also as common property in the sense that they should accrue to the benefit not only of himself but of others.
2. If a person is in extreme necessity, he has the right to take from the riches of others what he himself needs.
3. Let all individuals and governments undertake a genuine sharing of their goods.

Marxist maxims? Creeping socialism? Discredited liberalism?

None of the above. All are authentic teachings of Catholicism, taken verbatim from "The Church and the Modern World," the pastoral constitution of the Second Vatican Council. Nor are they newfangled notions that were slipped into the document by some woolly-minded clerics who managed to infiltrate the Vatican. Far from being novel or subversive, these ideas are hoary with age and thoroughly reputable. Their roots are in the central tradition of Christian thought. Solid theologians like Aquinas and Suarez would have considered them truisms.

Their lineage goes back even further. This we see in today's passage from Luke, which gives samples of the instructions John the Baptist gave to the penitents who crowded around him at the River Jordan. The first question they put to him was the most fundamental in life: "What then should we do?" They were not asking John to map out the path to heroic sanctity, but just to state the bare minimum a person *must* do to be saved.

John was a plain-spoken prophet who made his points with no fuss. They must, he answered, take care of their neighbor in need. Let anyone with an excess of possessions (two coats, second helpings at meals) dip into them and give to those who lack the necessities of a decent life (no coat, no food). This is not an option, but a must. Our obligation to relieve the destitute takes precedence over our right to private property.

John simply stated what a person must do. In later centuries Christians spelled out the underlying reason or an obligation that was self-evident to him. The Second Vatican Council reasons in this way:

"God intended the earth and all that it contains for the use of every human being...The right to have a share of earthly goods sufficient for one's self and one's family belongs to everyone.... By its very nature, private property has a social quality deriving from the law of the communal purpose of earthly goods." The Council goes on to cite a saying of the early Christians: "Feed the man dying of hunger, because if you have not fed him you have killed him." Helping the poor, then, is not playing Lady Bountiful for the tots in the slums, but simple justice. It obliges all who are not themselves paupers.

Justice, moreover, imposes specific obligations on particular groups of people. John singled out two for special attention, tax collectors and soldiers.

Tax collectors in Palestine were notorious for over-taxing and then pocketing the difference. Soldiers often ran roughshod over civilians, extorting their money and then grumbling that they were themselves underpaid. John's precepts were simple. To the tax collectors: "Stop collecting more than what is prescribed." To the soldiers: "Do not practice extortion, do not falsely accuse anyone, and be satisfied with your wages."

Note that John did not denounce the very notion of taxation, as some Israelites did. His concern was that the tax collector be honest. Interestingly, the Church today is still concerned with taxation, but now it is the taxpayer rather than tax-collector who needs warning. The Second Vatican Council condemned the many who "do not hesitate to resort to various frauds and deceptions to avoid paying just taxes or other debts due to society."

John's counsel to the soldiers was similar. He did not condemn soldiering as such. If there is anything intrinsically sinful about the military profession, it escaped John's scrutiny. What concerned him was the arrogance of the soldiers he saw, the way they trampled on the rights and convenience of ordinary citizens. A soldier is a public servant. Let him not turn into a public hoodlum. The same is true for all public servants.

John's task was to prepare for Jesus; he was not himself the Messiah. Of virtue like that of the Good Samaritan he possibly knew nothing. But he did know that if he was to make the world ready for the Messiah, his preaching must emphasize justice. There, after all, is where people mostly go wrong. Injustice, both private and social, causes the direst griefs.

As we prepare to celebrate the coming of Jesus, the Just One, we should give some thought to justice in our lives. In any examination of conscience, that is a good place to begin.

WHAT'S IN A NAME?

Fourth Sunday of Advent.
A: Mt. 1: 18-24.

❖❖❖

"What's in a name?" asked Shakespeare's Juliet. The answer this fictional heroine looked for was "nothing," or at least nothing of importance. But the answer actual men and women have mostly given is "plenty." Parents often agonize over the name to give their child. Its name is the badge of identity it will wear through life. On a check or on a will a name can make the difference between prosperity and penury. Most people take legitimate pride in their name and guard it as their honor. Those who ridicule another's name court danger. Duels have been fought over lesser injuries. Yes, Juliet, names are important.

The name given to Jesus was so important that Joseph, who would normally have the last word in choosing it, had the choice taken out of his hands. God revealed in a dream that Mary's child must be named Jesus, Hebrew for "God saves." In ancient times parents chose a name to fit their dream of what the child would grow to be. The name of Jesus expressed, not a dream, but a reality, for it came from God himself. The whole reason the second Person of the Trinity entered our world and joined our human family was to save us from our sins.

Jesus saved us from our sins in two ways. First, he won God's pardon for sins of the past, paying the penalty for them by his death on the cross and thus making it possible for us to be friends with God again. Second, he won for us the grace to avoid sin in the future. The greatest saints need this grace. Without it no human could last for long without serious sin.

People sometimes ask where the name "Christ" came from and what it means. Strictly speaking it is not a name at all, but a title. It means "Anointed One" or "Messiah," the liberator whom God had promised to send to the Jews and for whose coming they all longed. In his famous declaration at Caesarea Philippi, Peter proclaimed Jesus was the Christ. But because the Israelites had such a warped notion of the Messiah, imagining he would be a warrior-king, Jesus usually shunned the title.

With his Resurrection Jesus revealed himself openly as a Messiah who had surpassed all expectations by putting eternal life within the reach, not just of the Israelites, but of all mankind. In light of what happened at Easter, the early Christians began to combine the name with the title—Jesus, the member of Joseph's family, and Christ, the divinely appointed Messiah.

Like most people, Jesus had more than one name. At times he was called "Son of David," the same salutation the angel used to address Joseph. Jesus was not Joseph's son by blood. But when Joseph took Mary as wife, he became the legal father of the son she bore, making Jesus, like himself, a distant son of King David. Tradition says Mary shared the same royal ancestry. But in Jewish law it was the legal father's line that counted.

Not only was David Israel's most distinguished king. God promised that from his posterity the promised Messiah would come. When applied to Jesus, therefore, "Son of David" means more than royal lineage; it is also a Messianic title. During his triumphal entry into Jerusalem on the first Palm Sunday, Jesus allowed the crowd to acclaim him by this title. His life was now almost over and there was no longer reason to keep his Messiahship a secret. In a few days he would openly declare his identity to the Sanhedrin, the supreme council in Jerusalem.

This gospel passage gives one more name for Jesus, Emmanuel, meaning "God is with us." We have no record of Jesus going by this name during his lifetime. But the Church often uses it for him, especially at Christmas. He is the Word of God made flesh and therefore "with us." In the last sentence of Matthew's gospel Jesus says to his disciples, "Behold, I am with you always, until the end of the age." He is "God with us" still.

Why do Christians make such a fuss over the name of Jesus? Why call it a *holy* name? In doing so, aren't we indulging in a mild form of idolatry? How can a mere name, a puff of air, be holy? Isn't it the person the name stands for that counts?

That was Juliet's point, and she was wrong. Names do count, precisely because of the person they stand for. Those who disrespect the name of Jesus are like flag-desecrators. If this is their greatest offense, then in the catalogue of sinners they do not rank high. But just as flag desecrators win no prize for good citizenship, desecrators of the name of Jesus are sad specimens as Christians. Their loyalty to the man whose name they abuse is doubtful.

That at least is what Saint Paul thought. To the Philippians he wrote, "At the name of Jesus every knee should bend" *(2:10)*. If we do not literally bend our knees at "Jesus," at least let us bend our minds and hearts. In his name we are saved.

The Young Lady Who Out-Starred the Stars

Fourth Sunday of Advent.
B: Lk. 1: 26-38.

❖ ❖ ❖

Gazing at the stars on a clear summer night feasts our eyes. Thinking about the stars, however, or just trying to think about them, teases our minds. Astronomers assure us that the three thousand stars visible to the naked eye, each a sun in itself, are only a tiny fraction of those known to exist. When they add that the closest of these is more than twenty-five trillion miles away, our brains go blank. We cannot comprehend numbers so huge or distances so vast.

Which means we cannot comprehend God. In some quarters it is fashionable to say that scientific discoveries and religious convictions are at odds. What science reveals about the stars, however, leads more logically in the opposite direction. We have no greater evidence of the power and majesty of our Creator than the immensity and splendor of what he has created *(Rom. 1: 19-20).* If we are dumfounded by this visible universe, how much more should we stand in awe of the God who gave and gives it being? Astronomers are not the only people drawn to the stars . Saints have spent hours gazing at them.

This gospel is set, not in the star-studded heavens, but in a patch of earth that, if not as hard for us to comprehend as the stars, is hard enough. While the stars impress with their grandeur, Nazareth and its inhabitants do so with their lack of it. Here Luke tells the story of the greatest mismatch in history, when the power that governs the stars showered favor on a maiden in the tiny, unpretentious village of Nazareth.

By our standards, Nazareth of two thousand years ago was a wretched place. Hidden in the hills of Galilee, itself a little esteemed corner of a much despised nation, it was totally unknown to the great world. Its inhabitants, like millions of nameless peasants who have trudged through history, eked out an existence so humdrum it would have driven us to distraction. They had none of the diversions that the most countrified people today take for granted. A home there was not even a house, just a hillside cave with a crude board at its opening. How these rustics coped with boredom most of us find difficult to imagine.

There two thousand years ago a girl named Mary, betrothed to a carpenter named Joseph, had a day more exciting than any we will ever know. She learned she had been singled out by the creator of all things for the greatest honor ever bestowed on a human. This word was delivered by a herald from on high called Gabriel. In what form Gabriel appeared to Mary, Luke does not say, nor is it important. Scripture calls him an angel, which by definition is a pure spirit who acts as messenger from God. It was the message, not the messenger, that mattered.

He began by addressing Mary as God's "favored one," adding that the Lord was "with" her. These words troubled Mary. She knew how insignificant any creature is when measured against the Creator. Why, she wondered, should she have a special place in his bounty? Seeing her confusion, Gabriel went on to explain.

She was to bear a son, he told her, a blessing to any woman. And this would be no ordinary son, for he was destined to occupy the throne of David. To Mary, as to any Israelite, "throne of David" rang a bell. It meant her son would be the long awaited Messiah, the liberator God had promised Israel. And not only would he be the Messiah, to whose kingdom there would be "no end," but something greater. He would be called the Son of God.

Whether Mary yet realized the full meaning of these last words, that Almighty God was about to take human flesh in her womb and become a member of our race, is uncertain. But she had to realize that the promised birth would be out of the normal course of nature. When she protested that she was still a virgin, Gabriel revealed that the son she would bear would have no human father at all. The power of the Most High God, the Creator of the universe, would bring about his conception.

No event in history matches what happened when Mary said, "Behold, I am the handmaid of the Lord. May it be done to me according to your word." With those words the virgin of Nazareth gave flesh to the eternal Word, the second person of the Trinity, to whom every atom in the universe owes its origin and present existence. To say that Mary now out-starred the stars in the skies may sound flippant, but it is the simple truth.

As Christmas approaches, think not only of the birth of Jesus at Bethlehem, but of his conception at Nazareth, the mystery of the Incarnation. This mystery is mind-boggling, far more so than the stars. Why did the Creator of the universe step into our time and space? The answer is in his name, the name Mary was told to give him. Jesus means "God saves." The kingdom of Jesus is still with us. And he still saves.

A WORLD TOO GOOD TO BE TRUE?

Fourth Sunday of Advent.
C: Lk. 1: 39-45.

❖❖❖

Some people are confused when they see Catholics praying to saints, kneeling devoutly before their statues and belting out hymns in their honor. They associate kneeling and hymns with worship, and they maintain—quite correctly—that to worship anyone but God is idolatry. That, after all, is the point of the first commandment God gave to Moses on Mount Sinai.

The source of the confusion is possibly in the word "prayer." Sometimes it does carry the idea of worship, as in the principal prayer of the Church, the sacrifice of the Mass. But originally the word implied no such thing. Its root meaning is "to ask, entreat." A beggar pleading for a handout is praying, not worshiping. "Brother, Can You Spare a Dime," a popular American song of the thirties, was a prayer. And that is all we are doing when we pray to the saints—begging for handouts, pleading for a dime of their influence in the court of heaven.

How can the saints do anything for us? They are members of our human race and fellow Christians, brothers and sisters who have made it to the finish line. It is not idolatry when we ask them to take up our cause before the throne of God. We kneel to them as beggars kneel. If we can ask a living human being to say a prayer for us, we can certainly entreat the saints in heaven for the same favor. Here on earth they are listed among the dead. But they are all alive to God.

No saint in heaven is prayed to more often than Mary. Look at the churches named after her, the feasts in her honor, the Marian shrines all over the world. The very lavishness of our devotion to her, however, poses a problem. We place Mary on so lofty a pedestal that we are in danger of de-humanizing her, forgetting that she is after all a creature of flesh and blood, utterly sinless yet refreshingly human. At least that is the impression she makes in this passage from Luke.

Scripture is silent about her age when she received the message from the angel and set out on the journey to her cousin Elizabeth. From what we know of the marriage customs of the times, however, we can safely assume she was no older than 14 or 15. Although a mere child by today's norms, she was already engaged to Joseph, a carpenter and fellow villager of Nazareth.

A messenger from God had recently spoken to Mary. After praising her (excessively, she thought) he told her she was to be the mother of the Messiah. Then he added a more gossipy item. Her cousin Elizabeth, although advanced in years, was also to be a mother. And so Mary decided to visit Elizabeth. Nothing could be more human than this urge to see her cousin, so that the two could share the news of their good fortune.

We are not told exactly where Elizabeth lived except that it was in Judah. An ancient tradition places her home at Ain-Karem, about seven miles southwest of Jerusalem.. If so, the total distance from Nazareth in the northern province of Galilee was about eighty miles, a journey of at least four days.

When she saw Mary at her doorstep Elizabeth must have received an illumination from on high. Her first words prove she was already aware that Mary was bearing a child who, even more than her own, was destined for greatness before God. Elizabeth's words of greeting are as familiar to us as any in the Bible, for they are now part of a prayer familiar to all Catholics, the "Hail Mary." The first two clauses of this prayer are from the words the angel spoke to Mary when she announced that she was to be the mother of Jesus: *Hail, favored one! The Lord is with you.* It was left for Elizabeth to add, *Most blessed are you among women, and blessed is the fruit of your womb.*

In praying the "Hail Mary" we can picture Mary in these two scenes, the Annunciation and the Visitation. In the first she is bursting with surprise and confusion at the angel's words; in the second, throbbing with excitement at the good news she and her cousin exchange. In this prayer we take our place on a centuries-long line of Christians who have knelt before Mary, repeating the words of the angel and Elizabeth.

In time the Church added words of her own, summing up all the petitions Christians bring to their Queen in heaven. While acknowledging that we are sinners, we ask her to plead our cause with her son, now while we walk with the living, later when we are at the threshold of eternity: *Holy Mary, Mother of God, pray for us sinners, now and at the hour of our death.*

The favorite prayer of Catholics, the "Our Father," was authored by Jesus. The "Hail Mary," the runner-up, comes from an angel, Elizabeth, and the Church. Whoever doubts that devotion to Mary is rooted in Scripture and Christian tradition has this prayer to contend with. Its authors have impressive credentials.

A Man Rightly Called Righteous

Vigil of Christmas.
ABC: Mt. 1: 1-25 (or 18-25).

❖ ❖ ❖

Joseph is one of our most popular saints. The churches, schools, and hospitals named after him, not to mention the many individuals, are proof of how highly Christians have always regarded him. It may come as a surprise to some, then, to realize how little we actually know about Joseph. In Scripture, our only source of information, he is seldom seen and never heard. One senses this is how he would have wanted it.

His two big moments come early in Matthew's gospel, in the part he played, first in the events leading up to the birth of Jesus, and then in its sequel, the flight to Egypt. This passage from Matthew concentrates on the former.

About the actual birth of Jesus Matthew has nothing to say except that it happened in Bethlehem. His focus is rather on Nazareth and "how the birth of Jesus Christ came about," particularly on the dilemma Joseph faced when he discovered that Mary was with child. Unfortunately, most readers find Matthew's account of this dilemma a bundle of confusion.

He opens by telling us that Joseph and Mary were "betrothed," a word we normally take as synonymous with "engaged." That it was a mere engagement seems confirmed by the detail that the two did not yet live together. Yet the angel clearly refers to Mary as the "wife" of Joseph. Was she?

Their neighbors certainly did not yet consider Joseph and Mary to be husband and wife. If they did, Mary would not have been exposed to shame by being discovered with child. On the other hand, Joseph clearly looked on Mary as in some sense his wife. How else could he decide to "divorce" her?

Joseph's misgivings were not removed until the angel assured him that the child Mary bore had been conceived by the holy Spirit. We are told that after receiving this assurance, Joseph took Mary, "his wife," into his home. In biblical times it was the formal reception of the bride into the groom's home that constituted the marriage ceremony.

Clearly some of the language in our translation fails to capture Matthew's meaning. This is not the translator's fault. Because our marriage customs are very different from those in ancient Israel, we lack the words to describe Joseph's situation.

In ancient Palestine a man and a woman became engaged at a very early age. The woman might be a girl of fourteen. The two had little say in the matter, since arranged marriages were then the norm (as they still are in many parts of the world).

These engagements, or betrothals, were more binding than ours, so binding that the couple were already spoken of as man and wife, even though they lived separately and had no marital rights. That is the situation of Joseph and Mary at the beginning of this gospel story. Breaking a betrothal was not easy; so difficult, in fact, that the process was called a divorce.

Note the reticence of Matthew in telling the story of Joseph. In Luke's account of the conversation between Mary and the angel we are told how troubled Mary was on being told she was to give birth to the Messiah. All Matthew says about Joseph, however, is that he was a "righteous" man and would not expose Mary to shame. We are left to imagine the agony of doubt through which he must have passed, as well as his joy on learning of the privilege God had bestowed on Mary (and therefore himself).

Although this passage from Matthew ostensibly focuses on Joseph, it says more about Jesus and Mary than Joseph himself.

First, it confirms what we also know from Luke's gospel, that Jesus was conceived by the holy Spirit and born of a virgin. The virgin birth has from earliest times been one of the most firmly held beliefs of Christians. Those who challenge it have the authority of both Matthew and Luke to contend with. Few teachings are more firmly rooted in Scripture.

Second, Matthew's account tells how Jesus acquired one of his titles. By assuming legal paternity of Jesus, Joseph put the child in the line of King David, his own ancestor. To the early Christians this lineage was important. The prophets had consistently spoken of the Messiah as the son of David.

The first name the angel assigned to the child was "Jesus," meaning "God saves," indicating his destiny to save "his people" from their sins. We now know he did much more; that he is Savior, not only of his fellow Israelites, but of the entire human race.

The second name mentioned by the angel, "Emmanuel," is from Isaiah's prophecy *(7: 14)*, and is even more significant. It means "God is with us." The child born of Mary is more than a prophet sent by God to instruct and inspire us. He *is* God. In that name we read the deepest meaning of the season we are about to celebrate. On Christmas God came to dwell with us.

THE NIGHT GOD CRASHED INTO HISTORY

Christmas Mass at Midnight.
ABC: Lk. 2: 1-14.

❖❖❖

Travelers to West Africa who visit Victoria Beach in Lagos sometimes hear a tiny voice hawking what sounds like a "Native Tea Set." If they look to where the voice is coming from, they see a small boy holding up for sale, not African teacups, but seven wooden figurines—Joseph, Mary, three shepherds, an ox, and an infant in a manger—a nativity set. All are handcarved and, incidentally, reasonably priced by any standard. They are also proof of how widely known is the story Luke tells in this gospel. It would be hard to find a corner anywhere in the world where the good news of what happened two thousand years ago at Bethlehem has not penetrated. Everyone has heard it, and at Christmastime everyone wants to hear it again.

The story begins, not in Bethlehem, but in faraway Rome, in the executive chambers of Caesar Augustus, the first Roman emperor. The lives of little people are often upset by the decisions of the mighty. A ruler plunges his nation into a face-saving war, and a thousand young men have their lives cut short. A tycoon shuts a factory that has yielded meager profits, and half a town is thrown out of work. Caesar Augustus signs a decree for a census, and a young bride from Nazareth sets out on a journey with her spouse; and twenty centuries later people sit in churches throughout the world singing about the little town of Bethlehem instead of the little town of Nazareth.

Augustus was an excellent administrator, meticulous in keeping records. Three times during his forty-four-year reign he held a census of his subjects. So proud was he of the results that he included the totals in his autobiography. One thing he failed to include in this recital of the world-shaking events during his reign was the most important of all, that among the subjects born in his empire was the Savior of the world.

Joseph and his wife Mary, who was with child by the power of the holy Spirit, were living at Nazareth when they learned that a census was to be taken. They were obliged to go to King David's town, Bethlehem, to be counted, for Joseph was a descendant of David. To get there from Nazareth, a journey of eighty miles, would have taken them at least four days.

Luke's account of what happened when the couple arrived at Bethlehem is probably based on some recollections of Mary that were preserved among the early Christians, for there was hardly anyone else to tell the story. The details—the crowded inn, the manger and swaddling clothes, the visit of the shepherds—are just the sort one would expect to loom large in a mother's treasury of memories. The couple did not stay at the inn, and it was just as well. What passed for an inn in those days was merely a series of crude alcoves opening on a courtyard where animals were kept. Even if Joseph had found a free alcove, the place offered little privacy for a woman about to give birth.

Instead, Joseph brought Mary to an animal shelter, probably one of the limestone caves in the outskirts of the town. In it was a manger where oxen fed. Brushed clean and lined with straw, the feed-box made a comfortable bed for a newborn boy. Mary had brought swaddling clothes to wrap around the infant.

Joseph and Mary probably did not consider themselves particularly deprived because they had to spend the night in circumstances that seem inhumanly harsh to our cuddled sensitivities. Travelers in those days often slept in the open. Even if they found shelter, they did not expect the conveniences we take for granted. Of course the cave had none of the comforts of Augustus's palace, but these were luxuries that neither Joseph nor Mary had ever enjoyed, so they could hardly have missed them.

Such is the story of Bethlehem, and its lessons are many. We are reminded, as when we read about the humble beginnings of men like Franklin and Lincoln, that famous people are often born in poverty and obscurity. Contrasting the cave of Bethlehem with the court of Augustus, we realize that the measure of human worth is not in what a person possesses but what a person is. And the presence of the shepherds teaches that even those who are despised by neighbors for being crude and unlearned can be favored beyond kings by the only one whose favor counts.

Valuable as they are, however, none of these lessons gets to the heart of the Christmas story. The birth of Jesus was not just a human, but a divine event. On that unlikely night and in that improbable cave Almighty God came crashing into human history, took his place in our midst, joined our human race. No longer can we consider any human being just an insignificant speck in an uncaring universe. The cave of Bethlehem housed the Lord of all creation. By coming among us as a child in a manger he touched and transformed us all.

SHEPHERDS FAR FROM ANGELIC

Christmas Mass at Dawn.
ABC: Lk. 2: 15-20.

❖❖❖

Nativity scenes usually include three or four shepherds kneeling in wide-eyed wonder before the manger. They belong there. Probably they were not in real life as well-groomed or neatly-attired as artists have painted them, but no reproduction of the scene would be complete without them. Luke's gospel devotes only five verses to the activities of Joseph and Mary on that first Christmas, but thirteen to the shepherds. If Luke judged them that important, they certainly deserve our attention.

Their presence in the cave was no accident. They were there at the invitation of an angel, a messenger from God. The reason they were the first to gaze on the infant Jesus was that God wanted it so. Through them he taught two important lessons.

What kind of people were these men and boys who tended sheep in a field near Bethlehem? In biblical times the shepherds of Palestine had a reputation far from angelic. Most people regarded them as rough, tough, and thoroughly irreligious. Their occupation, dirty and round-the-clock, offered little opportunity for the ritual washings and other prescriptions of the Jewish religious law. They were even widely reputed to be thieves. Pharisees carefully avoided their company and warned others to do the same. In the eyes of most Israelites these shepherds were about as far from God as any Israelites could be.

The first lesson to draw from their presence at the manger, then, is to be wary of public opinion, especially when it condemns a whole class of people. Respectable members of Jewish society ostracized these shepherds. Obviously God did not concur.

All his life Jesus was to show how little stock he put in such blanket condemnations of groups. One of the chief accusations his enemies leveled against him was that he made friends with people most others regarded as sinners. Of this crime, at least, Jesus was guilty as charged. It was an ingrained habit, first observed when the shepherds were made welcome in the cave of Bethlehem, last observed when he held a friendly conversation with one of the thieves hanging alongside him on Calvary.

Most of us are aware of how unchristian it is to make rash judgments or spread nasty rumors about individuals. When an entire group is slandered by a good part of society, however, our Christian outrage is often muted. Say that our neighborhood is ringing with such slurs, that our acquaintances habitually speak of some race or people as lazy, incompetent, dirty, dishonest, shiftless, ill-mannered, and you know the rest. What do we do? It takes courage not to add our voices to the chorus.

It is precisely this kind of courage we should draw from the nativity scene. Try an imaginary substitution. Where the shepherds are, mentally place a few members of some group that has a poor reputation among our contemporaries. Far-fetched? Not really. Every age has its equivalent of the Palestinian shepherds, powerless members of a minority that is rejected by the majority. Picturing a few of them at the manger will remind us of what really took place at Bethlehem.

The shepherds teach another lesson. Luke says that after returning from the cave they praised God "for all they had heard and seen, just as it had been told to them." Now what the angels had told them, unequivocally, was that the child in the manger was the Messiah. This was astonishing news. Unlearned though they were, the shepherds knew what every Jew knew, that a Messiah would come to Israel and be a great king. That his actual birthplace was Bethlehem was also no surprise, for Scripture said so *(Micah 5: 1)*. But that he had been born on *this* night and that *they*, simple shepherds, had been invited to behold him within hours of his birth, were marvels beyond their dreams.

On arriving at the cave they received a shock. This infant did not at all resemble a king, not in this dingy cave, not with these plain parents. Kings are born in palaces. Music and feasting greet their arrival. But this birth was no more splendid than their own had been. This infant was one of them.

Yet the shepherds believed the angel and praised God for what they had seen. Gazing at the infant they must have been the first to grasp this simple lesson of Christmas, that true greatness does not consist in what a person *has*, but what a person *is*. Although born in a cave and as poor as the shepherds themselves, this infant was the Messiah. That at least is what he was in God's eyes, the only eyes that should matter.

The shepherds are famous today, not because of anything they did or said or owned, but because of what God did to them by placing them within a few paces of Jesus in the cave of Bethlehem. In God's sight they ranked high. So will we, if we heed the lessons God teaches through the shepherds.

A Prologue Worth Pondering

Christmas Mass During the Day.
ABC: Jn. 1: 1-18 (or 1-5: 9-14).

"Christmas" means, literally, Christ's Mass. Actually this day is so important that the Church gives us three Masses, at midnight, at dawn, and at daytime, each with its own readings. For midnight and dawn the gospel readings are from Luke's familiar telling of the Christmas story. For this daytime Mass we have the opening of John's first chapter, his "prologue."

Most people prefer the readings from Luke. As usual, he tells a good story. Even though we have heard it often before, we enjoy hearing again about the journey to Bethlehem, the crowded inn, the swaddling clothes, and the shepherds. John's prologue, by contrast, is anything but a story. Some scholars think it was originally a hymn; if so, we have lost the music, and to our ears it sounds more like a page torn from the lecture notes of some cerebral professor of theology. Most people find it forbidding—too abstract and not altogether clear. Even trained Scripture scholars can be baffled by parts of it.

But John's prologue is well worth pondering. Its main points are clear enough, and they get closer than anything in Luke to the central meaning of Christmas. John may well have known as much as Luke about the physical details surrounding the birth of Jesus, but these were not the focus of his interest. To him what happened at Bethlehem was more than a story about an infant born in obscure poverty who was destined for greatness. It was above all about the coming of Almighty God into our world. The cold and comfortless cave of Bethlehem was where the Eternal Word stepped into human history, became a member of our race.

In the beginning was the Word, and the Word was with God, and the Word was God. Jesus pre-existed Bethlehem. The child in the manger is the Word, John's designation for the second Person of the Trinity. Before any humans roamed the earth; before the sun, moon, planets, and stars were in place; before the big bang that sent trillions of atoms hurtling millions of miles into space; before there were any atoms to hurtle or anything big or small to make a bang, the eternal Word of God was.

He was in the beginning with God. All things came to be through him. What happened anterior to creation is an area our imagination cannot penetrate. There was only the three-Personed God, infinite, beyond space and time. But God spoke, "Let there be light," and our universe burst into being.

He was in the world...but the world did not know him. He came to what was his own, but his own people did not accept him. The story of mankind before Bethlehem is one of ignorance and sin. God gave to humans light enough to see how his goodness and beauty are reflected in his creation, but the mass of mankind preferred darkness to the light. Saint Paul says in his letter to the Romans, "What can be known about God is evident to them... in what he has made. As a result, they have no excuse" *(1:19-20).* To his chosen people God sent his prophets, but these received small honor.

And the Word became flesh. Paul says, "though he was in the form of God...*he emptied* himself" *(Phil. 2:6-7).* The Creed puts it, "he came down from heaven...and *became man.*" John's *became flesh* is starker. Its meaning is preserved in the English word, "incarnation," the root meaning of which is "enfleshment." All are faltering efforts to express the same overwhelming reality, that in the manger God became a puny thing of skin, blood, muscles, and bone, no different in appearance from any baby fresh from its mother's womb.

Our flesh is the feeblest part of us, infancy our most helpless period. At Christmas we should spend a few moments just gazing at the few pounds of humanity asleep on its bed of straw. This, we must keep hammering into our brains, is God.

And made his dwelling among us. John's Greek word means "pitched his tent among us." As he grew, Jesus shared camp life with the rest of the human race. Like us he needed food, water, air, and sleep; he knew what it was to shed tears or to laugh, to be scorched by the sun or cooled by the wind. He claimed no exemption from our daily routine of tedium and toil.

To say that this tiny bundle of frail flesh in the manger is the eternal Word, in the words of Paul, "the refulgence of his glory...who sustains all things by his mighty word" *(Heb. 1:3)* seems a blasphemous absurdity. Nothing that John says or a homilist adds can make it seem less absurd. But it is the central truth of Christianity, the truth the Church wants us to think about today, as we celebrate Christ's Mass.

Christianity does not consist in our search for God, but in God's reaching out for us. In the darkness of the cave at Bethlehem we catch a faint glimmer of how far he reached.

AN ORDINARY FAMILY IN A HUMDRUM TOWN

Sunday in Octave of Christmas: Holy Family.
A: Mt. 2: 13-15; 19-23.

A leading business executive once said that despite his almost legendary success and the fortune he had amassed he would consider himself a failure if his children had turned out badly. The remark raises some tantalizing questions. Should parents be judged guilty when their children grow up to be rascals? Conversely, how much credit do they deserve for the later success of their offspring? Don't children have wills of their own? History and experience suggest a somewhat blurred answer.

We all know instances where seemingly blameless parents have begotten scoundrels; and history tells of sterling heroes emerging from early homes that to all appearances were ideal breeding grounds for ne'er-do-wells. Ultimately, it is the individual, not the parents, who follows a crooked path or a straight one. Freedom to choose between good and evil is one of our most precious gifts. No one, not even our parents, can make this crucial decision for us.

But it remains true that upbringing counts for a lot. Teachers know that much in a pupil's conduct and performance can be traced to the family. Traits like fondness for books, respect for authority, even preferences in sports and politics, are nurtured in the home. So is reverence for God and respect for one's neighbor. So too is care for one's immortal soul. The family we grew up in stays with us for life. We can disown it , but cannot erase it.

One reason why the Church discourages hasty marriages is that it wants the couple to take a deep breath and have a good look at the waters before taking the plunge. Do they realize what it means to be parents, what their responsibilities will be? Mothers and fathers have custody over more than the physical well-being of their child. To them is entrusted the child's emotional, mental, and spiritual health. They are guardians of an immortal soul. Eternity begins in the home.

In recent times the family has been under attack. Prophets of the New Morality have propagandized for alternatives to the traditional family. Multiple spouses, same-sex parents, childless unions, and other bizarre combinations have been touted as legitimate improvements on the family as it has existed since long before the advent of Christianity. Not surprisingly, none of these substitutes has worked. As even the usually far-out sociologist Margaret Mead once pointed out, "No matter how many communes anybody invents, the family always creeps back." It creeps back for the same reason that hunger creeps back at night even though we have had a good lunch at noon. Like the need for food, the family is natural, the way God made us.

Today we celebrate the feast of the Holy Family. To Catholic families the world over our Church holds up Joseph, his spouse Mary, and their child Jesus as models of what the Christian family should be. At first sight it might appear to be a very strange model. After all, what do we really know about the Holy Family? About the circum-stances surrounding the birth of Jesus, two of the gospels tell us a great deal; but about how this family fared after settling at Nazareth we know next to nothing.

Luke tells us Jesus was obedient, but supplies no details. We also know Joseph was a carpenter and that Jesus followed him in this trade. The rest is silence. How can a Filipino family of today model itself on a Jewish family of the first century about which so little is known?

But wait. We do know the one important thing—how Jesus turned out. His human qualities—his thoughtfulness, courage, decisiveness, wisdom, compassion—all these must have had their origin at Nazareth. To Joseph and Mary belongs much of the credit. They set the course.

Can parents today expect the same success as Joseph and Mary? Not really, any more than children of today can expect to be perfect replicas of Jesus. But from the Holy Family the parents and children of today can learn the direction they should take. For a family to succeed, God must be a familiar presence in the home. Only then will parents and children alike have the mutual and genuine love that is the formula for a happy family. Only then will their children have the chance to grow into the Christians their parents want them to be.

Father Hesburgh once said that the most important thing a father can do for his children is to love their mother. We can add that the most important thing a mother can do for them is to love their father. And the children themselves can do nothing more precious to their parents than love one another. Love, after all, is what bound the Holy Family together. Jesus, the source of love, was always present.

ONE BIG FAMILY

Sunday in the Octave of Christmas: Holy Family.
B: Lk. 2: 22-40 (or 22; 39-40).

Today we honor the holy family of Nazareth. The whole world can chime out the full roster of its members: Jesus, Mary, and Joseph. Just three. Jesus was an only child.

The holy family was unique. Scripture tells us Jesus had no natural father, that his mother was miraculously a virgin at his birth. More-over, from earliest times Christians have believed that although legally married, Mary and Joseph showed their devotion to God in a special way: she remained a virgin. "Virgin Mary," one of her oldest titles, is Catholic doctrine.

If we were to travel back to biblical Nazareth, however, and ask Jesus how large is his family and who besides himself belongs to it, his answer could come as a shock. He might spend a minute or two just ticking off the names of all his brothers and sisters. That is because in those times all close relatives were "brothers" and "sisters." In Aramaic, the language Jesus spoke, the word for a sibling and a cousin was the same.

We have no idea how many brothers and sisters of this kind Jesus had. Scripture names no sisters; as brothers, James, Joseph, Simon, and Judas are named *(Mt. 13:55; Mk. 6:3),* possibly because they played roles in the early Church. But almost certainly there were many more. In those days everybody belonged to an extended family. That its members called one another brother and sister was not just a matter of terminology. Cousins actually felt closer to one another then than they do today.

In thinking of the life Jesus led at Nazareth, we should keep this larger family in mind. He must have felt for his cousins a kinship such as few of us have ever felt for relatives outside our immediate family. Thus he suffered none of the handicaps people often associate with an only child. The smallness of his immediate family was not confining. He had all the companionship and support that a large family gives.

When we speak of "the" holy family of Nazareth, however, as we do today, we usually mean family in its more restricted sense, just the threesome of Jesus, Mary, and Joseph. What do we know about their life at Nazareth? Quite honestly, not much.

Although not his natural father, Joseph was the legal father of Jesus. He was head of the family and like all Hebrew fathers of the time led its members in prayer, earned their bread, and made major decisions. Scripture calls him a carpenter *(Mt. 13:55)*, an occupation Jesus inherited *(Mk. 6:3)*. In those days carpenters worked more with metal than wood; in rural Nazareth their chief artifacts would have been such implements as wheels, plows, and yokes. This may explain the many agricultural images in the preaching of Jesus. The trade he learned from Joseph gave him a knowledge of farm life that lasted through life.

Apart from the infancy scenes, what do we know of Mary? Scripture hints that Joseph died before Jesus struck out on his own, but Mary certainly did not. Several times during his ministry she crossed her son's path, and she was present at his death on Calvary. *Acts (1: 14)* tells us she was even with the apostles in Jerusalem after his ascension. But about Mary at Nazareth while Jesus was growing up, Scripture is a blank.

What of Jesus himself during the Nazareth years? From what they had heard about him at the time of his birth, Mary and Joseph had every reason to expect mighty deeds of their son. At his nativity angels called him "Messiah and Lord" *(Lk. 2:11)*. In today's gospel Simeon hails him as a "light for revelation to the Gentiles" and "glory for your people Israel." But if Jesus did anything even slightly Messianic or remotely glorious during his years at Nazareth, Scripture knows nothing about it.

Luke records one unusual incident when Jesus was twelve and the family was visiting Jerusalem *(2:41-50)*. About the daily life at Nazareth, however, the silence of Scripture is almost total. We learn only that Jesus obeyed his parents (as we would expect), that he grew in physical strength (like all of us), that he was filled with wisdom (his parents deserve most of the credit there), and that God's favor was with him (inevitably, seeing that in him the divine and human were joined.)

Is there a lesson for us in this? Saints have suggested many, but one stands out. What Jesus was in later life he could not have been without what he had experienced at his home and on the streets of Nazareth. Even if he wanted to, he could no more shake his growing years out of his system than we can.

The debt we owe to Jesus, who lived and died for us, is obvious. But we owe a big one to Mary and Joseph too, as well as to the kinfolk in his extended family at Nazareth. Without the whole lot of them, the full-grown Jesus we know and revere would never have been. May all our families learn from his.

GROWING PAINS

Sunday in the Octave of Christmas: Holy Family.
C: Lk. 2: 41-52.

This episode has been called the losing and finding of the "child" Jesus in the temple. A child by our standards Jesus certainly was, only twelve years old. But childhood ended earlier then than now. At twelve Jesus was only a year short of the age when a Jewish boy became legally a man and subject to all the precepts of Jewish law. Joseph and Mary were fulfilling an obligation incumbent on Jewish adults by making their Passover visit to the temple, and this year they brought along their rapidly maturing pre-teener a year earlier than the law required. It turned out to be a trip to remember.

We should not fault his parents for failing to notice the absence of Jesus when they began their return journey. The departing caravans would have been scenes of great confusion, and in any case Jesus was now too old to require constant watching. Only at the first stopover after a day of travel did they miss him. The second day was spent retracing their steps to Jerusalem and the third searching through the city for him.

They finally tracked him down in the temple. There some Rabbis had gathered children together and were presiding over a question-and-answer session on Jewish religion. Among those sitting at their feet was Jesus. During festivals such informal classes were common in the outer court of the temple.

That the teachers were "astounded" at the answers of the lad from Nazareth is not surprising when we consider the sharpness and eloquence he displayed in later life. But we should not picture him as a Johnny- know-it-all. The modesty that marked him as an adult was surely there in embryo during his childhood.

"Son, why have you done this to us?" Mary's question reveals astonishment at the conduct of Jesus. In his reply Jesus affirmed that obedience to his heavenly Father took precedence over all other duties, including those towards his earthly parents. Luke's language implies that he was frankly puzzled that Joseph and Mary had scoured all Jerusalem in their search for him. They should have known where he had to be. "*Why* were you looking for me? Did you not know that I *must* be in my Father's house?"

Where else would he be but in the temple? This center of Jewish worship, one of the ancient world's wonders, must have enchanted Jesus. And the chance to learn more about his Jewish heritage from the learned Rabbis was too good to be missed.

Jesus returned with his parents to Nazareth, where for the next two decades he remained holed away without a deed worth recording. What had happened to his mission, so joyously proclaimed at his birth, to bring salvation to mankind? Why spend nine-tenths of his short life with this mission on hold?

The answer is that without those years at Nazareth Jesus would not have been truly human. To achieve full adulthood a human being must first pass through infancy and childhood. Had Jesus swooped down from the sky a full-grown man, equipped with all the skills needed for his mission, we would not recognize him as a member of our human family. His humanity would not have been, as the ancient theologian Hippolytus put it, "of the same clay as our own." At Nazareth Jesus *grew*, as all of us must grow, into the full bloom of his powers.

Luke tells us he progressed in *wisdom.* He attained this, not just from parents and teachers, but from the world of physical nature as well as the varieties of human nature he met in his trade as carpenter. No wiser man than Jesus ever lived. Getting that way took keen observation. He also advanced in *age.* His neighbors saw the gradual increase in the size and strength of his limbs and the skill of his carpenter fingers. Finally, he moved forward in the *favor*, not only of God, but of his fellow humans. It was at Nazareth that he acquired the charm of manner and tact in speech that marked his later years.

How could such grace and wisdom as Jesus later displayed come out of so unlikely a setting? Nazareth was a biblical Dullsville, so far from the mainstream of Jewish culture that its name was a joke among some Israelites. The story of Jesus proves that the highest grace and deepest wisdom can grow in a seemingly unfavorable environment if only one wants them to grow and is guided, as Jesus was, by wise and graceful elders.

The nearest thing we have to Nazareth is the family. Like Nazareth, the average family can appear to be narrow, dated, even dull. But within these limits the child can grow, not just in age, but in the wisdom of Christian values and the grace of Christian courtesy. They will do so only if the parents give wise guidance and encourage a gracious environment.

Our prayer today should be that all Christian families draw inspiration from looking at the holy Family at Nazareth.

A SCANDALOUS TITLE?

Octave of Christmas: Solemnity of Mary, Mother of God.
ABC: Lk. 2: 16-21.

❖❖❖

Biographies of famous people often open with a chapter about their parents. Knowing something about a person's forbears not only satisfies a natural curiosity; it often helps us understand the person. From our parents we receive the bodies we own along with some of their distinctive features. We also pick up from our parents' example many personality traits, possibly our manner of talking, our gestures, our sense of humor. Above all, mothers and fathers help to shape character.

This partly explains the importance Christians attach to the mother of Jesus. She had the honor of giving physical being to Jesus, was the source of his flesh and blood. In his looks he took after her. More than this, she nursed him as an infant and, along with Joseph, guided him through his early years at Nazareth. The human traits Jesus later displayed he owed, humanly speaking, to her more than anyone else.

Centuries of Christianity have awarded Mary many titles. Look through the telephone directory of any major city in the world and see the churches, schools, and hospitals that are dedicated to her. Many honor her with extremely poetic names, like Our Lady of Refuge, Our Lady of Victory, and Our Lady, Star of the Sea. But one title is more important than any other, because it is the source of all the rest: she is the Mother of God. Under this title every Catholic church in the world salutes Mary today, the first day of the year.

Some people are puzzled by this title, even scandalized. They consider it blasphemous to call a mere creature of God the mother of God, as though this somehow puts Mary on a higher pedestal than God himself. But that is not what the title means at all. It simply states that Mary is the mother of the man, Jesus Christ, who is also God. As Saint Paul put it, "When the fullness of time had come, God sent his Son, born of a woman" *(Gal. 4:4)*. Since the humanity of Jesus is united to the second Person of the Trinity, we can truly say that he is God. His mother, then, is rightly called the mother of God.

If we can call a woman a shoemaker's mother even though she knows nothing about making shoes, we can call Mary God's mother even though she is a creature of time, as totally dependent on God as any of us are. Once God chose to become a man, he needed a woman to give him flesh. Mary was that woman.

Our devotion to Mary should be rooted in Scripture and sound theology. We have no excuse for poking into legend or superstition to find ways of honoring her, since Scripture has more than enough honorable things to say. Just as, in the words of today's gospel, Mary reflected "in her heart" on what the shepherds told her, so Christians through the centuries have reflected in their hearts on what Scripture says about Mary. Anyone who doubts this should read the second Vatican Council's dogmatic constitution on the Church. Its explanation of why we honor Mary is loaded with references to Scripture.

In Scripture we learn that before the birth of Jesus an angel visited Mary and told her she had found favor with God. She was to conceive a king whose reign would have no end. Mary then visited her cousin Elizabeth who praised her good fortune, repeating the angel's compliment that she was "blessed...among women." From the words spoken to Mary on these two occasions the Church has fashioned the first part of one of the two all-time favorite prayers of Catholics, the Hail Mary.

Next we see Mary in Bethlehem, in Egypt, and back again at Nazareth where, as Luke tells us, Jesus was obedient to her and Joseph. Eventually the time came for his mission to the children of Israel, and during his years of active ministry Mary disappeared almost completely from the scene. One exception is recorded by John, the marriage feast at Cana. There we see as nowhere else the power Mary had with her son. It was at her request that he kept the wine flowing and the festivities alive.

Her finest hour was on Calvary, when she stood beneath the cross while Jesus gave his life for the salvation of the world. From the cross Jesus entrusted her to his beloved disciple, and his beloved disciple to her. Her final appearance in Scripture is only a mention, but an important one. Early in the *Acts of the Apostles (1:14)* we learn she was among the Christians who dwelt together in Jerusalem awaiting the coming of the holy Spirit. Thus Mary, as one would expect, played a role in the infant Church.

She still plays a role in the Church, a major role, just as any mother plays a major role in any family. All of us, members of Christ's mystical body, are her children. As we begin the year let us put all the needs of the Church as well as our personal needs in her motherly care.

WHAT THE MAGI KNEW

Epiphany.
ABC: Mt. 2: 1-12.

I

We all know the story of the three kings. As children we first learned of these wizards from the East who followed a star to Bethlehem, and now we are reminded of them whenever we pass a Christmas creche. There they kneel, just behind the shepherds, placing their gifts of gold, frankincense, and myrrh. Christmas would not be Christmas without Balthasar, Melchior, and Gaspar.

Doubts set in, however, when we read the only authentic source of their story, Saint Matthew's gospel, and discover how much of what we thought we knew about these men is not there. Matthew calls them "magi," which does not mean kings at all, but Persian priests of the Zoroaster religion, who derived much of their wisdom from the stars. The New American Bible once called them astrologers, a good enough translation as long as we do not confuse them with the charlatans of today who counsel politicians and write prophetic nonsense for the tabloids. Magi were learned men according to the standards of their times. Their belief that the future could be divined from the stars reflected the almost universal belief among the ancients that our destinies are some- how written in the heavens.

We have no basis for thinking the Magi were three. Matthew uses a simple plural. The names tradition has given them are pure fiction. The gospel is silent about when they arrived in Bethlehem except that it was "when Jesus was born." Since this could have been after Joseph and Mary had moved to better quarters, the Magi might never have seen the shepherds or even entered the cave at all. About the star we know absolutely nothing. All efforts to identify it with some verifiable conjunction of stars or planets are groundless guesswork.

But if a reading of Matthew challenges our preconceptions about the Magi, reading some of the commentaries is even more unsettling. Some reputable scholars dismiss the whole story as legend. "Midrash," they call it, or something similar to the style of writing that goes by that name, in which a fabulous tale is used to illustrate a biblical truth. The truth Matthew sought to convey by this tale, these scholars say, was important for his Gentile readers: that the Messiah came, not just for Jews, but for Gentiles as well—in fact, for all mankind.

The midrash theory is both unproved and unprovable. It certainly seems odd that God would foretell the birth of Jesus through a star, even odder that Zoroaster priests would trek all the way from Persia to Judea to check on an astrological prophecy. But we simply do not know enough about the ways of God or the habits of Zoroaster priests to dismiss such happenings as beyond credence. Some features of the story, such as the star and the gifts, seem at least partly symbolic. But even if the episode does have the "feel" of legend, we should remember that legends are usually rooted in some reality, not concocted out of thin air. Many sound biblical scholars are convinced that this story of the Magi has some solid factual basis.

We should, however, be grateful for the midrash theory. It has drawn attention away from the quaint details of Matthew's narrative and the astronomical speculations swirling about the star, putting the emphasis where it belongs, on the religious significance of this episode. What the Magi meant to Matthew and what the feast of Epiphany means to the Church are the same. "You revealed your Son to the nations," reads the prayer of today's Mass. "The Gentiles are coheirs, members of the same body, and copartners in the promise in Christ Jesus," wrote Saint Paul *(Eph. 3:6)*. The infant Jesus reached beyond Bethlehem, beyond Palestine. Herod plotted his death, but foreigners paid him homage. The child of Bethlehem belongs to the world.

Hilaire Belloc once wrote a book with the recurrent drumbeat "Europe is the Faith, the Faith is Europe." His admirers have been making excuses for this nonsense ever since. In the sixties I heard the leader of the Communist party in an Asian nation warn a group of Catholic students that Christianity was an alien import from the West. The students, whose Christian roots went back centuries earlier than the alien import of Marxism, were not impressed. In Africa I knew a university professor who liked to harangue his students with angry denunciations of Christianity and call for a return to the "authentic" religions of Africa. But the Christian churches throughout Africa remain filled. Their worshipers understand the significance of the Epiphany, the universal and timeless authenticity of Jesus Christ.

The appeal of Jesus leaps over national boundaries. Born a stranger in Bethlehem, he is at home everywhere. Christianity has no nationality because it belongs to all nations. This is the point of the Magi story, the message of Epiphany.

THEY CAME FROM THE EAST

Epiphany.
ABC: Mt. 2: 1-12.

❖❖❖

II

The Magi have always fascinated Christians. Their story blends marvel and mystery. Who were these roving oriental star-gazers, and what was the nature of the celestial light that guided them to the land of the Jews? What were their thoughts as they knelt before the newborn Jesus? What remembrance of Bethlehem did they bring back to their homelands?

Whatever answers appeal to us, we should remember that the Church sees in this episode more than a mind-teasing fairy tale or a thrilling sequel to the Christmas story. The Epiphany has for centuries been a major festival for Christians. Why? Because, in Matthew's words, the Magi came "from the east."

Unfortunately, we cannot pinpoint exactly where in the east. Scholars believe the word "magi" may mean they were priests of the Zoroaster religion who practiced the ancient art of reading the future in the stars. If so, their starting point was Persia, present-day Iran. In any event, and this detail is crucial to the importance the Church attaches to the Magi, Israelites they were not. They belonged to the hordes of non-Jews whom Israelites called Gentiles ("the nations"), the *goyim.*

Why is this significant? The early Christians saw it as a sign of the *universality* of the religion that Jesus founded. Even as an infant at Bethlehem he manifested himself, not just to the people of Israel, but to members of the vast non-Jewish world. Unlike Judaism, unlike all the religions that until then had flourished among mankind, Christianity would reach out to all the peoples on earth. None would be excluded.

On reaching their goal, the Magi worshiped the infant Jesus, hailing him as a king. Thus they were the first to give witness to his universal appeal. Legend has named them Gaspar, Balthasar, and Melchior. The idea that one of them (Gaspar) was black has no basis in Scripture, but the impulse that shaped the legend was sound. Jesus Christ belongs to all the races of mankind.

In his ordinary preaching Jesus did not stress the universality of his mission, even to his close apostles. He waited until after his resurrection to tell them they must preach his gospel to *all* nations; but this command, clear though it seems to us, did not immediately sink in. The early decades of Christianity saw the growing realization among Christians that the gospel was not meant exclusively for Jews and pagans willing to convert to Judaism. The first Christians had been children of the Old Covenant. It took time for them to be convinced that the New Covenant included the *goyim.*

All ancient religions were marked by exclusiveness. Most of us know what an exclusive club is, even if we have never belonged to one. Its fees are steep, its admission policy rigid, its facilities rarely soiled by the touch of non-members. Such was Judaism at the time of Christ. Within its fold were those who by blood or special adoption belonged to the chosen people. Outside was the vast mass of heathens, viewed by most Jews with distrust if not hostility, doomed never to enter God's kingdom.

Suddenly Christianity sprouted, and to the surprise even of many of its own members, it soon declared an open admission policy. Its preachers went to the highways and byways, searching out anyone willing to live by the gospel. Neither blood nor nationality mattered. The poorest slaves were welcome.

Imagine a father announcing to his children that henceforth any stranger from any land will be welcome to a place at their table and a bed in their home and should be treated just like all other members of the family. Fantastic? No more so than what Christianity announced as its policy in accepting new members. The policy rests on one of the fundamental truths of our faith: all humans have been redeemed by Jesus; therefore all are invited to join. His Church is universal.

Another word for universal is "catholic," and it is because the Church Jesus founded is world-wide in its reach that its title is the Catholic Church. In passing we may note how unthinkable should racial or national bigotry be for anyone posing as a Catholic. Presidents are expected to preside, prime ministers to minister, and governors to govern. Shouldn't Catholics be catholic?

The person who first propagated this policy among early Christians was Paul, apostle of the Gentiles. Overriding the blind objections of some fellow Christians, he insisted in letter after letter that the gospel was for Gentiles as well as Israelites, that Jesus Christ came to earth for people of all races and nations, that his arms are open for all.

Paul was first to shout this truth from rooftops. But he was not the first to manifest it. The Magi were.

WHAT UNHOLY COMPANY HE KEPT!

Baptism of the Lord.
A: Mt. 3: 13-17.

A surprise best-seller once hit our bookstores, a re-telling of the gospel story with the catchy title, *The Greatest Story Ever Told.* Actually, the title makes good sense. The first thing to note about Christianity is that at bottom it is a gripping story. The creed we recite on Sundays is packed with lofty theology, but its kernel is in the words at the center. There we proclaim that we accept as historically true the major events in the story of Jesus, events far stranger than fiction.

Take two events from the opening pages of this story. First, an obscure maiden is visited by an angel and no sooner says yes to the angel's invitation than the infinite God steps into our finite world and is locked in her womb. Next, her infant is born in a stable, his coming noted only by shepherds. Who would have expected the Lord of the universe to make so quiet an entrance into history? No spinner of yarns ever devised tales more marvelous than what in our creed we declare to be fact.

The baptism of Jesus also strains credulity. The infant of Bethlehem has grown to manhood and is now on the threshold of his career. What that career will be we state in our creed: he "came down from heaven for our salvation," that is, to free us from the bondage of sin. How does this crusader against sin launch his career? The gospel account defies logic: he submits to John's baptism, a ceremony designed for sinners.

Hard to believe, but true. Even those who do not accept Scripture as God's word concede that this episode rings true, for the simple reason that no believer would dare invent it. The early Christians guarded their faith fiercely. Among its doctrines none was more certain than that Jesus was the sinless son of God. Yet here Matthew shows him receiving baptism along with a crowd of self-declared sinners, as though he were a sinner himself. Even John protests, "I need to be baptized by you, and yet you are coming to me?" Unless the event had been recorded in Scripture, no Christian would be willing to believe it.

Why does Jesus ask John to baptize him? To "fulfill all righteousness," he says, without explaining why righteousness demands it. Many reasons have been suggested. Here is one.

When God entered Mary's womb, he became a complete human being. That was the whole point of the incarnation. He was now our blood brother, with an inside knowledge of what a child of Adam feels like. No longer can God be regarded as an uncaring taskmaster in the skies, with little patience for our weaknesses and failures. Another name for Jesus is Emmanuel, meaning "God is with us." Being with us, he can sympathize with us in our daily struggles. Whatever we experience, he experienced.

With one exception. He could not sin. He could not know how it feels to engage in a mugging or patronize a prostitute or exchange poisonous gossip with neighbors. Scripture says he ate and drank with sinners, not that he joined them in sin. If sin, as some seem to think, is the most human of human experiences, then in that sense Jesus was not fully human.

Although he could not join his fellow Israelites in sin, however, he could be with them while they repented of sin. That is what he is doing in this baptismal scene. He is companion to the sinners at the Jordan while they are in the act of renouncing their flirtation with evil and returning to God.

The people Jesus lines up with at the Jordan have been touched by the baptizer's words. Realizing how far they have strayed, they are working up courage to shut the door on the past and get a fresh start. Jesus can see shame for their faults in their faces and hunger for God in their eyes as they wait for John's baptism to cleanse them. Watching them, mingling with them, he comes as close as a sinless person can to experiencing repentance for sin. He sees how hard it is for a frail human being to turn from habitual vice. No wonder that in later life he will show such compassion for sinners.

By accepting baptism Jesus in effect says to his Father: these sinners are my people, I am their brother. They are often self-seeking, sometimes malicious, always weak; they pray bravely on Sabbaths and sin brazenly on weekdays; long to be cleansed one minute, then plunge into muck the next. But they are struggling to change, and I know from being with them how painful their struggle is. I will be their champion. Let my sufferings make up for their sins. My life and labors are for them.

That the Father accepts his offering is clear from the voice that speaks from the heavens, "This is my beloved Son, with whom I am well pleased." At this the sky opens and the Spirit descends on Jesus. The inauguration of Jesus is over. The career of the sinless one on behalf of sinners has begun.

When Ceremonies Count

Baptism of the Lord.
B: Mk. 1: 7-11.

❖❖❖

The evangelist Mark was a man of few words. Of the four gospels his is by far the briefest, less than two-thirds the size of Matthew's or Luke's. He omits the lengthy discourses of Jesus, making no mention of the Sermon on the Mount or the moving words Jesus spoke to his apostles at the Last Supper. What to many readers is even more surprising, he is stone silent about the birth of Jesus and his years of growth at Nazareth.

Instead, his gospel begins abruptly with a sketch of John the Baptist, the austere prophet who dwelt in the wilderness west of the Dead Sea. To the earnest Israelites who came swarming to his dessert hermitage, John's words urging them to abandon their sinful ways were like a clap of thunder. He warned that the Messiah, a man whose sandals he was himself unworthy to loosen, was sure to come soon. They must all prepare.

To help them prepare, John devised a ceremony he called a baptism of repentance. From the far corners of Judea sinners came crowding to the Jordan, eager for this baptism. This was their way of signaling their resolve to return to the Lord.

Suddenly, a mere seven verses into Mark's gospel, Jesus of Nazareth makes his appearance. He is already in full bloom of adulthood, about thirty years old. He has come to the Jordan for the same reason as the others, to submit to John's baptism.

Jesus was every inch a human being. Like the rest of us, he made use of ceremony to underscore important moments in his life. This day of his baptism was one of the most important.

If we humans were nothing more than thinking machines, we could dispense with ceremony. We are not, however, computers, but creatures of flesh and blood. Sights and sounds as well as the inner feelings that go with them are the stuff of our daily experience, and so the visible, tangible rituals of ceremony answer a need. The cake and candles at a child's birthday, the cap-and-gown procession at a graduation, the exchange of rings at a wedding—symbols like these fulfill a deep-seated craving. They express the meaning and emotions of the moment, help us to store them in the treasury of memory. Life stripped of all ceremony would be an emotionless wasteland.

John's penitents wanted to scrape away the grime of past sins, to start life again with a thoroughly clean slate. What more natural way to externalize this resolve for reform and call it to heaven's attention than with a ceremonial washing?

John's baptism was not in the same class as our Christian baptism, which owes its origin to Jesus himself. It did not issue, as ours does, in an outpouring of the Spirit, a real infusion of divine grace. Nor was it a rite of initiation into the Christian community, since the Christian Church did not yet exist. Viewed simply as a ceremony, however, it beats by a mile the pale ritual of baptism as administered in most churches today. Instead of releasing a mere thimble of water on the head of his penitents, John immersed them in the Jordan, plunging them head and shoulders into its waters. The good dunking John gave them made them feel clean all over. It was their way of telling God they were ready for a fresh start.

Baptism by immersion, which was customary among early Christians, is still an option in the Church, although for practical reasons it is rarely practiced today. If you want to see how it works, go visit Saint Joseph's church in Benin City, Nigeria, some Holy Saturday. There, unless the fervor of the parishioners and the vigor of the priests have ebbed since my last visit, you will see a multitude of adult converts baptized in true John-the-Baptist style. Unfortunately, Nigeria is an ocean away. But this ceremony is a sight worth traveling for.

Why did Jesus submit to John's baptism? With him there was no question of preparing for the Messiah. He *was* the Messiah, as the voice from the skies declared. Nor had he need to win pardon for sins of his own. As God's "beloved Son," in whom the Father was "well pleased," he was without the possibility of sin and had nothing to wash away. Then why seek baptism? What important moment in life did this ceremony mark for him?

The answer is not hard to find. The voice from the heavens told it all. This was the beginning of his career as Messiah. Up to now Jesus had been hidden in the hill town of Nazareth. With his baptism the curtain opened on his public career.

It was to be a career of rescuing sinners. He paid the price for our sin, accepting the punishment we deserve. Saint Paul said he "emptied" himself, took the "form of a slave" *(Phil. 2:7),* words that sum up the career of Jesus well. But this baptism ceremony, when Jesus stood side by side with the sinners he came into the world to redeem, sums it up even better.

"A VOICE CAME FROM HEAVEN"

Baptism of the Lord.
C: Lk. 3: 15-16; 21-22.

❖❖❖

If we were looking for a single scene to illustrate the entire career of Jesus Christ, we could probably find none better than the one Mark describes in this gospel. Picture him standing on the shore of the River Jordan, awaiting his turn for baptism. The crowd in line with him is typical of the crowds he will mingle with through the rest of his life. All levels of society are there—the rich as well as the poor, the daintily clad alongside the ragged, the learned rubbing elbows with the unschooled. All have one thing in common: they are sinners—some petty offenders, others steeped in vice. The reason they are at the Jordan is to be washed clean of their sins.

In this random sample of Israelites we see the kind of people who have always made up the mass of humanity. If Jesus felt discomfort in the company of any of them, he did not show it. He was in this world to redeem the entire human race.

Good Christians are sometimes puzzled by scenes like this, wondering how the sinless Jesus could mix so freely with the odious as well as the upright. But Jesus did not intend to spend the years of his ministry keeping his distance from those most in need of his presence. For the next few years he was going to live at close quarters with Israelites of all kinds, breaking bread and conversing freely with the worst as well as the best. From Day One he made friends with both sinners and saints.

The day Luke describes in this gospel was one of the most memorable in the life of Jesus, for on this day his mission as savior of the world officially began. After receiving John's baptism, he stood for a while knee-deep in the Jordan, wrapped in trance-like communion with his Father. This was a solemn moment, one of only three in the gospels when the Almighty spoke directly from the heavens. The skies opened, a dove descended on Jesus, and the divine voice came thundering down.

To the contemporaries of Jesus the words spoken from on high meant more than they can possibly mean to us, for they contained allusions to two biblical passages most Jews knew by heart. Both pointed to Jesus as the Messiah.

"You are my Son" is from the second Psalm of David, and a Jew would immediately recognize it as Messianic. At this time Israel was alive with rumors that the Messiah, the long-awaited king who would liberate Israel and save her sinful children, would soon appear on the scene. John the Baptist had to quash persistent speculation that he was himself the Messiah. To those who asked him, he insisted he was only the herald of the king who was about to appear. Now the divine voice announced that Jesus was that king. Thus did the Messianic Age begin.

The words "With you I am well pleased" are from Isaiah *(42:1)* where the mission of the Messiah is pictured as one of service and sacrifice. There he is poetically described as one who will bring freedom to the imprisoned, sight to the blind, and light to those in darkness. Thus did the voice define the *kind* of Messiah Jesus was to be: not a king who would lord it over his subjects, but one who would be their servant.

Jesus would say of himself that he was among us as "the one who serves" *(Lk. 22:27).* Messiah and king though he was, he never demanded the bowing and scraping that were due to royalty. Among that crowd at the Jordan he was completely at ease. He was going to spend the rest of his days serving them.

A genuine feel for the common people and desire to share their lot have always been rare commodities among the world's leaders. A Roman poet summed up the attitude of most people at the top in the words, "I detest the unholy mob and keep my distance." When told that her subjects had no bread, Marie Antoinette is said to have yawned back, "Let them eat cake." A business tycoon of the last century, whose family fortune had been made by milking the public, once snapped, "Let the public be damned." And a wealthy American candidate for high office, when asked to make a campaign stop at an inner city ghetto, quipped in reply, "If you've seen one slum you've seen them all." Leaders with a truly Lincolnesque touch are rare.

The greatest populist of all time is Jesus Christ, and today's gospel shows him in a typical moment. We can imagine ourselves standing with him in that crowd of newly baptized. It is a good scene to keep in mind when we become discouraged with ourselves or with the entire human race. Those who had been bathed in the Jordan by John were ready for a fresh start. So should we be when we have fallen from grace and have gone to our Savior for forgiveness. He will not run from us in horror.

Like the manger of Bethlehem and the cross of Calvary, this scene sums up his career: among sinners as one who serves.

A LAMB LED TO SLAUGHTER

Second Sunday in Ordinary Time.
A: Jn. 1: 29-34.

"Behold, the Lamb of God, who takes away the sin of the world." Shortly before distributing communion at Mass the priest holds up the consecrated host and echoes these words of John the Baptist. Many find them enigmatic. What did they mean to those who heard John utter them? What should they mean for us?

People today picture a lamb as a cuddly animal with snow-white fleece. To see how different a picture it might have evoked for John, I suggest an imaginary journey to biblical Jerusalem. Be prepared for culture shock. Animal rights activists and those who sicken at the sight of blood should stay home.

We join a gathering of early-bird worshipers in the court of the temple, facing the altar of holocaust. For centuries the ceremony we are about to behold has taken place twice daily, at dawn and dusk. John, whose father was a temple priest, knew the ritual well. Jesus, who frequented the temple on his visits to Jerusalem, must have witnessed it on many occasions.

A lamb is led to the altar, where a perpetual fire burns and a priest waits. The scene recalls the words of Isaiah, "a lamb led to the slaughter...smitten for the sin of his people" *(53:7-8).* The ceremony opens with the priest laying his hands on the lamb's head, offering it in atonement for the sins of the entire nation. Next he slits its throat and slowly sprinkles the blood over the altar. Then he skins it, quarters it, and washes the parts. Finally, the whole mess is thrown into the fire. The watchers remain until the carcass is totally consumed in the flames. That is what the word "holocaust" means.

Imagine the questions you might ask. Was the temple also the daily site for scores of private sacrifices? Did it reek with the blood, not only of lambs, but of doves, pigeons, goats, rams, and bulls? Did not Jerusalem have hungry people who could have feasted on all that food? Above all, was this butchering of defenseless animals really deemed a sacred act?

Yes on all counts. But we ought not judge the ancient Jews by our current norms. They did not lack affection for animals or take perverse delight in blood. To them God was a living presence in the temple, the source of all that is good, including the animals on which they fed. Then why slaughter a healthy lamb before his eyes? Because they believed that by so doing, by depriving themselves of its food, they gave the lamb back to God. This was their way of atoning for the sins of the nation.

That we find this notion strange says as much about ourselves as about the ancients. We have lost their sense of God's claims on his creatures, of our dependence on him and need for him. Animal sacrifice is one way of paying for sin (as well as praising God and seeking his help.) It was as natural as air to the ancients. It still is to some so-called "primitive" people. Rather than censure them we might ask if God has as high a place in our lives as he did and does in theirs.

After baptizing Jesus, John had seen the spirit descend on him like a dove, and by this sign knew he was God's Chosen One, the Messiah. By now calling him God's lamb, John showed that he glimpsed an even more astonishing truth: the Messiah would liberate his people by offering, not an animal, but himself as a sacrifice for their sins. In the words of Isaiah again, "He was pierced for our offenses, crushed for our sins... The Lord laid upon him the guilt of us all" *(53:5-6)*.

John would not live to see Calvary, a bloody sacrifice far more harrowing than any temple holocaust. It was there that the need for animal sacrifices ended. Jesus was the perfect, final sacrifice for the sins of mankind. By shedding his blood on the cross he paid the penalty for the sins of the entire world and made it possible for us to be friends with God again.

Jesus died only once. But at Mass he comes to the altar under the appearances of bread and wine and offers again to the Father the blood he once shed on the cross. He can suffer no more. But he can and does renew the offering of what he once suffered on our behalf. That is what the Church means when it calls the Mass the unbloody sacrifice of Calvary.

The daybreak holocaust at the temple was not a private ceremony. The lamb, which belonged to all the people, was slain for the sins of all. Those who watched the ceremony were united in heart with the priest when he laid his hands on the lamb's head. With him they offered its blood to God.

Nor is our Mass a private ceremony, and those attending should not be passive spectators. All should join the priest as the priest joins Jesus Christ in renewing the offering of Calvary. Our prayers and personal sacrifices can be joined to the holocaust of Calvary for our sins and those of the world.

MEETING THE MAN WHO WILL CHANGE THEIR LIVES

Second Sunday in Ordinary Time.
B: Jn. 1: 35-42.

❖❖❖

In last week's gospel the evangelist Mark described how Jesus was baptized in the Jordan by John, the penitential prophet of the desert. With this ceremonial washing, Jesus inaugurated his public career. He had arrived at the Jordan an obscure carpenter from Nazareth. Now, filled with the Spirit, he was about to turn into the most talked-about person in Israel.

The evangelist John takes up the story where Mark left off. Jesus had no intention of pursuing his mission alone. For the world-shaking enterprise he was launching, he needed co-workers, disciples to carry on after his days on earth were over. Here we learn where and how he found his first recruits.

It was no chance encounter. The Baptist himself did the introducing. Spying the newly baptized Jesus at the river bank, John pointed and said, "Behold, the Lamb of God." The two for whom he did the pointing were Andrew and an unnamed companion, two fishermen from Galilee among John's disciples. They were probably at a loss to know what "Lamb of God" meant, but were sure it must be important, so important it sent them trailing after this mysterious wayfarer in hopes of learning more.

John made no secret of his own insignificance, declaring bluntly that he was not himself the Messiah, God's promised liberator for Israel. All he was, he told his followers, was the Messiah's advance man. His task was to make them realize their liberation was close at hand. The two disciples must have wondered if this stranger, so highly praised by the Baptist, was the Messiah all Israel awaited. And so they sought a chance to meet him, to learn at first hand the kind of person he was.

The evangelist's account of what followed has all the marks of an eyewitness account. From earliest times readers have suspected that one of the two who chased after Jesus and spent the late afternoon with him, the unnamed one, was none other than the evangelist (also named John) himself. If so, it is one of the biggest days in his life he is describing, the day he first set eyes on Jesus, the day he fell under his spell.

There on the banks of the Jordan these two disciples met the man who was destined to change their lives. To say they were swept off their feet would be an understatement. At first they addressed Jesus as Rabbi, a term of respect for a teacher, especially a teacher of divine wisdom. After only a few hours in his presence they dared to think he was indeed the Messiah, the promised liberator of Israel. Andrew lost no time breaking this startling news to his brother and fishing partner, Simon.

And so it came about that Jesus had his first meeting with the man who was to be his chief apostle. In time, he told Simon, he would change his name to "Kephas" (Peter in English), a word meaning rock. The name, with good reason, stuck.

Important as this passage is for understanding where and how Jesus met his first disciples, some readers are disappointed. We are told that Andrew and his companion spent the afternoon conversing with Jesus and at the end of it were wholly won over, feeling he was the fulfillment of centuries of Jewish longings. But what words were exchanged? What did Jesus say to intimate to these men that he was who he was, the Messiah? We would give a world to know. But the evangelist supplies not a hint.

Although we will never know what words Jesus spoke, however, one lesson of the episode is clear. It was not what the scribes taught or John the Baptist preached that made the difference in the lives of these two, but their personal encounter with Jesus. In this brief meeting he radiated such sympathy and wisdom that they knew only God could be the source. That is how Jesus impressed others throughout his life. People were attracted to him not nearly so much by what he said or even did as by what he was. His gift to the world was not a system of theology or a compendium of moral instructions, but himself.

It will always be so. No pagan ever became a Christian and no Christian a better Christian just by reading what theologians say about Jesus or by weighing the pros and cons of apologetics. Other human beings, themselves imbued with his spirit, may introduce us to him, as John did these disciples. But ultimately we must encounter our Redeemer for ourselves.

Is this possible? Yes. The Jesus of history is dead. But the risen Jesus, the Jesus who reigns in heaven, still lives. He speaks to us in prayer, he comes to us in the sacraments. If we ask where he dwells, he gives us the same reply he gave to the two disciples, "Come, and you will see."

Jesus welcomes us today as gladly as he once welcomed these two disciples. He is always willing to talk with us. We too can be swept off our feet. We too can fall under his spell.

"THE BEGINNING OF HIS SIGNS"

Second Sunday in Ordinary Time.
C: Jn. 2: 1-12.

"Jesus did this as the beginning of his signs in Cana in Galilee and so revealed his glory." What a strange sign it was, and what an unexpectedly raffish kind of glory! Unless John's gospel had told us so, who would have dreamed that the Word Incarnate would inaugurate his career as a wonder-worker by adding to the alcoholic cheer of a wedding party? The episode seems out of character for so austere a prophet as Jesus. It has embarrassed preachers of teetotalism for centuries.

One escape, to be sure, is to focus attention on the symbolic nature of the sign. Thus one commentator assures us that "wine represents wisdom and teaching." True enough. But if wine is a symbol, it is also a reality. And this wine, according to the headwaiter, was a lip-smacking, rumpus-raising reality. We cannot understand the sign of Cana unless we admit that because of what Jesus did there the departing guests were at least a little less sober than they had been on arrival.

The quantity of wine, about 120 gallons, has raised eyebrows. The figure is not so staggering, however, when we consider the nature of wedding feasts in ancient Palestine. Our age has grown used to increasingly lavish wedding receptions, but few of these can match the extravagance of such events in biblical times. A wedding for the Israelites of old was cause for celebration, not just by the immediate family and friends, but by the extended family, indeed the entire village.

The festivities might last as long as a week, featuring choral songs, group dancing, and other forms of entertainment. Enthroned at the center were the bride and groom, both elaborately ornamented. For the final session of such a party, 120 gallons of wine would be generous, but not gargantuan.

The dialogue between Jesus and Mary can be puzzling. It proceeded, as conversations between intimates often do, by hints and suggestions rather than direct statement. Mary uttered no explicit request. She simply pointed to the awkward situation that had arisen, the potential embarrassment of bride and groom. By his reply Jesus showed that he understood Mary's unspoken plea. The translation of the lectionary is somewhat stilted. "Woman, how does your concern affect me?" A more colloquial rendition would be "Mother, what do you want me to do?"

When Jesus went on to say, "My hour has not yet come," a bystander might have interpreted these words as a refusal. But Mary, who could read the tone of his voice, knew otherwise. His mission had not yet officially begun, but Mary realized that her words had prompted him to consider anticipating its time. Cana could do as well as anywhere for his initial display of power. And so she immediately turned to the servers and bade them do whatever her son should ask.

Another puzzler in this colloquy is Jesus' use of "Woman" in addressing his mother. Scholars assure us this implied no lack of respect, as it would in modern English. This is certainly true. But the word still smacks of a formality we do not expect a son to use towards his mother, especially in a private conversation amid the relaxed atmosphere of a wedding feast.

The only other appearance Mary makes in John's gospel is at Calvary, and there again Jesus addressed her as "woman" when he entrusted her to the beloved disciple's care. Commentators have suggested that by using so formal a term in narrating these episodes John wants to stress that Mary should be regarded, not simply as the physical mother of Jesus, but as the mother of us all. In *Genesis*, Eve is "woman," for she is mother of all the living. Mary, the new Eve, replaced her and is now mother of all mankind.

For symbol-hunters the "changing water into wine" provides a rich mine. The trouble with their interpretations is not that they are false but that they may draw attention away from three plain but important lessons this story certainly embodies.

First, the mere presence of Jesus at such a scene of revelry tells a lot about Jesus; it also tells us more than a little about revelry and its place in the life of a follower of Jesus.

Second, Mary's alertness to her host's plight, along with her swiftness and tact in arranging to remedy it, reveals a thoughtfulness all children of Mary should emulate.

Finally, that Jesus replied to her suggestion so promptly and so much more than adequately is evidence of how powerful her influence was—and is. Those who question the traditional Catholic devotion to Mary will always have this episode to contend with. No son could be more loving to his mother than Jesus, no mother more caring for her children than Mary for this bride and groom. The power of Mary, Mother of newly-weds and Mother of mankind, is nowhere more triumphantly vindicated.

AN ORDINARY FOURSOME

Third Sunday in Ordinary Time.
A: Mt. 4: 12-23 (or 12-17).

"Jesus withdrew to Galilee." In modern idiom, he went off to the boondocks, for that is what Galilee was. His enemies never forgot the rustic origins of this carpenter-turned-preacher whom the rabble touted as the Messiah. To the polished urbanites of Jerusalem, Jesus was a hick. He hailed from the hilltop hamlet of Nazareth, made his headquarters in the remote lakeside town of Capernaum, and spent most of his energy haranguing yokels in the Galilean back country. Such slender credentials made them sure he could not be the divinely accredited prophet some said he was. Jesus was a nobody. He came from nowhere.

Matthew saw things differently. He wrote his gospel for Jews who had converted to Christianity, and so used a passage from Jewish Scripture as evidence that, far from being a place where no one should expect the Messiah to sprout up, Galilee had the stamp of approval from none other than the prophet Isaiah. The prophet Micah *(5:1)* had identified insignificant Bethlehem as the Messiah's birthplace; but for the locale where the Messiah's career would flourish, the prophet Isaiah pinpointed Galilee *(8:23-9:1).*

What was Galilee really like? This northernmost province of Palestine measured about fifty miles from north to south, twenty-five from east to west, making it roughly a third the size of Puerto Rico, a tenth the land mass of the Philippines. The prophet Isaiah called it "heathen," but this should not mislead us. In the time of Jesus its inhabitants were mostly Jews, many of them notoriously pious Jews. Galilee was heathen only in the sense that it was surrounded by Gentile country. If anything, this intensified the fierce nationalism of its inhabitants.

Physically, Galilee was one of the garden spots of the Mediterranean world. Rich soil, ample water, and a glorious climate made the land extremely fertile and hence, for a rural area, heavily populated. On its eastern border it featured a lake (somewhat pompously called the "Sea" of Galilee), a well-mined source of fish. Hundreds of fishing boats plied its waters.

Here it was that Jesus lived and labored for most of the days between his baptism and his crucifixion. This despised corner of a despised nation was the cradle of Christianity, where Jesus first proclaimed the kingdom of heaven and called on his fellow Israelites to reform their lives. Here also he found men who would carry on his work after he was gone. Matthew tells us how he called the first four of them, fishermen all, the brothers Peter and Andrew and the brothers James and John.

If we had only Matthew's account to go by, we might imagine these four made the most momentous decision of their lives with hardly a moment's reflection. His description of the episode is as delightful as it is unconvincing: Jesus makes a chance acquaintance with some fishermen at their nets by the lakeside, tersely bids them come after him, and lickety-split, off they trot, trailing like lapdogs at his feet. An unlikely scenario.

John's gospel supplies the missing detail. Jesus had made his first impression (a sensational one) on the four several months earlier, when he met them among the disciples of John the Baptist by the River Jordan. And we can presume they all furthered their acquaintance after he quit Nazareth and came to live in Capernaum. Matthew telescopes these events, focusing on the dramatic moment when Jesus finally disclosed his plan. They were to come with him and fish for men. Overjoyed at the prospect, they abandoned their nets and accepted his call.

How should we characterize these four men on whose shoulders the future of Christianity was to rest? They were neither at the top nor the bottom of the social and economic scales. Fishing was an undistinguished but honorable trade and, in a land where fish was a staple at table, must have provided a decent living. They did not belong to the educated class, but their future achievements reveal them as far from slow-witted. And their piety is beyond question. Had they been spiritual slouches, they would not have joined the company of John the Baptist.

In short, these were ordinary people, the kind you don't expect to run for mayor or make a million or be headlined in the tabloids. But ordinariness is no curse. Lincoln said God must love ordinary people very much, he made so many of them.

These four loved God so much in return that they are now among the saints in heaven. For those of us who count ourselves ordinary people, therein lies the lesson of this episode. If these men could make it, so can we. The Lord does not call all of us to such extraordinary labors as he did them, a lifetime of fishing for souls. But almost every day he calls ordinary people to do some labor for his kingdom. To join that foursome of fishermen in heaven, all we need do is answer these calls.

It All Started with Fish

Third Sunday in Ordinary Time.
B. Mk. 1: 14-20.

❖❖❖

From what economic level did the earliest disciples come? Certainly not the lowest. The fishermen Jesus found by the lakeside made a decent living. Affluent they certainly were not, but also far from indigent. How could they be when they plied their trade on waters as teeming with fish as the Sea of Galilee? An historian of the times counted 330 fishing craft on this lake. With meat a rare luxury, fish was a staple of the average family's diet. When they peddled the catch of the day, the disciples could never have been short of customers.

Nor ought we picture these disciples, rough men of the outdoors though they were, as being dull-witted or uncouth. They did not, it is true, belong to the learned class. But only a snob thinks brains and manners go inevitably or exclusively with formal education. Those who lack schooling are often better equipped for life, shrewder and more genuinely courteous, than those who have had their full of it. The later history of these disciples reveals them rich in these qualities.

In this passage Jesus finds four Galilean fishermen, two pairs of brothers, and bids them "come after" him. What coming after him will entail, they have no idea. The only clue Jesus gives is that he will transform them into "fishers of men," a job description that gives nothing away. Still, they are so captivated by him that they gladly say good-bye to their nets, although uncertain of what the future will bring.

We cannot reconstruct all the details of what the future actually did bring to these men of the lake. But we do know that all four went on to labors almost beyond their strength and to accomplishments far beyond their dreams. No historian questions the importance of what these followers of Jesus did. Although only fishermen, they changed the course of human events.

Of the four, Andrew's career is the murkiest. He appears several more times in the gospels, always in a subordinate role. *Acts* puts him among the twelve who gathered in Jerusalem after the ascension of Jesus, received the Holy Spirit on Pentecost, and set out to preach the gospel to the world. Regarding the particulars of his later activity, however, we have no reliable record. One tradition says he carried the gospel to Greece, where he was was martyred on a cross shaped like an X.

About James we know much more. He and his brother John were dubbed "sons of thunder" by Jesus *(Mk. 3:17)*, probably because they were inclined to rash, tempestuous conduct. (Those similarly inclined can take comfort in knowing such tendencies are not incompatible with high sanctity.) Along with Peter these two were closest to Jesus, the ones who beheld him transfigured and were with him during the agony at Gethsemane. After Pentecost James preached the gospel to his fellow Jews so well that a scarce decade later he was beheaded on orders of Herod Agrippa, one of the infamous Herods of Scripture *(Acts: 12: 2)*.

John, brother of James, is the only apostle about whom we have no tradition of martyrdom. Paul calls him one of the "pillars" of the Christian community in Jerusalem *(Gal. 2: 9)*. According to some sources he lived into the next century and died surrounded by disciples in the Grecian city of Ephesus. His greatest accomplishment, for which generations of Christians have been grateful, was the fourth gospel. Even if, as scholars suspect, he did not personally pen every word of it, this gospel is very probably based on his memory of his days with Jesus. People once credited him with *Revelation*, but that is less certain.

Peter is the only apostle who we know for a fact was married *(Mk. 1: 30)*. Whether his wife was a help or hindrance or even alive as he roamed through the world preaching the good news are among the unsolved mysteries of Scripture. All four gospels attest his pre-eminence among the apostles, a position bestowed on him by Jesus himself. *Acts* describes his leadership in the early Church. Although Paul is known as the apostle of the Gentiles, Peter was the first to baptize a non-Jew *(Acts 10)*, an act he would not have dared unless ordered to do so by the Holy Spirit. After settling in Rome, he was martyred there during Nero's persecution in 67-68 A.D. His burial place can be seen today under the main altar of the basilica that bears his name.

The Church urges us to imitate the saints. With saints such as these four, however, imitation is surely beyond our reach. But remember how they started, plain fishermen of Galilee. God doesn't ask us to match their works, but he does ask us to respond to his daily calls as they did, gladly and generously. When Jesus bade them come after him, they little suspected where the journey would end. As long as he was in the lead, however, none of them cared. Come to think of it, neither should we.

ALL EYES ON THE PULPIT

Third Sunday in Ordinary Time.
C: Lk. 1: 1-4; 4: 14-21.

❖❖❖

Tourists in Israel soon learn that the best way to get around that country is by bus. If they are traveling any distance on a Friday afternoon, however, they should be advised to get to the depot in good time. This was brought home to me when I found myself one Friday afternoon almost stranded in the town of Tiberias by the shore of the Sea of Galilee. Although I walked into the depot at what seemed the reasonably safe time of 1:55, I barely caught the last bus of the day for Jerusalem.

That is how I learned that the Sabbath, the seventh day of the week, officially begins at sunset on Friday. No Israeli bus driver dares start a journey unless confident of reaching his destination before the start of the day God set apart for rest and worship. The Sabbath is one of the most ancient and revered institutions of the Jewish religion, inscribed on the tablets Moses received from God on Mount Sinai.

What the Sabbath was and is for Jews, Sunday became and is for Christians. The choice of Sunday as our day of repose and worship goes back to the primitive Church. The Jews celebrate the seventh day of creation, when God rested; we celebrate the dawn of our Christian age, when Jesus rose from the dead.

This episode takes place on a Sabbath in Nazareth, the town where Jesus "had grown up." He was on a visit to the old haunts of his childhood, mingling with the neighbors and kinfolk he had left behind several months earlier when he set forth to launch his career as teacher and healer. Observant Jew that he was, Jesus went to the Sabbath service in the synagogue "according to his custom." There he took his place alongside the other worshipers, all familiar faces from his past.

The service in those days was lengthy, but simple: first a hymn and opening prayer, then a reading from Scripture followed by a homily, and finally a prayer capped with the concluding blessing. A male from the congregation was called on to read the Scripture and deliver the homily. On this occasion the choice fell on Jesus, whose reputation as a man of God was spreading.

The best way to envision the scene is to imagine how our Sunday congregation would feel if our church were hosting a newly ordained priest who once grew up in the parish. The people of Nazareth were curious about Jesus, just as we would be about our old neighbor turned priest. Will we recognize in him the child we once knew? How will he appear in the pulpit, and how well will his voice carry? What will he say in his homily?

The Nazarenes, in fact, had reason to be far more curious about Jesus than we would be about any new priest. In the months since setting out on his own, Jesus had turned into the most captivating preacher ever heard in the synagogues or on the hillsides of Galilee, and rumors had drifted back about the commotion he was causing. People said that in his words they sensed a more-than-human power. He spoke with authority.

Jesus did not elaborate on the numerous *do's* and *dont's* of Judaism, as did the scribes, the trained experts in Jewish religious law. *Good* news was what he dispensed, proclaiming that a new day had dawned for the children of Israel, that God himself was visiting his people and that his kingdom on earth had already begun. In short, the Messiah had arrived. The text Jesus chose to read to his old fellow villagers of Nazareth during this Sabbath service was a passage in which Isaiah *(61: 1-2; 58: 6)* describes the blessings of the Messianic age.

It is not easy for us to grasp the meaning of Isaiah's words. Taken literally, they read like a handout touting some candidate for public office, brimming with promises for blessings that will follow victory. Support this candidate and happy days will be here again: poverty will vanish and oppression cease, the handicapped will be helped and prisoners freed. This of course is only the literal meaning, while Isaiah was writing poetry. If we read his words as poetry should be read, for their inner meaning, we will see that, far from expressing the hollow promises of a politician, they hold the rich promises of God.

The new age that Jesus ushered in is still with us. We are assured of this every time we attend Mass on Sunday. Our world, like the one that Jesus walked in, is mired in spiritual poverty, polluted by sin, and rent with conflict. Left to ourselves, we are, all of us, captives of our own selfishness, caged in by unholy desires, blind to God's goodness and love.

But we are not left to ourselves. Jesus comes to our altars every Sunday just as surely as he attended the synagogue at Nazareth, and to us he delivers the same glad tidings he brought to the congregation there. We can all be spiritually rich, free, strong. We can all live our days in the favor of the Lord.

MUST A CHRISTIAN BE A WIMP?

Fourth Sunday in Ordinary Time.
A: Mt. 5: 1-12.

❖❖❖

What does Jesus mean when he says "the meek" are blessed?

Most people think of meekness more as a curse, that to be meek is to be spineless, submissive, passive—a wimp; and even a wimp would not call wimpiness a blessing. The early martyrs whose blood was the seed of the Church were far from spineless. The heroes of history who waged war on such outrages as slavery, colonialism, and segregation were anything but submissive. If history were shaped by the religiously and politically passive, where would we be today? Jesus must have had a different meaning for meekness.

He did. And since he once called himself meek, we can make a good guess at his meaning by looking at him.

A meek person is often viewed as someone not prone to anger, unwilling to take a strong stand against abuse. But if this were true, Jesus Christ himself was not meek. He was capable of towering anger. Twice in the gospels his wrath rose to fever pitch: when he drove the money changers and peddlers from the temple, and when he fulminated against the scribes and Pharisees.

But look at the kind of anger Jesus displayed on these occasions. It is best described as *meek* anger.

He never flared up merely because he felt personally injured. In turning the house the nation had built for divine worship into a market for private profit, the desecrators of the temple had sinned against God and the Jewish people. That alone was the reason for his anger. And although the scribes and Pharisees had slandered and obstructed his work, it was not for these offenses that Jesus lambasted them. Rather, he exposed them for perverting religion, for replacing piety with pride, and for putting intolerable burdens on the masses.

Jesus never directed his anger against individuals. On the last day of his life he endured with silence the insults and physical assaults of the Roman soldiers. In his trials before the Sanhedrin and Pontius Pilate he answered the charges with calm dignity. On reaching Calvary he asked God to forgive his murderers, even excusing them on the grounds that "they know not what they do" *(Lk. 23: 24)*. Jesus did not aim to hurt. Institutions and public abuses were his targets, not humans.

The anger of Jesus was always controlled. He never just blew his top. His rage was not a temper tantrum, but a means of drawing attention to corruption and abuse.

According to Aristotle, a virtue is the middle point between two extremes. On the one side, for example, is the vice of rashness, as in the warrior who exposes himself to enemy fire without good reason or ample protection; on the other is the vice of cowardice, bolting away on first sight of the foe. Bravery, the virtue, occupies the middle territory.

The meekness Jesus displayed fits Aristotle's formula. It is the middle ground between complacent acceptance of public injustice and corruption on the one hand and personalized or uncontrolled wrath on the other. If his followers achieve a like meekness, they will indeed be blessed.

Two other beatitudes shed light on the virtue of meekness.

"Blessed are the peacemakers." The genuine peacemaker must be meek. To maintain peace it may be necessary to remain silent even when sorely hurt. We cannot promote peace if we demand recompense for every real or supposed injustice we suffer. This does not mean a Christian must never sue for damages or seek payment for debts. But insisting always on the last ounce is unchristian. Standing up for one's rights can be wrong.

"Blessed are they who hunger and thirst for righteousness." The "righteousness" for which we are to hunger and thirst refers primarily to personal holiness, but it also includes the righteousness of society. No Christian should be content to accept without angry protest the injustices that permeate our world. We cannot all be among the leaders, but at least we can be loyal followers in the fight against abortion, racism, poverty, the arms race, and similar abominations. Those who sit on the sidelines are not models of genuine meekness but chicken-livered loafers. The beatitudes were not meant for them.

Saying that virtue is the middle point between two extremes does not mean it should be pursued with only a middling amount of effort. We cannot be too meek, any more than we can be too just or too brave. Once we find the midpoint between hot-tempered sensitivity to personal injury on the one side and wimpish passivity in the face of public corruption on the other, we should pursue it with passion. To parody an old political slogan: extremism in the exercise of Christian meekness is no vice, and moderation in making Jesus our model of meekness no virtue.

SPELLBINDER OF CAPERNAUM

Fourth Sunday in Ordinary Time.
B: Mk. 1: 21-28.

If asked what sites in Israel they would above all like to visit, most Christians would name three: Bethlehem, where Jesus was born; Nazareth, where he grew up; and Jerusalem, where he died and rose from the dead. Today all three locations have shrines under the reverential care of Franciscans, as well as hostels to accommodate pilgrims from all over the world.

A fourth location should be added, one repeatedly mentioned in the gospels: Capernaum. There, on the northwest shore of the Sea of Galilee, the fisherman Peter and his brother Andrew once shared a house in which Jesus was always welcome. During the two or three years of his public ministry he seems to have been mostly on the road, preaching throughout Galilee. But this house remained his base, the nearest thing he had to a home.

Not much is left of Capernaum today, certainly nothing to bring to mind the bustling port it was in biblical times. Even its name has changed; on maps it now appears as Tell Hum. But Tell Hum is well worth the journey there. Archaeologists have dug extensively, and among the antiquities they have uncovered is part of a splendid synagogue from about the fourth century and, beneath that, portions of what is probably the synagogue featured in today's gospel. Nearby are the remains of a fifth-century church built on the traditional site of Peter's house.

The pride of ancient Israel was the temple in Jerusalem, where twice daily priests offered sacrifice on behalf of the entire nation. But although the Jews had only one temple, synagogues were abundant throughout the land, even in hamlets where as few as ten families lived. A synagogue was not so much for worship as for religious instruction. On Sabbaths the Jews went there to listen and learn. The service could not have been simpler: no priest or music; just a prayer, a Scripture reading, and a lengthy explanation of the reading.

The reading and explaining could be performed by any male member of the congregation, whoever was invited to do so on a particular Sabbath. Thus the synagogue at Capernaum offered an ideal opportunity for Jesus to launch his career as a teacher, which is what he does in today's reading. Later, as official grumbling against his activities mounts, he will move his place of instruction outdoors, to the lakeside or the open fields.

Surprisingly, neither here nor elsewhere does Mark elaborate on *what* Jesus taught. Nowhere does he mention the Sermon on the Mount or the lengthy discourse Jesus gave at the Last Supper. To learn the content of what Jesus taught about morality and the mysteries of heaven, we must turn to Matthew, Luke, or John. Mark stresses rather the *effect* that his teaching produced on his listeners. From that first Sabbath, their response was the kind that every teacher dreams of—"astonished" and "amazed." The congregation at Capernaum had never heard the like of it.

Jesus did have one heckler, a man with an "unclean spirit." The same mastery with which he ousted the demon from this poor wretch ("Quiet! Come out of him!") Jesus also displayed in his teaching. He did both with unhesitating authority.

The Israelites of his day were used to the timorous teaching of the scribes, whose sole expertise was in the Jewish religious law of the Torah as well as in the usually rigid elaborations of this law that had been handed down by generations of scribes. Their years of study were spent putting these scribal traditions to rote memory. They rarely took a stand of their own or dared voice an opinion not supported by precedent.

Jesus needed no precedent. His listeners sensed he was his own authority whose words demanded acceptance simply because they were his. The "man with an unclean spirit" pinpointed why Jesus cast so electric a spell. He was no scribe fumbling for truth. His words *were* truth, for he *was* the "Holy One of God."

Do his words cast a similar spell today? They should. He is as present to us as he was to that congregation in Capernaum. We have no need to jet halfway around the world and visit Tell Hum to imagine what he had to say. Every time we attend Mass, we hear his words. If we are not as impressed as was the congregation at Capernaum, the fault is in ourselves.

Our world is filled with teachers far surer of themselves than the scribes of old, but just as blind. These self-appointed seers pronounce on everything from the difference between right and wrong to the ultimate origin of the universe. But their credentials are bogus. They do not, cannot, speak for God. Only the words of Jesus have the divine guarantee of truth, only he answers our deepest questions. If we listen closely, we cannot fail to be as astonished and amazed as was the congregation of Capernaum. He still teaches with the authority of God.

A Near Lynching

Fourth Sunday in Ordinary Time.
C: Lk. 4: 21-30.

This passage is a follow-up of last week's, in which Jesus led the Sabbath service in the synagogue of his native Nazareth. Here we learn that this service, which had begun so innocently, ended in near tragedy. The former neighbors of Jesus, some his own kinfolk, hounded him out of town. It is one of the grimmest episodes in Scripture. Jesus barely escaped with his life.

How could this happen? Luke's account describes three stages in the antagonism of the Nazarenes: first, envy; next, impossible demands; and finally, violence.

"Isn't this the son of Joseph?" The words betray a mood familiar to all. We often find it easier to acknowledge greatness in a total stranger than in someone close to us, someone with a stronger claim on our affection and good will. Jesus recalled a proverb that has found a place in many languages and cultures: "No prophet is accepted in his own native place."

Why? Partly because our very proximity to a "prophet" enables us to detect shortcomings that escape the eyes of strangers. A less excusable reason, however, is that if we acknowledge the accomplishments of one who has shared the same background as ourselves we implicitly admit our own failures. We resent a success that we were ourselves unable to achieve, an excellence we cannot match. The word for this mood is envy.

Medieval theologians distinguished seven capital sins: pride, greed, lust, anger, gluttony, envy and sloth. Actually, calling them sins is misleading, since these are not properly speaking sins, but dispositions that are the root causes of sinful actions. All are ugly, but none more ugly than envy. Envy is also the least rewarding of the seven. The others yield some measure of delight: pride, a feeling of superiority; greed, a fat bank account; lust, a few hours of fun; anger, the comfort of blowing off steam; gluttony, a good meal; sloth, some extra hours of sleep. But envy begets no pleasure. The only harvest the envious person reaps is a mood of sullen discontent.

Soon the attitude of the Nazarenes turned to brash insult. They challenged Jesus. If he were such a prodigy, they taunted, if the rumors that had drifted back from Capernaum were true, let him work some of his magic here. Why does he not perform his eye-popping miracles in his hometown?

This was not the first time Jesus heard such a challenge, nor would it be the last. Satan had urged him to inaugurate his mission with a display of aerial acrobatics from the pinnacle of the temple. On the final day of his life Herod would press Jesus to relieve the boredom of his court with some dazzling miracles. These were impossible demands, not because Jesus lacked miraculous power, but because such power was given to him to manifest God's goodness and spread God's kingdom. Not even for old friends of Nazareth would he turn into a stage magician.

The conclusion of the episode strains credulity. Who would have expected the peaceful hamlet of Nazareth to erupt in savage violence? Luke tells us that the congregation became so enraged at the reasoned reply of Jesus that they hustled him to the brow of the hill on which Nazareth perched. Absolute calm such as Jesus displayed in face of their opposition can be infuriating, and the fury of this crowd rose to such a pitch that they would have hurtled Jesus to his death had he not quietly slipped away. Madness had seized the people of Nazareth, lynch-mob madness. At such moments a group of people will commit atrocities that its individual members would tremble to think about in private.

Today we congratulate ourselves that the days of the lynch mob are over. True, but an insidious form of mob psychology persists. It is hard for an individual to hold out against the mob of public opinion. The pressure of the majority, the notion that "everyone is doing it," the fear of being branded old-fashioned, peculiar, a gutless wonder—these can be as forceful perpetrators of evil as any physical mob.

How many Christians are sturdy enough to hold out against widespread approval of ethnic intolerance, unjust wars, extramarital sex, petty corruption, abortion? Mobs easily turn violent, and the violence of public opinion today against the moral teaching of Jesus Christ is enormous.

Luke concludes that Jesus "passed through the midst of them and went away." It was a sad leave-taking, his first taste of rejection. What must have made it doubly sad was that the rejection came from kin and former neighbors, on whose friendship and support he had every right to rely. Contempt bred by familiarity had made Jesus an outcast from his own.

By baptism we are all kin and neighbors of Jesus. Pray that he may never be outcast from us!

A Pinch of Salt, a Ray of Sunshine

Fifth Sunday in Ordinary Time.
A: Mt. 5: 13-16

❖❖❖

Are the dictates of our conscience purely private business? In one sense, most people would say yes. Our neighbors have no right to pry into our moral convictions or to impose their own on us. The highest lawmakers cannot compel us to approve abortion or to give internal support to an unjust war. A conscience is a kingdom. No merely human trespassers may enter.

This gospel reminds us, however, that in another sense our moral convictions should be anything but private. Like salt and sunshine, they have a very public job to perform.

The setting is first-century Galilee, where a crowd listens as Jesus delivers what we now call his Sermon on the Mount, in which he outlines the code his followers are to live by. Alone among mortals Jesus is by nature endowed with power to bind consciences, for he alone speaks with the authority of God.

Here he tells his followers not to keep his moral code under lock and key, like a private treasure. They must season their surroundings with the salt of Christian morality. How? First of all by their conduct. A person's moral convictions, although under private ownership, are always on public display.

A Christian should be a living illustration of what Jesus preached. This does not mean we need to "edify" others. Just striving to shape our own lives by the Sermon on the Mount is enough. One-third of the people alive today are nominally Christian. Imagine a world in which all of them lived by the beatitudes, imagine our neighborhood if even a handful of the Christians there forswore anger and started to forgive injuries and love their enemies. Just by being salt, salt spreads its flavor. Just by being Christian, Christians spread Christianity.

Salt in ancient times not only seasoned food but was a means of preserving it. Without it meat turned rancid. By calling them the "salt of the earth," Jesus reminds his followers they must preserve his moral instructions intact. The instinct in all of us is to relax any code of conduct we find too taxing, to pare it down to what our unredeemed nature finds easiest. Here Jesus warns us not to let that happen in his Church.

When people deride the moral code of the Church, calling it old-fashioned, we should plead guilty as charged. Christian morality proudly dates back to the Sermon on the Mount. Instead of re-shaping it to fit the shifting moods of the day, our job is to keep it well salted, as fresh and unspoiled as when the disciples first heard it from the lips of their Master. Fashions in dress and hairdos change, but not the nature God gave us or the moral laws that govern our conduct. Hypocrisy and greed are as wrong today as when Jesus condemned them. Revenge, adultery, and assaults on human life will always be evil.

After likening his disciples to salt, Jesus compares them to sunshine, the light of the world. A tall order, but Jesus was never modest in the role he assigned to his Church. He knew the day would come when those calling themselves Christians would be spread across the globe. That day has now arrived. Does the world yet bask in the sunshine of his moral teaching?

Not exactly bask, but it does feel its rays. Two ideas that the world owes in great part to Christianity are that all humans are equal and that each has a priceless value. Not everyone today accepts these notions, but almost no one did before Christ. It was the Christian code that abolished slavery; the same code has made people conscious of their duty to care for the poor.

Despite these gains, however, the world is still mostly pagan, even where lip service is paid to the gospel. A Christian should be a beacon in this darkness. Most modern pagans are aware of where the Church stands on moral issues, for, like a city on a hill, its presence cannot be ignored. But without the example of Christians who actually live by the Sermon on the Mount, the Church's official teaching can do little. Like a lamp in a sunless room, we must light up our immediate surroundings, be propagandists for Christian morality.

"Propaganda" is today a dirty word. We think of military communiques exaggerating enemy losses and minimizing our own, of stories planted in newspapers claiming sagacity for some political ninny. But the word originally had a better meaning. It was the Latin title of a Roman Congregation founded in the seventeenth century to propagate Christianity in pagan lands.

In a less formal sense all of us are called to be Christian propagandists. To propagate means to multiply. Christians will never multiply unless individual Christians take seriously the words in this gospel. If they do not salt society with the moral code of Jesus Christ, if they do not light up the world with their enthusiasm for the Sermon on the Mount, who will?

A Night of Many Marvels

Fifth Sunday in Ordinary Time.
B: Mk. 1: 29-39.

Mark's gospel has at times been called the gospel according to Peter; not that Peter penned a word of it, but that much of what it contains seems to have come from his mouth. Mark, a Jew of Jerusalem, was probably too young to know Jesus in the flesh. But his mother was a convert to the gospel, and in her house one of the earliest Christian communities of Jerusalem used to gather for prayer *(Acts 12: 12)*. The boy Mark must have met many of the community's leaders, including Peter.

As a young man Mark accompanied Paul on several apostolic journeys. But by the sixties he was with the soon-to-be-martyred Peter in Rome, where he could hear the leader of the young Church tell stories of long ago when he walked and talked with Jesus. Papias, a second-century bishop, called Mark Peter's interpreter. Today we might call him the recorder of Peter's memoirs.

Certainly this passage from Mark's gospel has the ring of an eyewitness account. We can almost detect Peter's voice as he recalls the remarkable Sabbath in Capernaum shortly after he and his three fishing partners signed up with Jesus as fishers of men. After morning service in the synagogue, where Jesus astounded the congregation with his preaching and his cure of a demoniac, he and his four new companions walked a short distance to Peter's house. There they found Peter's mother-in-law bedridden, possibly with malaria. With a mere grasp of her hand Jesus dispelled the fever, and in an instant she was on her feet and bustling about, serving the midday meal.

Word swiftly made the rounds that a holy man with power to heal was in town. Jewish law forbade the bearing of burdens on the Sabbath, but as soon as night fell a crowd of townsfolk carried their ailing kin to Peter's door. Soon Jesus came out to this throng of sufferers; laying his hands on them one by one, he restored them to health. It was an evening of miracles.

The word "miracle" means "something to be marveled at," and what Jesus did that night in Capernaum must have struck the beholders as stupefyingly marvelous. In fact, the whole of Mark's gospel is an almost unbroken string of such marvels. As Saint Augustine explained, people marvel at a miracle because it goes "beyond the ordinary laws of nature."

Nature often heals, but rarely in extreme cases, and never—as was true for many of the cures performed by Jesus—in an instant.

Today many challenge the possibility of miracles. Nature, they say, admits no exceptions, its laws are unalterable. If this reasoning is right, then at least half of Mark's gospel is hogwash and the whole of Christianity a delusion. Those who believe in God, however, have no problem with miracles. If the Author of Nature cannot perform works beyond the power of Nature, then Nature is more powerful than its Author. In strict logic, whoever has power to make a law has power to make exceptions.

In biblical times no one denied either the possibility of miracles or that Jesus performed scores of them. Even his enemies acknowledged his mysterious power. Then how could they escape believing in him? They had only one refuge: they said he derived his power from the devil. But the devil, as Jesus pointed out, does not undermine the devil's own domain. Yet that is what the cures of Jesus did. Driving out unclean spirits and ridding people of infirmity and disease are acts of love and kindness. They have no place on Satan's agenda.

Nowhere do the gospels use the word "miracle." Rather, they speak of the cures of Jesus as "works of power" or "signs"—terms that point to the meaning and purpose of these cures. They were works of power because by them Satan's dominion over the world was thwarted and the power of a benign God revealed. They were signs because they pointed to Jesus as God's agent. Only someone approved by God can do the work of God.

That this was the meaning of the cures performed by Jesus we know from the aftermath of this night of miracles. The next morning Peter awoke to find Jesus had stolen away to a place where he could be alone with his Father. By the time he tracked Jesus down, Peter could hardly contain himself. Although elated at the success of Jesus so far, Peter feared his chance would slip away. "Everyone is looking for you," he cried. He wanted Jesus to return to Capernaum and receive the acclaim he deserved.

But Jesus had other plans. He was neither a circus performer nor a dispenser of medicine. His miracles were signs confirming his message, not the message itself. They proclaimed, as loudly as his words, that the kingdom of God, a kingdom of peace and love, was at hand. His task was to proclaim this good news, not just to Capernaum, but to all Galilee and, in time, through the words and works of his followers, to the entire world.

PETER'S MIGHTY CATCH

Fifth Sunday in Ordinary Time.
C: Lk. 5: 1-11.

This is a fish story and a vocation story wrapped in one.

Fish as food is often mentioned in the Bible. The common people of Palestine rarely ate animal meat. True, the Prodigal Son was welcomed home with a fatted calf, but that was because he had a father who was not only forgiving but rich. Such feasts had to be rare; only the moneyed class could afford them.

Fish, however, was abundant and reasonably priced. Along with bread, it was a staple of the family meal. Some fish came from the Mediterranean; but for those who lived in the northern regions, the Sea of Galilee was a principal source.

Peter and his partners worked these waters. With fish so much in demand, they must have made a comfortable living; when Jesus sighted them at the lakeshore, they were by no means numbered among the poorest of Palestine. Some day they would feel more than a pinch of poverty, but that would be after they had abandoned their nets to answer the call of Jesus.

This gospel tells the story of that call. Although it focuses on Peter, what happened to him was essentially true for his companions also. In fact, Peter's story has been duplicated through the ages in the lives of countless Christians who have heard the same call he heard and made the same response.

People often ask how a vocation happens. Very few Christians are called to follow Jesus as single-heartedly as Peter did, but even those who are not should know something about the process. Parents have good reason to be curious, since their child may someday surprise them by announcing the stirrings of a vocation. This gospel tells most of what they need to know on the subject.

As a first step, one must get acquainted with Jesus, as Peter did at the lakeside; but mere acquaintance is not enough. Before throwing aside everything and signing up forever, one must be overcome with love and admiration for the carpenter of Nazareth, absolutely bowled over by his power and goodness. Today's gospel shows us how Peter was bowled over.

First, Peter listened as Jesus preached to the crowd at the lakeside, and we know how strong an impression Jesus always made on his listeners. Thus when Jesus asked Peter to sail out into the deep waters and lower the net for a catch, Peter could not refuse. His fisherman's instinct told him the quest would be futile, but for this wonderful preacher he would do anything. Next came the catch itself, so huge and unexpected that Peter knew he was in the presence of a more-than-human power. Jesus was mighty in more than words; he was the Lord of Nature.

Christians today can come to know Jesus as certainly as Peter did, and they can be bowled over just as violently. When this happens, a vocation may be in the making. We meet Jesus in the Sacraments, of course; we also meet him in Scripture. I defy anyone to read thoughtfully through the gospels without the same tingle of excitement that comes when one finds a new and fascinating friend. Let anyone who doubts this try Mark or Luke for a start. The bowling over is sure to begin.

Finally—and for many this is the crucial step—we meet Jesus in other human beings, for he dwells in the members of his living Church, his Mystical Body. His spirit can be sensed in the words and gestures of many followers, living and dead, who once signed their lives over to him. Almost all who have answered the call of Jesus can point to men and women who reminded them of Jesus and fired their enthusiasm for his cause.

Peter cried, "Depart from me, Lord, for I am a sinful man." Are we to conclude that he was a gross sinner? Almost certainly not. The fishermen of Galilee were notorious among their fellow Israelites for piety. But in the presence of such sovereign holiness as Jesus radiated, Peter was overwhelmed with a conviction of his own unholiness. Conscious of his feeble creaturehood, he trembled in the presence of divinity.

Some such trembling is a prerequisite of any vocation. Those who consider themselves spiritually fit to be companions of Jesus should not think of presenting themselves at a convent door or seminary gate in quest of admittance. Paradoxically, only those who are convinced of their own unworthiness are truly worthy to join the ranks of God's special servants.

"Do not be afraid; from now on you will be catching men." Imagine how these words must have thrilled Peter. Some people still thrill to the same words—not spoken by a physical voice, but clearly heard in the depths of their hearts. They feel a strong urge to chuck everything and join the grand fishing expedition of Peter and Jesus Christ. Pray that more people heed this call, jump into Peter's bark, and have the joy of a mighty catch. The Church needs them. The world needs them.

THE BOMBSHELL HE DROPPED ON THE MOUNT

Sixth Sudnay in Ordinary Time.
A: Mt. 5: 17-37 (or 20-22; 27-28; 33-34; 37).

❖❖❖

Not all his fellow Israelites regarded Jesus as holy. His friendliness with sinners made him suspect. Even more damaging, he often seemed soft on sin itself. This was seen in his attitude towards religious law. He healed, for example, on the Sabbath; he did not object when his disciples omitted the ceremonial washing of hands before meals. No truly holy person, his critics urged, would have so little regard for sacred law. Jesus, they concluded, was lax, far less holy than the scribes and Pharisees.

In this passage from his Sermon on the Mount Jesus touches on the meaning of true holiness ("righteousness"). Some of his listeners, aware of his reputation for laxity, possibly expected him to proclaim a law easier than that of Moses. But he does nothing of the sort, professing instead the highest respect for this law. It must be obeyed, he says, to "the smallest part of a letter." Nothing could sound less like laxity.

How reconcile this with his reputation for tolerating violations of the law? Much depends on the kind of law one is talking about. When Jesus endorsed the law down to the smallest letter he meant the law God gave to Moses, a law summarized in the ten commandments and binding on all Jews. For the most part these also bind all humans, for they express the general moral law, the so-called "natural law" that is written in the hearts of all *(Rom. 2: 15)* and admits no exceptions.

Making exceptions, of course, has always been a popular pastime. It is said that in medieval times many felt that the laws of God were suspended during the celebrations that preceded Lent. I once knew a man who would shrink from cheating his neighbor but thought it a lark to defraud his insurance company or lie on a tax return. Some usually sober citizens drink themselves into premeditated oblivion every New Year's Eve.

Such people will find small comfort in these words of Jesus. There is no holiday from God's law, no time when we can count on his winking. Human laws may sometimes be bent, not God's.

For another kind of law, however, Jesus had little respect. This was the scribal law. The scribes felt that the law God gave to Moses on Sinai was not precise enough. It needed finicky footnoting by experts like themselves if one did not want to run the risk of even the slightest violation. For generations scribes had listed actions that they considered infractions of the Mosaic Law, prohibitions so detailed that no ordinary person could remember them, still less observe them.

God's law, for example, commanded the Jews to keep holy the Sabbath by abstaining from needless labor. What kind of labor did this prohibit? On the lunatic list of the scribes were such offenses as lifting a burden weightier than a fig or a swallow of milk. Some even extended the arm of the law to the barnyard, seriously debating whether one was allowed to eat an egg that had been laid on the Sabbath. Because the scribes and Pharisees observed such regulations scrupulously, many thought they were the epitome of holiness. Some of his followers must have gasped when Jesus declared that to be saved they must be more righteous than the scribes and Pharisees.

Obedience to a law may be down to the tiniest letter, yet rendered in a manner so mechanical, so foreign to the spirit of the law, that the whole purpose of the law is negated. It is such hollow obedience that Jesus here condemns: abstaining from outright murder, but not from anger or enmity; avoiding adultery, but harboring lustful desires; telling truth if under oath, but otherwise lying with reckless abandon.

The letter of the law says "Thou shalt not kill." Its spirit says far more. As Christians we must try to rid our hearts of any ill-feeling towards a neighbor. Long-standing grudges and the nursing of internal hostility may not land us in prison, but can be as sinful as many actions that would.

Only someone who looks merely to the letter of the law would be satisfied with a marriage in which neither party commits adultery. Christians guard their hearts. Infidelity in the heart violates the marriage vow as surely as physical infidelity.

Imagine going before God's judgement seat and pleading that we have heeded his command to be truthful, then citing as evidence that we have never lied under oath. Even without an oath the "Yes" of a Christian should mean "Yes," the "No" mean "No." We should guard the truth in everyday life as we would if under an oath in a court of law. A Christian's word is sacred.

God sees the heart. It was to the reform of our hearts that Jesus directed the Sermon on the Mount. Keeping the outside of the cup clean will never do. That is why Jesus warned that we must be more righteous than the scribes and Pharisees.

He Touches Us Too

Sixth Sunday in Ordinary Time.
B: Mk. 1: 40-45.

❖ ❖ ❖

Imagine what a painting of this gospel scene would look like: on one side, a leper kneeling before Jesus, his limbs rotting and his face so blotched with sores it scarcely seems human; on the other, touching the leper, the radiant Savior of the world. A sharper contrast could hardly be imagined.

The coming together of these stark opposites on a roadside in ancient Israel may not move people today as deeply as when Mark first described it. Few in our century, at least in America, have ever seen a leper in the flesh. We cannot comprehend how extraordinary was the response of Jesus because we do not conceive the terror the word "leprosy" once aroused.

Few words have aroused more. Although the term covers a wide range of maladies—from the fatal ailment known in medical texts as Hansen's disease to a host of disfiguring skin disorders that in popular (and biblical) usage go by the name of leprosy—all lepers have two things in common: they are sickening to behold and dangerous to be near. So sickening and dangerous that the rest of humanity has done its utmost to drive them away, banish them from sight. Lepers have always been outcasts.

Their disease is a slow death physically. Worse, it is often the equivalent of an instant death in the mind of others. The steps society takes to remove lepers from sight can make it seem they have ceased to exist. In lands where the disease is still a common scourge, its victims are herded out of sight and made to languish in colonies. Like the legendary Father Damien on his Hawaiian island of Molokai, brave men and women in remote corners of the world tend to the spiritual and physical needs of lepers. Leper colonies do not attract tourists.

In biblical times, keeping those infected with leprosy apart from the non-infected was deemed a religious duty and carried to extremes we find hard to believe today. Those who contracted the disease had to abandon their homes and settle in hovels outside of town, where they had only other lepers for company. If healthy humans came near, lepers had to ward them away with the cry, "Unclean!" A Jew of strict observance would neither greet nor walk within six feet of a leper.

One reason for this harsh treatment was that in the eyes of their fellow Israelites lepers were not just suffering from a physical malady. Their ulcerated skin and truncated limbs were thought to be punishment for some unspeakable sin, a view even the lepers did not challenge. The most pitiable people in Israel, they were as loathsome to themselves as to others.

Sometimes in reading Scriptures we find ourselves mulling over a tiny detail. A single word or phrase stands out, giving depth to the entire episode. This passage has such a detail in the sentence where Mark describes what Jesus did to the leper just before declaring him clean. "He stretched out his hand and *touched* him." That simple touch holds a wealth of meaning.

The onlookers must have shuddered with near disbelief. To touch a leper not only defied the law that made lepers outcasts, not only displayed disdain for our squeamishness at the sight of decaying flesh; above all, it was a gesture of friendship. With it Jesus declared, as though by a hearty handshake, his solidarity with all the outcasts of the world. Here was solid proof that Jesus of Nazareth was on their side.

Especially on the side of moral outcasts, the sinners. The picture Mark paints in this passage is a parable in action. As Jesus treated the leper, so he treats all sinners, that is, all of us; for we are all, as we acknowledge at the opening of Mass, sinners. By becoming man God reached out to our wayward race and became one with us. By dying on the cross Jesus touched us with his healing hand, cleansing us of our sins.

When grave theologians expound the doctrines of the Incarnation and Redemption, their words often ring hollow—too abstract, too removed from our experience. This gospel conveys these truths better than a thousand theological tracts, for it does it with a picture. In this picture sin is not just a vague "offense against God," but a disfiguring disease, a rotting away of the soul. And the Incarnate Word is not a pale abstraction, but a living human being whose heart is moved with pity at the sight of one of God's children degraded by sin.

The leper dared to approach Jesus, thus violating the law and exposing Jesus to contagion. But he trusted that despite the law and the horror his disease inspired, Jesus would not turn away. "If you wish, you *can* make me clean." Such trust should be ours. Jesus touches us in prayer, in the sacraments. The healing power of his touch can cleanse us too.

Blessings No Money Can Buy

Sixth Sunday in Ordinary Time.
C: Lk. 6: 17; 20-26.

"Blessed are you who are poor." To be blessed is to be favored, preserved from evil, happy. Do Christians really believe that poverty is a blessing? *Should* we believe it? To wipe out poverty or at least reduce its level is the aim of much of the social teaching in Papal encyclicals. Does this gospel urge us to refuse to join the struggle for fair wages, to resolve never to give a coin to a beggar? Am I spreading unhappiness when I contribute to a fund for the undernourished children of the street? Merely to pose these questions is to answer them. When Jesus called the poor blessed he was uttering a paradox, not advocating an absurdity.

To understand Christ's words in a way that is not absurd, we must first be clear on what he did *not* mean by "poor." He was not pronouncing as blessed people who are totally indigent, those who live on the margin of society. We are all appalled, and should be, when we see homeless people sleeping on the streets of Calcutta or in the back alleys of Manila. Poverty on that scale is a curse, not a blessing. As Christians it is our duty to do all in our power to stamp it out.

What level of poverty was Jesus talking about when he made this pronouncement? Look at his own life-style. Spiritual writers often rhapsodize about the "poverty" of Jesus at Nazareth. But his home there must have been moderately comfortable, supported as it was by a carpenter's earnings. Nazareth was not a slum. During the years of his public ministry throughout Galilee he was certainly poor by the standards of today. All Galileans were. We ought not, however, put them in the same category as those who are rightly called the "wretched of the earth."

They were poles apart from the many who today eke out their existence in the shanty-towns of the world. Historians say that in Christ's time Galilee was famed for its benign climate, rich soil, and abundant fish. The average Galilean ate simply, but adequately. Remember too that the gospels sometimes picture Jesus seated at the tables of the wealthy. He was not a stranger among the moneyed class, whose souls were as worth saving as those of the poor. Nor were his garments beggar's rags. If they had been, the soldiers on Calvary would not have cast lots for them. We can conclude that while Jesus was "poor" when compared with the rich, he was far from abject destitution.

We should not think, however, that blessing is automatically bestowed on those who, like Jesus, have no more than a modest sufficiency on the earth's goods. Far from it. Look at how frantically many of these labor to become rich. They are poor in what they possess, but rich in what they crave. Forever dissatisfied with what they have, they devote their energies to getting more, often committing crimes in the process, as our daily record of muggings and petty thefts reminds us. In no sense of the word can these be called "blessed." Clawing one's way to the top of the heap is no formula for contentment.

What then did Jesus mean by "poor"? The Hebrew word (*anawim*) for poor, which undoubtedly Luke here had in mind, designates those who accept their condition, although low on the economic scale, without complaint. Their aim is to walk in God's favor and live peacefully with their neighbors, not surround themselves with luxuries. One commentator says that to belong to the *anawim* is to be "resigned, abandoning oneself to God's providence, prompt and ready to obey the commands of God." It is God they seek, not riches or property; doing God's will is their goal, not multiplying dividends or maintaining mansions.

Even one who is rich in the ordinary sense of the term can belong to the *anawim*. That is why Matthew's "poor in spirit" is closer to the meaning here than simply "poor." For a rich person to be poor in spirit does not happen often or easily, as we learn from Christ's frequent warnings against riches. But it is do-able, perhaps just barely do-able. Some of our greatest saints (kings and queens have made the list) turned the trick. Whenever they did we find that their life-style was simple despite their lavish surroundings. They were always aware that their journey was like a camel's through a needle's eye. And they were generous to those in want, always eager to share.

Why are these poor blessed? What this beatitude says is that if we really want to be blessed (that is, happy, content) we must stop chasing after happiness, especially in the form of material possessions. This is a paradox, of course, perhaps *the* paradox of life. When happiness becomes our goal, it always eludes us. God is our only proper goal. Putting God first and loving our neighbors because they belong to God is the Christian formula. Happiness is the by-product.

HOW TO HANDLE SCAMPS AND SLOBS

Seventh Sunday in Ordinary Time.
A: Mt. 5: 38-48.

❖ ❖ ❖

A cyclone hit Bangladesh a few years ago, taking the lives of close to 100,000 and leaving at least that many without food, shelter, or potable water. News of the tragedy flashed around the world, and within days food and medical help were on the way, much of it from countries whose people could scarcely find Bangladesh on the map. This rush to rescue total strangers surprises no one. Today we take for granted that international relief will be mobilized whenever a major catastrophe strikes. Where or whom it strikes is inconsequential.

This was not always so. That we should reach out to needy foreigners is an idea the world owes to Christianity; it never occurred to people in ancient times. If you told a Roman soldier he should be kind to the barbarian in Gaul, he would probably have laughed in your face. The Israelites of old were keen on works of charity, but charity to their own. Their rule was "Love your neighbor," meaning love your fellow Jew. Few felt any obligation to non-Jews, that is, to more than 98% of humanity.

Jesus changed all that, and then some. His followers must do far more than lend a hand to strangers in distress. The word he used was "love," and the people he told us to love were not just strangers, but enemies. Such a command had never been heard before. Earlier religious leaders had urged followers to love family, tribe, perhaps passing wayfarers. But never enemies.

What did Jesus mean by "enemy"? The Greek word in Matthew covers not only people who are fiercely hostile but also those who are merely unfriendly. And the examples Jesus gives prove he is referring not just to bomb-tossing terrorists but also to the rude and inconsiderate slobs we meet in daily life.

First on his list is the person who humiliates us. Slapping someone on the right cheek was a stinging insult among Jews, as demeaning as a racial snub today. Next is the person who drags us to court, suing for damages without even trying for an amicable settlement. Then comes the pushy person who imposes on our generosity, not just asking a favor, but insisting on it, grabbing it. Finally Jesus points to the sponger, the neighbor who repeatedly cadges our dollars, rarely repays them.

The list could go on, but these tell us the sort of amateur enemies and everyday scamps Jesus wants us to love. This seems an impossible wrenching of human nature. How can our hearts warm to the neighbor whose midnight parties rob us of sleep, to the moocher who keeps pestering us for more, to the dangerously road-hogging motorist? What exactly did Jesus mean by "love"?

Certainly not "like." These are obnoxious people, and no power in the world can make us believe that obnoxious is really nice. I cannot force myself to enjoy their company any more than I can take pleasure in eating oat bran or listening to rock music.

What then did Jesus mean? Actually, the notion of loving wrong doers is not as far-fetched as it seems. Mothers and fathers do it all the time. They do not cease loving their child just because the child has done something that hurts them. To love is to wish a person well. Its test is that when people injure or annoy us, instead of hitting back, demanding eye for eye and tooth for tooth, we treat them kindly and wish them well.

A parent can punish a child without ceasing to love, just as a judge can send a terrorist to prison without feeling rancor. They do this in their official capacity, not because they take pleasure in inflicting injury. Those of us who have no position or authority, however, have no right to punish anyone. It is wrong to play God. Even God withholds full punishment while the sinner still lives, sending the sun and rain to good and evil alike. Who are we, not only to judge who has sinned, but to demand a retribution swifter than God's?

The Christian response to hostility is love, wishing well to those who wish us ill. If the word "love" seems too grandiose, try another formula. "Love your enemies" means: be kind to those who are unkind to you, a friend to those who are unfriendly.

Jesus does not say so, but this formula often yields unexpected bonuses. It is a great help to digestion and blood pressure, a good way to keep one's own eyes and teeth intact, and often the formula for turning enemies into friends.

Jesus concluded with the injunction, "Be perfect, just as your heavenly Father is perfect." This does not mean we must strive for divine perfection, an obvious absurdity. Rather Jesus meant that just as God has done his job perfectly, we should try to do ours perfectly. He has showered love on all human creatures; therefore we should be kind and friendly to all the men and women he has given us as companions in this world. Of course they are not all perfect. But, then, neither are we.

"He Is Blaspheming"

Seventh Sunday in Ordinary Time.
B: Mk. 2: 1-12.

Mark places this episode early in the ministry of Jesus. He was back in Capernaum after his first tour through Galilee, and a triumphant tour it had been. Wherever he went the acclaim for his preaching and healing preceded him, and hordes of ardent Israelites sought him out. His popularity was at a peak.

But popularity exacts a price. Like a superstar of today, Jesus was hounded by crowds on all sides. And crowds can hinder a prophet's work as well as help it. That is what we see going on as this gospel opens. Jesus was staying at what Mark calls his "home," actually the house of the brothers Peter and Andrew, fishermen and apostles. Once word of his whereabouts got around, the curious and devout of the town invaded this house, eager to see and hear Israel's new prophet at close range.

So great was the crush of the crowd that when four men carrying a paralytic arrived, they could not push their way through. Undeterred, they climbed the outside stairway, opened a hole in the thatched roof, and lowered the paralytic to where Jesus sat teaching. The eyes of all then turned on Jesus. From what they had heard of his conduct elsewhere, they felt sure he would make a show of his power by curing the paralytic.

But for the moment at least, Jesus did nothing of the sort. Instead, leaning over he said, "Child, your sins are forgiven."

Jesus was a man of many surprises. In reading the New Testament, so often do we find him doing the unexpected that in time the unexpected is what we come to expect. His surprises however, were never mere stunts to gain attention. All of them had a point, all should start us thinking.

This gospel is a good example. The surprise here is that Jesus forgave the sins of the paralytic when those watching expected a cure. In their hearts most knew that restoring God's friendship to a sinner is a far greater marvel than restoring movement to a paralytic. But it is also far less thrilling to behold. And so they were not just surprised, but disappointed.

The scribes who were present, however, were indignant. They dared not voice their feelings before the rest of the spectators, who they suspected were fans of Jesus. But while they kept their thoughts to themselves, their looks spoke volumes. They considered his words of forgiveness blasphemy.

The scribes, to give them their due, were half-right. Seeing the episode from hindsight, we readily accept Jesus at his word when he declares the paralytic forgiven. Our faith is an Easter faith. We see in Jesus the same fullness of divinity that doubting Thomas saw when he beheld the risen Jesus and cried out, "My Lord and my God!" *(Jn. 20: 28)*. But the scribes saw only his humanity, and so regarded what Jesus said as an outrageous affront to the Almighty. Since sins by definition are offenses against God, who but God can declare them forgiven?

The reasoning seems solid, but is not. If I can grant power of attorney to another, delegating someone to act in my name, God surely can give to humans authority to forgive sins in his name. Note that at the time Jesus claimed nothing more than such delegated authority. He did not even hint at his divinity. If he had, no one would have taken him seriously. But the power that he did claim he backed with miraculous proof. The reason he finally cured the paralytic was precisely "that you may know that the Son of Man has authority to forgive sins on earth."

Today, centuries later, his Church makes the same claim. The words of the priest in the sacrament of Penance (Reconciliation) are essentially the same as those Jesus spoke to the paralytic. Just as the scribes were shocked then, some people are shocked today. Understandably so, for the claim we make is truly a shocker: that through words of a priest, a mere human, offenses against Almighty God are wiped away.

How does the Church support this claim? Miracles like the one in this gospel are rarely seen today. But no visible miracle is needed. The power God's ministers have to remit sin in God's name was given to the Church by the greatest miracle-worker of all, Jesus Christ . After rising from the dead he breathed on his apostles saying, "Whose sins you forgive are forgiven them, and whose sins you retain are retained" *(Jn. 20: 23)*.

People sometimes moan that the age of miracles is over. How they would love to have been present to see the paralytic take up his mat and stride briskly away! But a greater miracle takes place every day. Jesus gave his Church power to restore God's friendship to souls immobilized by sin, and that power has been passed on through the centuries. Like the crowd in the gospel, we should be "astounded." The spirit that Jesus once breathed on the apostles remains alive in the world today.

Turning the World's Wisdom Upside-Down

Seventh Sunday in Ordinary Time.
C: Lk. 6: 27-38.

❖ ❖ ❖

Will Rogers, a popular American entertainer of the thirties, became famous for saying he never met a man he didn't like. Lucky Will! Most of us feel we have met more than our fair share of people we just cannot stand. What may bother us more, however, is knowing there are people who do not like us either, who fall into the category that Jesus in this passage calls "enemies."

We can distinguish two kinds of enemies.

First, the obvious ones, the heavy hitters. They slander us, cheat us, vandalize our property, do violence to our bodies. Perhaps we are lucky and have yet to meet an enemy of this sort. But they assault our fellow citizens everyday and may cross our path tomorrow. Proof? Read the daily papers with their record of armed robberies, unprovoked attacks, hijackings, and the like. Vicious, ruthless enemies are not phantoms. They exist.

Next come the less obvious foes, the bush league enemies. In its root meaning "enemy" denotes simply someone who behaves in an unfriendly manner, and of these we have all met plenty. They do not make the same headlines as the mass murderers or bank robbers, but paradoxically they are often harder to treat in a Christian way. Think of the neighbor who pesters you with humorless jokes, the boss who greets you with a scowl rather than a smile, the co-worker who welshes on ten-peso bets.

How should we handle enemies, both gross and petty? One way is expressed in slogans we have heard since childhood: hit back...get even...revenge is sweet...an eye for an eye...stand up for your rights...he started it, didn't he?...it's not the money, it's the principle of the thing...nice guys finish last. To many people these maxims seem self-evident. They are so much part of our culture that one can go through life without ever stopping to question them. Some who call themselves Christians seem amazed to learn that anyone ever did question them.

Jesus Christ not only questioned them, he assailed them head-on, turned them upside-down. His counter-slogans are in this passage from the Sermon on the Mount, and they are still as astounding a reversal of a human being's instinctive responses as when Jesus first uttered them:

love your enemies...do good to those who hate you...bless those who curse you...pray for those who maltreat you...be kind to the ungrateful and the wicked...be merciful...stop judging...stop condemning...forgive.

To treat our enemies in a Christian way it is not enough that we refrain from harming them. Jesus is not for a policy of armed neutrality. He commands us to take sides, the enemy's side. This means a personal program of affirmative action. Whether affirmative action is a wise public policy in dealing with the dispossessed is a question on which good people may disagree. But we cannot call ourselves Christians if we neglect it as a rule of personal conduct towards our "enemies," whether these be groups or individuals. Jesus Christ commands it.

Many teachers of morality have left their mark on history. With one exception their highest precept has been: do no injury to your enemies, do not retaliate when you are wronged. Jesus Christ is the exception. He alone teaches that we should switch loyalties, actually love our enemies, make them our friends.

What does he mean by love? Certainly not the kind of love we have for parents, children, or spouse. That would be unnatural. Nor does he mean the strong affection and regard we have for our closest friends. That would be impossible. The love Jesus speaks of we can have both for the muggers who assault us while taking our purse and for those everyday enemies, the people we do not "like" or who do not "like" us. This love comes down simply to this: we do what we can to make such people as prosperous and happy as we ourselves would like to be.

Here are some ways to test this love. Do we speak kindly of those who speak unkindly of us? Do we meet grumpiness with a smile? Do we lend a hand to those who passed us by when we needed help? Do we refrain from judging those who have misjudged us? Are we generous to the lazy, the wasteful, the mean?

These tests will not come in moments of high drama. We should not waste time imagining ourselves in the place of Saint Stephen, praying for those who are about to stone him; or Thomas More, wishing well to the king who had ordered his beheading; or Pope John Paul II, blessing the man who shot and nearly killed him. What Jesus demands is more the quiet, unpublicized, everyday heroism of turning the other cheek and walking the extra mile. Hardly a day goes by without a chance to practice it.

Why love our enemies? The gospel gives two reasons, as simple as they are compelling. First, God loves them. Second, God loves us. What right have we to be more choosy than God?

WHAT'S THE USE OF WORRYING?

Eighth Sunday in Ordinary Time.
A: Mt. 6: 24-34.

❖ ❖ ❖

Tourist guides in Galilee point to the hilltop where Jesus preached his Sermon on the Mount. Scripture scholars tell a different story. It is unlikely, they say, that the section in Matthew called the Sermon on the Mount records words Jesus spoke at a single sitting. Rather, these chapters (5-7) contain highlights from the preaching of Jesus, a collection of his memorable sayings on how he wanted his followers to live.

To appreciate these sayings, it helps to know something about the people of Galilee, for it was to them Jesus addressed the lion's share of his preaching. Today's reading comes into sharper focus when we consider two important features of their daily life—how they ate and how they were clothed.

In both respects the Galileans were blessed. So benign was their climate and rich their soil that having enough food at table was rarely a problem. And the sheep roaming their meadows yielded wool in such abundance that their need for clothing was easily satisfied. By our standards their meals were monotonous and their garments coarse, but few Galileans were in danger of going hungry or suffering from exposure.

Had they been, it is hard to imagine Jesus admonishing them not to "worry about your life." People on the edge of starvation in famine areas have good reason for such worry. It would be unfeeling to tell them to imitate the "birds in the sky." They are close to perishing precisely because, like the birds, they do not sow or reap or gather into barns. How they wish they could! And people so hard up they lack decent clothing *should* be anxious, at least anxious enough to take steps to garb themselves more sensibly than the wild flowers and grass. Had Jesus spoken the words of this gospel to the genuinely destitute, they could be read as a cruel joke.

Then what is Jesus driving at? What is he warning the Galileans not to worry about? Not *whether* they will have enough to eat and wear, but *what* they will eat and wear. Once their basic needs are satisfied, Jesus wants them to be at peace. They should not waste energy fretting over how to make their meals the tastiest in town and their apparel the trendiest.

We do not know how widespread such fretting was in ancient Galilee. Certainly some of the men must have been the Beau Brummels of their day, some of the women ancient versions of our gourmet cooks Otherwise Jesus would not have issued this warning. But the fretting Jesus denounced is surely more commonplace now than it was then. People in our century need this warning far more urgently than did the Galileans of old.

See the space our newspapers give to the latest fashions in men and women's apparel. Count the gourmet cookbooks in our bookstores. Visit our posh restaurants and watch the diners studiously downing their delicacies. Food for some people is less a source of nourishment than a lifetime preoccupation.

Let us not exaggerate or miss the point. We are not all called to dress in rags and dine on insects and herbs, like the desert monks of the early Church. Jesus did not say it is sinful to relish good food and take pleasure in being reasonably well dressed. In Scripture we see him attending banquets; his own garments were durable enough for the soldiers on Calvary to divide among themselves by lottery. It was worry over *trifles* that Jesus denounced, making the mere savor of food and the fashions of dress into matters of supreme moment.

One biblical scholar points out that the word here translated as "worry" means not so much anxiety as needless engrossment. Life is too short and the true God too good for us to make a god of our belly or a fetish of our appearance. Jesus did not want us to waste our energy on the unimportant when we have so many important matters to attend to.

One way to tell true Christians from pagans is that the former go through life with a healthy indifference towards the things that "the unbelievers are always running after," a devil-may-care attitude towards what they eat and how they are attired. Food and wardrobe do not soak up their time or money, because they have more serious things to spend time and money on. Prayer is one. Good works are another. Think of how improved the world would be if people spent as much time at prayer and helping others as they now spend pampering themselves at table and primping themselves before mirrors.

Pop psychologists have made fortunes telling people how to stop worrying. This passage beats them all. The best antidote to needless worry is to put fine food and fancy dress and other frivolities in their proper place. Seek first "the kingdom of God and his righteousness," and these petty concerns will fade.

Second Thoughts About Fasting

Eighth Sunday in Ordinary Time.
B: Mk. 2: 18-22.

❖❖❖

Fasting is a topic that few Catholics today know much about. In older times this was not true, so frequently did fast days appear on our church calendars. For good reason the Church has removed the obligation from many of these traditional fasts, or at least modified their rigor. But that does not mean the practice is outlawed. Christians have always fasted, starting with our founder himself. His forty-day fast in the desert put his seal of approval on the custom. The seal is still in place.

Fasting is a form of self-denial, and self-denial—of food or other pleasures of the flesh—has historically been a feature of every religion worth the name. Fasting is not to be confused with dieting. We diet to please our doctor or preserve our figure or perhaps even improve our golf stroke. We fast in the truly religious sense only when we reduce our intake of food with the express purpose of serving God better.

How does fasting help us serve God? In lots of ways, but here are a few to munch on. First, eating whenever and whatever we please makes us flabby spiritually as well as physically; it dulls our appetite for the things of God. Next, cutting down on food is a way of proving, at least to ourselves, that we take our religion seriously, that we put God first. Finally, by fasting we surrender a finite pleasure we like for the sake of the infinite God we love; if love for a creature proves its metal by sacrifice, all the more so does love for the Creator.

Not all fasting, however, hits its mark. Look, for example, at a kind of fasting that was censured by Jesus.

All observant Jews in his day did some fasting, at least on the one day of the year (the Day of Atonement), when a fast from sunrise to sunset was a matter of obligation. Some ultra-pious Israelites, however, found this once-a-year fast too effortless and displayed their superior virtue by fasting twice a week, every Monday and Thursday. The disciples of Jesus were conspicuous for not marching in step with these rigorists, and inevitably their laxity drew criticisms. If Jesus were truly a prophet, many Israelites wondered, why did his followers not fast as the Pharisees and disciples of John the Baptist fasted? That is the question they put to him in this gospel.

In his answer Jesus did not explain exactly what he found faulty in the fasting of the Pharisees. For that we must turn to the Sermon on the Mount *(Mt. 6: 16-18)*, where he denounced, not the fact of their fasting, but its manner.

They fasted ostentatiously, wanting the whole world to see the extent of their suffering, how they were wasting away from lack of food. To make sure others took proper notice, some even powdered their faces white and walked around with doleful expressions. Their manner proclaimed that religious observance took all the fun out of life, that their God was a killjoy.

Catholics today show no signs of aping these Pharisees in their manner of fasting. What little fasting most of us do is anything but ostentatious; the last thing we want is for others to notice. But in one respect the spirit of the Pharisees, with their powdered faces and dismal countenances, still lives. Many Christians today view the whole business of fasting as a gloomy leftover from the Middle Ages. When they fast, they do so, if not with long faces, certainly with heavy hearts.

Against this attitude Jesus was anxious to guard his disciples. Had he allowed them to model their fasting on that of the Pharisees, they too might be infected with gloom. But the salvation he announced on Easter was far from gloomy. In fact, it was the best of all good news. He wanted his followers never to lose their buoyant enthusiasm for his kingdom, their delight at being entrusted to spread it. Jesus put this idea in a bold metaphor, comparing the spirit he looked for in his followers to the merriment of revelers at a wedding feast. He was the bridegroom, they his guests. How dare they be morose?

And yet, he wanted us to fast (or at least do some form of penance). More accurately, he predicted that the day would come when "the groom would be taken away," and on that day we would *want* to fast. Why? Because by his death on the cross he gave us the chance to share in his work of redemption. That is what it means to be a member of his mystical body. All our sufferings, great and small, can be joined with his sacrifice on Calvary and help bring God's grace to a fallen world.

The fasting Jesus approved was as far from that of the Pharisees as new cloth from old. Fasting did not end with Jesus, but its spirit shifted from desolation to delight. Ask anyone—better, look at anyone—who has tried it. Good Christians, even when fasting, have light hearts and rosy features.

A Few Beads on a String

Eighth Sunday in Ordinary Time.
C: Lk. 6: 39-45.

❖❖❖

This is an unusual gospel. Instead of a single episode or a unified discourse, it contains a series of short, rapid-fire moral instructions, each in the form of a vivid picture, but seemingly with no central purpose. The term the biblical Jews had for this kind of exhortation was *charaz*, a favorite among the Rabbis. Literally, a *charaz* is a *stringing of beads*.

Like the makers of our TV commercials, the Rabbis had little faith in the attention span of listeners. Instead they liked to string one short directive after another, like a series of beads, each of them containing a striking picture or short parable. The Rabbis of old knew as well as the admen of today that they needed pictures to keep their listeners awake.

Jesus was a Rabbi. At least so his followers called him, for "Rabbi" means teacher, and it was to hear him teach that crowds flocked to his feet. Unlike other Rabbis, however, who had been schooled in the law of Moses, Jesus was a self-educated, free-lance Rabbi. His syllabus was his own, the New Law of the Sermon on the Mount. Much of his time he spent training his disciples in this Law, for soon they would themselves be Rabbis, passing on to the early Christians all they had heard from him.

The beads in this *charaz*, therefore, are not as disconnected as they seem. The string holding them together is that they were originally aimed at the disciples of Jesus, who would teach later generations the lessons of the Sermon on the Mount. But the *charaz* also applies to those who today have the same task as those early disciples, the clergy and lay people (parents especially) who instruct others in the code of Jesus Christ.

The first bead shows two men stumbling through a field. The second man grips the shoulders of the leader, while the leader, blind as his companion, gropes frantically ahead. Finally and inevitably, both tumble headlong into a ditch.

The point? Let no one who is spiritually blind try to guide others in the ways of the Lord. The gospel of Jesus Christ is a serious and demanding subject, far more serious and at least as demanding as medicine or law. Priests must study long and hard; seminaries need well- stocked libraries and well-trained staff. Parents and C.C.D. teachers can get by with less technical knowledge than priests, but not if they neglect study entirely. Asking an ignoramus to teach anything is dangerous; more than doubly dangerous when the subject is the gospel of Jesus Christ, especially what he said about good and evil.

The second bead is a caricature, a biblical cartoon. A man is calmly extracting a splinter from a friend's eye, totally oblivious of the huge chunk of timber in his own. This is a warning to all who teach the lessons of the Sermon on the Mount. How can they expect others to believe them if they live like pagans themselves? How can one who wallows in selfish affluence tell others to beware of riches or be generous to the poor?

We can be grateful that today no Catholic prelate lives in Renaissance style, aping the opulence of the Medici. But the lure of soft living affects everyone. Even people who preach to others the doctrine of the cross can be tempted to a life of sybaritic ease. Those who fall into this trap Jesus called hypocrites, one of the blackest names in our lexicon. Whoever preaches water should abstain from wine. This goes for parents and other teachers as well as prelates and priests.

On the third bead are pictured a healthy tree with ripe fruit alongside a diseased tree with barren branches. Nearby a foolish picker trudges through a thicket with his basket, vainly searching for grapes among the brambles. Here Jesus is warning us not to look to false prophets for moral guidance.

Who are the false prophets today? Astrologers for one, but happily few serious Christians seek guidance there. Other oracles, no more trustworthy than the stars, peddle their wares through the land; and since they are often touted highly in the press and given time on the airwaves, even good people can be misled. Think of the pagan humbug mouthed by some talk-show hosts and self-proclaimed sex therapists. Barnum is dead, but his spirit lives on. The gullible still pay to be fooled.

Among the false prophets at large are those who deify public opinion. Pollsters tell us where the public stands, not only on politics and perfumes, but on serious moral issues, everything from extortion to abortion. The sophistry of those who draw their moral code from these polls is crudely simple: if everybody is doing it, it can't be wrong.

What have these prophets produced? Look at the world today. By their fruits we know them. When public opinion is allowed to determine right and wrong, the morals of the nation decay.

The Lesson of Ruby Towers

Ninth Sunday in Ordinary Time.
A: Mt. 7: 21-27.

❖❖❖

Shortly after midnight in the late sixties an earthquake struck Manila, rousing all but the soundest sleepers. Earthquakes are an old story for Filipinos, and most sensed that this was no blockbuster. The next day proved them right. The overall damage was slight, with one exception: a posh apartment house, much admired for its elegance and modernity, was no more. In a matter of seconds its five or six stories had been reduced to one. The lone survivor, an infant, was dug out of the rubble a week later. Hundreds perished.

The apartment house was called Ruby Towers, and to this day Manilas refer to the quake by that name. The mystery of why it was singled out for destruction was soon solved. It turned out to have been built on an old army dump, as solid as sand. Corrupt contractors and negligent inspectors were blamed.

Today's reading is from the conclusion of the Sermon on the Mount. If Jesus were a contemporary Filipino, he might use the Ruby Towers disaster to make his point. No structure, spiritual or physical, can be sturdier than its foundations. The moral lessons Jesus proclaimed in his Sermon on the Mount are among his most famous. Even pagans often admire them and like to quote them, just as the people of Manila admired Ruby Towers. But admiring is not enough. We must put these lessons into practice. We must supply the foundation.

Jesus lists some of the people whose spiritual foundation is mere sand, and the list is a shocker—prophets, exorcists, miracle workers, the sort of people who today are called pillars of the Church. Why are these barred from Paradise? One might expect them to gain easy entrance, for they performed many works in the name of Jesus. Unfortunately, it turns out that their use of his name was the only thing Christian about them. The name of Jesus is sacred; the Church has always held it in honor. But like all names, his name is a mere thing, and a worthless thing if one does not live as he told us to live.

Parading under the name of Jesus Christ is not enough. We must prove we are worthy to march behind his banner by doing the will of the Father as he explained it in his Sermon on the Mount. Otherwise his name is reduced to magic. Imagining that a mere thing has miraculous powers is what is meant by superstition. And it is tragic how many would-be Christians build their lives on the fragile foundation of superstition.

Superstition among Catholics is more widespread than most people imagine. Take a scene that used to be commonplace in the gymnasiums of Catholic schools. A basketball player is fouled in the final seconds. Before taking his foul shot he makes the sign of the cross. Piety? Probably not. Almost certainly mere superstition masquerading as piety. For some people the sign of the cross is just a good luck charm. The same may be true of some of the medals they wear and prayers they mouth.

Some such superstitions can be relatively harmless. Even a genuinely good Christian may employ them unthinkingly, out of habit. But it is also possible for Catholics to erect their entire life as Christians on such foundations of sand. A person can possess and proudly display the external trappings of Christianity while ignoring its reality.

Even the Eucharist can be abused this way. Among those who crowd to the altar on Sundays to receive the sacred host, how many realize that the consecrated bread is not a mere thing, not a magic talisman, but Jesus Christ in the form of bread?

Superstition is not the only rot that can eat away at the foundations of one's life as a Christian. Sentimentality is another. This can take many forms, some relatively harmless. But this reading suggests a particularly virulent form. The sentimental person is the kind who expects all wishes to come true, all stories to end happily. Thus Christian sentimentalists cannot bear the thought that for some Christians, themselves included, the story may not end happily at all, that for all his goodness and forbearance, God can be pushed too far.

Jesus is no sentimentalist. Again and again in the gospel he speaks with brutal frankness of what awaits those Christians who hear his words but fail to act upon them. The warning in this passage is among his most frightening. The day will come, he tells us, when "many" who call out "Lord, Lord" will stand at the entrance to eternal life and hear those awful words, "I never knew you. Depart from me, you evildoers."

Earthquakes come with no immediate warning, and those who live where quakes are common know one may strike at any moment. Wise builders in those areas make sure their foundations are rock solid. So do wise Christians everywhere.

Keeping the Sabbath Holy

Ninth Sunday in Ordinary Time.
B: Mk. 2: 23-3: 6 (or 2: 23-28).

The Pharisees have such a negative press in the gospels that we are tempted to lump the whole crowd of them together, imagining they were all as spiteful as the specimens we meet in this passage. But that is not so. Some Pharisees who shared the same sky as Jesus in life now share his company in heaven.

One for sure is Nicodemus, who once sided with Jesus against the collective venom of his fellow Pharisees *(Jn. 7:51)* and later brought ointments to prepare his body for the tomb *(Jn. 19:39)*. Another is Paul, apostle of the Gentiles, who after training under the most learned Pharisee in Jerusalem became obsessed with a desire to crush Christianity. But even in his most fanatical mood, Paul would not have been at home among the sanctimonious spoilsports of today's gospel. Relentless in persecuting Christians the young Paul surely was, but anyone who reads his epistles knows he was incapable of being mean.

Still, enough Pharisees did fall into a pattern to give the word "pharisaical" the meaning of excessively legalistic. They paid niggling attention to the conduct mandated by religious law, but spurned the spirit that gave meaning to the law. Their religion began and ended with literal *do's* and *don't's.*

Most Pharisees never got the point that Jesus stresses here: that laws were made for us, not we for laws. They allowed no exceptions to the petty rules they concocted to regulate compliance with God's law. The plain command, "Keep holy the Sabbath," did not satisfy them. Through the years they listed thirty-nine different kinds of labor as violations, then treated this list as though each item had come from the mouth of God himself. On it were two that they now accused Jesus and his disciples of violating: plucking grain and practicing medicine.

Some laws, of course, do allow no exceptions. These are prohibitions that God has written in the hearts of every human being who ever walked the earth. In several epistles Paul lists some of these absolute prohibitions, sins like "impurity, licentiousness, idolatry, sorcery, hatreds, rivalry, jealousy" *(Gal: 5:19-20)*. Such dispositions of the heart are always evil. No emergency or appeal to a "higher good" can ever justify them.

But the interpretations the Pharisees gave to the Sabbath law should have allowed exceptions. The hunger of the apostles and the plight of the handicapped man were ample justification for breaking, not the Sabbath law itself, but the over-literal, pharisaical misapplication of that law. What Jesus and his disciples did, all God's children are free to do. That is the lesson Jesus tried to bang into the heads of these Pharisees.

How important is this lesson today? Not very. Contemporary Catholics have their faults, but pharisaical legalism is rarely one of them. Most know they are obliged to Sunday Mass, but I have not met many who were incapable of making exceptions. Few hesitate to miss Mass when a family member is sick and needs their company; most are ready to help a fellow motorist in trouble even if this means not getting to the church on time. Common sense knows when the literal law does not apply.

What, then, does this passage say to Catholics of today?

It should make us reflect for a moment on the age-old obligation of Sunday Mass, our equivalent of the Sabbath law. Like many other practices in our Catholic tradition, Sunday Mass attendance has fallen off in recent decades. But it remains our law, part of our Catholic identity. Almost anywhere one goes in the world, one of the things that makes Sunday different is still the sight of people on their way to Mass.

Why do they go? Not, let us hope, because they are pushed there by a spirit of pharisaical legalism. True, Sunday Mass is a duty. We are seriously obliged to attend if we can do so without suffering grave inconvenience or neglecting a neighbor in need. But this does not mean that those who obey the law should do so merely to fulfill a legal duty or that this duty is all they should think about as they struggle out of bed on Sunday morning. The Church, which has the task of dispensing the grace that Jesus Christ won for us on Calvary, wants us all to share that grace. That is what happens at Mass. That is why we should not only be there, but want to be there.

At Mass we are as close to Jesus as were the apostles who walked with him through the grain on that Sabbath long ago; as the man in the synagogue who held out his hand for healing; as Nicodemus when he prepared the body of Jesus for burial; and as Saint Paul when on the road to Damascus he beheld a blinding light and heard the voice of the Lord *(Acts 9: 1-9)*.

Nothing in our week surpasses in value the Mass we attend on Sunday. On the Lord's day we should be with the Lord.

THE GOOD ROMAN SOLDIER

Ninth Sunday in Ordinary Time.
C: Lk. 7: 1-10.

❖ ❖ ❖

One would not expect a centurion to enjoy a favorable press in biblical Palestine. As both a Gentile and a senior officer in the Roman army he had two strikes against him. It is pleasant to discover, then, that of the centurions we meet in the New Testament (two have minor roles in Luke's gospel, seven in his *Acts of the Apostles*) all are spoken of favorably; but none more favorably than the centurion of Capernaum in this gospel.

He probably commanded a peace-keeping force for Herod, the puppet ruler of Galilee. This posting in the boondocks of Palestine was hardly the answer to a soldier's prayer. How could he foresee that an incident in his life there would one day be read throughout the world to members of a religion not yet born? Or that centuries later his words, in slightly altered form, would be repeated by millions during a liturgy called the Mass?

Luke's portrait of him is a delight. He was what Spanish speakers call *simpatico*, a word for which we have no exact English equivalent. It is richer than our "sympathetic," for on Spanish-speaking lips it retains the flavor of its root meaning, *feeling with* other people, getting inside them, sharing their joys and sorrows. One who is *simpatico* easily crosses social and national barriers, makes friends with the most unlikely people.

See how this centurion got along with his neighbors at Capernaum, people whose background was miles apart from his own. They did not hesitate to use the word "love" to describe his manner of mixing with them. To realize how unusual this was, keep in mind that anti-Semitism was not born yesterday. Jew-baiting was alive and kicking among the ancient Romans, most of whom loathed God's chosen people, sneering at their provincial ways and scorning their clannish religion.

But this centurion, to the astonishment of his Jewish neighbors, was different. He did not just "tolerate" their religion, but actively encouraged them in their worship, even built the local synagogue. Mere tolerance is never enough.

For his sick servant he had a concern that would be rare in any age, but was truly remarkable in ancient times. Some translations call the boy a slave, which is probably closer to the mark, for in those days most servants fared little better than slaves (the Greek word for both was the same). Even today, when people pride themselves on their lack of social snobbery, the dishwashers and scrubwomen of the world are too often viewed as sub-human. Christianity should have changed all that.

What strikes us as most *simpatico* about the centurion, however, is the way he dealt with Jesus. He had heard of the marvelous cures Jesus performed, and in a desperate effort to save the ailing servant, sent for his help. Another centurion might simply have snapped an order: get the Galilean healer here at once and compel him to work his magic. After all, Jesus was only a Jew, a member of a conquered people. He would not dare ignore a summons from a centurion.

But the centurion was *simpatico*. Others had told him how god-like the prophet Jesus was. Did a sinner like himself have the right to receive a man of such holiness into his home?

Legend has it that when Socrates was told that the oracle at Delphi had named him the wisest Greek alive, he replied that if he was the wisest, it was because he alone acknowledged that in fact he knew nothing. This was not empty talk. Socrates had the wisdom to realize how vast were the areas of human learning he had not yet explored. He knew that compared to all there was to know, he knew virtually nothing.

The words of the centurion resemble those of Socrates. As Socrates knew how insignificant was his knowledge, the centurion knew how unworthy was his home. Although he represented the power and prestige of Rome, he was unfit to share the same roof with one as close to God as he had heard Jesus was. Merely being in his presence might smack of sacrilege.

There is no better starting point for a philosopher than an admission of ignorance. Out of it comes a thirst for knowledge and a readiness to learn. And there is no better starting point for a Christian than an admission of sin. Out of it comes a desire for reform and a craving for help that only God can give.

That is why the Church puts words modeled on those of the centurion into our mouths when we approach Holy Communion. In saying "Lord, I am not worthy to receive you, but only say the word and I shall be healed," we imitate the centurion's humility, acknowledging how unfit we are to be hosts to Jesus. Realizing our sinfulness, however, ought not keep us from receiving him in Communion. Since only he can cure us, it should make us all the more anxious to receive him into our souls.

SATAN'S WILY TRAPS

First Sunday of Lent.
A: Mt. 4: 1-11.

❖❖❖

A reader once asked why these gospel reflections put such stress on the human qualities of Jesus. I was happy that someone had noticed. That Jesus is (note *is*, not *was*) an honest-to-goodness member of the human race deserves stressing, for it is an important article of our creed. Few are more important.

Some people find the divinity of Jesus so overwhelming a truth that his humanity is all but eclipsed. They put him in almost the same class as those bloodless characters, drained of all recognizably human feeling, who populate science fiction. That such a view of Jesus is possible shows how sadly Scripture is neglected. The gospels paint a different picture.

There we meet a Jesus rich in warm human emotions. He wept at a friend's tomb; showed pity for a woman, a total stranger, who had lost her only son; felt the pangs of both hunger and thirst; was once so fagged out with preaching that he fell asleep in a moving boat. He even experienced the anguish of failure, of realizing how futile some of his best efforts had been. Yes, Jesus was as human as we are. Scripture leaves no room for doubt.

As in most matters, however, an exception must be made. In one important regard Jesus was unlike any of us. Saint Paul says he was "tested in every way, yet *without sin*" *(Heb. 4:15)*. Not only *did* he not sin, he *could* not sin. Sin by definition is an offense against God. It is unthinkable that Jesus, who was both God and man, could negate his divinity by sin.

We should remember this when we read that in the desert Jesus was "tempted by the devil." How could a man for whom sin was unthinkable be tempted to sin? Certainly not as we ordinary mortals often are. In our severe temptations we not only see evil dangling before us, but are enticed by its charms, lured almost irresistibly into its net. All the while we are aware of how easy it would be to yield. No ordinary mortal is immune.

Jesus was immune. The world, the flesh, and the devil could work their wiles to seduce him, but in vain. He never wavered, never toyed as we do with the prospect of doing evil, half saying yes and half saying no. He was always in total command.

Then what can his temptations, so unlike our own, teach us? Start by asking what Satan was up to in the desert.

His goal was to torpedo the mission of Jesus, get him off course from the outset. And so he tried to trap him, not into sin (he knew Jesus was too holy for that), but into attitudes that would spell disaster for his Messianic enterprise. Satan can employ a similar strategy on us, aiming more to poison our attitudes than to tempt us to this or that sin. He knows that if our attitudes are Christian, we can easily repent of a single sin and start afresh. But if we allow our attitudes to turn pagan, then many evils will follow, and his devilish job is done.

What three attitudes did Satan try to sell to Jesus?

First, sensuality. "Bread" here signifies more than a single slice of rye. It stands for gratification of the flesh in general. To gratify the flesh is not in itself sinful; in fact it is often a clear duty. But his miraculous powers were given to Jesus for a purpose higher than allaying his own hunger. If he had put his appetite ahead of God's purpose, his mission would have aborted. No one would heed a self-pampering prophet.

Second, egomania. To float down from the pinnacle of the temple would draw all eyes to himself and give him an audience worthy of a Messiah. All Israel would acclaim his wizardry, hail him as man of the hour. But that kind of notoriety was not what Jesus came in to the world to achieve. Service of others, not accolades for his own exploits, was the goal of his mission.

Third, lust for power. To have the kingdoms of the world under his sway would be ideal for a Messiah with the universal aspirations of Jesus. As ruler of all nations he could promulgate his law to the ends of the earth and issue decrees compelling obedience. But there was a catch. To attain such dominion, he would have to pay tribute to Satan, the prince of this world. Political power and religious purpose do not mix. If the history of the world's religions teaches anything, it teaches that.

What attitudes does the devil try to peddle to us? Not exactly the same as to Jesus in the desert. His were messianic temptations, and we are no Messiahs. But as Christians we have the duty to imitate the Messiah and help spread his spiritual kingdom. Clearly that would be impossible if we allowed our lives to be ruled by sensuality, egomania, and lust for power.

The season of Lent, which we enter today, is an occasion to confess our sins and start afresh. But even more important than our sins are our attitudes. How Christian are they? How pagan? Lent is a good time to take a close look.

Refreshment in the Desert

First Sunday of Lent.
B: Mk. 1: 12-15.

❖❖❖

Our faith affirms that Jesus Christ is both God and man. One might expect the first part of this statement to be the more difficult to hold onto, but that is not always so. We can be so overwhelmed by the divinity of Jesus that we lose sight of his humanity. Not that we consciously deny he was a man, but we can habitually think about him in a way that effectively strips him of any credibly human traits. We can find it almost impossible to picture him filing his fingernails or trimming his beard.

In one respect, it is true, Jesus was what many would regard as inhuman: he was not a sinner, not even capable of sin. He did not, like ourselves, inherit the guilt of our first parents, and so had none of our hankering for forbidden fruit. But in all other ways, italicize *all*, he was one of us.

When God joined our human race he was not putting on an act, like a king disguising himself as a peasant or a clown cavorting in lion skin. If the young men of Nazareth had wrestling matches, Jesus was not the automatic winner. If the adults had quiz shows, he could conceivably have muffed an answer. One preface for Sunday Mass says God became man because he "wanted us to be saved by one like us." The words are too tame. Jesus was not just *like* us. He *was* and *is*, one of us.

It is important to remember this when we picture the ordeal of Jesus in the desert when he had only wild beasts for company. We should neither exaggerate nor minimize what happened during those forty days. His survival was not miraculous. He was neither the first nor the last person to live that long without food. A healthy adult, experts say, can usually last up to forty days without nourishment. What Jesus did was skirt close to the edge of human endurance. In doing so, he experienced all the weakness, confusion, and anxiety any of us would if put to a similar test.

Have you ever seen photos of the skeletal survivors of Nazi concentration camps, staring with expressionless eyes, appearing more dead than alive? That is the sight Jesus must have presented as he staggered out of the desert after forty days. He certainly looked in no shape to launch a career as a preacher. Yet that is what he proceeded to do. Mark tells us his next move was to return to Galilee and start proclaiming the gospel that in time would sweep through the world.

Why did Jesus go into the desert? Scripture says the Spirit "drove" him there. This was the same holy Spirit that had surged through him while John was baptizing him in the Jordan. Why did the Spirit not plunge him into his preaching at once? Why delay him with an ordeal that could only weaken him physically?

Some people have gone on hunger strikes to make political statements to the world. But that could not have been the motive of Jesus. His desert fast, unknown to the world, was a private enterprise, witnessed only by Satan and beasts. Mark would not have had the story to tell at all if Jesus had not confided it to his apostles. Clearly he wanted them—and through them us—to learn from his experience. What can we learn?

For one thing, the importance of escaping occasionally from the hubbub of daily life, not just to relax in the sun, but to do what Jesus did—to think, to pray, to plan. If the holiest man who ever lived needed time alone to get ready for his mission in life, surely we need it to get ready for whatever he has in mind for us. And make no mistake. He has something in mind for each of us, some part in spreading his kingdom.

That is why many Catholics try to make a yearly retreat, to learn what God has to tell them when they listen for a few days. Everyone does not have that chance, but none is too busy to give God a few moments a day. We need to find out what we can do to bring God more into our world. Jesus astonished the crowds by telling them the kingdom of God was not in some never-never land, but here, in the reach of all. To realize this we must spend some time in a desert of our own making. Lent, the season we are entering, is a good time to grow in the habit.

But be warned. We ought not expect utter tranquillity in our desert. The evil spirit got to Jesus at prayer, and he will try to get to us too. His aim was not to entice Jesus to sin, but to steer him from the path of the cross that would bring success to his mission. He works a similar technique on all. As well as urging us to continue in the sins that make the world worse, he tries to block us from making it any better.

The conflict within our souls is not just between sin and no sin, but between not lifting a finger to expand the kingdom of God in our world and doing something that will have a lasting effect for good. What Jesus did in the desert prepared him for the task ahead. What we do in our private desert can prepare us too.

WHO'S *NOT* AFRAID OF THE BIG BAD IMP?

First Sunday of Lent.
C: Lk. 4: 1-13.

❖❖❖

Jesus was alone in the desert when the devil came and whispered barbed flattery in his ear. Details of this encounter could have come to his disciples only from the lips of Jesus himself. Were they shocked that Jesus, like themselves, was subject to temptation? Probably not, nor should we be.

As Son of God, Jesus could not offend God; he lived without sin. But immunity from sin need not mean absence of temptation; a thousand temptations do not add up to a single sin. We have all seen forbidden fruit dangle before our eyes and at the same time been aware we were free to say no. Jesus shared that experience. The difference is that he always said no.

What about the devil who wrangled with Jesus in the desert? Are we to take him literally? Is he a real person or an impersonal force? Does he work on us as he did on Jesus?

Theologians of the past were fairly unanimous in regarding the devil as a personal being, a fallen angel who roams the world and enters our imaginations, cluttering them with enticements to sin. Today some reputable Scripture scholars are not too sure. The temptations we call diabolic, they realize, are all too real; but the devil himself (always pictured as male) they see as more allegorical than real, a kind of myth employed by Scripture to portray the enormity of human malice and the seductive strategies of temptation.

Whichever view one favors, whether he is conceived as a person or a personification, the devil cannot control our fate; he may bewitch us with the glitter of evil, but he cannot compel us to grasp it. If sin is not freely chosen it is no sin at all. Forget about the fellow with horns on his head and a glint in his eyes who hurls innocents into hell. The Mephistopheles of legend belongs in the opera house, not the Christian creed.

Moreover, whether a reality or a myth, the devil is certainly not the only source of temptation. The lure of the world and the weakness of the flesh engender far more sins than Satan can. Only the more insidious temptations, those that threaten one's total allegiance to

Christ, deserve to be called diabolic. And not all humans are prey to such temptations. Gross sinners, those hardened in sin, the devil can safely leave alone. His energies are better spent trying to corrupt good people, important people, people in position to thwart his schemes, people who count. That is why he grappled with Jesus in the desert. More than any person who ever lived, Jesus counted.

A confidence man to the core, the devil pretended he was doing Jesus a favor. In urging him to turn stones into bread, he was not asking Jesus to pamper his palate. That would be too obvious. His aim was to undermine the Messianic mission of Jesus by suggesting a quack formula for quick success. Many Israelites expected a Messiah who would usher in an age of plenty. The devil took up this theme, telling Jesus to make bread, not the cross, the banner of his kingdom. Let him give people food for their bellies, not nourishment for their souls.

The next two temptations were also Messianic. Had Jesus accepted the devil's offer of power and glory, he would have become a political Messiah. The only price he had to pay was to make Satan his master. By prompting Jesus to leap from the temple, the devil proposed a showman's Messiah, one who would attract followers by displays of magic. Again, the price seemed small: just let the devil decide the meaning of Scripture.

Our own temptations are rarely diabolic; few of them threaten the fabric of our Christian life. But some do.

The desire to sleep over on a Sunday morning is hardly from the devil. It is not worth his time. But if we are tempted to reject the whole notion of Church's authority in matters like Sunday Mass, if we begin to think we can be good Christians without the Sacraments or the guidance of the Church, then we can be fairly sure the devil is poking into our lives.

A temptation to a single act of illicit sex is not diabolic. But the notion that sex is a plaything, that its pleasures are there for the plucking without reference to marriage, is straight from Satan's handbook. So is the idea that we should all design our own moral code, that only wimps seek direction from above.

This is the first Sunday of Lent, the season when Christians traditionally abstain from some innocent pleasures of life. But Lent should also be for us, as his stay in the desert was for Jesus, a time for serious thinking. We would have to be blind not to see traces of diabolic activity in the world around us. But what about our own world, our personal values? Has the devil made inroads there? How much have we allowed the sophistries of Satan to shape our world within?

Are We Listening?

Second Sunday of Lent.
A: Mt. 17: 1-9.

❖ ❖ ❖

To the apostles who witnessed it, the transfiguration of Jesus came as a total surprise. From their daily proximity to him they knew that, physically at least, Jesus did not belong to a superior species of humanity. Under the Palestinian sun he sweated as profusely as they did, at night he slept as soundly. Now, however, they discovered that the body of Jesus was capable of a swift transformation to a more exalted state. For a few moments on the mountainside they were transfixed with wonder as they beheld their Master in glory.

Our creed tells us that from the moment of his conception Jesus was both man and God. From the day the apostles first glimpsed him, however, his physical features gave no hint of divinity; no one gazing at his features would have reason to suspect that he was anything other than a splendid specimen of mature manhood. Now, during the transfiguration, his divinity came to the surface. He looked like a god because he was God; his flesh for a few moments was suffused with divine splendor.

No theologian has succeeded in explaining the internal mechanism of the transfiguration. But the external facts are clear. One night Jesus walked up a mountain trail, seeking a place to pray. His apostles found nothing unusual in that. They had often seen him steal away at dark to snatch a few moments of communion with his Father. This time, however, he broke the pattern of solitude and took with him Peter, James, and John, his favorite three. Coming to a clearing, he knelt on the ground and prayed. Weary from the climb, his companions slumped to the ground and were soon in the clutches of sleep.

Sometime during the night they started up, awakened by a mysterious brightness. As their eyes adjusted, they realized that the brightness was Jesus himself, his face shining "like the sun," his garments "white as light." Conversing with him were the lawgiver Moses and the prophet Elijah. Impulsively Peter blurted out a scheme to erect three booths on the spot. He wished to memorialize this meeting between Jesus and these two great figures of Jewish history.

Soon a luminous cloud spread over them, and from within a voice uttered the same words that had been heard at the baptism of Jesus.

"This is my beloved Son, with whom I am well pleased; listen to him." Awestruck, the apostles stumbled forward to the ground. Moments later, each of them felt the gentle touch of a hand and looked up to the familiar face of Jesus.

What had been going on? Theologians speculate on *how* this all happened, but there can be little doubt about *what* happened. The apostles had thought they knew Jesus. But after what they saw on the mountain they realized how fragmentary and superficial their knowledge was. In time the full truth of his identity would be revealed to them. But on this night they had been granted a strong hint of the truth, almost enough to start thinking what to a pious Jew was unthinkable. Jesus was a man, yes, but infinitely more than a man; not merely close to God, but penetrated to the depths of his being with Godhood. Looking back years later they would realize that the truly astonishing thing was not that God's glory had finally flashed forth from his flesh, but that it had remained hidden as long as it had.

What lesson can we draw from the transfiguration? Jesus once referred to himself as the "Way" to the Father, meaning among other things that he is the model for our daily conduct if we wish to win salvation. Imitate him and we please God. But how can we model ourselves on the transfigured Jesus? Do we, like him, possess a dual nature, human and divine?

Not exactly, but something much like it. Baptism is a kind of rebirth, giving us a second identity. After baptism we remain children of Adam, but are also in a special sense children of God, brothers and sisters of Jesus Christ, sharers in his life.

Some Catholics make the mistake of sneering at the term "born again Christian," wrongly associating it with some noisy form of holy roller evangelism. They should realize we are all, by reason of baptism, born again Christians. The term is straight from the mouth of Jesus *(Jn. 3: 3)*. Saint Paul says bluntly that Jesus won for us "the bath of rebirth" *(Tit. 3: 5)*.

At the transfiguration the apostles saw the reality of Jesus; not just a man, but the God-man. We should strive to see the reality of what we are as Christians; not just Children of Adam but in a special sense children of God, members of the family of Jesus Christ. As long as we do not embrace a life of sin, we are Christ-bearers and therefore God-bearers. As Paul says, we are called to a "holy life," *(2 Tim: 1: 9)*, which means a full awareness of the Christ who lives in us.

"It Is Good That We Are Here!"

Second Sunday of Lent.
B: Mk. 9: 2-10.

We all have our good days and our bad, the best of times and the worst. The fittest golfers go from brilliant seasons to busts. We should not be shocked that Jesus experienced similar swings from the heights to the depths and back. They go with being human, and human was what he came into our world to be.

Except for his dying hours on the cross, what was the lowest point in the life of Jesus? Undoubtedly his agony in the garden of Gethsemane on the night before he died, when he pleaded with his Father to spare him the pain and shame of the cross. Nowhere in the New Testament, possibly nowhere in literature, do we encounter anyone in the throes of more intense torment of soul. In Mark's words, he was "sorrowful even to death" *(14:34)*.

What was his high point? If we exclude the period after his resurrection, the gospels do not present Jesus in a more exalted state than in this passage. For a few precious moments on the mountain his divinity was made manifest. In everyday life his face could be as drenched with sweat and caked with the dust of the road as that of any wayfarer in Palestine, his tunic as in need of a good wash. But now, as the three awe-struck apostles looked on, he belonged to another world. His face was bathed in radiance, his garments immaculately white.

The same three who were with Jesus on the mountain, the apostles Peter, James, and John, would also be with him in the garden. Both times they were present by special invitation.

Why Jesus wanted them with him in the garden seems obvious. Like any person with a foreboding of suffering, he dreaded meeting it alone. He wanted the assurance of having fellow humans nearby, some intimate friends to witness his grief and feel for him in his anguish. Their mere presence would be a comfort.

Why he wanted them with him on the mountain to witness his glory is harder to say. Commentators have suggested that one reason was to prepare them for Gethsemane and Calvary. By this reasoning their presence on the mountain was meant as a kind of immunization process. Having seen him in his hour of glory, they would be less likely to have their world turn upside-down when they behold him in his hours of degradation.

But if this was what Jesus intended, it is clear that the stratagem did not work. Or perhaps, ironically, it worked too well. So well prepared were they that once his distress in the garden began, the three fell promptly asleep. Their inattention at the moment when he needed them most must have been one of the most agonizing aspects of his agony in the garden.

But although the stratagem failed with them, perhaps it will work for us. This may explain why the Church chooses one of the three accounts of the Transfiguration (Matthew, Mark, and Luke report the episode) for the gospel reading on the second Sunday of every Lent. She wants to prepare us for our coming commemoration of the passion and death of Jesus.

We should never read that story without realizing, not only that the disgrace of Jesus was only temporary, but that in the plan of God it was prelude to his Resurrection and Ascension. Gethsemane and Calvary together occupied less than twenty-four hours of his life. On the third day he arose and soon returned to his Father. What happened on the mountain was a preview of his eternal glory. We should remember this preview, even while reading the story of his passion and death.

Moreover, we should strive for the same double vision when we view our contemporary world. The Church Jesus left behind is often in agony. Its plight can appear as desperate as his own in Gethsemane. But the suffering of the Church, like that of Jesus, is redemptive. The cause that he died for will prevail. He is God's beloved Son, and we are his beloved Church.

Jesus was not the only person the apostles beheld on the mountain. Also there, conversing with him, were Moses, the great lawgiver, and Elijah, the revered prophet. The law God gave to Moses on Mount Sinai was perfected by the new law that Jesus proclaimed in his Sermon on the Mount. And Elijah, the most charismatic of the prophets, was the harbinger of the far more charismatic Jesus. The presence of these two on the mountain signaled that Jesus was the fulfillment of Jewish history.

Finally a cloud covered the mountain and from it came the voice of the Father. This is the climax of the passage, for the apostles its defining moment. Peter, James, and John became leaders of the early Church, revered by all for having walked and talked with Jesus. To their fellow Christians they had one clear message. They had seen the glory of Jesus on the mountain. They knew for a certainty that he was the "beloved Son" of the Father; that they—and we—must "listen to him."

WORDS OVERHEARD ON THE MOUNTAIN

Second Sunday of Lent.
C: Lk. 9: 28-36.

❖ ❖ ❖

During Lent we Christians often wonder if we are doing enough to mark the season. This gospel suggests an answer.

Along with three disciples, Jesus went up a mountain one night to pray. There was nothing unusual in that; nor in its sequel, when the watching disciples drifted off to sleep. But soon the sleepers awoke with a start to behold Jesus transformed, his garments a shimmering white and his face a blinding radiance.

What was going on? Those who have seen saints united with God in ecstatic prayer describe their features in terms that faintly those Luke uses here for Jesus. Was it the prayer of ecstasy that Jesus experienced on the mountain? Yes, and much more.

How much more we know from the words that thundered down from the cloud, "This is my chosen Son." The union of Jesus with God was infinitely closer than that of any saint in ecstasy. He was not just a beloved creature of God, but the eternal Son who shared the divine nature. On the mountain he allowed his divinity to flash forth, dazzling the disciples.

The voice added, "Listen to him." This crisp command was the climax of the Transfiguration and key to its meaning. The disciples were granted this sight of Jesus in glory, not for their personal gratification, but that they might realize how important it was that they listen to him. He was the "chosen Son," the Messiah, who came to teach mankind how to live. The disciples were the first to hear this teaching. The future of Christianity would depend on how well they listened.

This command to listen was not a vague mandate to heed the words of Jesus. In Luke's gospel it refers specifically to the doctrine Jesus had stated before ascending the mountain, the doctrine of the cross. It was then that for the first time he told them how his career would end. Instead of being crowned king of Israel, as they had hoped, he must "suffer greatly and be rejected...killed and on the third day be raised" *(Lk. 9:22)*.

That was not all. His followers should expect no better fate. They must willingly take up their cross and follow him. Otherwise they will never join him in the "glory of the Father."

To the disciples these words were deeply disturbing. A Messiah all Jews expected. A suffering Messiah, although foreseen by some of the prophets, most did not. That God rewards those who are faithful to him, all knew. That this reward does not always come in this life, that the path to glory is often painful, had to be taught by the word and example of Jesus.

This explains the presence of Moses and Elijah on the mountain. The doctrine of the cross had been foreshadowed in their own lives. Honored though this lawgiver and prophet now were, they had been rejected by many fellow Israelites while they lived. They spoke to Jesus about "the exodus that he was going to accomplish in Jerusalem," that is, about his journey through death and resurrection to his eternal kingdom.

How well these three disciples listened to the doctrine of the cross we see from their later lives. James was martyred for preaching the gospel, beheaded by Herod Agrippa a bare decade after Pentecost. Peter lasted a few decades longer, then shed his blood at Rome during Nero's persecution. Tradition has it that John died peacefully as an old man at Ephesus, but his lifetime of labors for the gospel had been far from painless.

The Church chooses the Transfiguration for the gospel today because she wants us to hear during Lent the same command the disciples heard. We too must *listen* to the doctrine of the cross. It is not true that this doctrine was easy for the early Christians to accept, that only in modern times do people find it repugnant. The cross was no more popular in the first century than it will be in the twenty-first. Through all history the chant of the world has been the same: get rich; get comfortable; step over anyone blocking your way; take care of Number One.

Directly opposing this chant is the doctrine of the cross. Some people think it glorifies suffering, but nothing could be further from the truth. Jesus did not embrace the cross because he loved pain but because he loved us. Love means giving; the ultimate gift, the way to prove the depth of one's love, is by giving what he and his disciples gave—their lives.

What should the serious Christian be doing for Lent? We can begin by listening to the doctrine of the cross as the disciples listened; make it shape our lives. Jesus gave his life for us on the cross; we can give a good part of our lives for our neighbors in need. That is the best penance. Forget about Number One. Rather, let our neighbor be Number One. Caring for our neighbor is caring for Jesus Christ.

HE JUST ASKED FOR A DRINK OF WATER

Third Sunday of Lent.
A: Jn. 4: 5-42 (or 5-15, 19-26, 39, 40-42).

❖ ❖ ❖

"If the Church is against bigotry, how come the priest never mentions it on Sunday? He must know we have plenty of bigots in the pews." I once heard this complaint from a student. Was it fair? Fair or not, it is worth thinking about. This passage, where Jesus confronts bigotry, is a good place to start.

In the time of Jesus the most visible targets of Jewish bigotry were the Samaritans, who nourished a reciprocal bigotry towards Jews. The Samaritans held a stretch of land smack in the middle of Palestine. Here we see Jesus conversing with a Samaritan woman. That this conversation took place at all tells what Jesus thought of bigotry. It was he who broke the ice.

He was sitting alone at Jacob's well, a resting place for travelers through Samaria. After hours of trudging along dusty roads he was thirsty, his throat parched. When a woman approached with a bucket, what could be more natural than his "Give me a drink?" But the woman was shocked, and with reason. In those days well-bred men did not strike up conversations with strange women at wells. Moreover, this man, she knew from his accent, was a Jew. And Jews did not converse with Samaritans at all.

Few Jews or Samaritans had even a clue to why they were enemies, but they did not need one. To a genuine bigot it is enough that the other is not "one of our kind." Actually, the quarrel was rooted in history, very hoary history. Centuries earlier the Samaritans had been contaminated by intermarriage with Gentiles. That alone made them an abomination in the eyes of pure-blooded Jews. Moreover, they were judged heretical, for they worshipped at Mount Gerizim in Samaria instead of the temple in Jerusalem. Thus the bigotry of these parties for one another was both racial and religious, the two most common types.

For racial bigotry there can be no rational basis. Anyone with the dimmest knowledge of biology knows that the concept of "pure blood" is pure poppycock. The contemporaries of Jesus had some excuse for their scientific ignorance. We have none.

Religious bigotry, on the other hand, has at least the veneer of a rational basis, since differences in religious belief are both genuine and profound. We should never in the interest of peace pretend these differences do not exist or are trivial. Notice how Jesus, without arrogance but with quiet firmness, tells the woman that "salvation is from the Jews." Well he knew. He was a Jew, fully conscious he was "the savior of the world."

To reject bigotry we need not hold that one religion is as good as another, a position that in strict logic means no religion is much good at all. Paradoxically, what we need is firmer belief in the truths of Christianity, especially the truth that God loves all and sent his Son, Jesus, to save all.

Possibly the most misunderstood doctrine of the Church is also one of the most ancient, "Outside the Church there is no salvation." It seems a perfect slogan for bigots. Rightly understood, however, it is the opposite. What it does not mean is that only those formally baptized in the Church can hope to reach heaven. What it does mean is that since Jesus is the sole redeemer of mankind, all power to do good comes from him. Outside Christ, who lives in his Church, there is no salvation. And his blood, as we read in the consecration at Mass, was shed "for all." No one reaches heaven without the grace of Calvary.

This grace is showered in thousands of ways, visible and invisible. Among those who receive it are some who never heard of Jesus, some who in good faith oppose him. On this, however, the Church's doctrine is clear: God wants all to be saved. No one goes through life without being offered the grace of Christ.

Ugly as bigotry is, we can take comfort in realizing it is not always a culpable fault. Often it has its origin in ignorance or environment, for which the bigot should not be faulted. People inhale it as they do germs in the air. Children catch it from parents, schoolmates, neighbors, even churches. They are not always to blame for carrying it into adult life.

Catholics, however, will have a problem pleading ignorance or environment as excuses for bigotry. Part of our environment since childhood has been the gospel of Jesus Christ. We have heard it often enough to know where he stands. The cure for bigotry is Jesus himself, whom the Samaritans learned to call "truly the savior of the world." His life and death refute all the sophistries that racial and religious hatred can invent.

We all have the job of bringing his grace to the Samaritans of our time. How? Begin by acting as he did at Jacob's well. We should treat everyone we meet, even people bigoted towards ourselves, as Jesus treated this woman, with Christian friendship and respect. We can all do our part in breaking the ice.

CRACKING THE WHIP IN THE TEMPLE

Third Sunday of Lent.
B: Jn. 2: 13-25.

❖❖❖

This is one of the few gospel episodes to which we can assign a precise date. The month was April (Passover time) and the year 28 A.D. (forty-six years after construction started on the temple). This does not mean, by the way, what it seems to mean, that Jesus was 28 years old. We now know that the sixth century monk who devised our calendar made an error in calculation, that Jesus was (paradoxically) born six or seven years before 1 A.D. That puts him in his mid-thirties when he drove the animals and money-changers from the temple.

If you have ever seen a movie version of this event, you know what a crowd-pleaser it is. Audiences are captivated by the sight of Jesus toppling the coin tables while the animals stampede through the market. They seem tickled to learn that even the usually calm and forbearing Jesus had a boiling point.

What provoked his anger? I used to think it was the thievery he saw in the market. I imagined him spotting a nimble-fingered money-changer shortchanging a customer or a smooth-talking sheep peddler bamboozling a peasant from the boondocks. A closer look, however, suggests graver reason for his anger.

Hordes of pilgrims flocked to Jerusalem every Passover, not just from elsewhere in Palestine, but from all over the Mediterranean world. Their goal was the temple, the center of Jewish worship. There they were obliged to pay the half-shekel temple tax (a laborer's average daily wage). Many also sought to make peace with God by sacrificing an ox or sheep or dove.

Thus a marketplace somewhere in Jerusalem was inevitable. Money-changers were needed, especially for pilgrims from abroad, since the only coin not defiled by pagan images or inscriptions was the Jewish shekel. The sale of animals also made sense, to supply the wherewithal for private sacrifice. The only question is why the market was where it was, in the outer court of the temple. Surely Jerusalem had other open spaces fit for a market.

Did petty thievery go on in this market? Of course. Has any market ever been free of it? The other evangelists report that Jesus denounced the place as a "den of thieves."

The thievery he was mostly incensed at, however, was not the occasional swindling by individual merchants. What Jesus saw in this market was one huge, centrally organized, officially sanctioned scam. Money-changers had no need to cheat their customers. They simply went along with the temple practice of charging an exorbitant fee for each transaction. Out of this they of course received their cut, but most of it went to the temple treasury and the pockets of the temple guardians.

The sale of animals was a temple monopoly. Since animals intended for sacrifice had to be approved, and since approval was almost never given for those purchased elsewhere, the temple prices were heavily inflated. Again, the lion's share of the extra profit was scooped up by the official overseers.

All this was within the law. The pilgrims who were fleeced could lodge no complaints, since it was the temple administrators who did the fleecing. Legally, all parties were clean. Morally all were thieves. And the chief thieves were the guardians of the nation's morals, the chief priests and scribes of Jerusalem.

Worse still, this gigantic rip-off was conducted on holy ground. The other evangelists have Jesus stressing that this den of thieves should by right have been a house of prayer. In John's version he does not mention thievery, just the scandal that his Father's house had become a market. That was why his anger reached red-hot fury. His disciples recalled the Messianic text, "Zeal for your house will consume me" *(Ps. 69: 10)*.

What Jesus was angry at, then, was, first, that a huge social injustice was conducted by and for the benefit of the temple officials, the guardians of morality, whose duty it was to oversee a just society; second and above all, that this vicious commerce violated the sanctity of his Father's house.

The lessons of this gospel are also two. First, we should never confuse legality with morality. Just because I can cheat my neighbor without being hauled before a judge does not make it right. The excuse that the whole system is rotten and everyone is doing it will not wash well on judgment day. Our judge will be the man who cracked the whip in the temple.

Second, remember that although our Church has no equivalent of the temple in ancient Jerusalem, each of us is a temple of the Holy Spirit. That, in the words of Saint Paul *(1 Cor 6:19)*, is what a Christian by baptism is. If we are consumed, like the temple market of ancient Jerusalem, with an unholy lust for money, we defile our personal temple. Money in itself is not evil. But God made us, his temples, for higher things.

"If You Do Not Repent..."

Third Sunday in Lent.
C: Lk: 13: 1-9.

❖❖❖

Towards sinners Jesus was always gentle, sometimes (his enemies charged) scandalously so; but never namby-pamby. His compassion for frail humanity did not hinder him from demanding total renunciation of sin. In picturing the punishment that awaits the unrepentant sinner, he even employed what some people today might call scare tactics, but was actually only realism. This gospel is a good example.

Jesus begins by recalling two disasters that had recently sent shock waves through Jerusalem: the massacre of some Galileans by Pilate's death squad while they were offering sacrifice in the temple; and the sudden collapse of a tower, fatally crushing eighteen laborers. If he were preaching today, Jesus might point to some typical headlines—a plane-load of tourists and business travelers blown to pieces by a terrorist bomb; or a high-rise condominium flattened in seconds by an earthquake. Mass murders and random catastrophes of nature like those Jesus pointed to occur on every land and in every age.

Do not think, Jesus tells his listeners, that the victims of such misfortunes must certainly have been guilty of some horrendous sin and thus incurred God's wrath. Their offenses were no worse than your own. But beware. All of you will suffer a fate like theirs if you do not turn from your sins.

And so, Jesus warns his listeners, they must begin to reform. But lest these words prove too discouraging, he adds a short parable to make the point that it is never too late to put one's life in order. The parable is about one of the most valuable trees in Palestine, the fig tree. Precious though it is, this tree is useless if it fails to produce fruit.

Wouldn't a sensible owner have a barren fig tree hacked down to make room for a healthy growth? Does anyone keep a broken TV set in the parlor? Or a dead canary in a cage? Should we expect God to spare the Christian who is barren of good deeds, whose example never brings others closer to God?

The tree's owner has made up his mind: the fig tree must go. But the vinedresser pleads: give me one more year, one more try. Perhaps with more careful husbandry I can get the tree to bear fruit again. It is not yet beyond repair.

The point of this parable is that God does give us such a second chance. However dismal our previous record, we are not yet beyond repair. The vinedresser in the parable stands for Jesus himself. Because he came to earth, because he gave his life for the human race, we can reform and start anew. The Church gives us this gospel during Lent because this is the season when Christians are asked to look at their lives, see what is in bad disrepair, and start the process of reform.

Reform is never easy. It begins with self-examination, a process no one can do for us. Admitting our true faults, even in the privacy of our hearts, demands uncompromising honesty. We are all afflicted with less than perfect vision when we play judge and jury on ourselves. Think of the alcoholics who insist they suffer from nothing more serious than an occasional tendency to take a drop too many; of the backbiters who defend their habit of poisonous gossip by pleading that they never speak a word against their neighbor unless it is true; of the racists who call themselves simple realists. Self-deception is easy; and because it is, self-examination is not.

Remember, however, that Jesus tells us we must *begin* to reform. He does not promise there will ever be an *end* to the process. We should not think that if we reform ourselves properly, some day we will wake to find we have no faults left to amend, no virtues yet to acquire. It doesn't happen that way. The life of a serious Christian is one of constant beginnings, many of them false starts; of repeated lapses, sometimes so discouraging we hardly have the heart to try again. This, if truth is told, is the story even of the greatest saints.

In a book she wrote on saints, the poet Phyllis McGinley made this point: "For the wonderful thing about saints is that they were human. They lost their tempers, got angry, scolded God, were egotistical or testy or impatient in their turns, made mistakes and regretted them. Still they went on doggedly blundering toward heaven." Well, some may say, that sounds much like ourselves. How did the saints differ from the rest of us? Precisely in this, that every day they "doggedly" seized their second chance and had the courage to make a new beginning.

Like the fig tree, we may have only one more year to go. But every day of that year we will wake to a second chance. On the day God calls us to our final account, may he find us, like his saints, "doggedly blundering toward heaven."

WASHING IN THE POOL OF SILOAM

Fourth Sunday of Lent.
A: Jn. 9: 1-41 (or 1, 6-9, 13-17, 34-38).

❖ ❖ ❖

This is the most spectacular miracle of its kind in the New Testament. John stresses that the blind man had not lost his sight through illness or accident, but had been in darkness since birth. Until this meeting with Jesus he had groped his way though life without even a memory of what color means or a human face looks like. Forced to beg for his bread, he sat daily in the same spot, crying out for alms whenever the sound of footsteps reached his ears. His life was a long monotony of begging until the day he heard the footsteps of Jesus.

Jesus could heal with a mere word and often did. For this beggar, however, he took his time. First, he formed a wad of mud by mixing his spittle with dirt from the ground; next he smeared the mud on the blind man's eyes (to us the process sounds wildly unhygienic, but it was the sort of ritual the ancients expected from a healer); finally he told the beggar to go bathe his eyes in the pool at Siloam. At this the beggar bounded up, found his way to the pool, crouched over its edge, splashed water in his eyes, stood suddenly upright, and let out whoops of pure delight. For the first time in his life he could see.

The gospel, one of the longest of the year, spends only two verses on the cure itself, although the entire process may well have taken hours. We can imagine with what solemnity Jesus shaped the wad of mud as he prepared to perform one of his greatest miracles. The Greek word the gospel uses for the application of the mud to the beggar's eyes is translated "smeared," but can also mean "anointed," giving the performance a sacred character. A healing by Jesus was a holy act.

Threading through the crowd to the pool must have been slow going for the blind man, and by the time he arrived there he would have attracted a circle of curious spectators. We can picture them buzzing with gratification as they watch the blind man jump with joy and make his way back to family and friends.

If we think this curing process resembled a ceremony, we are in good company, for that is exactly what the early Christians thought. They were struck by its likeness to the rite of baptism, which also has an anointing, uses water, and often attracts a group of beaming spectators. In the early Church, in fact, this passage was used to prepare catechumens for baptism. The scene was even painted on catacomb walls to illustrate the sacrament of initiation. The beggar's words, "I do believe," are echoed in the rite of baptism to this day.

When the once blind man returned to the place where he had spent his days begging, some neighbors refused to believe who he was. To settle the matter, they hauled him before the Pharisees, since the alleged cure had taken place on a Sabbath and might therefore have violated the Mosaic law. They felt sure that The Pharisees, who were not only themselves strict observers of the law but also its zealous enforcers, would know how to deal with the case. Those who failed to live up to their standards of Sabbath observance they expelled from the synagogue.

One of the principal laws God gave to Moses forbade labor on the Sabbath. The Pharisees insisted on interpreting this precept with inhuman rigidity. When we learn about some of their hairsplitting on the subject, we are tempted to call them madmen. To wear sandals that were made with nails, for example, broke their Sabbath, since in their eyes the weight of the nails was an excessive burden. Some even debated whether it was lawful to eat an egg that a chicken had laid on the Sabbath.

It is easy to see why people who indulged in this sort of nitpicking had no use for the compassionate and generous Jesus. They had decreed that medicine be practiced on the Sabbath only if necessary to preserve a human life. Since this man's life had not been in danger, healing him was judged a sin.

What strikes us most about these Pharisees is their inability to comprehend what religion is all about. Think of the privileges they had, living as they did in the time of Jesus. They had heard his parables and witnessed many of his works of compassion. Yet when he displayed his kindliness by giving sight to a blind man, all they saw was that he had violated their interpretation of the Mosaic law. In this gospel they are the ones who are truly blind. They sin against the light.

At the close of the passage the beggar tells Jesus he cannot believe in the Son of Man unless he knows who he is. "You have seen him," Jesus replies, "and the one speaking with you is he." The same words could be spoken to us. Our eyes were opened at baptism. We see Jesus in action every time we read the gospel. He speaks to us at every Mass we attend. We are not, thank God, blind like the Pharisees. May our eyes always remain open.

The Faith that Brings Eternal Life

Fourth Sunday of Lent.
B: Jn. 3: 14-21.

❖❖❖

Nicodemus was a very important person in Jerusalem, a Pharisee rich and powerful. He was also a very independent person, a man who made up his own mind. The other Pharisees were almost to a man opposed to Jesus, indignant that he dared voice opinions on God and morality not in harmony with their own. But Nicodemus liked what he had learned about the prophet from Galilee. Once when Jesus was in Jerusalem, Nicodemus visited and pumped him with questions, hoping to learn more.

He came by night, possibly because he did not want his brother Pharisees to know the way his mind was moving. John spends half a chapter describing this interview, and almost every line is packed with theology. That is not an unmixed blessing. Theology by its nature is cold, austere, often maddeningly dry. Most people prefer the stories and down-to-earth approach of the other evangelists to John's lofty abstractions.

In the segment for today's gospel, fortunately, Jesus starts with a story, an incident from the Book of Numbers *(21: 4-9)*. During their long, weary trek across the desert from Egypt, the Jews under Moses spent much of their time grumbling. They yearned for the promised land, but had not bargained for the hardships they had to endure to get there. In punishment the Lord sent a plague of deadly serpents. Later, to relieve their distress, he instructed Moses to fashion a bronze image of a serpent and lift it up on a pole. Whoever looked on this replica was rendered immune from the serpents' poison.

A strange tale, it makes little sense to us. But Jesus here uses it for his own purpose, as a parable of himself. Like the bronze serpent, he tells Nicodemus, he will himself be "lifted up." With these words he predicts his death on the cross. He then goes on to stress, first, what his cross will accomplish, and second, what our response to the cross should be.

The cross is the emblem of Christianity. But the words of Jesus to Nicodemus remind us that it is more than a mere emblem. "So must the Son of Man be lifted up, so that everyone who believes in him may have eternal life." The cross brought—and brings—salvation to the world.

To Nicodemus these words must have had a shattering effect. The Pharisees believed entry to eternal life was theirs by right and that the scribal law was their key. By obeying this law to the letter they thought they earned salvation. Here Jesus tells Nicodemus that this is not the way things are at all.

None of us *earns* salvation. We can no more conquer sin and win heaven on our own than the Jews could survive the desert without Moses and the bronze serpent. God has the initiative. The core of our theology is in the words, "God so loved the world that he gave his only Son, so that everyone who believes in him might not perish but might have eternal life." The key is not our obedience to God, but God's love for us.

I once heard a man boast of how his life turned around completely once he "found" Jesus Christ. He meant this statement as a tribute to God's grace, but unfortunately, the wording was theologically unsound. We humans do not find God. God found us. He did so because he loves us, from all eternity.

Does Jesus mean we have no say at all in the transaction? Not exactly. We must, he tells Nicodemus, be willing to receive God's love by believing in Jesus Christ. How God works out the process for those who have never heard the name of Jesus or been exposed to his gospel is God's business. We know that he finds a way, because the grace Jesus won on the cross was for all mankind, and God's will cannot be frustrated. But for those of us who have heard and been baptized in his name the answer is clear. We must *believe* that Jesus speaks with the voice of God, that his gospel is the light that has come into the world.

Jesus makes clear what kind of belief he is talking about. Merely assenting intellectually to the revelation of Jesus Christ is not enough. Satan and his minions in hell have that kind of barren belief. Our faith, the kind of belief Jesus recommends to Nicodemus, must be alive, that is, it must issue in action. Only with that kind of faith will we avoid the darkness of sin.

This is not the last mention of Nicodemus in John's gospel. Later we see him standing up to his fellow Pharisees for condemning Jesus without a hearing *(7:50-52)*. And on the day after they sentenced him to death, he helped take the body of Jesus from the cross and prepare it for burial *(19:39-42)*.

We have not the good fortune of Nicodemus, to speak person-to-person with Jesus and be physically with him on Calvary. But we can learn the same lessons Nicodemus learned. The light that entered his world has also entered ours.

WHO GETS TOP BILLING?

Fourth Sunday of Lent.
C: Lk. 15: 1-3; 11-32.

❖❖❖

If we were making a film of this parable, to whom should we assign the central role? Should our title be "The Wayward Son," or "The Disgruntled Brother," or "The Loving Father"? It depends on how the story is told. Here is one version.

The prodigal is far from an attractive young man. His leaving home is not an innocent episode of adolescent wanderlust, but a strategy of calculated selfishness. In biblical times the younger of two sons inherited a third of the estate. Realizing that decades may pass before the old man is in the grave, this younger son has no wish to spend the best of years of his life going to seed on the ancestral homestead. And so he puts his proposal bluntly: let his father give him his share of the family fortune now, and the two of them can be quits forever.

Some people wonder why the father agrees. Can't he foresee the outcome? Shouldn't he withhold the money and thus compel the boy to stay home? But there is wisdom in the father's indulgence. If he holds the son against his will, the lad will turn into an embittered prisoner in his own home. How then will he ever learn how much his father loves him? How learn to love his father in return? Better let him go. Love cannot be forced.

The prodigal's downfall is as predictable as soap opera: high living, low women; fair-weather friends, foul booze; down the slippery slope, resounding crash. Finally, penniless and among strangers, he lands a job as handyman on a pig farm.

What happens next is sometimes called the prodigal's conversion, but it is doubtful that it merits the name. As Jesus tells the story, the son shows not an ounce of remorse for the hurt he has inflicted on his father. He longs for home only because he realizes the pigs enjoy a better diet than he does. Perhaps his father will let him squeeze into one of the bunks where the farm hands sleep. At least he will be away from the swill of the swine and have a plate of edible food for supper.

Imagine sitting with the father as the prodigal appears in the distance, sheepishly creeping his way home. What advice would we give? Take the scamp in, of course. Can't let him starve in the streets. But don't treat him like visiting royalty. Bed him down with the hired help. Teach him a good lesson.

But the father is not built that way. As they watch him greet his son, the neighbors are flabbergasted. But no more so than the son himself. On spotting the lad in the distance, the father rushes to meet him, hugs and kisses him, showers him with gifts, proclaims a party to celebrate his return.

Imagine what goes through the son's mind as he sits in the place of honor, munching on meat from the fatted calf, feted like a prince and fussed over like a baby. This is not at all what he had expected. No groveling, no beating his breast in repentance, no tedious lectures to listen to, no thirty lashes in punishment. What did he ever do to deserve so loving a father?

The elder son is a different breed from his brother, but no prize either. (By what genetic quirk did so gracious a father spawn such an ungracious pair? The situation arises often enough in real life to keep us from challenging its verisimilitude here.) Among those who heard Jesus tell this parable and for whose sake he told it were some Pharisees, who were indignant that Jesus allowed sinners to come near him. They and the elder son were kindred spirits—cold, mean, vindictive, loveless.

On hearing the music and learning that his runaway brother has returned to a hero's welcome, the elder son stays outside in a sulk. When the father pleads with him to join the party, he pours out the resentment of a lifetime. Like many petty people, he has no lack of words to vent his grievances. It isn't fair, he whines. All these years he has slaved for his father and never once had even a goat to feast on. The word "slaved" gives him away. The father has never treated him like a slave. But he has acted like one, with no more affection for his father than a slave for his master. A son should labor for a father out of love. The elder son labored, but never got the point.

Yet even for this cipher of a son, the father has love, love to the point of folly. He pleads with him to be like himself, to have an open, generous, forgiving heart. "My son, you are here with me always; everything I have is yours."

The starring role is the film clearly belongs to the father, and perhaps the best title would be, "The Mystery of the Loving Father." For it is a mystery. Why does the father go on loving so unlovable a pair? What makes the story universal in its appeal is that it suggests an even greater mystery, the mystery of Christianity, which no one can ever fathom. Why does our heavenly Father go on loving such ungrateful children as ourselves?

Jesus Wept

Fifth Sunday of Lent.
A: Jn. 11: 1-45; or 3-7; 17; 20-27; 33-45.

❖❖❖

The great Houdini, a magician not content with plucking rabbits from hats, liked to create the illusion that he was toying with death. He was famous for having himself bound with ropes, packed in a trunk, and tossed into a lake. Although death by drowning seemed certain, within seconds he popped up from the waters unharmed. It was his most spectacular stunt.

But it was only a stunt. What Houdini escaped was only the appearance of imminent death. Jesus is the only person in history to return unassisted from the reality of death. That he did so is the foundation of our faith. If there were no Easter Sunday on the world's calendar, there would be no Christian religion. As simple as that.

Easter, however, was not the only time Jesus displayed mastery over death. Scripture records three occasions on which he brought others back to life. Near the city of Nain in Galilee he called a halt to a funeral procession, restored a young man to life, then returned him to his widowed mother *(Lk. 7: 11-15);* in the town of Capernaum, also in Galilee, he grasped the hand of the just-deceased daughter of an official named Jairus, and she breathed again *(Mt. 9: 25);* and at Bethany in Judea, a village two miles from Jerusalem, he summoned Lazarus from the tomb.

Of these three escapees from death, Lazarus had the most hair-raising experience to recount in later years. The other two had died only hours before Jesus came. A modern commission of inquiry might suspect they were merely in a coma and just appeared to be dead. Mistakes like that happen. But the most dyed-in-the-wool skeptic would not question that Lazarus was genuinely dead. By the time Jesus arrived, he had been four days in the fetid tomb, his body wrapped in burial cloths. Aside from his own resurrection, restoring Lazarus to life was the greatest miracle of Jesus, his most remarkable display of power.

His aspect was never more majestic than when he stood before the tomb of Lazarus, with the crowd of hushed mourners behind him, and boomed forth, "Lazarus, come out!" To the apprehensive Martha he had promised that if she believed in him she would see "the glory of God." Now, as they watched the blindfolded Lazarus stumble awkwardly from the tomb, Martha and the other onlookers realized what these words meant. Only divine power can bring the dead back to life. No wonder many of the mourners from Jerusalem became followers of Jesus on the spot.

Both Martha and Mary expressed confidence that if Jesus had arrived earlier, their brother would have lived. They had no doubt about the power of Jesus over physical ailments, for along with thousands of other Israelites, they had known him to heal the sick. It was only after their brother was returned to them, however, that they grasped the full truth. Jesus had power over life itself. He *is* "the resurrection and the life."

But power is not the only attribute Jesus manifested at the tomb of Lazarus, nor the only thing readers find striking in this episode. Just as striking to many is his simple humanity. Commentators keep telling us that in John's gospel Jesus seems more remote from everyday life than in the other three, more radiant with the aura of divinity. True enough, but in this episode John paints a more complex picture. In his raising of Lazarus the human attributes of Jesus play as memorable a role as the divine. Nowhere in Scripture is his dual nature more evident.

His humanity is first of all manifested by his very presence in Bethany. What brought him there was his affection for the household of Lazarus. He knew this threesome well, probably from staying at their home during visits to Jerusalem. When the illness of Lazarus grew serious, the sisters summoned Jesus with just, "the one you love is ill." No name was necessary. Later the evangelist says bluntly, "Now Jesus loved Martha and her sister and Lazarus." Jesus was, as Martha asserted, "the Messiah, the Son of God." But he was also, as we learn here, a very human Messiah, with very human ties of friendship.

At the tomb of Lazarus, Jesus was surrounded by the grief-stricken. For a heart as sympathetic as his, their tears were contagious. In the words of the evangelist, he "became perturbed and deeply troubled." The climax comes with the words, "And Jesus wept." That is not only the shortest verse in the New Testament but one of the most surprising. Jesus knew what he was going to do, that Lazarus would soon arise. And yet he wept.

Why did he weep? John does not tell us. If we focus only on the divinity of Jesus, his weeping makes no sense. Omnipotence cannot grieve. But Jesus was one of us, as human as we are in everything but sin. John does not have to tell us why Jesus wept. We have all buried dear ones of our own. We know why.

"If It Dies, It Produces Much Fruit"

Fifth Sunday of Lent.
B: Jn. 12: 20-33.

❖❖❖

Andy Warhol once quipped that someday each of us will be famous for fifteen minutes. For most of the huddled and nameless masses of mankind that surely is a lie, but it proved marvelously true for some Greeks who passed through Jerusalem a few days before the death of Jesus. They had the good fortune to be within earshot as he spoke some of his most memorable lines. Just being among his listeners for those few minutes earned them the fame of this mention in John's gospel.

How much did they grasp of what he said? Probably little, since he spoke of events still to come. We look back on these events, however, and soon along all Christians will celebrate them. During Holy Week these words will be well worth pondering.

"The hour has come," Jesus began, "for the Son of Man to be glorified." Knowing what kind of death he was soon to die, we may wonder what hour he meant. Death by crucifixion is anything but glorious. The crosses people hang from neck chains or we see in churches give hardly a hint of the reality.

Can you imagine a TV documentary about that Black Friday on Calvary, with neither the groans of the crucified convicts nor the blood they shed left out? No advertiser would touch it, knowing most viewers would find it unbearable. Jesus knew what butchery a crucifixion truly was, how its victims died in direst agony and disgrace. Why call it his hour of glory?

That is what he went on to explain. Once we get a grip on his meaning, we will see why we ought never think of his crucifixion in isolation from its aftermath. Christians believe that Jesus redeemed us by his death. Sound doctrine though it is, that statement can mislead. Jesus redeemed us by dying *and* rising. Without Easter, Good Friday is a pointless horror tale. Only by coupling the two can we view the crucifixion as glorious.

To illustrate this point, Jesus fetched an image from the rural world he knew well, the world of farmers and wheat fields. Hold a grain of wheat in your hand, and it remains just a grain of wheat. Bury the same grain in the soil, and in time it will sprout as wholesome food. Its seeming death is prelude to life, its burial the first stage of its rebirth. That is the law of sacrifice, and we see it in the death and burial of Jesus.

Jesus rose from the dead and still lives. He dwells in his Church, now spread throughout the world. And he will reign forever in the company of all who, because he died, will win eternal life. They are the "fruit" produced by his death.

Jesus went on to apply the notion of death and rebirth to all humans: "*Whoever* loves his life loses it, and *whoever* hates his life in this world will preserve it for eternal life." That saying, so much a favorite of Jesus that his disciples could probably repeat it in their sleep, is *the* Christian paradox. If we wish to share in his glory, we must follow him on the path of service and sacrifice. Note that "hating" one's life is a Semitic expression. It means being willing to sacrifice all one holds dear, even life itself, for someone or something one holds dearer. That is what Jesus did on Calvary. Our role, he added, is identical. "Whoever serves me must follow me."

All this may make Jesus sound coldhearted, without fears for himself or compassion for us. But that is not so. We should not imagine that he approached death without a quiver of fear or that he expected us to follow him with stoical calm. Like all humans Jesus would have preferred a gentler, more commonplace form of death. "Father," he prayed, as he would again in the garden of Gethsemani, "save me from this hour."

But as he was soon also to do in the garden, he here reminded himself that he had come into the world to redeem the world and that death on a cross was the way his Father had chosen for him to accomplish this. By choosing to submit he gave glory to his Father. "Father," he cried, "glorify your name."

Twice before in the life of Jesus the voice of his Father came from the sky, at his baptism and his transfiguration. Both times the Father expressed approval of his mission. Now he does so again, "I have glorified it and will glorify it again."

What happened to the visiting Greeks after this brief encounter with Jesus, we are not told. Non-Jews are rare in John's gospel. These left the scene as mysteriously as they came, but not before Jesus showed awareness of their presence. When he dies (is "lifted up from the earth") he declared, he will "draw *everyone*" to himself. His victory over Satan, the "ruler of this world," will be a victory for all mankind.

In the glory of his heavenly kingdom, not only Greeks, but all the races and nationalities of the world, have their share. The shadow of the cross covers the entire world.

When Mercy and Misery Met

Fifth Sunday of Lent.
C: Jn. 8: 1-11.

❖❖❖

The Church has for centuries encouraged devotion to the Sacred Heart of Jesus. This gospel tells much about the kind of heart Jesus had—his deep respect for all humans, however wretched their present or blemished their past. The most loveless and unloved among his fellows he regarded as children of God. It was to save all these children that he came into the world.

While visiting Jerusalem, Jesus often trekked by dawn's early light to the temple, where groups gathered around him as he sat in their midst and taught. This gospel describes an occasion when such a session was brusquely interrupted. Some scribes and Pharisees pushed their way through the circle of listeners, dragging with them a shamed and cringing woman. After forcing her to stand in full view of the assembly, they declared that they had caught her in the very act of adultery.

To the Israelites few crimes were more serious. For any woman found guilty, the punishment prescribed by Moses was death by stoning. The intruders now threw their challenge at Jesus. Should this slut be stoned or not? They knew that if Jesus endorsed stoning, his reputation for clemency would erode and the ranks of his followers shrink. But if he said nay, he would be assuming an authority higher than Moses himself. A neat dilemma, they thought, for this reputedly sharp-witted preacher.

As he sat there, aggrieved at their effrontery, Jesus faced a different dilemma. About the fate he would favor for the woman, he had not a moment's hesitation. His voice, even if it did not prevail, must favor compassion. But how was he to handle her accusers? He knew what was in their hearts; they wanted to trap him, and the woman was only a pawn in their game. Her fate meant nothing to them; he himself was their target.

He could have scored an easy triumph by unmasking their hypocrisy. Reading hearts was his specialty. Why not disclose their own sexual records, hold these humbugs up to the ridicule of the crowd? But this he would not do. Such a tactic could easily backfire; the woman's accusers might stone her just to get even with Jesus. Moreover, it would leave the accusers defeated, but simmering with resentment. To make an opponent lose face never pays. It would be especially anathema to Jesus, who came to win the hearts of all sinners, hypocrites included.

How to get these accusers to see for themselves that stoning the woman would be wrong? Idly drawing figures on the ground, Jesus kept the onlookers in suspense as he mulled over this problem and formed his plan. Finally he stood, faced the scribes and Pharisees, and with neither accusatory anger nor sarcasm but only a touch of sadness in his voice, gave conditional assent to a stoning: "Let the man among you who has no sin be the first to cast a stone." These words appealed to their sense of fair play. All people, despite other faults, like to feel that at least they are fair and are known to be fair.

While Jesus sat and resumed his tracing, his strategy worked. Instead of crushing his opponents, he had forced their own consciences to take over. As he watched from the corner of his eyes, the assembly slunk away one by one, beginning with those who had least to lose, the eldest.

Finally Jesus and the woman were alone. With her no strategy was necessary. Her life had been saved, and her only problem now was to comprehend why this stranger had taken the trouble to save it. She was not used to being treated with respect, even by herself. Was she, after all, worth saving?

Many sinners have asked the same question. Can the Son of God bother about a single sinner? This gospel delivers a ringing answer. No one ever hated sin as Jesus did. Merely being in the presence of this woman could not have been easy for the sinless Son of God and chaste son of Mary. But his heart had no room for ill feeling. He did not condemn her for her past, nor does he reject us because we have failed him. His concern is for the future. "From now on, avoid this sin."

One of the prayers in today's Mass asks God to help us "transform the darkness and pain of the world" into "the life and joy of Easter." A single Christian, of course, cannot transform the whole world. But each of us does control one world, the inner world of our thoughts, aspirations, attitudes—in a word, our hearts.

If we make the values of the Sacred Heart reign in our own hearts, replacing our grudges and resentments with a deep respect for all other humans, we will go a long way towards transforming the tiny world in which we live and work. The lives of people we touch will be touched by him. Some of their darkness and pain will disappear, replaced by his life and joy.

Conduct Wildly Out of Character

Passion Sunday (Palm Sunday).
A: Mt. 21: 1-11.

❖❖❖

When someone we know, or think we know, acts in a manner clearly out of character—imagine a tongue-tied acquaintance starring on a quiz show or a local hooligan entering the Trappists—we start wondering. Why the sudden change? We are even more baffled when the person is the steady type, not the sort to engage in bizarre conduct. Jesus Christ, for example.

That is why the gospel for the blessing of the palms initially puzzles many people. This is not the Jesus Christ they learned about in catechism class. Matthew describes him entering Jerusalem amid the hoopla we associate with a victory parade or a political rally. The crowd escorting him, wild with excitement, spread cloaks and branches in his path. Their song proclaimed him the Son of David, a title that unmistakably means Messiah. Throughout it all Jesus lifted not a finger to still their voices. Instead, he reveled in this moment of triumph.

This demonstration, moreover, was at least partly his own doing. He did not prepackage it to the last detail, as a campaign manager might do today, but he had certainly been aware it was in the works and taken steps to get himself ready. He had even directed his disciples to commandeer the ass he rode on.

This gesture may not mean much to us, but to all who beheld him it sent a clear signal, for the prophet Zechariah once described the Messiah as mounted on an ass *(9: 9)*. No wonder all Jerusalem was shaken as Jesus passed through the gates. Word raced through the streets that a claimant to the title of Messiah was within the walls and with him a near army of followers.

For Jesus such conduct was wildly out of character. All his life he had shunned notoriety and discouraged people from referring to him as the Messiah. To his close disciples he had once confided his true identity, but then pledged them to secrecy. How explain the dramatic shift we see in this gospel?

Recall that Jesus knew something these cheering Israelites did not, that this was not only his first but his last hurrah. In less than a week he would die. After that, no one except his close followers would set eyes on him again. That meant he no longer had reason to keep his identity secret.

Most Israelites expected a political Messiah, one who would end their subjection to Rome. Had Jesus made an earlier claim to the title Messiah, his followers would have started agitating for an insurrection. That kind of commotion, in turn, would have provoked the authorities to move against him before his work was done. But now that his days were numbered, this consideration no longer held. Let the people shout from the rooftops that he was the Messiah. Both Romans and Israelites would learn soon enough how little interest he had in politics.

But Jesus had another and more cogent reason for allowing this clamorous reception. He reveled in the role of triumphant hero for the simple reason that this was his moment of triumph. The work he had begun on the day John baptized him was now complete. He had proclaimed the kingdom throughout Israel, gathered apostles, and prepared them to carry on without him. In a few days he would give his life as a sacrifice for the sins of the world. The redemption of mankind would be history.

He did not enter Jerusalem a prisoner in chains, cornered and captured by superior force. Rather, he approached his final hours willingly, even joyfully. All his life had been prelude to this hour. Now it had come. Why should he not feel triumphant?

We should keep this mood in mind during Holy Week, as we recall his passion and death. Jesus did not go through this final ordeal like a man defeated, someone who suddenly finds to his horror that he is on the losing side. Nothing in Scripture warrants such a view. On Thursday night he spent a few crushed hours in the garden of Gethsemani, readying himself for the ordeal to come. But once that agony was over, he regained command. And he remained in total command until the end.

In recent decades the word "triumph" has had lost favor in some circles. It stands for a kind of poison ("triumphalism") that is said to have infected Catholics since the Reformation—a patronizing contempt for other religions, a feeling that we Catholics are always in the right, a gloating over our supposedly irrefutable answers to all questions.

Perhaps too many Catholics did once act like that. The word "triumph," however, has a good pedigree and need not carry unpleasant overtones. Christianity is by definition triumphant. Triumph was the mood of the first Palm Sunday, a mood we should make our own. We are not on the losing side. Jesus defeated sin and death, and now he invites us to share in his victory. He had reason to revel in the cheers of Palm Sunday. So do we.

A Wilful Act of Defiance

Passion Sunday (Palm Sunday).
B: Jn. 12: 12-16.

❖❖❖

Jesus was no politician. Like all of us, however, he was affected by politics. To appreciate the drama of his entry into Jerusalem a few days before his execution, we must see what was going on among those who held political power in Jerusalem, the chief priests and Pharisees who made up the Sanhedrin, the supreme council of Judea. Almost to a man they opposed Jesus.

We can think of plenty of reasons for their opposition: envy of his success as a preacher and healer; anger that he had exposed their hypocrisy; fear that he would totally discredit them with the masses. But these were mean motives, and the members of the Sanhedrin were professedly religious men who at least paid lip service to virtue. They were hardly willing to admit such motives to themselves, much less voice them openly.

Instead, they masked their malice, as scoundrels often do, in the rhetoric of patriotism. Jesus, they said, was a menace to the nation. For Israel to survive, Jesus must go.

Rome, they reasoned, would not tolerate civil disorder. In recent decades several would-be Messiahs had staged uprisings, but so far none had mounted a serious threat. With Jesus the outcome might be different, for his following was vaster and more ardent in their support. Throughout Palestine people were whispering that in him the real Messiah had surely come, that under his leadership Israel could achieve its nationalistic goals. The only kind of Messiah most of them could conceive was a political one, a king who would lead them all to freedom.

This kind of talk frightened the Sanhedrin. They had an uneasy alliance with Rome. As long as no one rocked the boat, many affairs of the nation were in their hands. But if Jesus made a move, Rome might strip them of what power they had.

Passover was at hand, a dangerous time. Tens of thousands, many from Galilee and loyal to their fellow Galilean Jesus, were on pilgrimage to Jerusalem, lodging in the city or camping in nearby fields. The Sanhedrin met in an atmosphere of near panic. The high priest put the matter bluntly. It was better, he counseled, that one man die for the people than that the whole nation perish *(Jn. 14: 47-53)*. Not for the first or last time in history, expediency mandated murder.

Thus was the plot to execute Jesus hatched. The Sanhedrin immediately issued an order for his arrest.

Jesus soon learned he was a hunted man and why. His response on this Sunday morning was an act of unmistakable defiance. All his life he had shunned applause, run away from titles of honor. But now, with a sentence of death hanging over him precisely because it was feared that he might call himself a king, he made an about-face and allowed a mob of politically impassioned pilgrims to acclaim him as "King of Israel."

Make no mistake about it. What the people chanted as Jesus rode along the two-mile stretch from Bethpage to the gates of Jerusalem was a political statement. The words they sang were the same that had once welcomed military commanders returning from conquest. Even the palm branches had political significance, since the Israelites of the past had celebrated victories with waving of palms. The donkey Jesus rode may seem far from kingly to us, but to the Jews it suggested a king on an errand of peace, and specifically the long awaited Messiah-king. They could recall that according to the prophet Zechariah the Messiah would make his appearance "seated upon an ass's colt" *(9: 9)*.

The pilgrims who took part in this impromptu procession were wild with enthusiasm, and their hurrahs echoed throughout the Kidron Valley. This was the very kind of popular outpouring the Sanhedrin had dreaded. Now for a certainty the fate of Jesus was sealed. He had accepted the title of Messiah and king. He must accept the consequences and be destroyed without delay.

Why did Jesus step deliberately into his enemies' hands? One reason must have been that he wanted all Jerusalem and all posterity to know that he was going to his death with eyes open. That he could have escaped if he wished was now manifest. This crowd was in his hands, and he had power to provoke a disturbance so serious that arrest would be impossible. But he chose not to escape. Long ago he had rejected the devil's offer to make him a military and political Messiah. He chose instead to be a Messiah on a donkey, a king on an errand of peace.

As we go through Holy Week and watch Jesus in the final hours before his death, we should keep this scene in mind. He was not a captured felon who had no choice but to submit to an ignominious punishment. He endured his sufferings without complaint; in the words of the Mass, he "freely accepted" his death. He accepted it for us, a willing sacrifice for our peace.

A Victim in Command to the End

Passion Sunday (Palm Sunday).
C: Lk. 19: 28-40.

❖❖❖

Today we begin Holy Week, an odd name for a week that recalls some of the unholiest events in history—the capture, trial, and execution of Jesus. One might expect Christians to pass these days in unrelieved sadness. Yet the procession and hymns featured in today's ceremonies are anything but sad. The Church's liturgy for Palm Sunday is a festive celebration.

Rightly so, for that is what the first Palm Sunday was for Jesus himself, whose heart must have swelled with joy on seeing the crowd that hailed him as he approached Jerusalem. Hundreds of its inhabitants, along with hordes of Passover pilgrims, cheered him on with songs and palm branches, acclaiming him the Messiah, liberator of Israel. Our Palm Sunday procession is a pale re-enactment of the noisy welcome Jesus then received.

Although this demonstration was not a staged event, it was one for which Jesus had carefully prepared. He knew a crowd of admirers would line his path from Mt. Olivet to Jerusalem, and for this once he was willing, even eager, to bask in their applause. Before starting out he mounted an ass that his disciples had on his instructions commandeered in a nearby village. Thus he reminded the crowd of Zechariah's prophecy that the Messiah would arrive "meek, and riding on an ass" *(9: 9)*.

In the past Jesus had shunned the title of Messiah, confiding his identity only to close disciples, whom he pledged to secrecy. Once, when he realized that some followers were getting ready to declare him a king, he simply fled *(Jn. 6: 15)*. Throughout his career he did nothing that might be seen as a grab of power. He had no itch for high office or public acclaim.

But this day was an exception. He made no move to hush the noisy multitude that hailed him as a king on a mission of peace. Some Pharisees scented danger in the tumult he was creating and ordered him to silence the mob. Jesus refused.

Why this change? He wanted the whole world to know that he was walking into the hands of his enemies willingly, with eyes wide open. He knew what the rulers in Jerusalem were scheming, what fate threatened him once he set foot on their territory. The crowd that strained their lungs with songs of joy and praise was proof that he could, if he wished, lead a revolt against the powers that ruled over Israel. But he was in control of his destiny, and he chose not to do so.

The point is important. Some years ago a movie with an oddly grim view of the life of Jesus made the rounds of our theaters. A few of the reviews were more interesting than the movie itself. One well-known journalist observed that the plot was built on what he considered a novel and ingenious idea—that Jesus, had he so chosen, could have escaped crucifixion and sought to redeem our race by some less ignominious means; in other words, that Jesus freely accepted the cross.

The notion is hardly novel. In fact it is a perfectly orthodox truism of Christian theology. Scripture leaves no room for doubt on the subject; the Church has always taught it. During the Mass the priest proclaims that Jesus "freely accepted" his death. If not freely, where would be the merit? What distinguished Jesus from the two thieves who were executed with him was not just that they were guilty while he was innocent. Even more important, they could not escape, but would have if they could; he could have escaped, but did not.

In viewing the events of the first Holy Week, we should keep this in mind. Some artists and actors show Jesus going through his final hours like a whimpering, spiritless dog—subdued and impotent in face of superior forces. Nothing could be further from the picture painted in the gospels, especially that of St. John, who witnessed most of the Passion first hand.

When the soldiers came for him in the garden, Jesus went forth to meet them, refusing Peter's offer of physical resistance. To both the Sanhedrin and Pilate Jesus spoke out boldly, affirming his origin, his kingship, his mission. On Calvary he forgave his enemies, prayed for his torturers rather than cursed them, provided for his mother's care, and promised the good thief that both would soon be in heaven. At every moment of his Passion he, not his enemies, was in command.

This command of events began on Palm Sunday. He still had time to turn back; he even had the opportunity to lead a popular revolt. But he did neither. With full deliberation he chose to redeem the human race by the greatest and holiest act of love possible, placing his life on the line for love of us. No wonder Palm Sunday, in the words of the prayer for this Mass, is the day when we "joyfully acclaim Jesus our Messiah and King." No wonder this week is called Holy Week.

STRANGE DOINGS AT DAYBREAK

Easter Vigil Midnight Mass.
A: Mt. 28: 1-10.

❖❖❖

A friend once asked why the homilies priests preach on Sundays dwell so much on sin. Our "obsession" with the topic, he thought, casts a pall over religion and instills unhealthy guilt feelings. Shouldn't we use our few moments in the pulpit to brighten people's lives with a message of hope and cheer?

An unusual protest, I thought, from someone living in this century. Most people plead with us for homilies more relevant to the realities of the modern world. What could be more relevant than sin? It is all around us. Scan the headlines, watch the evening news, turn the pages of newsmagazines. A frightening percentage of the coverage is about murder, muggings, mayhem, and the whole dreary catalogue of sensuality, perversion, and greed. In short, sin. How can an honest homilist ignore it?

Still, the man with the complaint had a point. We should never be so shaken by the enormity and abundance of evil in today's world that we regard the situation as helpless. Pessimism is not a Christian mood. Sin is a large part of the human story, the first chapter in any unexpurgated history of our race. But Christianity has added a second chapter, the Easter story. Never did our plight seem darker than when viewed from Calvary at midday on Good Friday. But never was it brighter than when the women entered the tomb on Easter morning and heard an angel announce that Jesus had been "raised from the dead."

The women had set out for the burial place at the crack of dawn. As they scurried through the murky lanes of Jerusalem, the events of the past few days were more than enough to make them view the human situation as hopeless. They had stood by the cross during the hours when, in Matthew's account, darkness covered the land. But this physical darkness was nothing compared with the moral darkness that had brought Jesus to his death.

For a few years he had given the world hope, made some of the most degraded sinners feel they could follow the path he had shown them in his Sermon on the Mount. But those hopes were now dashed. The Pilates, the Herods, the high priests had won. The light of the world had been snuffed out, and darkness seemed certain to cover the world until the end of time.

We can imagine ourselves arriving at the tomb with the women and finding the stone rolled away, the guards lying on the ground like dead men, the burial chamber empty, and a radiant stranger greeting us with word that Jesus was alive again. Reading the gospel as we do from hindsight, we have trouble recapturing the drama of that moment. There is no surprise for us, for we know what had happened during the night. But for these women it was a moment of total shock.

As they raced back to tell the disciples what had happened, tremors of fear and tingles of joy coursed together through their veins. Soon they learned that everything the angel at the tomb had said was true. Jesus himself waylaid them with the greeting, "Do not be afraid." They no longer had reason for pessimism. Sin had been the cause of his death. But by overcoming death he had given humans power to overcome sin.

Saint Paul had it right. What happened at Easter long ago resembles what has happened at baptism ever since. "Are you unaware that we who were baptized into Christ Jesus were baptized into his death? We were buried with him through baptism...that, just as Christ was raised from the dead...we might live in newness of life." Through baptism we rise from the death of sin. That is why the Easter vigil service has room for baptism.

If every church had at least one adult baptism at this vigil, all present would have a clearer idea of what Easter means. In Africa I used to go to a church at Easter where the service was more impressive than any I have seen elsewhere. Dozens of adults, all raised as pagans, were literally immersed in a tub of water for baptism. Today in this same church the adult baptisms at the Easter vigil number in the hundreds. Watching an adult baptism like those I witnessed in Africa, or even renewing our own baptism vows as we do during our vigil service, helps us to understand Easter. As Jesus was restored to life on Easter morning, we also received new life at baptism.

The man who complained that our homilies dwell too much on sin was half right. Talking about sin is useless unless it includes also the Easter truth. Because of Christ's dying and rising, because of our symbolic death and spiritual rebirth during baptism, we can all "live in newness of life." We need no longer be slaves to sin. We may—indeed do—live in a distressingly pagan and sinful world. But we are no longer part of this world. By baptism we are different, and proud to be different. We belong to Jesus Christ, who still lives.

A Morning Chock-full of Surprises

Easter Vigil Midnight Mass.
B: Mk. 16: 1-8.

❖ ❖ ❖

Among the good things that diminish with time is our capacity to be surprised. Children, to whom the world is an ever-changing garden of new delights, are in an almost constant state of surprise. As we age, however, most of us grow immune to all but the most spectacular of nature's marvels. Chesterton thought that by rights we should be wonder-struck every time the sun goes down or returns in the morning. Most of us need something closer to an earthquake to be roused from our torpor.

The women who visited the tomb of Jesus on the first Easter morning, hoping to anoint his body with spices, experienced a series of events more surprising than a score of earthquakes. Mark tells the story in his unruffled style, but the women he describes were far from unruffled. Among the words he uses to describe them are "frightened," "amazed," "bewildered," "trembling, " and "in great fear." As we read his account of the women's movements, we should try to blot out our knowledge of what is to come and recapture their moments of surprise.

The tomb to which the body of Jesus had been carried at dusk on Friday was just outside the walls of Jerusalem, only a stone's throw from the foot of Calvary. Its owner was a rich Pharisee named Joseph, a secret follower of Jesus from the town of Arimathea. The part he played in the Easter story, although minor, was significant. Had he not come forth with the offer of his tomb, the corpse of Jesus would probably have been tossed into the common heap of executed criminals.

Instead, Joseph wrapped it in a shroud and placed it in his newly dug family tomb, a natural cave hollowed into a sepulcher. The low, narrow opening led through a vestibule to the burial place, a chamber equipped with stone slabs as resting places for the dead. Another huge stone covered the tomb's entrance.

It was this stone that concerned the women as they made their way to the tomb in the wee hours of Easter, for they doubted that without assistance they could roll it away. Their first surprise, then, was finding that this worry had been needless. The stone had already been rolled aside.

This puzzled the women, who wondered who could have reached the tomb before them. But they had a task to perform and did not let their misgivings hold them back. After stooping through the opening they passed across the vestibule and into the chamber of death itself. There they had a second and larger surprise. The stone slab where the body had been placed was bare.

As their eyes grew accustomed to the murky interior, the women could see that the chamber itself was not empty. Sitting in the gloom of the interior was what appeared to be a young man in white but in reality was a messenger from heaven. This, of course, the women had at first no way of knowing, and the sight of the intruder gave them the scare of a lifetime. It is not hard to picture them standing there, speechless with terror, their teeth chattering and spines tingling.

Finally came the fourth and greatest surprise. How the body of Jesus came to be missing, these women were unable to fathom, but now the young man spoke words even harder to fathom. Jesus of Nazareth, he told them, was not there. Let them see for themselves the place where the body had been. It was empty. He had been "raised" and was alive again. The messenger even told them where Jesus could be found—in Galilee, where they had first known him and learned to hope he was the Messiah, the savior of Israel. Return to Galilee, the messenger told them. There Jesus would meet his followers again.

Mark ends the episode abruptly. The women had heard the words of the messenger distinctly and in time would remember them well enough to repeat them for others. But at the moment it was as though they had heard nothing at all, for the words made no sense. The women were so traumatized that for a while they told no one of their experience at the tomb. No one would believe them. They hardly believed what had happened themselves.

Their story is still next to impossible to believe. A man once walked this earth, breathed the same air we breathe, grew to full maturity, endured a horrible death, and then was placed in a tomb. But his flesh did not rot. He not only came to life again but was still alive and would meet the women in Galilee. That was the truth that sank slowly into their minds as the minutes of that first Easter Sunday ticked away.

Jesus Christ, who never tired of jolting his followers with surprises, had delivered his last jolt, as overwhelming today as it was then: he was alive again. We could do nothing better today than spend some time letting this surprise sink slowly in: Jesus, who once rose from the dead, is *still* alive.

The Empty Tomb

Easter Vigil Midnight Mass.
C: Lk. 24: 1-12.

❖❖❖

The word "Easter" means dawn. No wonder, for the story of Easter began at dawn, with a band of women hurrying through the alleys of Jerusalem as the first lights of morning streaked the skies. They were on their way to the tomb, where they intended to anoint a body they had seen expire on a cross three days earlier. The Sabbath had prevented them from visiting the tomb on the day following, and now they were impatient to perform a final act of kindness and respect for the man they had revered as the Messiah. His life had ended in failure, their hopes in gloom. Rendering this service might help soften their grief.

The French preacher Bossuet once said that the Resurrection of Jesus is the central fact of human history. What would the world be like today if the women found in the tomb the corpse they were looking for? Jesus might still receive mention in our history books and be remembered, as a man like Socrates is remembered, for his wisdom and courage. Scholars might still ponder the writings of his disciples, searching for a clue to the spell he once cast on a generation of ancient Jews. A few of his sayings might have found their way into the world's treasury of proverbs. But his mark on history would be slight, his influence on the way people live today close to zero.

Bossuet was right. Without the Resurrection there would be no Christianity. And without Christianity the story of the past twenty centuries would have to be re-written from scratch. Everything depends on what those early-bird women found in the tomb; or rather, on what they did not find.

The stone that had been in front of the tomb was rolled away, the guards had fled, the tomb itself was empty. As the women gaped at the bare stone slab where the corpse had been placed, the turmoil of the first Easter Sunday began. It turned into a day of wild confusion: frenzied running back and forth from the tomb, excited talk among the disciples, a wild jumble of emotions—bewilderment, fear, disbelief, doubt, glimmers of hope. Only at the end of the day, when they had actually seen Jesus, touched him, heard his familiar voice, watched him eat and drink at their table, did the gladness of Easter settle on this group of men and women who had once staked everything they had on the prophet from Nazareth.

In those first moments at the tomb, however, the women simply stared, speechless with shock. Suddenly they were not alone. Two men in white joined them, messengers from God. Theirs was the first Easter greeting: "Why do you seek the living one among the dead? He is not here, but he has been raised."

He has been raised. In the portion of his epistle to the Romans read at today's Mass, Paul says that Jesus "once raised from the dead, will never die again." Of other famous men all we can say is that they lived, they died, and that was the end. Their books may fill shelves in our libraries, their faces may be carved on Mount Rushmore. But books are made of perishable paper, and the most enduring stone is dead.

Only Jesus returned from death to life and to this day remains alive. This truth is the foundation of Christianity. Those who deny it may find solace in what Jesus said and inspiration in what he did; but they are not Christians.

To assert "I am a Christian" is to make an affirmation totally different in scope from "I am a Marxist" or "I am a Jeffersonian." No one today says, "I am making this sacrifice for Karl Marx," or "I am helping my neighbor because Thomas Jefferson wants me to." But these are precisely the kind of things Christians say about Jesus Christ.

Christianity is not just a theory Jesus once taught or a set of rules he left behind. No one can understand our religion without realizing we believe that the man who founded it still lives. Jesus returned to life on Easter Sunday and is with us now. To be fully a Christian is to share his life and be, in Paul's words, "dead to sin and living for God in Christ Jesus."

Nowhere are we reminded of this more forcefully than in the sacrament of baptism. That is why the Easter Vigil service makes room for a baptism ceremony and includes a renewal of baptismal vows. In this sacrament a person moves from the death of sin to "newness of life." In Paul's time baptism was usually performed by immersion in a pool of water. As Jesus emerged from the tomb, the new Christian emerges from the waters of baptism, cleansed of sin, to begin a new life of service to Christ. This is what we pledge when we renew our baptismal vows.

Easter means dawn, the dawn of a new life for Jesus Christ. It also means our dawn, the new life we received at baptism. Our job is to keep the light of that dawn aglow in our souls.

FOOT-RACE AT DAWN

Easter Sunday: Morning Mass.
ABC: Jn. 20: 1-9.

❖ ❖ ❖

On the second morning after the crucifixion Simon Peter and another disciple (the one "Jesus loved") awoke with heavy hearts. Only a week earlier Jesus had entered Jerusalem to the cheers of a palm-waving mob that hailed him as the Messiah. Now, as far as these two disciples knew, his corpse lay rotting in the cold chamber of a tomb. His followers were scattered and desolate, while his enemies gloated over his death.

To Peter this death was especially painful. After the arrest of Jesus on Thursday night Peter had wilted before the taunts of a few servants and denied ever knowing him. Now, with Jesus gone forever, he would never have a chance to make amends.

The second disciple, "whom Jesus loved," is identified by tradition and many reputable scholars with John, once a fellow fisherman with Peter and like him chosen by Jesus as an apostle. Evidence also points to him as the source of the fourth gospel, making "whom Jesus loved" John's way of describing himself. This would explain why today's reading is so fresh and vivid, coming as it does from a principal participant. How much he loved Jesus in return is evident from his conduct on Calvary, where he remained standing by the cross to the end.

Anyone who has ever lost a job knows how empty and useless one feels on becoming just another figure in the anonymous statistics of the unemployed. Something of that feeling must have been shared by Peter and his companion on that first Easter morning. Their occupation was gone. They had lost not only the best friend they ever knew but the best job they could ever hope to have. Jesus had assured them that in his kingdom they would share his labors, becoming fishers of men. Now all their training as preachers, their anticipation of glorious careers in his new kingdom, had gone up in smoke. The sinners they had helped bring back to God would return to their sin. They themselves had no choice left but to return to their fish.

To these Galilean followers of Jesus, Jerusalem was now hostile territory. As the two shrugged off their sleep, their first thought must have been to pack their things and beat a swift exit from the holy city. But before they could stir, Mary Magdalen came bursting in. Breathless from running and almost incoherent with excitement and grief, she poured out her story. Along with some other women she had gone at dawn to visit the tomb. There they found that the corpse of Jesus had been "taken," and she had no idea where "they," the takers, had put it.

Unlikely though her story sounded (why would grave-despoilers be loose in Jerusalem?), Peter and John got up and rushed to see for themselves. And so it happened that the first Easter parade was an early morning running race, each of the two vying to be first from the cenacle to the tomb.

John eventually pulled ahead and reached the finish line first, noting as he did that the stone had been rolled away from the opening (another mystery). Peering in, he saw the burial cloths but not the body of Jesus. Out of deference to his elder he did not enter until Peter arrived and preceded him. Then both inspected the tomb together.

At a glance they could see it was empty, with no sign of an intruder. But the body of Jesus had certainly vanished. As they took in the rest of the scene they proved themselves good detectives, focusing on details that did not fit the hypothesis of a stolen corpse. The linen wrappings that Joseph of Arimathea and Nicodemus had wound around the body after covering it with precious ointments were neatly folded and in place, making it look as if the body had simply passed through them like a mist. The head cloth, carefully folded, was separate.

What corpse-snatcher would take the trouble to remove these wrappings? And if he did, wouldn't he just discard them hastily and leave them crumpled on the ground? Would he, *could* he, arrange them in such a fashion that the corpse seemed simply to have evaporated from within?

We can try to retrace John's thoughts as he gazed at the scene. If no one *took* the body, then it must have...no, that cannot be...but it *must* be. Didn't he often speak mysteriously about *rising* from death?...and doesn't that fit what he said about a grain of wheat having to die before it can produce fruit?

John "saw and believed." His was the first instance of what we call "Easter faith." What John believed and what we celebrate today are the same. Only in realizing what the empty tomb means can we make sense of Good Friday. While his enemies murdered him Jesus offered himself for the sins of the world. The Father accepted his sacrifice, and Jesus returned to the land of the living. In the empty tomb is proof that Jesus has conquered sin and death.

A Morning to Remember

Easter Sunday: Alternate Morning Mass.
A: Mt. 28:1-10; B: Mk. 16:1-8; C: Lk. 24:1-12

❖❖❖

Our two biggest holy days of the year are Christmas and Easter. Think for a moment of how different in quality are the mental pictures we have of the events these feasts commemorate.

For Christmas the picture is sharp—the cave, the shepherds, the travel-weary couple, the infant on his bed of straw. These details in themselves are utterly unspectacular, for nothing is more universal than birth or more commonplace than poverty. But scores of artistic renditions have stamped the nativity scene indelibly on our imaginations. No one has trouble visualizing the event we celebrate on Christmas.

For Easter the situation is reversed, and we do have trouble. We feel that Christ's emergence from the tomb, if we could see exactly how it happened, would be super-spectacular. But what we mostly see is a blur. All four evangelists describe the goings-on in Jerusalem on the morning Jesus rose, pieced together from reports of many witnesses. One feature all four accounts have in common: none attempts to depict the day's main event, the very event that makes Easter worth celebrating.

We learn of the earthquake at dawn; the stone rolled away from the tomb's entrance; the guards stretched out like dead men on the ground; the women coming to anoint the corpse and encountering angels instead; and finally, Peter racing to the tomb and finding only burial cloths where the body should be. But we never see what we above all want to see—Jesus himself striding forth from the tomb in a blaze of glory.

Scripture does not describe this scene for a good reason: no one was there to witness it. Although dawn had barely broken when the women reached the tomb, the main action was already over; Jesus had risen. Thus, while Christmas has its well populated cave, Easter has only an empty tomb.

God could have arranged things differently, supplied a host of witnesses to satisfy our curiosity. That he did not do so suggests where our attention should go. The essential message of Easter is not in the physical triumph of Jesus over the corruption of the grave, but in his spiritual triumph over sin and the eternal death that is consequence of sin.

The battle itself was waged on Calvary. We know this battle

ended in victory only because Jesus rose from the dead. His resurrection tells the world that Calvary was not just a hill where a promising career was cut short by evil men. It was rather an altar of sacrifice where Jesus gave his life for the sins of mankind. His return to the land of the living is proof that the Father accepted his sacrifice and our redemption was won.

Although Scripture does not describe Jesus in the act of rising from the dead, it describes the physical evidence he displayed of his victory. The risen Jesus was unmistakably the same flesh-and-blood Jesus the disciples knew well, but he was in many respects much changed from the man they had lived and labored with. His body was still a human body; he invited his disciples to touch his wounds, even ate and drank in their presence. But his body was now transformed, spiritualized, less weighed down than it had been by the terrestrial laws of nature.

The accounts of his appearances during the forty days after his resurrection make this change clear. His voice and features were not always immediately recognizable; on the evening of the first Easter he entered the room of the apostles suddenly and soundlessly, although the doors were all locked; later he vanished just as mysteriously; and during the following weeks he moved undetected and with uncanny ease from one part of Palestine to another, appearing and disappearing at will. This was the same Jesus they had known, yet somehow not the same.

What was the difference? The risen Jesus was more than a re-animated corpse. On Calvary he did not just die; he conquered death. As a result, during his stay in the tomb he entered an entirely new phase of existence. Paul says, "Death no longer has power over him" *(Rom. 6: 9).* Neither did many everyday signs of human mortality. Although he still moved on earth, he was unfettered by the limits of space and time. As the triumphant lord of creation, his body was already in glory.

Where is the lesson for us? The prayer of today's Mass reminds us that by conquering death Jesus "opened for us the way to eternal life." We have not yet joined him in heaven, but the way has been cleared. We must never forget that we are destined for a resurrection like his, for an eternity in his company when our bodies, like his, will be in glory.

Easter reminds us never to lose sight of this goal. We must prepare ourselves, in Paul's words, by setting our hearts on "what is above, not what is on earth."

DISILLUSIONMENT AT EMMAUS

Easter Sunday (for an afternoon or evening Mass).
ABC: Lk. 24: 13-35.

❖ ❖ ❖

"Oh, how foolish you are! How slow of heart...!" Strong words, almost insulting words, especially from an utter stranger. Imagine some busy body on a bus plumping himself beside you, prompting you to pour out your troubles, and then, instead of offering sympathy, calling you a nitwit, incapable of adding two and two. Wouldn't you be quick to change your seat?

Fortunately, these two disciples did nothing like that. Something in the manner of this mysterious wayfarer attracted them, made them eager to hear him out. Soon they were enraptured. Their hearts, as they put it later, burned within them.

Before long the two were astonished to find they had covered the entire seven miles from Jerusalem to Emmaus. Nightfall was nearing, and at their urging the stranger stopped with them at a local inn. As the bread was served this new acquaintance was still talking, the pair of them still listening.

Little wonder they were enthralled by his words. No more moving Easter homily has ever been preached. After all, the homilist, as we now know and as the two came to know during the breaking of the bread, was the Lord of Easter himself.

Why Jesus chose to approach these two in disguise, why he trapped them into disclosing their naive notions about his kingdom, the gospel does not say. But this was certainly an effective teaching strategy. On later reflection they realized his words had changed their whole way of thinking about him and his kingdom. That is what an Easter homily should do.

Jesus had one central purpose: to disillusion the two disciples—and through them to disillusion all who in future generations would call themselves Christians. Disillusion? Isn't that a bad word? Haven't we often been warned not to disillusion others? Aren't grown-ups told to be especially on guard lest they disillusion the young, the inexperienced, the innocent?

Such warnings are both misinformed and dangerous. Disillusionment is essential to the maturing process. To disillusion someone is to do that person a favor, for when we disillusion we remove an illusion; and an illusion is by definition "an erroneous concept of belief." The one who disillusions should be gentle, of course, as a doctor in lancing an infection. But to correct an error, to replace a falsehood with a truth, a pipe dream with reality, cannot result in anything good. No one should build a life on falsehood. Those who retain the illusions of childhood are doomed to remain always children, unfit for the harsh realities of life.

The gist of what Jesus said to these disciples was this: You call yourselves followers of Jesus Christ, a man you say was mighty in deed and word before God and all the people. You say you hoped that he would liberate Israel. But this was a vain hope, an illusion. You should have known better.

Read the Scriptures. See what Moses and the prophets really said about the Messiah. They did not promise someone who would win a glorious victory over Israel's political and military enemies. The liberator they promised was to be a suffering Messiah, a lamb of sacrifice led to slaughter. And the enemy he was to battle with is internal, the sins of the human race.

Remember the words of your Master. He never encouraged you to look on him as a political leader who would overthrow Rome and gain independence for Israel. Over and over he told you his kingdom was spiritual and would be won only by the cross. That is the lesson of Easter. The Messiah had to suffer in order to enter into glory. So also, he always insisted, must you.

Above all, do not be downcast, brooding over the loss of your leader. Good Friday is behind you, the battle is over, the crucified Jesus has won. His victory is also yours.

What did these two disciples mean when they later told the apostles that Jesus was "made known to them in the breaking of the bread"? Probably they had been part of the crowd by the lakeside months earlier when Jesus multiplied the loaves and fishes. As they now sat down at table with him at Emmaus, he repeated the same gestures of breaking and blessing bread that they had watched that afternoon in Galilee. Their memories were suddenly jolted, their eyes opened. This was Jesus himself they had been listening to! No sooner did they experience this shock of recognition than Jesus somehow vanished from their sight.

The lesson he had taught them, however, remained and became the substance of Easter homilies from that day to this. Before entering his glory Jesus *had* to endure the cross. He was not the liberator of Israel that some had hoped for. That was all illusion. The reality is a thousand times grander. By his death he liberated all of us, invited all to share in his glory.

NO WONDER HE HAD HIS DOUBTS

Second Sunday of Easter.
ABC: Jn. 20: 19-31.

I

The gospels tell a lot about Jesus Christ. Almost everything we know, in fact. They also tell a lot about his apostles, those loyal companions who never doubted his word. But the gospels do not tell all we would like to know. For that, in the words of John the evangelist, "the whole world would not contain the books that would be written" *(21: 25).* Even as it is, questions pop up at almost every page. Some will never be answered.

Still, being curious animals, we cannot help rummaging for answers. Take this story of doubting Thomas. Many readers are puzzled, want to know more. Why, for a start, was Thomas not with the other ten apostles when Jesus came to them on the first Easter evening?

Many possibilities have been proposed. One commentator calls Thomas an introvert who, after the death of Jesus, was "so broken-hearted that he chose to be alone with his grief." A good guess, but no more. It is as likely he had a headache and took a stroll in the evening air.

For whatever reason, Thomas was not where we would expect him to be, in the room with his fellow apostles. He had shared thousands of thrilling moments with their company, but on this Easter evening he missed the biggest thrill of all.

The vexing question about Thomas, however, is not why he was elsewhere that night, but why he was so bullheaded towards the others when they told him what they had seen. Again, we can never be certain. But we can explore the possibilities.

Did he think his fellow apostles were willfully circulating a falsehood? Hardly. Thomas knew them too well to suspect them of hatching a hoax, least of all for his benefit. The loss of Jesus on Good Friday had been the saddest event of their lives. Was it conceivable that grief had transformed this group of earnest, God-fearing men into a band of godless bamboozlers?

Why then did Thomas doubt their word? Only one answer seems plausible. If they were not consciously fooling him, then they must somehow have been fooled themselves, tricked by a phantom. What kind of phantom? Perhaps they wanted so badly to see Jesus that they imagined they had in fact seen him. Even in those pre-Freudian days people must have suspected that imagination can play strange tricks, that wishing hard enough can give birth to a phantom, make something that isn't so seem to be so.

For centuries skeptics have resorted to similar logic. Like Thomas, most of them have realized that the idea of a deliberate scam by the apostles does not stand up. Confidence men do not cook up stories for the fun of it, but for profit. And there was surely no profit for the apostles in this tale. The only outcome they could expect was what they mostly got: after a lifetime of labor, death for their pains.

And so for these doubters the only possible solution has been that the apostles underwent a collective hallucination. The trouble with this theory is that it forgets Thomas. Suppose the other apostles were credulous fools. Suppose they yearned to see their master so strongly that they only thought they had heard his voice, inspected his wounds, and watched while he ate a fish in their presence. What about Thomas?

Thomas's loyalty to Jesus was as strong as that of his companions. He once boasted he was willing to die for him *(Jn. 11: 16)*. No one could have wished Jesus alive more than Thomas did. But wishing did not make him think it so. He knew it *could* not be so. In this episode he is the man from Missouri, as hard to convince as the most stubborn skeptic. "Unless *I* see the mark of the nails in his hands and put *my* finger into the nail marks and put *my* hand into his side, *I* will not believe."

To us these words seem to have an impudent ring. Who, after all, was Thomas to set down terms of surrender to the Lord? Fortunately for Thomas, and for us who profit from his obstinacy, Jesus saw no such impudence. In fact, he yielded on every point. Thomas, after all, was his high card. If it were not for doubting Thomas, think of how many doubters in generations to come would in good faith grasp at straws to explain why the early Christians believed so strongly in the resurrection. Thomas is the final refutation of the theory that the Easter story was a collective hallucination, the product of wishful thinking by the apostles.

Thomas exclaimed, "My Lord and my God!" Nowhere in the New Testament is there a stronger, more explicit act of faith in Jesus. Mere mortals, when endowed with talent and virtue, can work marvels. But returning to life as Jesus did, and sending apostles to preach his gospels to the world for the rest of time, belong in another category. Jesus is Lord of all creation, the Eternal Word who came to dwell among us, *our* Lord and *our* God.

THE PEACE THAT COMES WITH A PRICE

Second Sunday of Easter.

ABC: Jn. 20: 19-31.

II

How Jesus dealt with doubting Thomas is so gripping a drama that it almost makes one lose sight of the first part of this gospel. But what happened when Jesus appeared to the other apostles on the evening of the first Easter is worth pondering. It was then that our Church was born; then also that Jesus gave to mere mortals the power to forgive sins.

The apostles were huddled behind barred doors, probably in the same room where they had supped with Jesus three nights earlier. Their ears were alert for steps on the stairs, fearful that those who had contrived the death of Jesus might move against themselves as well. Suddenly, they knew not from where he came, Jesus was standing in their midst.

From Luke's gospel we learn that they thought he was a ghost, that it was not until they had seen his wounds and watched him devour some food that their doubts were dissolved. This passage from John mentions briefly that Jesus displayed his wounds, but then concentrates on what he said to his apostles.

Alone among the institutions of the world the Church can boast of a divine rather than merely human origin. Jesus Christ, the word of God, came to earth to bring salvation to mankind. But since he could not dwell among us forever, he commissioned others to form a Church and continue his work. They and their successors would pilot this Church through the centuries.

During his first Easter appearance, Jesus conferred this commission on his apostles, saying, "As the Father has sent me, so I send you." Then, as God once infused life into Adam, Jesus *breathed* on his apostles, thus imparting the life of the Holy Spirit. With this simple ceremony our Church was born.

Usually we think of Pentecost, fifty days after Easter, as the birthday of the Church. It was certainly on Pentecost that the apostles got started on their mission and the Church began to grow; but it was not then that they first received the Spirit. Pentecost was rather the public manifestation of the Spirit that Jesus had already breathed into them at Easter.

Before bestowing the Spirit, Jesus said "Peace." This was the ordinary oriental form of greeting, but here it had a more than ordinary meaning. By his death and Resurrection Jesus had made a triple peace possible for us children of Adam—peace with God, peace with our fellow humans, peace within ourselves. The obstacle to this triple peace is sin: rebellion against God, conflict with fellow humans, restless cravings within ourselves. Now with the word "Peace" Jesus told his disciples that he has made it possible for mortals to overcome sin.

This explains why he went on to give his apostles power to forgive sins. His words were unambiguous: sins that the apostles forgive will be forgiven by God; those they retain will be retained. This same power Jesus himself had exercised throughout his career. Hereafter the apostles and their successors will be his proxies in the world, imparting his peace by absolving the sins of those who are truly repentant.

These words are therefore among the most important in Scripture. On them the Church rests its claim to absolve sins in the Sacrament of Penance. It could as well be called the Sacrament of Peace, for peace is what Jesus wanted it to give.

Unfortunately, some penitents fail to achieve this peace, not because the sacrament is defective, but because they regard it as mere magic: tell the priest your sins, bow for his blessing, listen to some mumbo-jumbo called absolution, and presto!—your sins are washed away and you can start all over again with a clean slate. But that was not what Jesus had in mind at all. He paid a price to make it possible for us to achieve and hold onto his peace. We too must pay a price.

Unless we desire God's friendship and intend to live as his friend, unless we retain no rancor against neighbor or desire for revenge, the words of absolution are empty noise. Jesus put the peace of Easter within our reach. But to obtain and keep it we must accept what he taught, reject what he rejected. Peace is not handed to us on a platter. It must be won.

Winning it requires a struggle. I once met a Polish-American priest who for twenty years had been held on trumped-up charges in the Soviet Union, five in Moscow's infamous Lubianka prison, fifteen in the wilds of Siberia. The prayers of many friends and some deft diplomacy in Washington eventually brought him home, but nothing could erase the wisdom or diminish the serenity he had acquired during those years of lonely captivity.

I asked if he thought the world would ever achieve genuine peace. With a spark of irony in his eye, he fairly shouted his paradoxical answer: "Peace is something you have to *fight* for."

JESUS CONDUCTS A BIBLE CLASS

Third Sunday of Easter.
A: Lk. 24: 13-35.

❖❖❖

Christianity has inspired many to abstain from fine food and strong drink. The hermits of ancient Egypt subsisted on water and whatever herbs they could scratch from the desert. Even in our indulgent age the Church has monasteries and convents where meals are mostly meager helpings of coarse vegetables.

Such austerity pleases God; those who practice it win graces for us all. Even a casual knowledge of the New Testament and Church history, however, reveals that constant fasting is not the only way to God. It was not the way chosen by some of the greatest Christians, foremost among them Jesus Christ himself.

The evangelists are fond of picturing Jesus at table, frequently a banquet table. On the night before he died he shared the Paschal feast with his apostles. Astoundingly, he continued to take food even after his resurrection. Peter boasted that the apostles "ate and drank" with Jesus "after he rose from the dead" *(Acts 10: 41)*, making us wonder if there will be gourmet repasts in heaven. From Scripture we learn that the risen Jesus shared food with disciples on at least four occasions.

The first of these took place on Easter afternoon at Emmaus, a small town seven miles from Jerusalem. It was a heart-warming scene, often reproduced in art: Jesus stopping at a tavern with his two companions of the road, the three bent over their food in spirited talk. We are not told what the fare was (the phrase "breaking of the bread" is a biblical expression for a meal of some sort), but we do know something about their table talk. It was a continuation of the conversation Jesus had struck up with the two soon after joining them during their journey.

They had met Jesus after leaving Jerusalem that morning, and for reasons that are not clear failed to recognize him. But Jesus recognized them. He must have often seen them among the disciples who watched with astonishment as he cured the sick or multiplied bread and who had listened to his parables with delight. Now their faces were glum, their mood black.

Both were still in shock, as were all the disciples of Jesus who had been in Jerusalem on Good Friday. When this seeming stranger joined them on the road and asked why they were talking so excitedly, they poured out the whole story. Had he not heard of Jesus, the great prophet, and how he had been put to death? That Jesus could die so ignominiously, with his mission still unfulfilled, had seemed to them unthinkable. Yet the unthinkable had happened, and when it did their whole world had come crashing down. They had staked everything on Jesus and lost.

One sentence gave them away: "We were hoping that he would be the one to redeem Israel." They had revered Jesus as the Messiah, and to them the Messiah had one clear mission: to drive the hated Romans from the land of the Israelites. For a century now Rome had ruled over Palestine, actually occupied the promised land. Jesus, they had been sure, was the one to put an end to this abomination. But nothing of the sort had happened. Instead, the Romans had put an end to Jesus. The dream of his followers was all over.

Except that one of them was named Cleopas, we know nothing about these two, not even why they were bound for Emmaus. But their words tell us that although they had thought they were themselves followers of Jesus, they had missed the whole point of his mission. Jesus now proceeded to set the record straight.

His words to them, explaining the scriptural prophecies about the Messiah, have been called the most famous Bible lesson in history. It was certainly the most authoritative. Imagine hearing a definitive explanation of all the prophetic texts about the Messiah, and this from the lips of the Messiah himself!

Patiently he explained to them that God had never promised a Messiah who would be a political wizard or a conquering warrior. Isaiah, for example, had spoken of the Messiah as a servant who by suffering would atone for the offenses of all. His task was to release, not Israel from bondage to Rome, but humanity from bondage to sin. Thus what had happened on Calvary did not signal the failure of his mission, but its fulfillment.

While listening to Jesus on the road, the two disciples had burned with enthusiasm for the man who had died three days earlier, the leader they had never truly understood. Now, sitting with this seeming stranger in the tavern at Emmaus, they felt a veil was lifting from their eyes. Slowly they grew aware that their eloquent companion was none other than Jesus himself.

No sooner did they realize this than he vanished from their sight. His task was finished. He had opened their eyes to the meaning of the cross and the reality of the Resurrection.

As we attend the breaking of the eucharistic bread at Mass, may the veils be lifted from our eyes as well!

WHY HE ROSE FROM THE DEAD

Third Sunday of Easter.
B: Lk. 24: 35-48.

❖❖❖

"On the third day he rose again" is a key clause in our Christian Creed. It is also a favorite target of rationalists, those who deny the possibility of miracles or anything supernatural. One has to be gullible, they say, to give credence to any miracle recorded in Scripture; super-gullible to give credence to the resurrection. Dead men do not rise.

The charge of gullibility is rarely made against Jesus himself. His evident wisdom and eloquence shield him from any such accusation. The fault, these rationalists say, was with his disciples, who spread the fable that Jesus had risen. They were probably not conscious liars, just naive enough to be taken in by their own daydreams, a textbook case of what psychologists call wish-fulfillment. So strongly did they wish Jesus to be alive that they imagined he was alive and then gave reality to the figment of their own imagination.

How well does the case against the disciples stand up? This passage from Luke, describing events in Jerusalem on the Sunday after the burial of Jesus, is a good place to test it.

The disciples were in the room where Jesus had shared his final meal with them. Suddenly, they saw him in their midst, bidding them peace. As far as they could tell, he had simply materialized out of thin air. What was their initial response? Far from whooping with joy at the sight of their wish fulfilled, they shuddered with surprise and terror. They were so sure this apparition was not the real Jesus that they called it a ghost.

If they had been gullible types, ready to believe anything, they would not have been surprised at this sight of Jesus. All day others had tried to convince them he was alive again. First, some women returned from the tomb, saying they had found it empty and met an angel who said the Lord had risen. Later, even the normally sober-minded Peter claimed he had seen Jesus. To top it all, two agitated men had just burst into the room with a tale of having broken bread with Jesus in a tavern at Emmaus.

But these disciples stood firm, certain as any rationalist that the dead do not come back. Even when they saw Jesus standing before them, they were sure he was not for real. They needed evidence more solid than sight that this was not a ghost.

Such evidence was what Jesus proceeded to give. First, since neither a ghost nor a figment of the imagination has flesh and blood, he had them touch his hands and feet. After feeling how solid these were, they became "incredulous for joy." That is, although exultant, they still held back belief. Like the big winners in a lottery, they found it all too good to be true.

Finally, as irrefutable proof he was no phantom but a living human being like themselves, Jesus sat down and ate some fish in their presence. Only when they saw the morsels disappear into his mouth did they yield to the evidence of their senses.

The disciples, then, were not gullible. A good thing, too, for the sake of people like us who listen to the gospel they proclaimed. Because of their slowness to believe on that first Easter, we know they were not the type to spend the rest of their lives proclaiming pious hokum. Only after they had seen Jesus, touched and shared food with him, did they believe.

As believers they listened attentively while he spoke his final words to them, making sense of all that had happened.

First, he pointed out that his suffering, death, and resurrection should not have taken them totally by surprise. As devout Jews they had always believed Scripture to be God's word. Now he patiently opened their eyes to passages they had hardly noticed before, showing it was all there, the whole story of how the Messiah must suffer and rise from the dead. As our Creed says, what happened was "in fulfillment of the Scriptures."

Next, he commissioned them. His task on earth was over, theirs about to begin. Their mission for the rest of their days would be to "preach repentance for the forgiveness of sins" to "all the nations." This commissioning of the disciples is the climax of this passage (as well as of Luke's entire gospel). For us, whose faith rests on what they preached to all nations, it is almost as important as the Resurrection itself.

Miracles played a big part in the life of Jesus, but he did not come to earth to astound us with miracles. His rising from the dead was not just a stupendous piece of wizardry, the last piece of magic from his bag of magic tricks. Everything he did had one purpose: to win mankind from sin and lead us back to God. That is why he died and why he rose from the dead.

His return from death to life made possible our return from the death of sin to the life of God's children. For us that is his greatest miracle and most amazing Easter message.

LIGHT BRUNCH FOR EIGHT BY THE LAKESIDE

Third Sunday of Easter.
C: Jn. 21: 1-19 (or 1-14).

❖❖❖

The body of water where the apostles once fished has several names in Scripture—sometimes the Sea of Galilee or Tiberias, sometimes the Lake of Gennesaret. "Sea" seems an outsize label when we consider its actual dimensions. Shaped like an inverted pear, it measures only thirteen miles from top to bottom, a little less than eight at its widest. Capernaum, once a thriving town on the northern shore, is now a scattering of ruins, while the hill town of Nazareth lies almost thirty miles to the west.

The lake ranks with the world's most beautiful. Although the flora now surrounding it are sparser than in biblical times, it rivals the tourist-haunted lakes of Europe or the Americas. That the Incarnate Word chose so lovely a region as the principal locale for his activities must contain some lesson, although I am not sure what it is. At the least it should give heart to today's environmentalists. It may also remind us that holiness is never enhanced by squalor. The beauty of England's lake district led the poet Wordsworth to reverence for God, beauty's author. Nature's wonders should do no less for us. The world, the poet Hopkins wrote, is "charged with the grandeur of God." One would have to be a thickheaded oaf or an atheist to disagree.

Several decades ago I gazed on the waters of the Sea of Galilee that Jesus once sailed on, and they seemed charged with the peace he came among us to give. An afternoon bus trip had brought me from Jerusalem to Tiberias, a town built by Herod Antipas on the west shore of the lake. It is now a popular watering place for vacationing Israelis. After a meal featuring a fish named after the apostle Peter and a sound sleep in a room overlooking the water, I took a bus north along the shore to a stop about three miles from the remains of Capernaum.

Walking alone along the shore, I came to a stone ledge jutting out into the lake. On it was a tiny chapel with an inscription relating the local tradition that this was where Jesus played host to his apostles on the misty morning we read about in today's gospel. Without any planning on my part, I had arrived at the very spot where that famous lakeside brunch had taken place almost two thousand years ago.

No cookout was ever more informal. Peter was dripping from his impulsive dive into the water. The others, bleary-eyed from a sleepless night and reeking from the fish they had just hauled in, exchanged with Jesus the traditional greeting of peace. The meal itself was delayed until they had made a careful tally of the fish they had netted. That done, they all sat around the charcoal fire while Jesus did the cooking and serving.

John has preserved the exchange that took place between Peter and Jesus after the meal. At the Last Supper, Peter had boasted that his loyalty to Jesus surpassed that of all other apostles, but before the night was over he three times denied even knowing him. Now Jesus gave him a chance to make amends. Three times Peter was asked if he loved Jesus; and three times he replied that he did, finally adding in desperation that since Jesus knew all things, he well knew how much Peter loved him.

After each reply Jesus, the Good Shepherd, reminded Peter that he was now leader of the flock and must feed its lambs and sheep with the same care that Jesus himself had shown. But this was not the only way he was to follow Jesus. As the Good Shepherd laid down his life for his sheep, Peter must prepare to do the same. Years later, during the persecution by Nero in Rome, Peter was to fulfill this prophecy. The method of execution would be the same as his Master's, crucifixion.

The lake of Galilee is as serene a spot, as conducive to contemplation, as any I have looked on. Standing on the ledge I thought of how much the world had changed since Jesus spoke those words to Peter a few weeks after rising from the dead. The human family is not yet Christian, but the peace of the risen Jesus has found its way into more hearts than the apostles who shared that picnic could ever have thought possible.

Much remains to be done. How much I soon learned, as my reverie was broken. The bus that was to take me back to Tiberias did not appear on schedule. Eventually a scarred station wagon marked "U.N." came rumbling along, and I hitched a ride. To the driver, a member of a United Nations observation team, I ventured, "Well, things sure look peaceful here today." "Not where I've just come from," he replied. "People are shooting one another on the Golan Heights this morning."

Peter preached the gospel of peace and was killed for his pains. People still labor for peace, and some die in its cause. May the Lord Jesus, who preached of peace by the lake of Galilee long ago, answer the prayers of all who labor for peace today.

The Enemies at Our Gate

Fourth Sunday of Easter.
A: Jn. 10: 1-10.

❖❖❖

Jesus introduces the parable of the Good Shepherd with "Amen, amen" ("Truly, truly"), a Hebrew expression underscoring the solemn importance of what one is about to say. With these words Jesus alerts his listeners that this will not be just another parable, but a key one. The Church has always regarded it as such, and so has a portion of it read at Mass every fourth Sunday of Easter. Hence the name "Good Shepherd Sunday."

"Amen, amen" is also a transitional phrase. It never introduces a completely new topic, but rather a comment on what has just been said. To understand the Good Shepherd parable, then, we must look at what precedes it. Surprisingly, we find that this seemingly peaceful parable was first spoken in the midst of a heated dispute between Jesus and some Pharisees.

In earlier confrontations the Pharisees had attacked Jesus for such infractions as allowing his disciples to violate tradition by eating without a ritual washing of hands. The alleged crime this time was graver. It was a Sabbath, and Jesus had just given sight to a man born blind. To the Pharisees this violated the prohibition against labor on God's day. To express their outrage they denounced Jesus as a devil-possessed sinner.

Jesus retorted by branding the Pharisees as blind. They could not see what was plain even to the unschooled, that anyone who performed such works as he performed must have his power from God. It was at this point in the debate that Jesus interjected the parable of the good shepherd.

The point of the parable is not just that the good shepherd guards his flock and leads them to pasture, but that enemies are at large, strangers and thieves who sneak unobserved into the sheepfold at night, aiming to snatch as many sheep as possible. In contrast, the good shepherd is admitted by the gatekeeper each morning. He knows each of his sheep by name and labors to protect them from all kinds of danger.

As the good shepherd stands for Jesus himself, the strangers—"thieves and robbers"—stand for the Pharisees. Thus the parable is not as peaceful as it seems. It reflects the ongoing conflict between Jesus and the Pharisees. We should never forget how much at odds with the authorities

Jesus was, how much hatred from on high he provoked. A biblical scholar has called him a "marginal Jew," meaning someone outside the mainstream. That certainly was how he was viewed by the Pharisees, who considered themselves the authentic guardians of Jewish religion.

What most infuriated the Pharisees was that despite their opposition, Jesus continued to attract followers who regarded him as holy and wise. Thus the conflict between Jesus and the Pharisees was critical. They were locked in a struggle for souls. Protecting his followers from the clutches of pharisaical legalism was of vital importance for the mission of Jesus.

If the shepherd in the parable stands for Jesus and the robbers for the Pharisees, for whom do the sheep stand? Originally, the Israelites Jesus addressed. Today, all who by baptism are in the sheepfold of the Church. That is, ourselves.

While marauders still threaten God's sheepfold, they are a different breed from the ones who opposed Jesus. The Pharisaism he encountered is happily dead in our century. In place of the blind legalism that saw sin where sin surely was not, the enemy today is a blind permissiveness that sees no sin where sin surely is. Thus, although the nature of the conflict has changed, it is still Jesus against the establishment, protecting his sheep from false shepherds in high places.

Officially established religions are rare in the nations of the world today. But would anyone deny that almost everywhere in our century one finds an unofficially established irreligion, a secularism that aims to wipe out any remnant of religious values in society? The atmosphere fostered in many educational institutions, by the media and the entertainment industry, makes the dedicated Christian almost an endangered species.

So pervasive is this atmosphere that people who believe that the latest public opinion poll is not the criterion of morality, the flesh not a plaything, the unborn child not disposable biological tissue, and homosexuality not an acceptable alternate life-style, are in some quarters deemed hopelessly out of date. Thieves and robbers have not just invaded our sheepfold; they have hoisted their flag in our midst.

While the identity of the marauders has changed, their goal is still to "steal and slaughter and destroy." The goal of Jesus also remains what it was, that we "might have life and have it more abundantly." The Good Shepherd leads us to eternal pastures. His is the voice we must listen to.

What Every Pastor Should Know

Fourth Sunday of Easter.
B: Jn. 10: 11-18.

❖❖❖

Now that Latin has gone out of fashion in most of our schools, how many realize that *pastor* is Latin for shepherd? When parishioners speak of their pastor, does the image of a shepherd flicker even faintly across their minds? It should. The pastor is *their* spiritual shepherd. They are *his* flock.

This passage from John is a self-portrait by Jesus Christ, the eternal Good Shepherd. It is also a personally compiled job description of the kind of pastor he wanted in his Church, the ideal pastor. It applies to the Pope, the shepherd of the universal Church; to bishops, shepherds of their dioceses; and not only to the priest who is shepherd of the parish to which he is assigned, but also to all who assist him in his shepherding by dispensing the sacraments or teaching the truths of our faith. All are called to model themselves on the Good Shepherd.

The Catholic Church is a world-wide organization, vaster and more complex than any multinational conglomerate. But gigantic though it is, it is not supposed to conduct its affairs in the impersonal fashion we expect from the overseers of General Motors or I.B.M. Its leaders are not business executives; the people they lead are not a collection of paying consumers. What holds the entire structure together is Jesus Christ, present among us through the holy Spirit. He should also be recognizable in our leaders, the shepherds he has placed over his flock.

Making the duties of a pastor the topic for Sunday homily or a reflection in a diocesan paper is a delicate matter. Most exhortations to virtue are directed at lay persons, the people in the pews. These are usually content to leave it to the bishop to instruct his priests on their need for shepherd-like behavior, and to the Pope to do the same for his bishops. No one expects such instructions to be promulgated for the laity.

But it is not a bad idea for the ordinary lay Catholic to think for a while about the kind of person Jesus wanted his shepherds to be. No human will live up to this ideal perfectly, of course. An ideal by definition is a goal one aims for but never fully attains. The prayers and cooperation of parishioners, however, can help our shepherds come closer to this ideal.

In describing the ideal pastor, Jesus stresses three points.

First, the good pastor is not a hired hand whose overriding goals are his comfort and his paycheck. The hireling of Palestine scurried for safety if his flock was attacked by wolves or menaced by thieves; he turned slack if his duties became too demanding. The good shepherd, on the other hand, labored out of concern for his flock, with no eye for comfort or gain.

The Church needs leaders with that selfless dedication. When her shepherds act like hirelings, all her members suffer. The sheep are rarely fooled. They are quick to sense when their shepherd puts his ease ahead of the needs of his flock.

Second, as far as possible the good shepherd knows each member of his flock intimately. "I know mine and mine know me." Those of us who have never lived on a farm or become close to animals find it hard to comprehend the affectionate familiarity a human can have for an animal. It was this kind of affection that moved the Palestinian shepherd to tend his sheep that were sick, to rescue those caught in brambles or found at the bottom of a ravine. The bond between these shepherds and their sheep was legendary. Both the Bible and secular history attest it.

Such affection cannot be faked. If even dumb sheep can detect its presence or absence in their shepherd, certainly parishioners can in their pastor. Those who have business in the rectory have a right to expect this kind of bond to exist between themselves and the shepherd who stands before them.

Finally, the good shepherd "lays down his life for the sheep." This was literally true of Jesus Christ. The lesser shepherds who inhabit our bishop's houses and parish rectories may not actually shed their blood in the line of duty (although I have known a few who did), but they should be willing, if called on, to die for their flock. The test is how hard they work. Selfless labor for others is a daily martyrdom. We have all seen such selflessness in many shepherds of the Church.

Finally, a word about the parishioners, the members of the flock. We have just examined what they can legitimately look for in their pastor. But what can their pastor expect in return? If *pastor* means shepherd, what does *parishioner* mean?

It comes from a Greek word meaning neighbor. If the parishioners have the right to demand that their pastor live up to his name and be a good shepherd, then the pastor has the right to ask that they do the same. And so—live up to your name, you parishioners. Be *good* neighbors to your pastors.

ONE WITH HIS FATHER

Fourth Sunday of Easterd.
C: Jn. 10- 27-30.

❖ ❖ ❖

The gospel is short; perhaps too short, for it completely omits the setting in which Jesus spoke these words. For that we must look at the verses immediately preceding.

There we learn that Jesus was in Jerusalem during the feast of the Dedication. This winter celebration, also known as the Festival of Lights or Hannukah, is still observed by Jews on a date that almost coincides with our Christmas. When present in Jerusalem on such a feast, Jesus would often go to one of the porches of the temple, where he usually found an eager audience. On this occasion, however, he met hostility.

He had gathered a group in the Portico of Solomon (on the east side of the temple, protected from the cold desert winds). Among his listeners were some whose patience was wearing thin. They had heard whispers that Jesus might be the Messiah, the king all Israelites longed for. Was he? So far, they felt, he had been evasive. Now they insisted on a clear answer. "If you are the Messiah, tell us so plainly." Let's have no more shilly-shallying, just give us a straight yes or no.

But a straight yes or no was not easy. For one thing, the word "Messiah" had more than one meaning, just as the world has known more than one kind of king. Many expected the Messiah to be a military monarch who would avenge Israel by crushing its heathen foes in bloody battle. Jesus certainly did not want to raise hopes in that direction. Moreover, he had to be careful not to ignite the enmity of both Jewish and Roman authorities before his time had come. A public revelation of his identity as Messiah, and especially of the kind of Messiah he was, must wait until his death on Calvary and his rising on Easter Sunday.

Meanwhile he spoke in images. The more perceptive among his listeners might begin to grasp them, but only to later generations of Christians would their full meaning unfold. Here he used the most vivid image of all—the Good Shepherd.

To us a shepherd may seem as far removed from a king as a cow-hand from a congressman. But in ancient times, among both Jews and other oriental peoples, the image of a shepherd often stood for a king. The analogy is not as far-fetched as it sounds. Israel's great king David started out as a shepherd. And the prophets often pictured the Messiah in a shepherd's garb.

Forget the artistic renditions of the Good Shepherd you may have seen. One popular Sunday Missal illustrates this reading with a drawing of an anemic Jesus sitting under a palm tree and cuddling a snow-white lamb in his lap. "Lazybones" would be a fitter caption than "Good Shepherd." Think rather of how strong and gritty the Palestinian shepherd had to be, how ready to risk his life. When the young shepherd David stepped forward to accept the challenge of Goliath, he declared that his record proved him equal to the task. To protect his flock, he boasted, he had already slain both a bear and a lion *(I Sam 17:36)*.

In calling himself a shepherd, then, Jesus indirectly answered the question put to him. Yes, he was a king, but only in the sense that a king can be likened to a shepherd, that is, a *good* king to a *good* shepherd. Not only is he, like David, strong, daring, and courageous, but he knows the members of his flock as individuals, protects them and leads them to safety. He is not cold and selfish, seeking the perks and pomps of royalty. He loves his subjects and wants them to love him.

His sheep follow him because they do in fact love him and are familiar with his voice. Ordinary kings win obedience by instilling fear into their subjects; Jesus attracts followers by gaining their trust. His flock is confident that he can lead them through the dangers of this world to eternal life.

How can Jesus know all the sheep as individuals? We know that parents with a dozen children can know each of them as intimately as parents with two. But the Christians in the world, along with the potential Christians, are numbered in the millions. Can our Shepherd care for each of them personally?

At the close of this passage Jesus gives the answer, declaring that "The Father and I are One." Scholars today may debate the precise meaning of these words. Those who first heard them, however, had no problem. John says that as soon as Jesus spoke them, some listeners "picked up rocks to stone him," accusing him of blasphemy. "You, a man, are making yourself God."

Precisely. And this is what most of all distinguishes his authority from that of any merely human authority. He knows each of his millions of followers intimately because as the Incarnate Son of God he has the infinite knowledge of God. And he can lead us to eternal life because no one better than he knows how to find it. Heaven, after all, is his turf.

THE MONSTROUS CLAIM JESUS MADE

Fifth Sunday of Easter.
A: Jn. 14: 1-12.

❖ ❖ ❖

Among the more insidious enemies of our religion are the people who call themselves Christian but reject Christian doctrine. They quote approvingly from the proverbs and parables of Jesus, praise his works of mercy, applaud his heroic death. In their view he was the most perfect specimen of humanity ever to inhabit our globe, and they wish we would all learn to live as he did. But that is as far as they will go. The creeds that Christians have formulated about Jesus, the theology that has evolved over the centuries, they dismiss as irrelevant nuisances.

Above all, they reject the notion that Jesus was in any meaningful sense divine, preferring that we scrap all discussion of the topic. Jesus, they insist, was simply a good and wise man, perhaps the best and wisest ever to walk this earth. We should be content to leave the matter there.

How these people come to regard Jesus so highly is a mystery, since they have little regard for the New Testament, our only source for knowledge about him. When a passage fails to agree with their pre-set notions, they either deny its plain meaning or ignore it. Two otherwise honorable men belong in the latter class. Gathering dust in the libraries of the world are two curious editions of the gospels, one according to the American statesman Thomas Jefferson, the other according to the Russian novelist Leo Tolstoy. Both had towering egos. They simply expunged from the gospels whatever did not suit their taste (such as reference to the divinity of Jesus) and kept what they liked. A censor could not do a more thorough hatchet job on a piece of writing than these two did on the New Testament.

Those who say Jesus never claimed to be more than human will have rough going when they come to today's gospel passage, which is from John the evangelist's record of the words Jesus spoke to his apostles at the close of the Last Supper. If these were spoken by a mere man, then he was certifiably a madman. We label as a lunatic anyone who claims to be Napoleon. Far greater would be the lunacy of a mere human claiming to be the central figure in all history, the one on whom the salvation of the entire world depends. Yet that is what Jesus claims here.

He has just told his apostles he is going away. Seeing how upset they are at this announcement, he now tells them the place where he is going is his "Father's house" and that when he gets there he will prepare places for his faithful followers. There is, he assures his apostles, ample space for all. Are these the words of a mere human? One with all faculties intact?

Philip interrupts with a request that Jesus show the apostles the way to his Father's house. No more important question has ever been asked. In one form or another human beings have been asking it since the beginning of history. Where is the road to eternal happiness? What is the ultimate truth about our destiny? How can we achieve everlasting life? Jesus replies with one of his boldest and best remembered statements. "*I* am the way and the truth and the life." What does he mean?

The author of *The Imitation of Christ* gives a famous paraphrase: "I am the way you must follow, the truth you must believe, the life you must hope for." A contemporary commentator suggests a slightly different emphasis: "I am the true and living way that leads to an everlasting dwelling place in my Father's house." Whichever version one prefers, this much is clear: Jesus is not merely promising to *show* us the way, not just presenting himself as the *model* all human beings must imitate. Rather, he says he *is* the way to eternal life. As he puts it in the following verse, "No one comes to the Father but *through* me."

In other words, Jesus is the only road to salvation, the only revelation of eternal truth, the only source of the supernatural energy we need to do God's will and win heaven. This is true for all mankind and until the end of time. By his death on the cross Jesus paid ransom for the sins of the world.

Does this mean salvation is denied to pagans simply because through no fault of theirs they have never known Jesus Christ? Not at all. The Church teaches that even though they are unaware of its origin, pagans too can be "moved by grace" to "seek God" and "strive to do his will" (*Lumen Gentium*, second Vatican Council). Their impulse to do good comes, although they know it not, from Jesus Christ, who shed his blood "for all." For them as truly as for Christians, he is the only way to eternal life.

We will never fathom the entire mystery of Jesus. We know this much for sure, however, that he was not just another good man whose example we would do well to emulate and whose counsel we would be wise to follow. He is the Lord of all creation, the Alpha and Omega, our Way and our Truth and our Life.

KEEPING IN TOUCH

Fifth Sunday of Easter.
B: Jn. 15: 1-8.

This reading is from the parting words Jesus spoke to his apostles on the night before he died. They had just eaten the Paschal supper together. Except for a few meetings with him after the Resurrection, these disciples were to share his company no more. He wanted them to remember him after he was gone; and not only to remember, but to stay in touch with him. The key sentence in the passage is, "Remain in me, as I remain in you."

It would be a mistake to imagine Jesus intended these words only for the apostles who were physically at table with him as he spoke, listening to his actual voice. He was also addressing future generations of Christians who would try to live by his code without ever having his physical presence to guide and inspire them. In other words, he was speaking to us. Few of his words speak as urgently across the centuries.

Nor should we think these words were intended primarily for those few people among us who have scaled the heights of mystical prayer. They were intended also, perhaps especially, for average Christians, those who have trouble enough fulfilling their basic religious duties and staying on the sunny side of God's grace. To all of us he says, "Remain in me."

How can one person "remain" in another? We can take much of the mystery out of these words if we recall leave-takings that take place among us every day, whenever friends or dear ones realize they will not be together again for a long time.

Go to any railway station or airport where students are going off to boarding school or soldiers to overseas duty. Listen to snatches of what is spoken to them before they leave. "Stay well...Don't get into trouble...Think of us while you are away...Write often...If you need anything, be sure to let us know...Keep in touch."

That is what Jesus said to his apostles at the Last Supper and says to us every day of our lives: *Keep in touch.* He added a warning: If you don't keep in touch and seek my help when you need it, everything may be lost. "Without me you can do nothing. Anyone who does not remain in me will be thrown out like a branch and wither." But he also appended a promise: "Ask for whatever you want and it will be done for you."

The image Jesus used to illustrate the necessity of our keeping in touch was more familiar to his apostles than to most of us. Palestine was a grape-producing land. Vines with their precious clusters were everywhere. The grape vine was the symbol of the people of Israel, the emblem on one of their coins, a golden decoration in their temple. In Scripture the Israelites were often compared to a vine in the vineyard of the Lord.

Thus the image Jesus used here was not original. Strikingly original, however, was the use to which he put it. In the old dispensation the chosen people were the vine. Here Jesus himself is the vine, the source and center of life for his followers. No greater claim was ever on his lips than "I am the vine, you are the branches." In the new dispensation, with the inauguration of his kingdom, all Christians will draw strength from him and from him alone, just as branches do from their vine.

We can draw some practical conclusions from this image.

First, for the Christian, prayer is not a luxury but a necessity. To keep in touch with our fellow human beings we need devices like the telephone or the mails. To keep in touch with Jesus Christ, the source of all our spiritual strength, there is no substitute for prayer. To start our days habitually without asking for his help, or to let the weeks slip by without being present at his sacrifice of the Mass, is to lose touch with the vine that sustains us. We may become barren branches.

Second, God expects us to bear fruit. In fact, in a sense the vine needs us as much as we need it, for if it is to produce any fruit at all, it must produce it through us. It is on its individual branches that are grown the grapes that bring nourishment to mankind. Likewise, it is through individual Christians that the spiritually nourishing grace of God is brought into the world. Our task is not just to draw our own strength from the vine. We must share it with others.

Finally, the image reminds us that the Christian world should be both united and ever expanding. The vine that started to grow on the first Pentecost Sunday had only a few hundred branches to boast of, and it covered only a small patch of ground. Today that vine is gigantic, leaping from continent to continent. Each of us is only one among millions of branches.

We pray, then, not only for our own strength and health, but for that of all branches. Jesus Christ has made us one. Together we must remain in him. Together we must bear fruit.

"SEE HOW THEY LOVE ONE ANOTHER"

Fifth Sunday of Easter.
C: Jn. 13: 31-33; 34-35.

❖ ❖ ❖

Christianity created a sensation when it exploded into history. It was not just a new religion, but a new *kind* of religion. Religions were an old story in the Roman Empire, as commonplace as grasshoppers. Without exception, however, they stressed externals—rituals, rules, taboos. Christianity alone demanded—more accurately, *produced*—a profound internal change in its members. It was this internalization of their religion that set Christians apart from their pagan neighbors. They lived—more accurately, strove to live—by an inner code that governed their everyday activities.

What was the most novel part of Christian behavior, the feature that most attracted the notice of their pagan neighbors? Simply this, the love that bound Christians together. Tertullian, a second century observer, exclaimed in his description of Christians, "See how they love one another!" In a world where selfishness was a universally acceptable mode of conduct, people who acted as selflessly towards one another as Christians did stood out like a pack of freaks. (So, incidentally, should we).

Minucius Felix, a contemporary of Tertullian, remarked that Christians "love one another even before they know one another." A Christian could arrive a total stranger from a distant land and be welcomed among the local Christians as one of their own. This was because they were convinced they were all related to one another through the union they shared with their crucified founder. Lucian, a Roman satirist, looked at Christians and marveled that "their Master has made them believe they are all brothers." That people could consider themselves brothers and sisters without blood ties or prior acquaintance was to their pagan contemporaries an astonishing novelty.

Possibly these accounts exaggerate the harmony that existed among the early Christians. Some passages in Paul's letters indicate that much. But these early witnesses certainly put their finger on the single feature that Jesus wanted to be the identifying badge of his followers. In today's gospel passage, an excerpt from his discourse to his apostles at the Last

Supper, Jesus put the matter bluntly: "This is how all will know that you are my disciples, if you have love for one another."

This does not, of course, mean a Christian must love only fellow Christians, that we are free to despise or do injury to the unbaptized of this world. In the parable of the Good Samaritan Jesus made that much clear. An attitude of coldness or a spirit of vindictiveness, whether directed against Christian or non-Christian, is a violation of our code. (That is why the term "Christian war" is an absurdity, a contradiction in terms). But in addition to the love he wanted us to show to all humans, Jesus told us we must have a special love for one another. That is why at the Last Supper he called this a "new" commandment.

This is hardly surprising. We all have, and should have, a stronger love for members of our immediate family than for strangers. We should also have a special place in our hearts and a special urgency in our prayers and charitable works for those who belong with us to the family of Jesus Christ.

In a further sense this commandment is "new." The Old Law said we must love our neighbor *as ourselves.* Here Jesus gives us a new and higher norm, to love one another *as he loved us.* "As I have loved you, so you also should love one another."

What was special about the love Jesus had for us? It was *sacrificial,* a love unto death. We tend to think of love the way poets have always described it, as a warm glow in the heart. True enough, but the only test that this glow is strong and enduring is one's willingness to sacrifice for one's beloved, to give as well as to take. Real love is gritty, tough. It proves itself in sweat and fatigue, in patience and (most important of all) in forgiveness. The supreme model for such sacrificial love is Jesus on Calvary. Our love for fellow Christians must also be sacrificial. It is not for real unless it costs.

"Love one another" was not just a new but the final commandment of Jesus, promulgated the night before he died. "My children," he said, addressing his disciples as a dying father or mother might address sons and daughters gathered around the deathbed, "I will be with you only a little while longer." His tone was urgent, almost pleading. Whatever good or bad fortune attends their mission, however much they may fail in other matters, let them not fail in this, his final wish.

His words are as fresh today as when he first uttered them that Thursday night in Jerusalem. He wants us never to forget that we bear his name, never to discard the identity badge he fashioned for us at such cost to himself—"Love one another."

THE ADVOCATE

Sixth Sunday of Easter.
A: Jn. 14: 15-21.

❖❖❖

Students today are sometimes fond of a teacher, but rarely so fond that if the teacher dies they consider themselves orphans. It was different in ancient times. When a learned Rabbi in Israel died, his pupils often spoke of themselves as having been orphaned, for the Rabbi had nourished them with fatherly wisdom. And Plato wrote that after Socrates drank the cup of lethal hemlock, his pupils mourned that "they would have to spend the rest of their lives as children who had lost their father."

Jesus had been a source of wisdom for the apostles who gathered around him at the Last Supper. They had been his pupils, and from him they had learned eternal truths. But Jesus knew, and had just warned them, that this was soon to end, for he was going away. Now he added that although he was departing, he had no intention of leaving them orphans. Their loss, although severe, would not be total. He was going to send them "another Advocate, to be with you always, the Spirit of truth."

What did Jesus mean by "Advocate"? The previous edition of the New American Bible used the word "Paraclete," which is closer to the original Greek but means little to most people today. Actually, "Paraclete" was a term borrowed from the courtroom, meaning a defense attorney or a witness for the defense. The legal term "advocate," meaning "someone who pleads in another's behalf," is probably our closest equivalent.

Other terms in use through the centuries have been "Strengthener," "Consoler," even "Comforter." All are suitable as long as we know they refer to the third Person of the Trinity, the holy Spirit, and that what he consoles and strengthens us with is eternal truth. Jesus names him the "Spirit of truth."

Why did Jesus call him "another" Advocate? Who was the first? Clearly, Jesus himself. For roughly three years he had dispensed truth to the apostles. This new Advocate would preserve in truth both the apostles and those who would come after them.

Between Jesus and this new Advocate, the holy Spirit, however, are two important differences.

First, Jesus was present to his apostles and the world physically, a being of flesh and blood. His truths had been conveyed by words and gestures, in parables the simplest peasants could understand and with images from the fields and villages they knew well. His classrooms had been the temple of Jerusalem as well as the synagogues, lakeside, and hillsides of Galilee.

The new Advocate is neither seen nor heard. He is "Spirit," whose presence among us is gentler than dew, stiller than dawn. This does not make him less real, except for earthbound people to whom all spirit is mere phantom and only the flesh is real.

Secondly, the new Advocate, unlike Jesus, will remain in the world "always." The visible presence of Jesus ceased at the Ascension. But the holy Spirit, the Advocate, continues to work on our behalf and will continue. The history of the Spirit's labors in the world is the history of Christianity.

Imagine what the consequences would have been if Jesus had left his apostles orphans. They would have grieved, of course, as the disciples of Socrates grieved, and the rest of their lives would have been empty. But how much greater a difference it would have made for Christians who have come after the apostles, to ourselves who live twenty centuries later!

Without the Advocate, the New Testament would never have been written. We would know little more about the teaching of Jesus than that of the Rabbis who were his contemporaries. Jesus might still be the object of academic research by dusty scholars in musty libraries, as Socrates and Plato still are. But that is all. No one would live for him, still less die for him. Why should they? His teaching, his wisdom would be dead.

But it is not dead. The Advocate has been alive in the Church ever since Jesus breathed on his apostles after rising from the dead. He has been especially present whenever bishops, the successors to the apostles, have met in general council. Through them the Advocate has consoled and strengthened the people of God with the truths first taught by Jesus Christ.

The Advocate, however, does not need an ecumenical council to make his presence felt. He is present—defending, strengthening, consoling—in all individual Christians who live by the faith they professed at baptism. He is present whenever parishioners assemble for Mass, whenever at prayer we bless ourselves in the name of Father, Son, and Holy Spirit.

The "world" does not recognize the Advocate, any more than it recognized Jesus when he walked the earth in the flesh. But we can recognize him, both in ourselves and in other Christians. The Spirit of Jesus lives in his people. We are not orphans.

Friends of the Lord

Sixth Sunday of Easter.
B: Jn. 15: 9-17.

❖❖❖

Defining the word "Christian" is not as easy as it might seem. Here are a few attempts I have heard:

(1) Someone who has received the sacrament of baptism.

(2) Someone who not only accepts the teachings of Jesus Christ but lives by them.

(3) Someone who tries to obey the final commandment Jesus gave his apostles—to "love one another as I love you."

How would you score these? Here is my grade sheet:

Number One: B. Good, technically accurate, but of little practical use. Certainly with baptism one formally joins the Christian community. The story of Cornelius in *Acts*, describing how at baptism this Gentile was welcomed among Christians, supports this understanding of the sacrament. But the definition is static, identifying a person by a ceremony that took place in the past rather than by how a person lives in the present. It is like defining education as the process of earning a degree or a teacher as someone who belongs to a teacher's union.

Baptism is more than a rite of initiation. With its waters, Saint Paul tells us, our souls are flooded with divine grace and we are made heirs of heaven *(Rom. 6:3-10)*. To be on the roll of currently active Christians, a person must strive to hold onto this grace and keep on the path to heaven. Merely being recorded on a baptismal register is no guarantee of that.

Number Two: A. Excellent, with one flaw. Jesus was certainly a teacher, and it would be a lie to bear his name and at the same time reject his teaching about God and morality. What he taught about God, although often hard or even impossible to understand (such as the doctrine of the Trinity), most people can accept without a struggle. What he taught about morality, on the other hand, although usually easy to understand (like his words on marriage), is often very hard to live by.

Thus, while the first definition asks too little, this asks too much. If we used the word "Christian" only for those who never fail to live up to the teachings of Jesus, the list would contain only saints. The net of Christianity is wider than that. I suggest we amend the definition to "...who accepts the teachings of Jesus and *strives* to live by them." To be truly Christian is to be engaged in a constant struggle. A Christian does not always win, but never stops trying. Really trying.

Number Three: A plus. This definition wins the prize. Coming as it does from Jesus himself, it gets to the heart of what it is to be a Christian. Loving one another as he loved us is the special commandment he kept repeating to his apostles on the night before he died. Even non-Christians recognize this as *the* Christian commandment. We are told that in the first century, pagans would point to Christians with astonishment and exclaim, "There go the Christians; see how they love one another!" The world had never seen anything like it.

That we should love one another as he has loved us was the farewell commandment of Jesus. How much did he love us? Enough to lay down his life for us. "No one," he said, "has greater love than this." But did he mean that to be his followers we must all lay down our lives? To remain in his ranks, must we literally die for others? Are we all called to be martyrs?

Clearly not. If we were, our churches would be nearly empty and our graveyards overflowing. Martyrdom in the service of God or one's neighbor is a rare grace granted sometimes to the most unlikely people (I have known a few). Most of us, like the rest of mankind, will die in bed. The martyrdom demanded of the ordinary Christian is a matter of daily living rather once dying. Living for others can be as hard as dying for them.

The point is that our love must be limitless, no strings attached. It will certainly demand a price (how high, only God knows). Where there is no sacrifice, there is no love. But whatever God should ask us to suffer in the service of others, we should pray for the strength to accept.

One final point. Jesus tells us that the spirit in which we should carry out this commandment is joy. Someone has said that a glum Christian is a contradiction in terms. Once we start moaning over the price we have to pay in order to show love for others, we have lost what it takes to be a good Christian. Little is accomplished by the cheerless giver.

Why be cheerful? Because of what the Lord has done for us. In the words Jesus spoke to his apostles on the night before he died, he revealed the reason for our joy. We did not choose him; he chose us—to be, not his slaves, but his friends.

Isn't that another good definition of a Christian—someone who is a friend of the Lord and who tries to remain his friend?

God Is Not Silent

Sixth Sunday of Easter.
C: Jn. 14: 23-29.

❖❖❖

Most of us find prayer a struggle. That should be no surprise, since the good things in life (and prayer is surely one of them) often come only after a struggle. The problem is that in the struggle of prayer we seem always to be losers. Ideally, we are told, prayer is a conversation with God; and a conversation, we know, should be a two-way affair in which one listens at least as much as one speaks. But in our prayer we do all the talking. We plead, complain, cajole, whine. But through all our chatter God remains silent. Or so it seems.

Some privileged souls, to be sure, have had better success in making contact with God. Once when he was at prayer, St. Thomas Aquinas received an illumination from on high so powerful that on rising from his knees he declared that all his theological writings were mere straw compared with what God had laid bare to him in those few moments of rapture. Other saints tell of similar experiences. From their accounts it almost seems that God routinely made person-to-person calls to them. But never, alas, to us. Never to us.

Or doesn't he? Perhaps we are expecting the wrong kind of communication. Are we like the Israelites of old who expected the Messiah to come in such splendor that, when he did arrive as a carpenter from Nazareth, they failed to recognize him? Prayer does not have to reach mystical heights to be genuine.

The truth is that, even though we are far from being ready for induction into prayer's Hall of Fame, God does speak to us. His words are on every page of the Bible. Simply reading Scripture or listening attentively when it is read at Mass is a kind of prayer. In today's passage Jesus says, "The word you hear is not mine but that of the Father who sent me." To hear the word of God, then, we need only to open the pages of the New Testament and read the words of Jesus Christ.

Moreover, in Scripture Jesus not only *speaks* the word of God, he *is* the Word of God clothed in human flesh. Simply to read of his doings as he traveled through Palestine—preaching, healing, consoling, forgiving—is to read the script of a drama composed by and about God. We are the intended audience.

Today's passage is from the words Jesus spoke to his apostles on the night before he died. They had finished their meal together; Jesus had just given them himself in the form of bread and wine. To these beloved pupils of the past three years, Jesus now presided over his last class. In four chapters of his gospel, the fourteenth to the seventeenth, the evangelist John gives the gist of what he said to them.

This final discourse was meant, not just for the apostles at table with him, but for all who in time to come would inherit the faith of these apostles. That is why years later John recorded his memory of these words, why the Church has preserved them intact. A man about to die spoke them to his dearest friends. No words in Scripture are more moving.

Jesus not only wanted his words to last; he guaranteed that they would. "The Spirit that the Father will send in my name ... will teach you everything and remind you of all that I told you." At Pentecost the Father sent his Spirit to the entire Church, but to the four composers of the gospels the Spirit came in a special way. Their accounts relied on the memory of the apostles and of other eyewitnesses. But human memory is fallible and human power of expression feeble. That is why Jesus assured his apostles that his holy Spirit would be with them. The four evangelists wrote their accounts of the deeds and sayings of Jesus with the help and guidance of this Spirit.

The Spirit is still with us. When the Church explains Scripture, she does not ape the methods of classical scholars who feel they have done their job once they have explained what the words of the classics meant to the ancient Greeks and Romans. The words of Jesus were meant, not just for the people who first heard them, but for all Christians and for all time. Thus they were meant to be applied to the changing circumstances of the world throughout history. It is the Church, guided by the successors of the apostles and with the help of the holy Spirit, who opens our eyes to the meaning of God's word for us.

The Church does not, indeed cannot, give us new revelations from on high. But it can and does apply the words of Jesus to the concerns of today. We trust her to do this wisely because we have faith in Christ's promise that the holy Spirit (whose other name is holy Wisdom) would remain with her. When we listen to the Church expound the words of Scripture, we are listening to a human voice, but a voice guided by the Spirit.

None of us has the right to complain that God is silent.

A Quiet Leave-Taking

Ascension.
A: Mt. 28: 16-20.

❖ ❖ ❖

The departure of Jesus from this world was as quiet and unpublicized as his arrival. After escorting his remaining eleven apostles to a hill outside Jerusalem, he ascended to his Father and was never seen on earth again. Today's first reading, from *Acts*, describes this leave-taking. The third reading, from Matthew, contains the commission Jesus gave his apostles only days before his ascension. Among the world's "famous last words", these certainly rank as the most famous.

All power in heaven and earth has been given to me. The power of Jesus on "earth" is evident above all in his moral teaching, his warrant as Son of God and author of life to tell us what is good and what is evil, what leads to salvation and what does not. Those who heard him explain the moral law were impressed by the note of authority in his voice, how much his manner differed from the shilly-shallying of the scribes. He spoke with the certitude of one who *knows*, whose knowledge was from heaven. "You have *heard*...But I *say* to you...." *(Mt. 5).*

Another reason why the moral instruction of Jesus was so firm and clear is that a single law was its bedrock. This was the law of love. Over and over he repeated the formula: we must first love God; when we do love him and because we do, we will love our neighbors as ourselves. Anyone guided by this law has no time for the sophistries and evasions propagated by self-appointed pontificators on moral issues.

The absolute power that Jesus wields "in heaven" we will witness on Judgment Day. Elsewhere *(Mt. 25: 31-46)* he describes how, seated on his throne and with the nations of the world gathered before him, he will divide mankind into those destined for Paradise and those doomed for eternal darkness. The law he will judge us by will be his law of love. Did we show towards others the same compassion that Jesus has shown towards us? Whatever we do to our neighbor he will take as done to himself.

Go, therefore, and make disciples of all nations, baptizing them...teaching them to observe all that I have commanded you. Before leaving this world Jesus gave his apostles a mission similar to his own. As he had taught and made disciples of them, they were to teach and make disciples of others. Their teaching was not to deviate from his, by more or by less. Through baptism and instruction their ranks would soon swell. Their words and example would make his law of love known to "all nations."

The key word is "all." The eleven and those who were to come after them needed a vision that would reach to every corner of the world. Matthew composed his gospel only a few decades after the Ascension, when the Church was still in its early infancy. To the scattered pockets of mostly poor and persecuted Christians who first heard these words, the universal scope of that vision must have seemed absurdly out of reach, just as it did to the Eleven to whom Jesus first proposed it.

Yet the people of God made Christ's vision their own, and in the centuries since never doubted that their goals were worldwide. Jesus did not found a Church to serve the needs of a few initiates or limit its membership to particular races or nationalities. The gospel must go everywhere. Christ's law of love must be given the chance to transform the entire world.

History has vindicated the confidence Jesus placed in his apostles. Outside U. N. headquarters in Manhattan fly the flags of every nation in the world. Does even a single one represent a land to which the gospel is a total stranger? Globetrotters report that wherever in the world they go, at least some evidence of Christianity is present. Throughout history leaders of the Church Jesus founded have been guilty of many lapses, but never of forgetting his mandate of multinationality. Jesus did not say his gospel would be accepted by every individual on earth. But he wanted it preached wherever people are. And it is.

And behold, I am with you always, until the end of the age. The name the angel gave to Jesus even before he was born was Emmanuel, meaning "God is with us" *(Mt. 1: 23).* Jesus, who is God, is still with us, living not only in the Eucharist but through his holy Spirit in all Christians who obey his law of love. Without this presence the Church would not have lasted for twenty decades, still less for twenty centuries. She would never have spread, as she has, across the globe.

Because Jesus is present, he is still heard—in the voice of parents teaching children their prayers, of catechists preparing people for baptism, of Popes and bishops urging us to apply Christ's law of love to current social problems. The voice of the teaching Church is the voice of Jesus Christ. It has the task of making itself heard "until the end of the age."

"TAKEN UP INTO HEAVEN"

Ascension.

B: Mk. 16: 15-20.

❖❖❖

Although they bring Mark's gospel to a close, these lines are not the work of Mark. So at least the biblical scholars assures us. If Mark did write a conclusion to his gospel, it seems to have been lost and had this passage inserted in its place by some nameless member of the primitive Church.

This does not mean the passage is worthless. It is actually a compilation of details from other parts of the New Testament where the risen life of Jesus and the early years of the Church are described. Thus, although not Mark's, these belong among the inspired words of God. What they tell us is particularly appropriate for this feast of the Ascension.

The gospels portray Jesus with his apostles in different parts of Palestine during the forty days after his Resurrection. Both in the last chapter of his gospel and the first of *Acts,* Luke records how, after meeting with them for a final time, he parted from them on a hill near Jerusalem. It is not easy to form a clear picture of how this happened. Artists have tried to capture the scene on canvas, often with spectacular results, but many of their details have little basis in Scripture.

The point of the Ascension, however, is not how it looked to those who were with Jesus during those final moments he spent on earth, but what it meant from the vantage of heaven. Mark puts the essential truth of the Ascension in these words: "The Lord Jesus, after he spoke to them, was taken into heaven and took his seat at the right hand of God." Thus his sojourn among us as a man of flesh came to a close and he passed into his eternal glory. It is this passing that we celebrate today.

Today's reading contains some final instructions Jesus gave his apostles. They provide a picture of the Church, not only in the first century, but through all centuries thereafter, our own included. We do not have a proper picture of the Church today unless we realize there is an unbroken link between ourselves and the apostles who first heard these words of Jesus.

The reason it is unbroken is that the apostles were not left entirely on their own. Jesus parted from them, but not completely. His Ascension meant loss of his physical presence; no one in the days since then has gazed upon his features as the apostles did on that final day. But his

Spirit came to them at Pentecost, remained with them, and remains with those who have come after them. Jesus is still here, present in his Church.

The key sentence in this passage is its last, stating that the apostles "went forth and preached everywhere, while *the Lord worked with them* and confirmed the word through accompanying signs." After twenty centuries he continues to work with us, who are descendants of the apostles. Although far in time from when the Word was clothed in human flesh and dwelt among us, we are his Church, empowered with the same mandate he gave his apostles. Our message, like theirs, is confirmed by signs.

His mandate was that they "go into the whole world and proclaim the good news." The good news, simply put, is that God loves us and has made it possible for us to return his love. The command to bring this news everywhere put a staggering responsibility on the shoulders of these scantily educated apostles and the nobodies who became their first converts. As far as we can see, however, they accepted it without a wince.

The early Church set out to penetrate the cold paganism of the Roman empire and subdue it with the warm charity of Jesus. As centuries passed, the world grew larger, but geography was no barrier. Wherever new lands were found, bearers of the gospel were sent. We are still sending them. The world is our parish.

What of the signs that Jesus promised would confirm the good news? Some of the examples he mentions—speaking new languages, handling serpents, and drinking poison—seem strange to our ears, but they were all verified in the early Church. For later ages, including our own, signs of a different kind are required, and these have been granted by the Spirit.

Among them are many we take for granted. Think of the Christian works of mercy, our care for the sick, the aged, the homeless, and those crippled by drugs and the neglect of society; think also of the education the Church supports, her labors to overcome bigotry and prejudice, her battles against the many errors of our age that have brought so much suffering to mankind.

Yes, signs still confirm the gospel. Let anyone who doubts this imagine for a moment what our world would be like if tomorrow all memory of Jesus ceased, all bearers of his word struck mute, and all doers of his word turned idle. The message of the Ascension is not that Jesus is gone, but that he is still here—in his Church and, please God, in each of us.

Great Joy After Losing Their Lord

Ascension.
C: Lk. 24: 46-53.

❖❖❖

"They...returned to Jerusalem with great joy." A reader might wonder what in the world the apostles had to be joyful about, seeing that they had just had their last glimpse on earth of the man they revered as their Lord and Master. Once before, after his death on Calvary, they had been convinced he was gone forever, and on that occasion only sorrow filled their hearts.

But then came the marvel of his Resurrection, followed by forty days of pure delight in their repeated meetings with the risen Jesus. During those meetings Jesus "presented himself alive to them by many proofs" and instructed them about the role they were to play in propagating his kingdom. Now the last of these meetings was over. After leading them out to the "Mount called Olivet" Jesus parted from them for the last time.

Why did they rejoice to see him go? And why does the Church commemorate this leave-taking with a feast, a Mass in which we ask God to "make us joyful" in the Ascension?

First of all, let us be clear on what we are commemorating today. The best biblical scholars remind us that the Ascension was not primarily a physical event, a kind of circus performance in the sky. In popular imagination (as well as in some dazzling artistic renditions), the Ascension looks something like this: the disciples stand in a circle on a mountain top, watching in solemn stupefaction as Jesus glides majestically upward and finally disappears behind a cloud. Nothing in Scripture excludes such imaginative embellishment, but nothing demands it either. In any case, it misses the point of the Ascension.

Luke states that Jesus "parted from them *and was taken up to heaven.*" What was the physical reality behind these words? Did Jesus dramatize the event by a slow ascent through the empyrean or did he just vanish in the wink of an eye? Either could fit the account Luke gives here and in *Acts*. At one moment Jesus was visibly present to his disciples; at another he was nowhere to be seen. The point of the narrative, its essential truth, is that the mission of Jesus on earth was definitively over. By his Ascension he returned to his heavenly Father.

What the disciples witnessed on Mount Olivet, then, was the final manifestation of the human Jesus on earth. He was no longer physically present among us. The next time he is seen by human eyes will be on the Last Day, at his second coming.

The end of his days on earth was for Jesus also a beginning, the inauguration of his reign in heaven. This was the first reason the apostles had to be joyful as they drifted back to their lodgings in Jerusalem. They were glad because for Jesus, to whom they now felt more attached than ever, the Ascension meant fulfillment. The battle was over. He had won.

They had a second reason to rejoice. For the apostles as well as for Jesus, the Ascension marked a beginning. "Men of Galilee," asked the messenger of God after Jesus had departed, "why are you standing there looking at the sky?" This was like saying, "What are you gaping at? You have a job to do. Get on with it." God did not want the apostles to spend their days like aging tennis bums, nostalgically recalling their former days of glory. The real game was yet to be played.

Jesus had promised to send his Spirit, "the promise of my Father." With his coming they would be "clothed with power from on high." Their lives thereafter would be spent as witnesses to Jesus, preaching in his name "to all the nations." In and through them the Spirit of Jesus would remain in the world.

Saint Paul learned of this continued presence of the Spirit when Jesus spoke to him on the road to Damascus. "Saul, Saul, why are you persecuting *me*?" *(Acts 9: 9)*. Paul had thought he was hounding fellow Jews who lived on the memory of a dead prophet. To him that was all Jesus was—a memory, a molding corpse. Now Jesus let him know he was still alive in the members of his Church, that any assault on them was an assault on him. Later, after Paul became an apostle, he was conscious of the presence of Jesus in himself. "I live, no longer I, but Christ lives in me" *(Gal. 2: 20)*. No human can claim to be closer to Jesus than that. And no Christian should claim less.

On this feast of the Ascension, then, we do not mourn the loss of Jesus. Much as we would all willingly give our right arms for the privilege of seeing and working with him as the apostles once did, we know that the work of the historical Jesus is over. He now reigns in heaven. But he is still present in the world as truly as when he once walked the roads of Galilee. He is present wherever he is preached, wherever he is served. He is present in us all, as long as we accept his reign.

Today we celebrate, with joy, this continued presence.

A PRIEST'S BRIEF PRAYER AFTER DINNER

Seventh Sunday of Easter.
A: Jn. 17: 1-11.

❖❖❖

What is probably the most famous after-dinner address in history took place in an upper room of Jerusalem two thousand years ago. Its occasion was a paschal banquet, one of many thousands served that same evening in every household of the holy city. This ceremonial meal was the Israelites' traditional way of thanking God for an event that had taken place centuries earlier, the escape of their ancestors from bondage in Egypt.

Presiding over the meal and delivering the address at its conclusion was Jesus Christ. Eleven of his apostles formed his audience. Only Judas Iscariot was missing. Earlier in the evening he had had scooted off on some undisclosed business.

For Jesus this address was a swan song, his farewell to the men he had lived and labored with for the past several years. He had performed many marvelous works during those years—given sight to the blind, health to the sick, comfort and pardon to sinners. But his most important work was with his apostles. Besides teaching them God's word ("the words you gave to me I have given to them"), he had trained them to deliver that same word to the world after his departure. The future of his gospel, of God's word to mankind, was to be in their hands. If they failed, then his lifetime of labor had been in vain.

Alone at the banquet Jesus knew that one apostle had in fact already failed. At the very moment Jesus was speaking, Judas was preparing to hand him over to his enemies. This awareness of Jesus that his "hour" had finally come made the words he now spoke all the more precious. With betrayal and certain death less than twenty-four hours away, all his care was for those he was leaving behind and to whom he was entrusting his gospel. That was the main thrust of this farewell address. His days were over. The future was in their hands.

Our readings for the past two Sundays have been from the evangelist John's account of this address. With today's reading, however, comes a significant shift in focus. Up to this point Jesus had directed his words exclusively to his apostles. Now, raising his eyes, he addressed his heavenly Father. The words he spoke to him are today known as his "high priestly prayer."

Picture him getting to his feet as he opened this prayer with the words recorded in this gospel reading. Among Jews of biblical times, standing was the customary posture one took in addressing God. And praying aloud, as Jesus did here, was not unusual, since the person praying often wanted the bystanders to overhear. Certainly Jesus wanted his apostles to hear this prayer. It was for their benefit that he prayed.

We should be glad for the chance to eavesdrop, since in praying for his apostles Jesus prayed also for us. In a later passage he specifically included in this prayer all future generations who would believe in him because of the preaching of the apostles *(17: 20)*. Thus the scope of this priestly prayer was vast. It reached out to all Christians to the end of time.

Jesus began by speaking of his death, his "hour," as something glorious ("The hour has come. Give glory to your son"). How could he speak of death by crucifixion as something glorious? The answer is that a person's motive can transform even an ignominious death into a thing of glory. To lose one's life while rescuing someone from death has always been considered the highest heroism. Jesus saw it as the surest proof of love, saying that "No one has greater love than this" *(Jn. 17:13)*. His own death was the peak of heroism inspired by the deepest love, for he died that we might have "eternal life."

It is because Jesus here offered himself for this sacrificial death that this prayer is called a "priestly" prayer. People today do not usually think of Jesus as a priest. But that is what he was—and is. Historically, the proper function of a priest is to offer sacrifice on behalf of the people he represents. In biblical times the high priest of the Old Covenant performed the sacrificial rite daily in the temple, slaying a lamb on the altar of holocausts to atone for the sins of the Jewish people. Jesus, high priest of the New Covenant, shed his own blood on Calvary to atone for the sins of mankind.

What is the most important task in the day of a Catholic priest? Although he has many important functions, none approaches his offering of the sacrifice of the Mass, which he does on behalf of all mankind. The Mass has value only because it is a re-enactment of the sacrifice Jesus once offered on Calvary. He became both our high priest and our sacrificial victim by shedding his blood, thereby freeing us from sin and winning for us entrance to heaven. He remains our high priest, coming to our altars at every Mass and renewing the offering of Calvary.

THE WINNING SIDE

Seventh Sunday of Easter.
B: Jn. 17: 11-19.

❖ ❖ ❖

Paintings of the Last Supper often picture only eleven apostles gathered around Jesus, although the table has room for twelve. The absentee, of course, is Judas. Scripture is not clear on exactly when Judas made off, but it was certainly before Jesus prayed aloud for his apostles at the close of the meal. Although the tone of this prayer is generally jubilant, a note of anguish can be heard in the passage chosen for today's gospel, where he deplores the defection of Judas. The empty place at table represents the one great failure of Jesus.

All twelve apostles had been hand-picked. Here Jesus declares he has "protected" and "guarded" them, that only one, "the son of destruction," has slipped through his watch.

Not only slipped through, but crossed over and joined the other side. As Jesus uttered this prayer, the apostle-turned-traitor was meeting with the enemies of Jesus, arranging a time and place to hand his master over, settling on a price.

Christians have always been fascinated by Judas. Partly this is because to our sin-clouded minds, as any good novelist or scriptwriter knows, vice is perversely more interesting than virtue. The case of Judas, however, rouses special curiosity. We cannot help wondering what made him tick. Why abandon his glorious vocation? Why plunge a knife into the back of a friend as good and generous as Jesus? Why seal his treason with a kiss?

Blaming the devil, as two of the evangelists seem to do *(Jn. 13:2, Lk. 22:3)*, is not enough. The devil certainly played a major role in the downfall of Judas, and that is probably what these evangelists had in mind; but even the devil needs something to work on, some weakness a person has nurtured for years. Often it is a weakness of the flesh, but there is no suggestion of that in Judas. What was it? Scripture gives hints, but no certain answer. All one can give is an educated guess.

Judas seems to have been shrewd in assessing odds, skilled in reading the signs of the times. He could see the crash coming, the disaster into which Jesus seemed so heedlessly heading. The people Jesus had offended were too highly placed for a mere preacher from Galilee to withstand. It was an uneven match.

Who were these people? Prominent among them were the high priests of Jerusalem, men of considerable prestige and also considerable means. Their most notorious collision with Jesus took place when he expelled the animal-hawkers and money-changers from the temple. For them that market had been a steady source of revenue, and for disrupting it they considered Jesus a meddling fanatic, an extremist in his opposition to wealth.

In short, these high priests, supposedly dedicated to God, were in fact enamored of riches, in love with the world. Judas, who also had an itchy palm *(Jn. 12: 6),* instinctively sided with them and their cohorts among the proud Pharisees. These, he could see, were the smart-money people, the winners. Jesus, on the other hand, who lived like a pauper and appalled Judas with his incessant tirades against riches, was a failure, a sure loser. Judas could not bear being a follower of a failure, least of all a financial failure. And so, while he still had time, he cut his losses and joined the side that had made peace with the world. He felt sure that this was the winning side.

It was no accident, then, that immediately after his mention of Judas, Jesus warns the remaining eleven against "the world." The term means money as well as all the money can buy: not just everyday creature comforts, but power, prestige, entry into the smart set, the company of the beautiful people. "The world" and the gospel are at opposite poles. The world "hated" Jesus. It will always hate his true followers.

Jesus does not pray that his disciples be taken out of the world. He has himself been sent into the world by his Father, and into the world he in turn will send his apostles. The world is where they will live, for there they must plant his gospel. But while they live in the world, they must reject the world's values, steer clear of its traps. Especially the trap that snared Judas, the conviction that the world's side is the winning side.

In a sense, of course, it is. In the short run, the world always wins. And the short run was what Judas chose—instant success, cash in the bank. He could not bear to put his money on a loser. In his eyes and the eyes of many like him, the side that rejects the values of the world will surely lose.

Jesus knew the world would do its best to seduce the remaining eleven, and their followers, and the successors of their followers. As long as we have among us Christians who forget that we "do not belong to the world," that the only run that counts is the long run, Judases will appear in our midst.

STAYING TOGETHER

Seventh Sunday of Easter.
C: Jn. 17: 20-26.

❖❖❖

This passage has a ring of finality. It brings to an end the words Jesus spoke to his apostles at the close of the Last Supper. The rhetoricians of old called this part of a discourse its peroration, decreeing that it should among other things restate the speaker's main theme with an added dollop of emotion. This passage does exactly that. Although unschooled in the secrets of rhetoric, Jesus was master of them by instinct.

John spends four chapters (14-17) on this final discourse of Jesus, and one theme dominates: his pledge that, although he is about to leave his apostles, he will return. Thereafter, he will remain with them in a mysterious but real way, provided only they stay true to his teaching. "If you love me, you will keep my commandments," he stated at the outset, adding "I will not leave you orphans; I will come to you" *(14: 18)*.

Jesus here repeats this theme, but with a new twist. So far he has seemed to limit his remarks to the band of apostles who have been sitting with him amid the leftovers of the Last Supper. Now he expands his vision to include a prayer for "those who will believe" in him through the words of his apostles, promising that these disciples of future generations will enjoy his continued presence. He will also be "in them."

Who are included among these future disciples? The apostles began to preach the word on Pentecost. Before long, their preaching was put in writing and thus the gospels, the record or our faith, were born. All Christians who for the past twenty centuries have believed in the Jesus of the gospels are included in the prayer that Jesus uttered at the close of the Last Supper.

What gift does Jesus pray they will have? Unity—that "they may all be one." Do today's followers of Jesus have that unity? Sadly, no; at least not the perfect unity Jesus prayed for.

Consult a recent almanac and see how deep are the divisions among Christians. In mine I find that out of a world population of 5.2 billion, about 30% call themselves Christian. That is the good news. But of these, less than 60% are in union with the Pope, the successor of Saint Peter. That is the bad news.

The two most serious quarrels within the Church gave birth, first to the orthodox churches of the East, next to the Protestant churches of the West. The Protestant break-off led inevitably to further fragmentation, so that today the protesting churches are divided and subdivided into sects too numerous to count. Christianity suffers from no greater scandal or more serious threat to its health and growth than this disunity among those who profess allegiance to the one Lord and Savior.

Jesus foresaw the harm that a multiplicity of denominations would bring. He prayed that his followers would remain one, "that the world may know that you sent me." Think of how hard it is for an honest, inquiring pagan to know which Christian church to choose when Christians cannot agree among themselves.

Few Catholics today feel the urge to challenge the authority of Rome by nailing protests to the door of their parish church. But all should be on guard against attitudes that may weaken their esteem for the unity Jesus prayed for. This does not mean Catholics should agree on everything. In politics they may range from rock-ribbed conservatives to flag-burning liberals. In science one may believe in UFO's, another dismiss them as illusions. Even in religious matters absolute uniformity is neither desirable nor possible. Some prefer hymns with a rock beat, others care only for Gregorian chant or Palestrina.

But on essentials our unity should be absolute. The essentials boil down to the three C's of Creed, Code, and Cult—what we believe, the way we try to behave, and how we worship. All three must be governed by what Jesus taught and his Church has recorded in the gospels. If they are, then Jesus will truly, as he promised at the Last Supper, "live" in us.

We have one *creed*, preserved through the centuries. Saint Paul once said that even if an angel from heaven should preach a gospel other than that of the apostles, he should be cursed *(Gal. 1: 8)*. So should we, if we water down an iota of the creed.

We have one *code*, the code Jesus Christ preached, especially in his Sermon on the Mount. We can never perfectly observe it, but it is our goal. All true Christians agree, for example, that wealth is perilous, that human life and marriage are sacred, that all neighbors should be loved and all foes forgiven.

Finally, we have one *cult* or central form of worship. This is the Mass, which unites us all with God and with one another. Whatever its language, it is the same Mass everywhere, whether in a cathedral or a nipa hut. Never should the unity of Catholics be firmer than when they join in the Sacrifice of the Mass.

Living Water, Real Spirit

Pentecost Vigil.
ABC: Jn. 7: 37-39.

❖ ❖ ❖

The most sublime doctrine of Christianity is the Holy Trinity. It is also the most incomprehensible. No human mind, however high its IQ, can grasp it. Whenever we say the Creed, we affirm that the Trinity is not the absurdity it seems to be, but an eternal truth revealed by Jesus Christ. In so affirming, we say something about both ourselves and God. First, that our intellects, proud of them though we are, are in fact puny, provincial things; and second, that the Author of the universe, the three-in-one God, is infinitely beyond our reach. A human straining to comprehend the inner workings of God is like a cat sniffing at a computer, unable to figure out what the thing is. No more can we figure out God.

But that is not all. For most people, the Trinity contains within itself another mystery. Who or what, they wonder, is the third Person, the one we call the holy Spirit? Neither the Father nor the Son poses so great a problem. Although we know that the first Person is only *like* a human father and the second only *like* a human son, still we feel that these names give some inkling of who these Persons are and how they affect our lives.

The first Person watches over creation as a father over his family. The second Person came on an errand to earth, where in obedience to his Father he lived and died for us. But what about the third Person? What role does the holy Spirit play?

It must be an important role. Pentecost has through the centuries been celebrated as one of the principal holy days of the year. It was on the Jewish Pentecost, fifty days after the Passover on which Jesus died, that the third Person came to the apostles and the work of the Church began. Tomorrow we celebrate this entry of the holy Spirit into the world.

But how are we to celebrate Pentecost if we are fuzzy about who the holy Spirit is and the place he has in the world and in our lives? Even the name of the third Person poses a problem. When I was growing up we said "Holy Ghost," while now we say "Holy Spirit." What is the difference, and why the change?

At first sight "Ghost" seems a satisfactory word. On the night before he died, Jesus had promised to return to his apostles in a new form of existence and to remain with them and their successors until the end of time *(Jn. 14,15)*. A ghost, according to common usage, is the shade of a dead person haunting the places where the person once lived. To call this new presence of Jesus in the Church his ghost, then, seems natural enough.

Through the years, however, the word "ghost" has acquired unwelcome associations, reminding people of haunted houses and little children trembling at spooks that go bump in the night. Many felt that this somewhat comic-book flavor of the word "ghost" made it an undignified way to refer to the third Person of the Trinity. The conviction, and not any profound theological insight, was why "Ghost" was dropped and "Spirit" won the day.

"Spirit" signifies a presence that is invisible but real. We cannot see or touch "school spirit" or the "spirit of the nation" that patriotic orators invoke. Still, we know when such spirits are present and when they are not. Insubstantial things can be real, and these are real. The holy Spirit, the third Person of the Trinity, is infinitely more real, as real as the first and second Persons. Since the first Christian Pentecost, the holy Spirit has made its presence felt wherever Christians have gathered and carried on the work of Christ.

The name "Spirit," moreover, tells us something important about the third Person of the Trinity. "Spirit" means breath, and breath means life. The holy Spirit is like the breath of God in *Genesis*, which gave life to dust and thus created our human race; the breath that the prophet Exekiel spoke of when he described the Lord breathing life into dry bones and raising up an army of living soldiers; above all, like the strong breath of wind that God sent roaring through the house where the apostles were gathered on the first Christian Pentecost. Filled with new life, these men who had been passing their days in idle silence rushed into the streets and started shouting out the good news of Jesus Christ. Our Church was born.

In the third reading Jesus compares the holy Spirit to living water. To the Jews of his day the expression "living water" meant moving water, the invigorating water from springs or streams as opposed to the stagnant water of pools and swamps; water that refreshes dry throats and brings soothing coolness to weary travelers; water that restores the vigor of youth.

All this the holy Spirit does for the Church and for those who go to her for refreshment. The holy Spirit keeps the Church alive, healthy, strong; and ancient though she is, forever young.

WE'RE ALL ON STAGE FOR ACT THREE

Pentecost.
ABC: Jn. 20: 19-23.

I

Pentecost is a drama in three acts. The setting for Act One is the room in Jerusalem where the risen Jesus spoke to his apostles on the evening of the first Easter Sunday. Act Two opens on the same room fifty days later, on the Sunday the Jews called Pentecost (their festival for the fiftieth day after Passover). Act Three is still being played out.

The first act features one of the best known lines of Jesus, "As the Father has sent me, so I send you." This was the mandate from which the apostles drew their authority. What Jesus preached, they were to preach. As he healed and forgave sins, they also were to heal and forgive sins. Through them and their successors, Jesus would remain at work in the world. In fact, his work would vastly expand in their hands. He had confined his labor to a few years in Palestine. Their labors would know no boundaries. From their lips the good news of Jesus Christ would go out to all nations until the end of time.

Next, Jesus breathed on his apostles, imparting the holy Spirit. As far as we learn from Scripture, this reception of the Spirit had no immediate effect. The apostles seem to have remained as tongue-tied as ever, daring not to go among their fellow Israelites and tell the story of Jesus. Without heaps more of courage as well as a strong infusion of eloquence, they could not hope to carry out the mandate of Jesus. Just to get started, they needed a powerful push from on high.

Fortunately, they were soon assured that this push was on its way. Before ascending to his Father, Jesus told them to remain in Jerusalem until the full power of the holy Spirit was given to them. When and how this Spirit would make his presence felt, they had no idea. But they knew it would be in Jerusalem, and so there they waited and prayed. With them were the mother of Jesus and about a hundred of his close followers.

Suddenly, on the day the city was crowded with pilgrims who had come from afar for the Jewish Pentecost, their waiting was over and the curtain opened on Act Two of the Pentecost drama. Jesus had imparted the Spirit noiselessly at Easter, by a mere breath. Now that breath turned into a wind that came roaring out of the sky and was heard throughout Jerusalem. This was the public manifestation of the Spirit that Jesus had breathed into his apostles at Easter, the Big Bang that gave Christianity its start. With it, heaven served notice on all Jerusalem that the Spirit of God was at work in their midst.

Suddenly what appeared to be tongues of fire settled over the heads of the apostles, and soon their own tongues felt loosened. At that, they rushed out and began proclaiming the good news of Jesus Christ. All who heard them, pilgrims from distant nations as well as natives of Jerusalem, understood what they said as though it were spoken in their own language.

This was an omen of what was to come. The gospel of Jesus would spread to all nations, cross all language barriers. When the first day was over, three thousand of their listeners asked the apostles for baptism. The expansion of the Church had begun.

No New Testament event had a greater impact on history than the coming of the Spirit at Pentecost. It rocked Jerusalem, it rocked the world. The birth of Jesus had been a private affair, witnessed only by his parents and a handful of shepherds. His death on Calvary was the talk of Jerusalem for a while, but without its sequel would hardly have merited a footnote in the chronicles of mankind. As dawn broke on that Pentecost day in about the year 33 A.D., the prophet of Nazareth, as far as most people knew, was just another dead prophet whose teaching had died with him. Pentecost changed all that, transforming a tiny band of untested, ill-educated rustics, into preachers who would shake the world. Today we celebrate their first day on the job, the day the Church went public.

Turn now to Act Three of Pentecost. *When* does the action take place? Through all the centuries that have elapsed since the first outpouring of the Spirit. The Spirit is still at work. *Who* are the characters in this act? All Christians, including ourselves. We all have roles in the current Pentecost drama, for we have all received the same Spirit. *Where* is the action set? The whole world. More immediately important, our world—the church we attend, the places where we work and live.

Luke describes the beginning of Act Three of Pentecost in *Acts*, telling how the followers of Jesus fanned out, first to Samaria, then to other parts of the Roman world, bringing the gospel to Jews of the diaspora. In time Paul joined their ranks, reached out to the Gentiles, and Christianity exploded. We are all part of that explosion. The Spirit is with us still.

The Breath that Turned into a Tornado

Pentecost.

ABC: Jn. 20: 19-23.

II

Not long ago the third Person of the Trinity was almost always called the Holy Ghost. Today most people say Holy Spirit. The aptness of this title we can see in this gospel. "Spirit" means breath, and it was by breathing on his apostles on the evening of the first Easter that Jesus gave them the holy Spirit.

Breath is a sign of life. When Jesus breathed on his apostles, he roused them from their lethargy, filled them with new vitality. "As the Father has sent me, so I send you." Today we celebrate this infusion of life, the birth of the Church.

The connection between breath and life is natural. One way to determine if someone still lives is by holding a finger to the lips. That life and breath go together is also a biblical notion. In *Genesis* "God formed man out of the clay of the ground and blew into his nostrils the breath of life" *(2:7)*.

We should read the story of Jesus breathing on the apostles in light of this passage. When he breathed on them, he imparted the living presence of the third Person of the Trinity, whom we now call the holy Spirit. What happened at that moment was arguably as important as what happened when Jesus was born.

Although Jesus was soon to ascend to his Father, his Spirit did not leave them, nor has it ever left the Church they were soon to launch. Without this Spirit they would have remained powerless, mute, paralyzed with fear. With it they soon proclaimed to the people of Jerusalem the same gospel Jesus had given them; with it they also had power to bring the forgiveness of God to people who had lost his favor through sin.

The Spirit Jesus breathed into the apostles was no fiction, no mere figure of speech. If a Fourth of July orator rhapsodizes that "the spirit of our forefathers" is still alive, Americans know he is talking poetically. Washington and Jefferson breathed their last several centuries ago, and even the windiest declaimer cannot summon their dry bones back to life. But when Jesus said to his apostles, "Receive the holy Spirit," he gave them the real Person he had promised at that Last Supper, saying, "I will ask the Father and he will give you another Advocate to be with you always, the Spirit of truth" *(Jn. 14:16)*.

We usually associate the actual coming of the Spirit, not with what happened to the apostles when Jesus appeared in their midst and breathed on them only hours after rising from the dead, but with what happened seven weeks later, on Pentecost Sunday. This is described in the first reading, from the second chapter of *Acts*. The word "Pentecost" means fiftieth, and the fiftieth day after Passover was a Jewish festival long before the Christian Age. It commemorated the ascent of Moses to Mount Sinai, the event that signaled the birth of the Jewish religion.

During this celebration the apostles were together in Jerusalem, possibly in the same room where the Last Supper had taken place, wondering how on earth they could get started on the mission Jesus had given them. They had trained under him, yes. For the past three years no one had been closer to Jesus than themselves. But without his physical presence to instruct, encourage, and correct them, how could they hope to carry out his command to preach the gospel to "all nations"? Without any proven skills in preaching, how hope to preach the gospel of Jesus in the very city where mobs had recently applauded his death? As they languished in fear and self-doubt, they little suspected that on this day their period of inaction would end.

Suddenly the whole city heard a loud wind as the holy Spirit approached where the apostles were gathered. This time it was not the gentle breath of Jesus that they felt on their faces. Instead the Spirit came rushing in with a roar like that of a tornado, while tongues of fire leaped from head to head. Almost immediately they rushed out to the streets of Jerusalem to tell the story of Jesus. The Christian era had begun.

What happened at Pentecost was not a separate coming of the Spirit. The apostles had already received its fullness at Easter. But it was a separate manifestation of the Spirit's gifts, of the marvels the Spirit was to work through them. The wind was a sign of the power of their preaching, which would sweep from Jerusalem to the ends of the earth, replacing the old ways of the world with the new and good news of salvation. The tongues of fire were a sign of the newly found eloquence on the tongues of the apostles and the fire of God's love that their words would ignite. Pentecost was when they got started.

Today, then, is the birthday of our Church. Birthdays are joyous occasions, and today we should all rejoice. The Spirit that came upon the apostles still dwells in our midst.

MORE REAL THAN THE AIR WE BREATHE

Trinity Sunday.
A: Jn. 3: 16-18.

❖❖❖

Villains in the New Testament are usually either Pharisees or member of the Sanhedrin or very rich. John's gospel features one man, however, who was all three without coming close to being a villain. Nicodemus by name, he once stood up to fellow members of the Sanhedrin when they were rushing to judgment against Jesus *(7: 50-52).* After the crucifixion, he and a brother Pharisee removed the body of Jesus from the cross and laid it in the tomb *(19: 38-42).* That he was wealthy we know from the hundred pounds of costly spices he added to the burial cloths.

John also describes a visit Nicodemus once paid to Jesus by night and the query he put to him about the way to salvation. The reply Jesus gave is one of the most precious passages in Scripture. The portion in this gospel is its climax.

God so loved the world. A common mistake people make about religion is thinking it consists essentially in our quest for God, as if the business of salvation started with us. The reality, as Jesus tells Nicodemus here, is the other way around. The poet Francis Thompson put his finger on the essence of religion when he described God as a "hound of heaven" who chases us across the sharp cliffs and through the dark caverns of life. The initiative is his, not ours. Unless he loved us first, we could never love him. Our very power to love comes from God.

God showed his love the only way love can be shown, by giving. First, he created the human race, giving life itself. Next, even more marvelously, he reached out to us after we sinned by sending his only Son into the world "that the world might be saved through him." He does not compel any of us to return his love, for love is not love unless free. He invites us by pursuing us. Even if we wished, we could not escape his pursuit.

So that everyone who believes in him might not perish but might have eternal life. Why does Jesus put such stress on belief? Does just rattling off the Creed win us a pass to paradise? Is just believing an adequate return for love? Are not good works the only way we can show our love for God?

The relative importance of faith and good works was once hotly debated among theologians, one side rooting for faith, the other insisting on good works. Is Jesus here taking sides in this hoary debate? Not really. The quarrel was largely about words. Correctly understood, both sides had it right.

For a Christian, explicit and abiding faith in Jesus is the indispensable avenue to salvation. No one familiar with Scripture questions that. But Scripture also makes clear that this must be a living faith, not just arid intellectual assent. And when faith is alive, when we are convinced to the roots of our being that Jesus came from God and his words are God's will for us, faith inevitably issues in good works. Conversely, our works are salvific only when they spring from living faith. That is the kind of faith Jesus here demands from his followers.

Would we believe a doctor who told us to exercise more and eat less? We may say we do, but our words are mere air if we ignore the advice. Similarly, mouthing the Creed does not guarantee our salvation, no matter how lustily we ring out its phrases. Unless, for example, we forgive our enemies from our hearts and give alms to the poor, our Christian faith is dead.

Did Nicodemus respond to Jesus with living faith? The gospel does not say in so may words, but from what he did for Jesus on Calvary, the odds are heavy that he did. Only one filled with living faith in Jesus could show such solicitude.

At first sight this reading seems out of place for Trinity Sunday, but actually it is not. We are all in danger of regarding any discussion of the Trinity as theological hair-splitting about a medieval dogma of no concern to the ordinary Christian of today. But this passage should make us take a second look at this greatest mystery of our faith. It shows how intimately the Trinity is intertwined with our daily lives. The Trinity is not just an abstract theological proposition: three distinct persons, one God. Rather, from what Jesus said to Nicodemus, we can see how it contains the whole story of our salvation.

Salvation began when in his love for us the Father, the First Person of the Trinity, sent his only Son, the Second Person, to save our sinful race. When Jesus came he not only lived and died for us; he also left his Spirit, the Third Person, to strengthen and guide us after he was gone. We can have living faith in his word only when this Spirit dwells in us.

How three Persons can be One God our minds cannot grasp, any more than Nicodemus grasped all that Jesus said. But that the Trinity is closer to us, more real than the air we breathe, is certain. It is the reality of God's love for the world.

"UNTIL THE END OF THE AGE"

Trinity Sunday.
B: Mt. 28: 16-20.

❖ ❖ ❖

Each of the four gospels has its own style, just as each author had his own vision of Jesus. Had he been a film director, Matthew would probably have made his name with panoramic spectacles. In reading him we often sense the multinational dimensions of the gospel story, how the aspirations of Jesus extended far beyond the borders of Palestine and the inward-looking children of Israel. Matthew makes us realize that the words of Jesus were intended for the entire world.

Thus Matthew alone relates how some wise men of the orient came laden with treasures to pay homage to the infant at Bethlehem. Humble though its circumstances were, the birth of Jesus was of overwhelming importance to those travelers from afar, the first of millions of Gentiles to honor him as king.

An episode central to Matthew and which only he gives in full detail is the Sermon on the Mount. He describes how early in his career Jesus took a seat on a mountainside before a vast multitude and began to speak. In the history of human eloquence, no words have carried a weightier message or were intended for a wider audience. With a presence more commanding than the great lawgiver Moses, Jesus promulgated the new law—*his* law—by which he wanted all human conduct henceforth to be governed.

Matthew is also the only evangelist to tell us that, shortly before the close of his career, Jesus described for his followers the day of universal reckoning. Every tribe and people who ever inhabited the earth will be gathered before his throne. As lord of history he will pass judgment on all the nations of mankind and assign to every man and woman their place in eternity.

In today's reading, the conclusion of Matthew's gospel, Jesus makes his final appearance to his apostles. The setting itself is not extraordinary; it would hardly have impressed a casual observer from outer space. On a hilltop (what Matthew calls a mountain is by our standards little more than a high hill), in an insignificant corner of the Roman empire, a discredited prophet, thought by most people to be rotting in the grave, is speaking to a tiny band of die-hard disciples, none of them distinguished for learning or other accomplishments.

But listen to what Jesus says. The claims he here makes for himself and the commission he now gives to his listeners are nothing short of breathtaking. Nowhere in Scripture is the world-embracing character of his vision more forcefully stated. Looking back from twenty centuries of history, we easily miss the impact it must have had on the Eleven. To us the vision is in great part a reality. But imagine how wildly impossible a dream it seemed to the Eleven who first heard these words!

All power in heaven and on earth has been given to me. This means exactly what it says. Jesus is claiming to be nothing less than the most important human being who ever walked on earth. Ordinary titles fail to do justice his exalted position, for the power he claims is more than material. He oversees the consciences of human beings and passes judgment on their eternal destinies. No ruler in history, however deep in despotism or drunk with power, ever made a boast as sweeping as this.

Make disciples of all nations, baptizing them...teaching them to observe all that I have commanded. The tutelage of the Eleven is now over, and here for the first time Jesus outlines the magnitude of the task for which he has trained them. The prospect is staggering. This unpromising band of eleven is to do nothing less than change the course of history. As Jesus has taught and sanctified them, they must teach and sanctify others. Their message and blessing must reach out to all people.

Since it will be physically impossible for them to visit every corner of the globe and to keep teaching through the centuries, this commission implies that the Eleven will in turn commission other disciples. Thus the teaching and power of Jesus will remain alive and be handed down through all generations.

I am with you always, until the end of the age. In Matthew's first chapter an angel gives Jesus the name Emmanuel, meaning "God is with us." It is an apt name, for the Word Incarnate, the eternal Son of the Father, came to dwell with us in the person of the child born in Bethlehem. Now, at the close of his earthly stay, as he prepares to return to his Father, Jesus declares he is "with" us for keeps. His Spirit will be an abiding presence in human history, instructing and sanctifying the peoples of the world through the apostles and their successors.

On this feast of the Trinity we are as close to Jesus, and through him to the Father and the Spirit, as were the apostles on that hilltop near Jerusalem long ago. The trinity of Father, Son, and holy Spirit still fills the world.

The Relevance of the Irrelevant

Trinity Sunday.
C: Jn. 16: 12-15.

❖❖❖

As children, we learned to start and finish our prayers with the sign of the cross, invoking the Father, the Son, and the holy Spirit. Before long, we were told that these three Persons were really one God, that this one God was really three Persons, and that the name of this conundrum was the important "mystery" of the holy Trinity. Since life was already a rich garden of inexplicable mysteries, we did not balk at one more.

It never occurred to us to ask why the Trinity was deemed important. Would the world be different if there were only one Person in God? If more, why stop at three? Why not four or five?

A few years ago, the papers carried remarks by a Christian preacher appealing to students and ministers of the gospel to scrap all talk about the Trinity. Modern life, he pointed out, challenges us with problems enough—crime in the streets, nuclear arms, poverty, drugs, crooked politicians, and so on. Wouldn't we all be better off if our theologians and pastors stopped wasting their time on the Trinity and applied their considerable talents to untangling problems like these? Why bother about a doctrine that doesn't make a spark of a difference to our everyday life, a mystery even the greatest theologians have been unable to unravel? Perhaps the Trinity was a hot topic in the Middle Ages. Today it seems hopelessly irrelevant.

But is the doctrine of the Trinity really irrelevant?

On one point, at least, those who say it is are dead right. No one understands the Trinity. If anyone ever proposes to explain it, don't waste your time listening. The Church has always considered the Trinity a mystery, the most incomprehensible in our creed. Some important passages in the gospels, like this from Saint John, imply *that* there are three persons in one God, but never tell *how* this can be so.

What the Church means by a mystery is not what writers of murder mysteries mean. The whodunit does, after all, have a solution, and the clever reader who follows the clues can usually work it out. But when the Church calls an article of our faith a mystery she means that no human, however brainy, can figure it out. It goes beyond the capacity of the human intellect. We can no more comprehend it than a pigeon can the purpose of a power line or a chicken the meaning of human love.

The doctrine of the Trinity states that although God is one, there are three Persons in God, all completely distinct from one another, yet all sharing the same divine life. Our minds revolt at such a seeming absurdity. Our pride bids us refuse to acknowledge that something is true if we are incapable of ever understanding how it can be true.

Yet Jesus Christ, God's emissary on earth, told us it is true. To accept his word is to take a giant step towards acquiring the Christian virtue of humility. We thereby admit how insignificant we are, how far from God, at least as far as a pigeon is from an electrical engineer or a chicken from the emotion of human love. Infinitely farther away, in fact.

Now such an admission is very relevant. Religious wisdom, like philosophical wisdom, begins with self-knowledge. "Know thyself" is the first step towards knowing God. What we must first of all know about ourselves, if we expect ever to know anything about God or the universe he has placed us in, is how limited even the cleverest of us are. We are poor, puny, insignificant creatures. Even the best brains among us are dwarfed to sputtering ignorance in the face of eternal truth.

And here we come to the second reason for the relevance of the seemingly irrelevant Trinity. If there were no Trinity, we would hardly know anything at all about God. Saint Paul assures us that a pagan without revelation can, indeed should, come to the conviction that there is a supreme being who made and governs the universe *(Rom. 1:19-21)*. But that is all. To understand what is important to us about God we need the Second person of the Trinity, Jesus Christ. Without Jesus, God would always seem remote, unapproachable, uninterested in human affairs. But Jesus is not. His life reveals God's compassion, forgiveness, love. When we watch Jesus in action we watch God.

But Jesus, you may object, is gone. His followers no longer see him in the flesh or hear his voice. We only read about him in Scripture. How can we know that we read Scripture properly?

The answer is that we have also the third Person of the Trinity, the holy Spirit, whom this Scripture passage calls the "Spirit of truth" and who guides us "to all truth." Isn't a guide relevant? The holy Spirit dwells in the Church and will dwell there, Jesus assured us, until the end of time. Doesn't this guidance make a difference in our everyday life?

A CONGREGATION IN UPROAR

Corpus Christi.
A: Jn. 6: 51-58.

❖❖❖

Not long ago the Church switched from Latin to the vernacular at Mass and the other sacraments. About the only trace of Latin left in the liturgy is the name of the feast we celebrate today. Church authorities probably figured that the words "Corpus Christi" are too familiar and too firmly embedded in the history of the Eucharist to be abandoned.

Today the entire Catholic world proclaims its faith in the Eucharist, Corpus Christi, the Body of Christ. We believe that Jesus Christ, last seen on earth saying farewell to his apostles on a hill near Jerusalem, is still with us. In the form of bread, he comes daily to the altars of the world during the sacrifice of the Mass. We worshipers consume him as food.

Now this belief of ours—let us face the fact—is viewed by almost everyone else as an arrogant absurdity. They think it rash enough for us to say that the prophet from Nazareth was both human and divine. How can we go on to say that this God-Man has somehow been trapped in a wafer of bread? And believing this, how can we presume to eat this bread?

We should not be surprised at this incredulity. It has always been so. One day at Capernaum, according to John's gospel, Jesus gave a discourse on the Bread of Life, preparing his followers for the mystery of the Eucharist. His preaching usually stirred wonder and delight, but these words provoked anger and disbelief. Today's reading is part of that discourse.

Jesus often made statements that even his most ardent followers found hard to take. To some who heard his words that day at Capernaum, however, he seemed finally to have gone totally haywire. The claim he made, "Whoever eats this bread will live forever; and the bread that I will give is my flesh for the life of the world," was preposterous.

The congregation erupted. Was Jesus a madman? What did he mean by saying he would give them us his flesh to eat? Was he proposing that they become butchers, carve his body to pieces and serve him at table in some monstrous blood ritual?

Jesus persisted, became even more explicit. "My flesh is true food, and my blood is true drink. Whoever eats my flesh and drinks my blood remains in me and I in him." Dazed disbelief came to the eyes of many listeners. Some of his close disciples turned on their heels and walked with him no longer. Eat his flesh and drink his blood? Not even this miracle worker could convince them that God would approve so outrageous a meal.

The disciples who remained with Jesus could not fathom what he meant any more than those who abandoned him. But they knew he spoke only truth and trusted that someday he would make his meaning clear. They were right. On the night before he died, while at table with the apostles, he took bread, broke it, and said, "This is my body which will be given up for you." Next he took the cup of wine saying, "This is the cup of my blood....It will be shed for you and for all so that sins may be forgiven." At these words his apostles could at last begin to get a glimmering of what Jesus had meant that day at Capernaum when he called himself as the Bread of Life.

Among the Jews "flesh and blood" referred to the whole person. What Jesus said over the bread and wine changed what had been ordinary food and drink into himself, his whole person. But the appearance of bread and wine remained. The apostles saw Jesus reclining with them at table. But now they knew he was also *on* the table, present in the form of bread and wine, ready for them to eat and drink. To accept this as true took enormous faith, the kind only Jesus could command. But at least they now knew he was not proposing an act of cannibalism.

Jesus added, "Do this in memory of me." His followers have been doing it in his memory ever since. When the priest at Mass says, "This is my body...This is my blood" over bread and wine, Jesus Christ comes to the altar. The Mass is a re-enactment of the Last Supper, performed at the command of Jesus himself.

The early Christians gathered regularly in homes for this re-enactment. The Mass was for them, as it still is for us, the central act of Christian worship. Saint Paul once described what the Mass meant to those first century congregations: "The cup of blessing that we bless, is it not a participation in the blood of Christ? The bread that we break, is it not a participation in the body of Christ?" *(1 Cor. 10:16)*.

As bread nourishes the life of the body, the Eucharist nourishes the life of the spirit, prepares us for eternal life. Jesus said, "Whoever eats my flesh...has eternal life, and I will raise him upon the last day." This is the mystery of the Body of Christ. Today we proclaim it as our faith.

Words That Do What They Say

Corpus Christi.
B: Mk. 14: 12-16; 22-26.

❖❖❖

The word "church," comes from the Greek *kurikon* meaning "the Lord's house." Of course, people who build churches as well as those who worship in them are aware that we cannot box the Infinite in a structure of wood or stone. Lay waste all the churches in the world, and God is still, as the catechism says, everywhere. His power sustains the universe from the tiniest atom to the most distant star. We can adore him wherever we please, in a shopping mall or trans-oceanic jet as fervently as in a cathedral or parish church. His house is all around us.

From earliest times, however, members of all religions have constructed special buildings for God. We want a place where together we can sing out the praises of our Creator; or where, alone and away from the bustling streets, we can converse with him in the silence of our hearts. All religions have such houses. Moslems call them mosques, Hindus temples, Jews synagogues, and Christians churches.

For Catholics, however, a church is in a special sense the Lord's house. Somewhere in every Catholic church, on a side or main altar, is a tabernacle, a word meaning "small hut." In that hut is at least one wafer of bread that has been consecrated during a Mass. Our faith tells us that once this wafer was consecrated it was no longer bread but the Body of Christ, *Corpus Christi.* And it is this Body of Christ, dwelling in all the tabernacles of the world, that we honor today.

As liturgical feasts go, Corpus Christi is relatively young, dating back only to the thirteenth century. From almost the day after the first Pentecost, of course, Christians obeyed the command of Christ by coming together, especially on Sundays, to re-enact what he did at the Last Supper, as we still do every time we assemble for Mass. We also give special honor to the Eucharist on Thursday of Holy Week, when we hear Paul's account of what he had learned about the Last Supper *(1 Cor. 11: 23-26).*

Holy Week, however, is mostly a time for sorrowing. Its ceremonies focus on the sufferings of Jesus during his Passion. The feast of Corpus Christi, on the other hand, was instituted so that we could reflect on the joyful aspect of the Eucharist. The word

"Eucharist" means "good gift" or "splendid favor." Today we rejoice in this gift, the splendid favor Jesus bequeathed to his followers followers on the night before he died.

The Eucharist is not a permanent memorial to Jesus in the same way a graveyard monument is a memorial to a dead person. In the Eucharist Jesus gave us his *living* self. That is what Body of Christ, *Corpus Christi*, means. Jesus called the bread he distributed to his apostles his "body," and the wine he passed around to them his "blood." Neither term was used in its narrow, physical sense. To the Hebrews of old a person's "body and blood" meant the whole person, physical and spiritual, body and soul.

Thus what Jesus meant when he said to his apostles "This is my body" and "This is my blood" was that the bread and wine were no longer bread and wine, but himself. He was now present to them in two ways: as a man with visible features, standing before them, speaking to them; and as a man in disguised form, under the appearance of bread and wine.

The Eucharist, therefore, is a deep mystery. What Jesus distributed a*ppeared* to be bread. The wafers in our tabernacles and distributed at Communion also *appear* to be bread. To a scientist, who deals only with empirically verifiable phenomena, they *are* bread. To the person of faith, however, who knows the story of what Jesus did at the Last Supper and who relies on two thousand years of devotion to this sacrament, they are not bread. What appears to be so is not so. The reality is that Jesus Christ is present. How, we know not. But he is there.

In the fourteenth century Catholics began to celebrate the feast of Corpus Christi with huge outdoor processions. The Eucharist was carried in a monstrance through the streets while crowds sang out their gratitude that Jesus Christ was housed in their midst. Even today, although in most places secularists have succeeded in ridding the environment of any traces of the divine, Corpus Christi processions have not entirely died out. I once witnessed one threading through the narrow streets of Valleta in Malta. On the campus of the University of Nigeria, I have joined hundreds of students and staff as they marched through the winding lanes singing praise to the Eucharist.

Even without a public procession, however, we can join all those voices from the past and sing out to the Eucharist on this feat of Corpus Christi. In our own house of God, in the hut that we call the tabernacle, Jesus Christ still dwells in the form of bread. He is neighbor to us all.

PILGRIMS HUNGRY FOR THE LORD

Corpus Christi.
C: Lk. 9: 11-17.

❖❖❖

At first sight this gospel seems out of place. Today the Church honors the Holy Eucharist, using the title *Corpus Christi*, Latin for Body of Christ. What does the feeding of a horde of first century Hebrews have to do with the consecrated bread that is passed around at Mass with the words, "Body of Christ"?

The French have a saying that hunger is the main ingredient of a good meal. If so, then the meal served in this gospel, sparse though it seems by modern standards, must have been a feast for the Israelites lucky enough to partake of it. Although far from starvation, they had taken nothing to eat since morning. As evening drew near, their stomachs started churning. But they were in such an out-of-the-way place that relief seemed out of the question. Imagine, then, the murmur of astonishment that rumbled through their ranks as the apostles passed among them with their generous giveaway of loaves and fishes.

The apostles themselves, however, were even more astonished. They knew how little food had been at hand when Jesus issued his command to feed the crowd—a mere five loaves and two fishes. After the last of the five thousand had eaten their fill, even the apostles must have gasped with disbelief as they collected the fragments. Twelve baskets full of leftovers!

The early Christians had no difficulty seeing the connection between this incident and the Eucharist. To them the story of the apostles distributing loaves to the multitude was prophetic, a preview of the Eucharist that was to come. Sometimes in a movie one scene dissolves into another, and then that scene into a third. Imagine the scene that Luke here describes dissolving into two later scenes: first the Last Supper, with Jesus passing morsels of bread and a cup of wine into the hands of his apostles; then the Sacrifice of the Mass, with worshipers surging forth to receive consecrated bread at Communion time.

That the early Christians saw similarities among these scenes is clear from the words Scripture uses to describe them. Before feeding the multitude, Jesus *said the blessing* over the loaves, *broke* them, then *gave* them to his apostles. Almost identical words are used in the gospel accounts of the Last Supper; and from the first century to today similar words have been repeated by the priest at the Consecration of the Mass.

What do the three scenes have in common? Not just bread as food, but bread as food for hungry travelers, sustenance for people on a journey.

Those who received the loaves and fishes from the apostles were travelers. They had been on the move since early morning, searching for Jesus. After finding him, they had passed the afternoon listening to him preach and watching him heal. So absorbed had they been that they almost forgot their need for food. But Jesus realized their plight, knew they still had miles to go before finding a place to rest and satisfy their hunger. The food he gave them would keep them strong for the journey.

The apostles who received the bread and wine from Jesus on the night before he died were also travelers. They had been on the road ever since he invited them to leave their homes and tramp with him through Palestine, proclaiming the good news of God's kingdom. Now they were about to set out on their last and most challenging journey. Jesus would soon leave them, and it would be their task to preach his gospel through the world.

What did Jesus give them for nourishment? Not material bread, but himself under the appearance of bread. To the Israelites in biblical times the word "body" referred, not just to the flesh, but to the whole person. The words of Jesus, "This my body," meant "This is myself." He will be the bread to sustain them during their future wanderings as preachers of the gospel.

All who receive Jesus today under the form of bread are travelers passing through this world to eternity. In the hymn written for today's Mass by Saint Thomas Aquinas, the Eucharist is called "pilgrim's food." A pilgrimage is not just any journey, but one to a holy place for a holy purpose; and that is how a Christian views the journey of life.

We travel through this world with a goal, to dwell with Jesus Christ in his heavenly court for eternity. Through the Eucharist Jesus becomes our traveling companion as well as our goal. Among our other companions are the men and women, wayfarers from all over the world, who also receive the Body of Christ.

With them we form one vast pilgrimage, all feasting, not on bread to nourish our bodies, but bread to nourish our souls. Our hunger is real, our need for spiritual nourishment urgent. Most of us still have miles to go before we can rest. Only a fool would refuse this pilgrim's food, the Body of Christ.

PARTY-POOPERS

Tenth Sunday in Ordinary Time.
A: Mt. 9: 9-13.

This passage describes a going-away party. Matthew, the tax collector of Capernaum, had invited his friends to his house to say good-by. He was bidding farewell to Capernaum as his home and to tax collecting as his occupation. From now on his career would be nomadic, following Jesus wherever he went.

Many of his friends must have been stunned. Tax collectors, and Matthew was no exception, had little reputation for piety. Their profession was so notoriously corrupt that they were barred even from setting foot in a synagogue. Ever since he had started listening to the prophet from Nazareth, however, Matthew had been a man under a spell. Before long he told his friends of his intention to chuck everything and become one of the apostles.

The decision was not entirely Matthew's. No one joined that band of close companions to Jesus without being beckoned by Jesus himself. While Matthew had been busy watching Jesus as he preached, Jesus had been just as busy observing Matthew as he listened. Something in Matthew attracted Jesus, something he knew would be a help in the spreading of the gospel. And so one day he stopped at Matthew's tax booth and with a voice both firm and friendly said, "Follow me." At once Matthew bounded up from his seat, walked away from his money table, and took his place alongside the other apostles.

Soon Matthew invited some friends to his home to celebrate his new mode of life. Like all tax collectors he was well off, and his house well equipped for a party. We can picture him beaming with delight as he led Jesus and the apostles around his courtyard, introducing them one by one to his other guests.

Unfortunately, his delight did not last long. Some Pharisees heard the din, looked in at the gathering, and proceeded to create an ugly scene. These meddlers were indignant, not at Matthew (a tax collector was beneath their contempt), but at Jesus. They approached some of his disciples and exploded with indignation. Why was their leader, they demanded, gracing this party with his presence? Didn't he know who these people were? Matthew was a lawbreaker, a sinner. So were his other guests. Merely to sit at table with these dregs of society was a scandal.

The Pharisees had good reason to think ill of Matthew. Tax collectors were not only collaborators, agents of imperial Rome; they were crooks who lined their pockets with money they extorted from fellow Jews, amassing fortunes through fraud and chicanery. All decent people shunned them.

What lesson ought we draw from this incident? Certainly not that we should imitate Matthew by opening our homes to the modern equivalent of the people at Matthew's table, that we extend our hospitality to a drug dealer or two, perhaps some racketeers and corrupt politicians. No, the lesson is simpler. It is implicit in the explanation of his conduct Jesus gave the Pharisees, "I did not come to call the righteous but sinners."

The fault of the Pharisees was not that they abhorred sin. Sin cannot be abhorred too strenuously. Their fault was that in their self-righteousness they failed to see that they too were sinners, with as much need for the compassion of Jesus an any mortal. As long as they considered themselves morally superior to people like those at Matthew's party, however, they could never be objects of that compassion. A physician cannot heal all who are sick, only those who come in for healing.

If their reason for shunning the kind of people at Matthew's party was that they could not endure scurrilous talk or that they feared they would themselves be enticed into sin, they cannot be faulted. But their reason was that they thought they were truly better than these others. Perhaps in many respects they were, but this was not for them to decide. Only God knows the heart. We are all sinners. Self-righteousness, however, the conviction that one is freer than others from sin, is an especially dangerous sin. The self-righteous person feels no need for repentance and therefore cannot repent.

An underlying difference between the Pharisees and the company at Matthew's party was that the Pharisees were socially respectable, welcome in the best of circles, while the others were outcasts. The sins of the Pharisees were overlooked by the powerful and the trend-setters of the day (as, unfortunately, many of the most serious sins still are). Between respectability and genuine goodness, however, is an ocean of difference, an ocean the Pharisees knew nothing about. Neither do many of the most respectable people today.

It is a difference we must all learn—if we want one day to be welcomed at the everlasting party where Jesus and Matthew and the other apostles will be present to greet us.

“HE IS OUT OF HIS MIND”

Tenth Sunday in Ordinary Time.
B: Mk. 3: 20-35.

This passage finds Jesus in Capernaum at the peak of his popularity. The house where he is staying, probably Peter’s, has been invaded by a crowd so dense that he and his disciples have scarcely space to eat. But not all in the crowd have come to cheer. Some kinfolk from Nazareth are present, hoping to entice him back home. Others, scribes who have come all the way from Jerusalem, are determined to denounce him as a fraud.

Mark tells us that the “relatives” of Jesus want to “seize” him. These relatives, we later learn, consist of his mother along with some brothers and sisters. The mother we know, but who are these brothers and sisters? Probably some cousins from Nazareth. The words “brother” and “sister” did not have the same narrow meaning for the ancient Jews as they do for us. Any close relative would fit. Those who have lived in Asia or Africa know that to this day a “brother” there can be anyone from a sibling to a fourth cousin or even a fellow villager.

News of the kind of the kind of vagabond life Jesus has been leading has filtered back to Nazareth, the town where he grew up. The reports are disturbing enough to prompt his people to wonder if he has gone “out of his mind,” that is, turned into an unbalanced religions fanatic. To rescue him from what they consider an ill-chosen and possibly ill-fated career is why these Nazarenes have journeyed the twenty or so miles from Nazareth. Their intentions are all for the best.

What they find at Capernaum convinces them that the carpenter’s son they once knew well is in dire need of help. He is overworked, surrounded by strangers, and without regular meals or sleep. And so they are intent on using force if necessary to bring him back with them to Nazareth. There he can find decent employment and live in peace and privacy among his own. The presence of his mother among these relatives is proof that their motive is not malicious.

Jesus, however, knows what he is doing. Since his baptism he has been on a mission for his Father, the mission he was born for. His ties to the people he grew up with at Nazareth, much as he reveres them, cannot be allowed to steer him off course. And so he declares to all present that he now has a new family, that anyone who "does the will of God" is henceforth his "brother and sister and mother." One day this family will include you and me and the millions of others in his Church. We are all brothers and sisters to him and to one another. To prepare for this extended family he must say no to the offers of protection even from his nearest and dearest.

Another group is in Capernaum, having journeyed from Jerusalem to conduct an inquiry into Jesus, the would-be prophet who has been attracting crowds throughout Galilee. These men are scribes, trained experts in Jewish religion, the theologians of Palestine. They have now completed their investigation, and to whoever cares to listen they announce their verdict. Jesus, they have found, is a fake. His so-called cures and other marvels have nothing to do with the God of Israel. They are the works Beelzebub, prince of devils, in whose clutches Jesus is.

Jesus demolishes this calumny with ease. If the devil is working through him, then the devil is a paper tiger indeed. Only a bungling, butterfingered devil would undermine the devil's own cause by performing the works Jesus has performed. No one who beholds his works or listens to his words can honestly conclude that he is not on God's side and God not on his.

Jesus goes on to accuse these scribes of blaspheming against the holy Spirit, a sin that "will never have forgiveness." He does not say God *cannot* forgive this sin, a notion that is patently absurd. Those who use the term "unforgivable sin" in discussing this passage are misreading the words. What Jesus says is that God *will not* forgive those who after seeing his works persist in saying he is in league with the devil. To investigate Jesus as the scribes have done and still call him an agent of Satan, to be in the presence of the Light of the World and call him darkness, is the blackest blasphemy. Such blasphemers, Jesus foresees, will refuse even the grace of final repentance.

These words are a warning against mushy Christianity. Jesus never fostered the notion that in the end all malice will melt away, all vice turn out to be virtue in disguise. That view of life is sentimental rot. Whoever is determined to do so can escape the net of God's mercy. All one has to do is behold good and call it evil, taste vice and pronounce it virtue.

That is how Satan fell from grace. That is how the scribes and Pharisees came to reject and ultimately murder Jesus. Any man or woman who wishes to do so is free to follow their path.

A Mother's Tears

Tenth Sunday in Ordinary Time.
C: Lk. 7: 11-17.

❖❖❖

All funerals are sad. But the funeral procession that Jesus met near the town of Nain was gripped by a threefold sadness: the corpse was of a man who had died in the bloom of youth; he was an only son; and his mother was a widow. Pity for this weeping mother welled up in the heart of Jesus. He was no Stoic, nor did he counsel his followers to stifle their emotions. Where nature called for tears, like most people he let them flow.

That is why the words Jesus spoke to the mother, "Do not weep," must have struck the onlookers as unnatural. Why should the mother not weep? Only in view of what followed did these words make sense. As the incarnate Son of God, Jesus had power over life and death, and now he intended to use that power to the full. The widow's tears need flow no longer.

Usually Jesus waited for some outward request before exercising his mastery over sickness or death. This was early in his career, however, and the people of Nain had probably not yet set eyes on him or heard of the wonders he had already performed elsewhere. But once they saw him touch the young man's litter and return the son to his mother, they hailed him as a mighty prophet. A new and glorious age had dawned for Israel.

Heart-warming though this episode is, a modern Christian might wonder what message it holds for our time. Those whom Jesus called back from the sleep of death were few. The gospels mention only three, although in his wanderings through Palestine he must have beheld dozens of funerals as pitiful as the one featured here. And certainly no one attending a Christian funeral today, not even the most fervent believer, expects the corpse to spring from the coffin and start comforting the grieving mourners. Perhaps our prayers are not powerful enough. Whatever the reason, the age for that sort of miracle seems to be over.

And yet the story of the widow of Nain and her restored son does have a lesson for all generations. By its vivid picture of Jesus as the Lord of all creation with absolute power over the here and the hereafter, it reminds Christians of what should be their habitual way of thinking about death. Here is a litmus test for Christians. Their attitude towards death, like their love for one another, should mark them off from pagans.

To the pagan, death is the final curtain. Once it closes, nothing follows but total annihilation; on the other side of the grave stretches unbroken oblivion. How profoundly this attitude towards death affects one's attitude towards life is evident to anyone who scans our daily headlines or walks our city streets. To the pagan, only the here and now, with whatever pleasures one finds ripe for plucking, counts. To the Christian, life on this side of the grave counts also, but mostly as prelude. The visible world is the vestibule of eternity.

What is death to a Christian? Look at the Church's liturgy. In one of the acclamations after the Consecration we declare that Jesus *destroyed* death; and a Sunday Preface states flatly that he *freed* us from death. What can such affirmations mean? Christians are as subject to death as other mortals; no human is free from its clutches. Baptism bestows no elixir to ward off aging, disease, decay, and ultimate dissolution.

Elsewhere the liturgy puts its meaning clearly. The death Jesus freed us from was what the pagans mean by death, that is, "unending death" (Sunday Preface II). God did not destine us for the unending death of annihilation or eternal damnation. The first optional Preface for use at a funeral Mass puts this idea in unforgettable terms: because Christ rose from the dead, "The sadness of death gives way to the bright promise of immortality...When the body of our earthly dwelling lies in death, we gain an everlasting dwelling place in heaven."

Since this is our faith, some may wonder if it is not unchristian to be sad at the funeral of a friend or dear one who has lived a good life. Should not the words of Jesus, "Do not weep," apply to us? Will he not raise the one we have lost as surely as he did the widow's son? Our tears at the death of a loved one—let us face it—are largely for ourselves. We feel sorry because of the loss we have suffered. Should not this sorrow be cancelled out by our Christian hope that the deceased has reached or will soon pass to eternal glory?

In a completely logical world, yes. But we are not logic machines, any more than Jesus was a Stoic. What God asks is, not that we Christians never weep at death, but that we never shed tears of despair. We may have lost someone dearer than all the world, and the ache may take years to heal. But our eyes of faith should be on the Lord of Life and his "bright promise of immortality" on the other side of the grave.

FIELDS STILL READY FOR HARVEST

Eleventh Sunday in Ordinary Time.
A: Mt. 9: 36-10: 8.

❖❖❖

"Say it with pictures" has been a slogan for journalists and admen since the invention of photography. But long before the first camera clicked, preachers and politicians were in on the secret. The best of them were skilled at painting pictures with words, verbal images that delivered their message instantly and effortlessly. Not surprisingly, Jesus was a master of the technique. When he spoke, however lofty the subject, images came tumbling from his lips. This passage has two of his best.

A crowd of Galileans has assembled, and as Jesus scans their faces his heart wells up with pity. The first image he finds to sum up the sight is a herd of sheep without a shepherd—lost, confused, and angered by wolves. Just so does Jesus view the spiritual plight of these Galileans. Their religious leaders, the legalistic scribes and the proud Pharisees, have left them untended. If only they could all hear the good news that the kingdom of heaven is at hand! If only they all had shepherds to guide them to their true home!

The second picture is a field teeming with wheat, radiant in the sun and just waiting to be reaped. Harvest time has arrived, but the field hands are few. Only a scattering of them stoop in the noonday heat, collecting what they can of the abundant crop. More harvesters must be found, sturdy and willing laborers, or much of the remaining wheat will wither and die.

These images are prelude to what follows. Turning to his followers, Jesus picks out twelve, summoning each by name. These will be the shepherds of his flock, the laborers in his field.

Why twelve? The number was sacred to the ancient Israelites. The chosen people was composed of twelve tribes, each sprung from one of the twelve sons of the patriarch Jacob. By settling on the same number Jesus indicates that from these twelve he wants his Church, God's people of the new covenant, to spring.

To the Twelve, after Jesus himself, our Church owes its origin. So important did his followers consider this exact number that after the defection of Judas the remaining eleven felt obliged to fill his empty slot. It had to be with someone who, like themselves, had been in the company of Jesus from his baptism to his resurrection. The story of how they elected Matthias to this post is told in the first chapter of *Acts*.

Why were the Twelve called apostles? The word "apostle" means someone who is "sent." It is sometimes rendered as "messenger," a good translation as long as we realize these apostles were more than mere mailmen delivering a sealed letter from Jesus Christ. They were rather his fully accredited proxies, empowered to speak and labor in his name, sent not merely to declare that the kingdom of God was at hand, but actually to make that kingdom visible by their own presence in the world. When Jesus told them to cure the sick and raise the dead, he meant more than bodily ills. They must battle above all against the diseases and demons that attack the soul, the leprosy and spiritual death of sin.

In this reading Jesus tells the Twelve to limit their labors to lost sheep of Israel, those in the surrounding towns and villages of Galilee. This is merely a training mission, a warm-up session to get them in trim for the main event. Their definitive commissioning will not take place until after the Resurrection, when Jesus will send them to "all nations," with a promise to remain with them until the end of time *(Mt. 28: 29-30)*.

Who have inherited the mission of the Twelve today? Strictly speaking, the successors of the apostles, those officially empowered to shepherd Christ's flock, are our bishops. But the bishops cannot do this job alone. They need co-workers alongside them. These must come, not just from the ranks of priests and nuns, but from all the faithful, all parents and parishioners. As all Israelites were heirs of the twelve sons of Jacob, all Christians are spiritual descendants of the Twelve apostles.

Imagine Jesus gazing at the hordes of humanity alive today, just as he did on the Galileans in this gospel. What does he see? In most places, confusion and bewilderment, shepherdless sheep. The fields are still ready for harvest, but laborers are still too few. His Church needs, not just more parishioners, but parishioners willing to labor alongside their priests.

The key images in this reading are the shepherdless sheep and the field teeming with wheat. But the key word is "laborers." Warm bodies are not enough to tend Christ's flock and gather his harvest. The Church today needs bodies not afraid of hard work. All are called to the field. No baptized child of God is exempt. Pray that the harvest master send us true laborers.

TWO BASIC LESSONS IN AGRICULTURE

Eleventh Sunday in Ordinary Time.
B: Mk. 4: 26-34.

❖❖❖

Here are two of the shortest parables ever uttered by Jesus. Both have a rustic setting, but this need not discourage those of us who have never lived on a farm. Even if our experience of country things has been limited to watching plants sprout in flower pots, we have all the agricultural expertise we need.

Together the parables make two points.

The first is that the process of growth, slow and mysterious, is essentially out of the hands of the planter. The farmer scatters the seed and gathers the harvest, but it is Nature—another name for God—that keeps the seed alive and growing. The second is that the size to which things grow often exceeds all expectations. From tiny seeds bumper crops and massive trees come into being. The mustard seed, the tiniest in Palestine, grew into a bush that towered high as a tree.

In themselves there was nothing profound or surprising in these ideas. They were garden-variety platitudes for the peasants to whom the parables were originally addressed. For them the cycle of planting and reaping was an annually recurring miracle that must have long since lost its power to amaze.

Jesus did not, however, intend these parables as a refresher course in crop science. His real subject was the kingdom of God. To bring that kingdom to mankind, to help the children of Adam live by God's rule and thereby prepare for an eternity in God's heavenly mansions, was the mission of Jesus. That is why he founded a Church and entrusted it to his apostles.

These parables are above all about this Church, the visible instrument of God's kingdom or earth. Before ascending to his Father, Jesus promised to remain in the world until the end of time *(Mt. 28: 20)*. It is by his living presence in his Church and therefore in human history that he has kept that promise.

If Jesus were not present in the Church, all the labors of its members would be futile and all its visible trappings turn to dust. Church buildings are important, of course, as are the tedious hours that both clergy and laity put into them. Every diocese needs its busy chancellery, just as the entire Church needs the humming activity of the Vatican. But these are no more what keeps the Church alive and growing than the farmer and his equipment are what keep crops alive and growing. The main business of the Church, like the main business that goes on in a farm or in a flower pot, is out of human hands.

This does not mean we might just as well call quits to our labors and leave the future of the Church to God's care alone. But it does confirm the old truth that while we should work as industriously as we would if everything depended in ourselves, we should never forget that the success of the Church's enterprise depends ultimately on the presence of Jesus in our midst. He alone keeps the Church alive and growing.

Look at the Church today, see how she has fulfilled the prophesy of growth implicit in the image of the mustard seed. She is huge beyond the wildest dreams of the apostles, and her branches hold people from all over the world. That the Church Jesus founded has weathered the centuries and reached out to all mankind is now part of history. One of the first hints that this would come to pass was this parable of the mustard seed.

The Church is not, however, just another multinational company. What sets her apart is that her aim is to enrich mankind spiritually rather than materially, to promote God's glory rather than the wealth of nations. This means she is radically different from any business conglomerate, as different as a human being from a house or a cat from a computer. The secret of her continuance is that she is alive. Running through her veins is the divine life of Jesus Christ, the source of all her spiritual strength. He alone gives her power to grow, despite assaults from without and inevitable corruption from within.

When I was in the seminary one of our teachers used to make a big issue of the corruption that has plagued the Church throughout history. Far from being reason for dismissing the Church as a merely human organization, he insisted, this corruption is the most convincing vindication of her claim to enjoy the continued presence of Jesus Christ. His point was that no organization that relied on merely human efforts could have survived the fits of incompetence and downright depravity that have periodically afflicted leaders of the Church since the beginning.

This may seem an odd way to argue for the supernatural credentials of the Catholic Church. But give some thought to these parables and it makes sense. The seed, not the farmer, is what counts. And the seed that gave birth and still gives life to the Church is none other than Jesus Christ.

THE PARTY-CRASHER

Eleventh Sunday in Ordinary Time.
C: Lk. 7: 36-8: 3 (or 7: 36-50).

❖❖❖

Imagine having Jesus Christ as a dinner guest! Wouldn't just sharing a meal with him brighten our lives, make us better people? Scripture paints him as a person of radiant charm who with a word could captivate, comfort, heal, or uplift; the kind of person in whose presence almost everyone grew more gracious.

Almost. One exception was Simon the Pharisee, whose story belongs in a Guiness Book of wasted opportunities. Why this paragon of self-righteousness invited Jesus to his home in the first place is hard to fathom. Perhaps he hoped to impress the other guests by hosting this much-touted holy man, the most celebrated rabbi in Palestine, at his table. Jesus was now at the peak of his fame. Everywhere he attracted crowds who hailed him as a holy prophet and were electrified by his preaching.

Much as he prized Jesus as a conversation piece, however, Simon himself did not revere him as a holy man. See the shabby way he greeted him, omitting the usual signs of courtesy—the kiss of peace, the anointing with oil, the washing of feet. Simon did not expect to learn anything about holiness from this carpenter's son. Holiness, after all, was the specialty of the Pharisees. The very word "Pharisee" meant "separated one," for they thought they belonged to a breed of humanity higher than the unholy mass of common sinners.

Before the meal was over, however, Jesus showed Simon that even a notorious sinner can become holier than a Pharisee. The dinner was held in Simon's courtyard, where the guests reclined Roman-fashion at low table. Such gatherings often attracted intruders from the townsfolk, gate-crashers who liked to listen to the learned conversation. Suddenly a ruckus erupted behind Jesus. A woman from among the intruders knelt at his feet, bathing them with her tears and drying them with her hair.

Luke says she was "known in the town as a sinner," code words for a woman who made a living by selling her flesh. Most Israelites abhorred prostitution, ostracizing its practitioners. Not all, of course, were so fastidious; the Bible contains ample evidence that sexual delinquency was not unknown among the Chosen People. Their society as a whole, however, had much we can admire in this regard, and not just in the lesser role sex played in individual lives. More important, their public opinion did not condone sexual license, still less glorify it, but saw it as the personal and social cancer it truly is.

The woman in the gospel had come to realize the cancerous enormity of her sins. The preaching of Jesus had made her eager to make up for the past and return to God's favor. To those with no tolerance for loud emotional scenes, her conduct may smack of vulgar ostentation. But in fact it was a courageous act of public reparation for a career of public sin.

Simon, however, was not pleased. Note that he does not voice his displeasure. But looks can speak as severely as words, and we can well imagine the look of disgust on the face of this "separated one" when the elegant decorum of his dinner party was disrupted by the rude blubbering and wailing from this woman of the street. He also saw the incident as proof positive that Jesus was a fraud. If he were truly a holy man, would not Jesus order this unholy monstrosity out of his sight? How could he bear even to be touched by her?

Jesus knew Simon's thoughts. His rebuke is as timely today as when Pharisaism flourished.

Mankind is not divided, as the Pharisees thought, into sinners and non-sinners. We are all sinners. Some, however, admit their failures and seek God's forgiveness. These are the loving ones, like the woman Simon scorned. God rewards their love by remitting all their debts, however huge. Others are convinced they owe no serious debts to God and feel no need for forgiveness, no urge to return to God. These are the smug, self-righteous ones. Like Simon and all the Pharisees of this world, little is forgiven them, because their love is so small.

It is by no means certain that the sins of Simon and his tribe are trivial when compared with those of the sinful woman. Pharisaical sins are not as offensive to public decency. But pride is fouler than promiscuity, more harmful to the soul. For all we know, the snobbery in the houses of the elite cries out for divine vengeance more stridently than the raucous conduct of the slums. If Jesus lived among us, where would he feel more at home?

At Mass we are guests at a banquet hosted by Jesus. Let it not be a wasted opportunity. The greatest saints did not think their debts to God where trivial. Neither should we. Love of God means owning up to these debts, making amends, starting over again. Only those as smug as Simon refuse to do that.

THE SMILE ON THE FACE OF THE MARTYRS

Twelfth Sunday in Ordinary Time.
A: Mt. 10: 26-33.

❖❖❖

"Do not be afraid of them." Who are the "them" the apostles are not to be afraid of? In the previous passage Jesus warns his apostles of persecutions to come. "Them," then, refers to the persecutors—wolves, Jesus calls them, among whom his followers will seem mere sheep *(10: 16)*. Informers will denounce his followers, courts condemn them, synagogue leaders scourge them, rulers harass them, family members consign them to death. "You will be hated by all because of my name."

If Jesus has himself been rejected by the rulers in his own land of Israel, how can the apostles expect a friendly welcome from the strangers to whom they will bring his gospel? But let not the fear of persecution muzzle them in their preaching. What Jesus has taught them in the seclusion of Galilee, they are to proclaim from the housetops of the world.

The early Christians must have pored over every word of today's reading. With this warning in mind, they could hardly have been surprised that their history was written in blood. The first in their long litany of martyrs, the deacon Stephen, met death at the hands of fellow Israelites, the same cabal of high priests and elders that once sentenced Jesus to death. How Stephen courted martyrdom by his fiery preaching before the Sanhedrin was a treasured memory among early Christians. It is told in the sixth and seventh chapters of *Acts*.

Once Christianity started to filter throughout the rest of the Roman empire, persecutions began in earnest. Why this was so is no mystery. The Roman Empire was steeped in paganism. Such Christian values as humility, turning the other cheek, and faithfulness to a single spouse would strike the average pagan as pietistic pabulum, fit fodder for babes and weaklings. The notion that there is only one God who deserves our total allegiance, the doctrine of the cross all with its corollary that salvation is possible only through sacrifice—how could these be welcomed by people brought up to worship a whole cartload of gods who themselves indulged in the grossest sensuality?

The first of the general persecutions took place at Rome in 64 A.D. under the notorious emperor Nero. It was then that both Peter and Paul gave their lives, Peter according to tradition by crucifixion, Paul by beheading. How many more Christians forfeited their lives for the faith during the next 250 years no one knows. One historian puts their number close to 100,000.

Mass martyrdom by no means ceased with the end of the Roman Empire or at the borders of Europe. During the sixteenth and seventeenth centuries, even faraway Japan caught the fever. As many as forty thousand Japanese Christians, mostly converts, chose death over apostasy. The church has never lacked heroes.

Stories abound about the joy that lit the face of martyrs as they surrendered their lives for Christ. In the third century the deacon Lawrence, reputedly roasted on a gridiron like a piece of meat, is said to have lightheartedly asked his torturers to turn him over, as he was sufficiently cooked on one side.

That tale is probably legend, but there is no doubt about Thomas More's mood when King Henry VIII had him executed for refusing to bow to Henry's claim of sovereignty over the Church in England. Witnesses describe how More exchanged pleasantries with the executioner just before placing his head on the chopping block. But his final words were both in dead earnest and defiant—"I am the king's good servant, but God's first."

Miguel Pro was a young priest in Mexico when the authorities waged a campaign against the Church. His refusal to give in was an affront they could not tolerate. Finally captured, he faced the firing squad with a shout of triumphant defiance, "Long live Christ the King!" He knew whose was the winning aside.

It seems blasphemy to mention the petty price we must pay to remain Christians in the same breath as the sufferings of these martyrs. But even though it is unlikely that any of us will have to choose between Christ and the preservation of our skin, we all face choices: Christ or physical comfort, Christ or popularity with our peers, Christ or the approval of the trend-setters who decree where the world stands on moral issues. Paganism is not dead; it has just changed tactics. Instead of attacking the gospel head-on, it either ignores it or ridicules it. The result can be as daunting to the Christian as a firing squad or the prospect of being cooked on a gridiron.

Either by our conduct we acknowledge before men our allegiance to Christ or by our silence we disown him. If we let fear determine where we stand, he will disown us. May God give us a drop of the joyful defiance that marked his martyrs. May we never forget that ours is ultimately the winning side.

"MAYDAY!"

Twelfth Sunday in Ordinary Time.
B: Mk. 4: 35-41.

The catechism in use when I was a child described Jesus as "true God and true man." While doctrinally sound, this catechism was, for children at least, a miserable volume—no stories, no dialogue, no pictures. If we wanted two gospel scenes to illustrate the two parts of this answer, the humanity and the divinity of Jesus, we could find none better than the key scenes of this gospel: first, Jesus asleep in the fishing boat, his humanity visible to all; next, Jesus commanding the storm to relent its fury, a command any man could utter, but only God, lord of Nature, could both utter and make stick.

Together these scenes make the episode of the storm on the lake one of the most theologically significant, as well as personally consoling, in the New Testament. Watch it unfold.

As professional fishermen who made their living on the Sea of Galilee, the apostles were no strangers to its moods. The voyage described in this gospel could not have been the first that saw them sail out on a surface smooth as glass and in a short while plunge without warning into trouble. These waters were, and still are, famous for squalls that come suddenly out of nowhere and just as suddenly turn to calm. The only explanation for the shrill alarm of the apostles on this occasion is that this was, even for this lake, a freak storm, unusually ferocious. They had probably never run into its equal.

As they saw the waves cascading over the sides of their craft, terror seized them. These apostles were realists, not prone to panic. They knew that unless the tempest soon subsided, their bark was certain to sink and all in it likely to drown.

Through it all, Jesus was in the stern, serenely slumbering on a cushion. The stern was the place of honor in the small crafts of antiquity. As the revered leader of the apostles, it was natural that Jesus be placed there; natural, too, that he should initially fall into deep sleep, for he was bone-weary from a day of preaching parables to the multitude at the lakeside. What seemed eerily unnatural was that he could remain so utterly dead to the world once the storm had struck. To the first shouts of the apostles he made no response at all.

Their final outcry, "Teacher, do you not care that we are perishing?" betrayed not just frustration at the fury of the sea, but exasperation with the sleeping Jesus. He seemed indifferent to the disaster that loomed. They had often seen him rescue others in distress; he did not hesitate to heal the crippled, cleanse lepers, restore sight to the blind. Why did he not now display a similar concern for his friends in their hour of need? Was he going to allow these loyal and loving disciples to perish? Was he about to perish himself?

Since they first joined their fortunes to those of Jesus, the apostles had felt they were living in a dream. With this worker of wonders on their side, what misfortune could befall them? Now, suddenly, their enchanted world seemed about to fall apart. Soon they would all be engulfed in the waves.

Sound familiar? I do not mean, have you ever been literally trapped in a boat that seemed about to sink, but have you ever felt you were caught in a spiritual storm comparable to the physical storm that swooped down on the apostles? That the temptations assaulting you were beyond your power to resist? That your years of Catholic upbringing had been reduced to ashes?

Or have you ever felt that, not you alone, but the entire Church and all it stood for were being swept away? That the evil in society was overwhelming the good? Worst of all, that God, if there was a God, was fast asleep, that he did not care?

We would not be human if such dark moods never came over us, sometimes like a storm out of the blue. That is why the climax of this gospel is worth burning into our memory. When things were at their worst and total shipwreck seemed certain, Jesus stood erect in the pitching craft and rebuked the wind and the waves with the word, "Quiet!"—the same word he once used to silence a demon and send him scurrying away *(Mk. 1:25)*.

The disciples had never had doubts about the humanity of Jesus. Now, after watching him quell the storm with a word, their awareness of his divinity began to take shape. They eyed him with awe. "Who then is this whom even wind and sea obey?" When the demon of despair threatens, we should recall this scene. It can do for us what it has always done for Christians—remind us of who the man in the stern really is. Jesus is Lord of all.

"Do you not yet have faith?" Jesus asked. The faith the apostles needed is what we too need in time of spiritual upheaval, faith in the old catechism answer: that Jesus, truly man, is also truly God. If we call, he will calm the storm.

THE PRICE HIS FOLLOWERS MUST PAY

Twelfth Sunday in Ordinary Time.
C: Lk. 9: 18-24.

❖❖❖

"Who do the crowds say that I am?" One day Jesus put this question to his disciples. They knew well what the crowds were saying, for they had been caught in crowds ever since the day they started to follow Jesus. Some had themselves been part of the crowd at the River Jordan when Jesus arrived there for John's baptism. Others had joined him in Galilee as he moved from town to town, from crowd to crowd, healing and preaching.

The disciples knew how curious about Jesus the people in these crowds were, how they whispered among themselves, trading guesses about his identity. Some confused him with John the Baptist, who according to reports had been beheaded by Herod. Now they wondered if John had been restored to life and was completing the work that Herod had cut off. Others suggested that Elijah, the wonder-worker of old, or some other prophet of the past, had returned to earth in the person of Jesus.

Jesus now invited his disciples to speak for themselves. Forget about what the crowds are saying. You have been with me long enough to have an opinion. Who do *you* say that I am?

The reply was instant. "The Messiah of God." The voice was that of Peter, the natural leader of the Twelve. He could hardly believe the words had come from his mouth, so far-fetched they seemed. This Jesus who stood before him was as unlike what people looked for in the Messiah as a man could be. Most Jews thought the Messiah, when he came, would be a glorious ruler, a warrior-king in the mold of King David. But Jesus lived simply, shunned publicity, and favored the company of the poor and humble. He cared not at all for the approval of the political and religious leaders in Palestine, the clique that held power in Jerusalem. In fact, he sometimes seemed to cultivate their enmity. How could he be the great Messiah?

Despite these counts against Jesus, however, Peter stood firm, convinced that only someone sent by God to deliver Israel could speak with such authority and display such compassion as Jesus did. To be his chosen companion and to help him prepare for his kingdom were privileges beyond a fisherman's wildest dream. Yes, Jesus was the Messiah, and Peter was proud to be the first to say so out loud. The other disciples listened with approval, proud that they too walked with the Messiah.

The disciples had long ago learned to expect the unexpected from Jesus. He delighted in uttering paradoxes and springing surprises, upsetting the preconceptions of his listeners. Now, in what should have been a moment of celebration and unalloyed joy, he proved true to form. Instead of congratulating the disciples for recognizing they were riding high on the bandwagon of the Messiah, he spoke in a sober tone. He would not, he told them, be the kind of Messiah they had dreamed of.

He would not, at least not yet, ascend a Messiah's throne. Instead, he would suffer disgrace and defeat. Rejected by the chief priests and scribes, the official custodians of the Jewish religion, he would be put to death. He added, although in their astonishment they hardly seemed to hear and certainly did not understand, that on the third day he would "be raised."

The bad news continued. His disciples themselves, he went on, would have to pay a heavy price for their allegiance to him. They would live without the perks that they thought belonged by right to a king's close companions. Their daily life would be a kind of crucifixion; and crucifixion, they knew, was the most disgraceful form of death mankind had devised.

Needless to say, the disciples did not understand.

I once knew a man who said there was one thing about his Catholic religion he did not understand. He loved his Church, had loved it since childhood. He admired its ceremonies and the grandeur of its cathedrals, cherished the Sunday readings from Scripture and the stories of missionaries wasting away among infidels in fields afar. But what for the life of him he could not understand was the Church's emphasis on self-denial and the cross. Christianity, he said, seemed bent on taking the fun out of life, turning harmless pleasures into sins.

What this man wanted was what the early disciples of Jesus had in mind when he first mentioned the cross. To them a suffering Messiah was unthinkable. Just as unthinkable was the idea that his followers would have to share his cross.

Now, twenty centuries later, it still seems unthinkable. This passage from Luke invites us at least to start thinking.

What Is Different in the Demands of Jesus

Thirteenth Sunday in Ordinary Time.
A: Mt. 10: 37-42.

❖❖❖

Jesus opens this passage by demanding three things of his followers. It is sometimes said that no other leader in history ever made demands as exacting as these, that they are unique to Christianity. Is this in fact so?

First, Jesus tells his followers they must be ready to brush aside their most precious family ties. Even the love of parent for child or child for parent will have to take second place. Well, what is unusual in that? Have not nations always demanded as much of their youth in time of war? Doesn't the world of business feel free to put a comparable burden on its managers? Top executives sometimes complain they are so often on the road or at the conference table that they have scarcely time to get to know their children, let alone give them the companionship and guidance they deserve.

Second, Jesus insists that his followers be prepared to carry a cross. To Israelites the word "cross" was a familiar metaphor, for crucifixion was the normal sentence the Romans meted out to vicious criminals in conquered nations. The sight of fellow Israelite shouldering a cross while being whipped to a place of execution was not unusual in first century Palestine. Thus for the people whom Jesus here addresses "cross" stands for severe suffering. In saying that his followers must take up their crosses, then, Jesus is saying at least this, that the path on which he leads them will not be strewn with roses.

But if that is all he means, there is nothing very new in it. Do not all the children of Adam have to endure their share of adversity between the cradle and the grave? As the saying goes, into every life a little rain must fall. And as we all know, sometimes misfortunes do not merely rain, they pour. Bad guesses, bad health, and bad luck are inseparable from the human condition. To expect ever to be free of them is a delusion excusable only in the young. No, learning to bear crosses is not uniquely Christian. It is part of growing up.

Third, Jesus here repeats a favorite theme, often called the Christian paradox: those preoccupied with saving their lives are sure to lose them; only those prepared to lose their lives will save them.

Severe as some formulations of this paradox may sound, isn't it—when rightly understood—a piece of wisdom familiar to sages throughout history? Even simple folk sense that people who spend their days and nights pampering themselves in the pursuit of pleasure are on a free fall to misery. Only those who devote themselves to making others happy succeed in winning genuine happiness for themselves.

What then is new and unique in what Jesus here says to his followers? Simply this, that he places himself at the center of each demand. *He* is the one who must take first place in our lives. Risking happiness for *his* sake is what guarantees our happiness. It is *his* cross we must take up, *him* we must follow.

The key word is "cross." When Jesus pronounced these demands he had not yet ascended Calvary. Although his listeners knew what the word "cross" meant, they could hardly grasp how much more it meant to Jesus and would mean to people like ourselves, who read this passage centuries later in light of what happened on Good Friday. We know that the suffering of Jesus was redemptive. He accepted death on the cross that we might live forever. In demanding that we follow in his path he does not mean merely that we should stoically endure the routine hardships of life. Rather, he wants us to accept our crosses as he did his, knowing that our sufferings also can be redemptive. All we have to do is join them to his.

Remember the Morning Offering? It used to be taught to all Catholic children, and I hope it still is. There we bundle together all the mishaps, big or small, that will come into our lives during the day and place them on the altars of the world along with what Jesus Christ suffered on Calvary. His sacrifice becomes our sacrifice. This doesn't make a toothache less painful or a neighbor's rude remark easier to take. But it does work a kind of alchemy, turning the hardships of the day into prayer. By trying to accept them as Jesus accepted the pains of Calvary we transform their base metal to gold.

This is especially true when hardships strike precisely because we are striving to live by the moral code Jesus gave us. Keeping the ten commandments involves hardship, sometimes heroic hardship. And living by the Sermon on the Mount involves even more. To show charity and forgiveness to our neighbor, to be utterly sincere towards God and our fellowmen—these involve a daily martyrdom. What makes them bearable is that the goal is in sight and that the goalkeeper is Jesus himself.

"SHE SHOULD BE GIVEN SOMETHING TO EAT"

Thirteenth Sunday in Ordinary Time.
B: Mk. 5: 21-24; 35-43 (or 21-43).

❖❖❖

At first sight Mark's account of how Jesus restored the daughter of Jairus to life reads like just another miracle story. But some of its details merit a closer-than-usual look.

One is in the words Jesus speaks at the climax of the drama, "*Talitha koum,*" meaning "Little girl, I say to you, arise." Here Mark treats us to a sample of Aramaic, the language Jesus grew up with. This is one of the six places in his gospel that record actual sounds once uttered by Jesus. Another occurs two chapters later, where he describes how, in healing a deaf-mute, Jesus placed a finger to the man's ears and in his tongue, exclaiming, "*Ephphatha!*"—Armaic for "be opened" *(7: 34).*

Some people are surprised to learn that the language of Jesus was not the language we know as Hebrew. By his time, however, Hebrew was for practical purposes a dead language, reserved almost exclusively for liturgical services. (In the same way, Latin lingered on in our Mass and sacraments long after this language of Cicero and Caesar had ceased being a language in everyday use.) From at least the third century before Christ the everyday language of Palestine was Aramaic.

Why does Mark, who composed his gospel in Greek, hold onto the Aramaic here? Probably because Jairus himself, along with his household and neighbors, attached importance to the precise sounds Jesus uttered at the moment of the girl's resuscitation. It was not every day, after all, that a girl who had been declared dead was called back to the land of the living. The exact verbal formula Jesus employed in telling the girl to arise must have passed from mouth to mouth as though it held some special power, like a magical incantation.

Another feature worth noting in this passage is that Mark is careful to name the man on whose behalf Jesus performed this wonder. This is unusual. Most of the people who benefited from the healing power of Jesus are nameless in Mark's gospel. Along with Bartimaeus, the blind beggar on the roadside of Jericho *(10: 46-52),* Jairus stands out as an exception.

Why does Mark preserve his name? Remember that Jairus was an official of the synagogue in Capernaum and therefore a man of great prestige and widely known. As the story of what Jesus had done for his daughter made the rounds, Jairus's name would have naturally been part of it, for it was at his request and in his home that the girl had been brought back from death.

But was it really from death? Had the girl died? Biblical scholars, unlike the mourners who greeted Jairus with wailing and Jesus with ridicule, are not sure. Even in our time seasoned medical workers have been known to pronounce living people dead. With their far less sophisticated knowledge of medicine, these mourners might easily have mistaken a coma for death.

The best reason for thinking this is what happened is the statement of Jesus himself, "The child is not dead but asleep." Perhaps, as some think, he meant the girl would soon awake from death. But if we take his words literally, and we have no reason not to, we will not put this event alongside the raising of Lazarus, of whose death there can be no doubt. This girls seems to have been raised from apparent death, not death itself.

What Jesus did for the girl was still, of course, miraculous. Only someone with more than human insight could know, as Jesus knew, that the girl was still alive. And even if Jesus did not save her from actual death, he saved her from a fate many would consider even worse. Since the Jews buried their dead before sunset, she would soon have been buried alive.

Mark closes with a seemingly trifling detail. While the bystanders gazed with amazement at the strutting child, Jesus thought of something even her parents seem to have missed. Since the start of her illness, the girl had not eaten. She must have been famished. Get her, Jesus told the bystanders, some food.

Of the three evangelists who describe this miracle (Matthew and Luke are the others), only Mark gives this detail. He must have learned of it from Peter, the source for most of his gospel and an actual witness of the event. Without his testimony we would not have this evidence of how thoughtful Jesus was.

Thoughtfulness, care for the needs of others, is not usually listed among the specifically Christian virtues. Perhaps it should be. Ordering food for the child was in itself a trifling gesture. But as the poet Homer observed, a gesture that is only a trifle to the one who makes it can be as precious as gold to the one for whom it is made. It is pleasing to know that the Lord of the universe and savior of mankind was not above such trifles. And that Peter, prince of the apostles and foundation rock of the Church, was not too busy to notice.

A REBUKE FOR TWO OF HIS FINEST

Thirteenth Sunday in Ordinary Time.
C: Lk. 9: 51-62.

❖❖❖

James and John, blood brothers as well as fishing partners, were among the first recruits rounded up by Jesus. And they made splendid recruits, too, unlike those who declare their eagerness to enlist but only on the condition that their cots be soft and their active service deferred. Once James and John quit their nets to follow Jesus, they never turned back. With Peter they formed a trio closer to him than any other apostles.

As the gospels unfold, however, the reader realizes that these two were hardly prepackaged candidates for canonization. So headstrong were they, so fierce in their zeal for the gospel, that Jesus dubbed them "sons of thunder" *(Mk. 3: 17)*. Here Luke gives an instance of the kind of conduct that earned them this nickname. Christian warriors on the warpath against real or supposed enemies of Jesus have splashed blood across many sad chapters in the history of the Church. Happily, James and John did not succeed in their efforts, but this was not for want of trying.

That a Christian should never indulge in bigotry is clear. Nothing could be more alien to the Sermon on the Mount. What is not always clear is how to respond when Jesus and his gospel become targets for the bigotry of others. That was the challenge that faced James and John. Luke describes how they sought to deal with the situation and how Jesus in turn dealt with them.

Since the Samaritans harbored a centuries-old hostility for Jews, they put out no welcome mat when Jewish pilgrims to Jerusalem passed through their territory. It is useless to ask why they refused hospitality. Bigotry needs no why, only a who—someone with the wrong religion or nationality or ancestry.

Thus when Jesus, en route to Jerusalem with his disciples, requested safe passage through a Samaritan town, he received a flat refusal. At this, James and John exploded. Jesus could work miracles. Let him set fire to this town and roast its inhabitants to a crisp. Such inhospitality deserved such a fate.

History is rife with instances of holiness twisted to hatred, of would-be saints hell-bent on incinerating the foes of God. Soon after his decision to reform and walk in the path of the Lord, Saint

Ignatius Loyola came within a whisker of slaying a Moslem for having denied the virginity of Christ's mother. Christians have joined in the massacre of fellow Christians and defended the carnage as the only way to rid the Church of turncoats. Women branded as witches have been burnt at the stake while onlooking zealots praised God for the flames.

Few today have witnessed scenes as lurid as these, but most have seen seemingly good Christians answer the bigotry of others with bigotry of their own. Catholics do not usually blame the Jew next door for the murder of Christ or abhor every Protestant for refusing to honor his mother. But it is rare for a Catholic to grow up without inheriting a grudge or two against members of other religions or nations. Ancestral antagonisms simmer for centuries. But whether the wrong one resents happened yesterday or ages ago or (as likely as not) never at all, the Christian response should never be another wrong. There is no such thing as holy vengeance. Punishment for sin, like judgment of whether there is sin at all, should be left to God.

How did Jesus reply to the request of James and John? Luke says he turned "to reprimand them." Sometimes the silence of the gospels can infuriate the reader. What exactly did the boy Jesus say to the elders in the temple that so amazed them? What passages in Scripture did Jesus cite during his conversation with the two disciples at Emmaus? We will never know. No more can we know the exact words he used to reprimand James and John.

In a sense, however, we do not have to know. Jesus was on the way to Jerusalem, and it was there, during his passion and death, that he taught by example how his followers should respond to those who in any age treat them unjustly. If ever a man had good cause to lash out at foes, it was Jesus during his final hours in Jerusalem. But he endured the savagery inflicted on him without complaint. This was his way of teaching that hatred can never dispel hatred. Only love can do that.

To judge by their later conduct, James and John learned this lesson well. James met a martyr's death, beheaded by Herod ten years after the death of Jesus. John lived on for so long that some thought he would never die. Among the writings to which he gave his name, one of the most treasured is his first epistle, where on page after page he repeats the lesson of love. His words are worth recalling whenever one is tempted to answer hatred with hatred: "If anyone says, 'I love God,' but hates his brother, he is a liar, for whoever does not love a brother whom he has seen cannot love God whom he has not seen" *(4:20)*.

What the Wise and Learned Never Learned

Fourteenth Sunday in Ordinary Time.
A: Mt. 11: 25-30.

❖❖❖

Scholar-bashing is an ancient and ever popular pastime that even scholars occasionally indulge in. Some scholars, of course, deserve all the pummeling they get, they make themselves such inviting targets. The simplest schoolchild soon learns that erudition is no certain antidote against silliness. That is why the absent-minded professor is the butt of a thousand jokes, why eggheads rarely win elections.

Jesus opens this gospel with some scholar-bashing of his own. He is not just poking fun, however; his words are spoken in sadness. The scholars of his day were the scribes, whom the gospels paint so often as villains that we easily forget what their profession actually was. As doctors of law, a title they acquired only after years of arduous study, they were the closest thing in biblical Judaism to what we call an educated class, an intelligentsia. Since the law they expounded was religious law, their expertise was supposedly in matters religious. That is why their story is so sad. As their rejection of Jesus makes clear, in religious insight they merited a flunk.

Religious insight begins with a readiness to listen to God's word. Yet when God's revelation came to these scribes in the person of Jesus Christ, who as the eternal Son of the heavenly Father is the source of all wisdom, they refused him a fair hearing. Intellectual pride was at the root of their refusal. Neither his words nor his works could make them re-think the arid lessons that had been drummed into them at school. Thus in calling them "wise and learned," Jesus spoke ironically. Their learning was an empty shell, their wisdom a sham.

Who did listen to Jesus? He was certainly no box-office flop. Wherever he went—in synagogues, in the fields of Galilee, in the pavilions of the temple—crowds gathered and hungrily devoured his words. What especially made them treasure his message was that it was so unlike that of the scribes.

Mostly these admirers were plain folk—farmers, fishermen, traders, the common run of humanity. In calling them "childlike," Jesus was far from implying they were simple-minded. That they were uneducated does not mean they were unintelligent; it never does. But they were like children in their willingness to accept guidance from someone they recognized as wiser and more virtuous than themselves. It is hard to find a higher wisdom than that.

They had little trouble choosing between the guidance of the scribes and that of Jesus. Why did the teaching of the scribes repel them, even frighten them? In the hands of a typical scribe, the ancient and pure religion of Judaism was reduced to an endless list of dry rituals and rigid laws; in place of the law God had given to Moses, they composed a catalogue of man-made interpretations of that law. Obey these, they told the Israelites, or forfeit entrance to God's kingdom.

To journey through life burdened by this load of scribal laws was a labor the common people could scarcely endure. No wonder they opened their hearts to Jesus when he revealed to them his route to God's kingdom. Instead of a set of rules, he presented himself—"learn from me." He did not promise life without a struggle, salvation without a cross. Of course there would be a yoke on their shoulders and a burden to bear. But their yoke-mate would be Jesus himself. With him as companion the journey would be endurable because the goal would be sure.

This is a key passage in the New Testament. It contains a fundamental truth about Christianity (some would call it *the* fundamental truth.) Our religion is not, like that of the scribes, made of taboos and pious rituals. It is a person, Jesus Christ, as alive today as when he spoke these words. He invites us to walk through life with him. Only if we get that straight and accept his invitation can we truly live as Christians.

Scribal legalism masquerading as religion is dead today. But intellectual pride masquerading as wisdom is not. Many members of today's educated class are at least as hostile to the revelation of Jesus as were the scribes of old. Although they sing the praises of an open mind, they want us to close our minds to the revelation of Jesus Christ. They even succeed in convincing some people that one cannot be a genuine scholar or deep thinker if one belongs to the Church Jesus founded.

That is their Big Lie. No institution in the world has done more than the Church to foster education and disseminate learning. The list of Catholic scholars, living and dead, is long and illustrious. What Christianity opposes is intellectual pride, thinking that the unassisted human mind can know the ultimate meaning of life and find a sure formula for human happiness. Only Jesus Christ, eternal Wisdom, can do that.

The Harm Our Tongues Can Do

Fourteenth Sunday in Ordinary Time.
B: Mk. 6: 1-6.

❖❖❖

Idealizing the past is a universal addiction. We all dream of a world golden with virtue in days gone by, immune from the atrocities that plague us today. We also put halos around small towns and rural settings, imagining that only good neighbors dwell there, far from the mean streets of the cities. But especially do we idealize the biblical past. Nazareth, the rural town where Jesus grew up, is for many a name synonymous with holiness. How gracious the people must have been who had Mary, full of grace, and Jesus, the author of grace, as neighbors!

This gospel skips the myth and reports the reality. Were the people who grew up with Jesus any kinder and gentler than people today? Was the graciousness of the Holy Family catching? See how Mark describes a visit Jesus paid to his old neighbors.

The episode took place when Jesus was well into his public ministry. His days were spent touring the towns and villages of Galilee, teaching and healing. Everywhere people hailed him as a prophet. Eventually he came to the hill country he knew well and stopped at Nazareth, his "native place." But Jesus was not visiting his hometown just to chat with chums from his childhood. Here, as everywhere in Galilee, he presented himself as a Rabbi, a teacher of divine wisdom.

And so, when Sabbath came Jesus went with his disciples to the synagogue of his childhood, mounted the pulpit, read from Scripture, and taught. The congregation was a sea of familiar faces. But not, he soon learned, of kind and gentle faces.

For a while they were wide-eyed with wonder. They had never dreamed that the lad who once did their carpentry and whose kin still lived down the street could acquire such a way with words. Soon, however, their astonishment turned to heckling resentment. Where, they asked, had Jesus learned to speak like this? What newfangled wisdom was he peddling? How did this mere carpenter come to be known as a miracle-worker? Weren't his people just plain Nazarenes, no better than themselves?

Instead of attending to his message, these old neighbors drowned out his words with sputtering indignation. This would-be prophet did not impress them. They dismissed him as a charlatan.

Jesus responded with a piece of folk wisdom about a prophet having no honor among his own people. The proverb is one of the world's oldest, with versions in scores of languages. All make essentially the same point, all warn against envy. Distant people, people we have never met, are rarely the objects of our envy. Old acquaintances are. It shames us that someone who had the same chances as ourselves, whose equal we thought we were, has left us far behind. When that happens, the easiest way to make things equal again is by tearing that person down.

The people of Nazareth were not monstrously evil—unless we consider the average person monstrously evil. We miss the point of Mark's narrative if we fail to realize how thoroughly average, how much like ourselves, these neighbors of Jesus were. Even if, please God, we have never sunk to their level of nastiness, we should recall how close we have come. It is not hard to imagine ourselves completely at home among those neighbors of Nazareth, adding our snippets of envy to their spiteful chatter. Wherever we go we can hear people sneering at others the way these did at Jesus. Have we never joined in?

We average people are hardly ever tempted to sins of Satanic pride. We go through life without contemplating mass murder or grand larceny. But like the people of Nazareth, we find it hard to rid ourselves of petty vices, especially vices of the tongue. Badmouthing our successful neighbors, carping at the gifted and the industrious, taking pleasure in exposing the flaws of our betters—these are the sins we must guard against.

The epistle of James is not the best known book in the Bible, but it contains the best remembered warning against sins of the tongue *(3: 1-12)*. Our tongue, James says, is "a restless evil, full of deadly poison" which "no human can tame." James should know. Scholars identify him as the James who in the early Church was leader of the Christians in Jerusalem, the same James who in this gospel is called a "brother" of Jesus. He may well have been in the synagogue on the day Mark here describes and heard his neighbors hoot down the Son of God.

Of course the people who did the hooting did not know Jesus was the Son of God. Even James did not know this at the time. To the hooters he was just plain Jesus, their old neighbor. We, however, have no such excuse. We have been told over and over that what we do to our neighbors, for good or ill, Jesus takes as done to himself. When we hoot them down, we hoot him down. When we praise them, the Son of God is praised.

LAMBS AMONG WOLVES

Fourteenth Sunday in Ordinary Time.
C: Lk. 10: 1-12; 17-20; (or 1-9).

❖❖❖

Galilee, the northern section of Palestine, is only a speck on the map of the world. About fifty miles from top to bottom and twenty-five a cross, its area is roughly equal to that of Rhode Island. The ancient historian Josephus probably exaggerated when he put its population at three million, but his estimate suggests that it was heavily populated for its day. For about three years Jesus crisscrossed through Galilee with his apostles, giving joy to the poor and spiritually hungry, assuring them that God cared for them, that his kingdom was at hand.

No preacher, however charismatic, could make a mark on world history if he confined himself to so tiny a patch of land for so brief a time. How, under these circumstances, could Jesus hope to accomplish his universal mission to mankind? How fulfill the prophecy made by Simeon in his infancy, that he would grow up to be a "light for revelation to the Gentiles" *(Lk. 2: 32)*?

Only by deputy. Others would have to perform the lion's share of the work for him. Here Luke tells who his first deputies were and how he sent them out on their first training mission.

Jesus had already chosen twelve companions whom he dubbed "apostles," a word meaning people who are "sent" *(Lk. 6: 12-16; 9: 1-6)*. Now he expanded his deputies to include an additional seventy-two. These in time came to be called "disciples," meaning pupils. Henceforth much of Christ's time and energy would be spent, not preaching directly to the people of Palestine, but instructing these men. The work for which he was readying them would not begin in earnest until after his ascension, when the Church would be born. Through the labors of these men and of their successors the Church would spread throughout the world.

This passage summarizes the instructions Jesus gave to the seventy two when he sent them out on their first training exercise. Some of these instructions—the prohibition against money bags, for example, and the injunction to eat what is set before them—are obsolete today. But the idea behind them still holds. The emissary of Jesus, now as well as then, should not load up with material possessions or fret over personal comfort. Jesus was an itinerant preacher, content with what came his way. So too should be his disciples.

Why did Jesus settle on the number seventy-two? Luke does not say, but it may be connected with the belief then current among the Jews that the nations of the world were exactly seventy-two. Thus the number would signify the challenge these disciples would face after the first Pentecost, to bring the word of Jesus to every corner of the globe.

Jesus never guaranteed that every man, woman, and child in the world would hear his message. But he did promise that it would be preached wherever mankind would be. Thus the missionary activity of the Church is neither an option nor a luxury, but a necessity if she is to live up to the original mandate from Jesus. The Catholic Church is by nature expansive, sending preachers to lands where, like the towns these seventy-two visited in Galilee, the message of Jesus has not yet penetrated.

Our Catholic people sometimes wonder why we cannot leave well enough alone. After spending time and money to train priests and nuns, why pack them off to distant outposts where, as likely as not, no one has asked them to come? Can't we find good use for them here? Shouldn't charity begin at home?

The answer is that the Church must maintain its missionary character or else cease to be the Church Jesus founded. "The missionary spirit," wrote Pius XII, "and the Catholic spirit are one and the same thing." Indeed, the missionary spirit is the same whether the pulpit is in Leyte or Little Rock. Disciples must be everywhere and be missionaries wherever they are. Thus we have urgent need for a continuous flow of disciples. They must go to where the Church is flourishing, where it is faltering, and where it has not yet taken root.

It is no secret that in recent decades the number of priests and nuns has dropped dramatically and dangerously in most parts of the world. What is less well known is that in some regions the reverse is true. Almost without exception these are places where life is harsh and the Church desperately poor. Many seminaries and convents in eastern Europe are bulging at the seams. The same is true in parts of Asia and Africa.

There is a lesson here for us. The way to spiritual prosperity is never through material abundance. Jesus said his disciples would have to live as sheep among wolves. The daily lot of sheep among wolves is far from easy. But sheep who live among wolves grow up tougher, stronger, and probably far happier than sheep who live among sheep.

The Sower and His Soil

Fifteenth Sunday in Ordinary Time.
A: Mt. 13: 1-23 (or 1-9).

❖ ❖ ❖

Jesus was not only a tireless teacher, but an unusually obliging one as well. Unlike many in the profession, he was never fussy about physical surroundings. Any out-of-the-way corner would do, as long as people were willing to gather there and lend him their ears. Often in Galilee this meant an impromptu assembly in an open field. Today we see him holding forth from the most makeshift podium of all. A throng has hurried to the lakeside to hear him, and to escape their crush he steps into a fishing boat, settles himself on a cushion in its stern, and turns to face the audience lined along the banks.

A stunning panorama stretches behind them. Galilee in biblical times was a near paradise of agricultural plenty: well-tilled fields of wheat and barley, abundant sunshine, an intricate network of tiny canals and dams. The region around the lake was particularly luxuriant. Americans abroad sometimes irritate their hosts by calling their homeland "God's own country." The Galileans of old were just as boastful of their native soil, naming it *Jezreel*, meaning "God's own plantation."

Imagine that before speaking Jesus sits silently for a moment, gathering his thoughts. His topic today will be the Word of God—how generously he has uttered it and how variously his hearers have responded. The eyes of Jesus drift across the landscape and catch sight of a sower in the distance, holding a sack in one hand, scattering seeds with the other. Just the image Jesus needs to illustrate how the word of God works!

Back and forth the sower walks, flinging his seeds in heaps to left and right. Some the wind carries to the path, where feet will trample them or birds gobble them up; others fall on stony ground, where the topsoil is thin and they cannot take firm root; others fall on ground thick with thorns that will eventually choke them. But the seeds are abundant, with plenty to spare, and many do land on rich soil. The harvest will be ample, with some seeds yielding up to a hundredfold.

Jesus points to the sower. His audience is rural; for them the sight makes a powerful parable for the question he wants them to ponder. They have all noticed that the words from the mouth of Jesus produce different results in different people. Why? Is God's word sometimes defective? Not at all, the parable implies. The receiver is the variable. There are as many ways of receiving God's word as places for the seed to fall.

People today are little different from those who saw and heard Jesus in the flesh. Take any Sunday congregation and think of the way its members respond when God's word is read at Mass. Some sit in the pews as alert as bumps on logs, hearing but hardly listening; others do listen, but their thoughts drift away as soon as the book is closed; still others let the words sink in, but once Mass is over, the pressures and pleasures of everyday life crowd them out. Finally, some take the words in gladly, mull over them on their own, make them a part of their lives. That is what we should all strive for. A brief passage from Scripture totally changed the young Saint Augustine. The Scripture readings on Sunday can change our lives too.

If the flesh and blood Jesus were to return to earth today, how would he get this lesson across to a congregation of city dwellers who have never lived on a farm? What machine age parable would fit his purpose? Who or what would replace the sower?

Perhaps a city's electrical power plant, feeding thousands of outlets, but all with very different results. The same electricity that illumines the screens in moviehouses also floods the highways with light and glows in the midnight lamps of students cramming for finals. Or perhaps instead of a sower he would point to a gas station attendant, pumping fuel for a long line of trucks, automobiles, and motorcycles, all heading off to different destinations.

But neither of these images really does the job. The point about the image Jesus uses is that the soil is not just a passive receptacle for the seed, the way a lamp is for electricity or a tank for gasoline. The soil contributes actively to what grows within it. Without its nutrients the seed will never germinate. A plant owes its life to the soil as well as to the seed.

The point of this parable is that we are the soil, and we must actively nourish God's word within us, mull over it, make it our own. Among those who heard God's word from Jesus were his disciples. How these nourished his words and produced fruit of a hundredfold is a wonderful chapter in history. But the age of Christian wonders is not over. The seed of God's word is as alive among us as ever. It is read to us every Sunday.

What kind of a hearing do we give it?

BAGGAGE CHECK

Fifteenth Sunday in Ordinary Time.
B: Mk. 6: 7-13.

To Christians of the first century the apostles were known as "The Twelve." These were the men Jesus had "sent out" to spread the gospel (the word "apostle" means "someone who is sent"), and because he sent them, they were the living links between himself and the primitive Church. Most Christians of the first century knew the Lord only second-hand. The Twelve, however, had walked and talked with him, received their lifetime commissions from him. No wonder they were held in awe.

Possibly it was Jesus himself who first used the term. As a football coach today might speak of his "Eleven," Jesus could have referred to his "Twelve," for it was he who had chosen them, journeyed through Palestine with them, and above all trained them. In this gospel Mark gives a glimpse of the training program he made them undergo. It was, you will agree, austere.

"Austere" is in fact too mild a word. Listening to Jesus describe how they were to live, the apostles must have felt the way an army recruit of today might feel on his first night in boot camp, wondering why in the world he had been so quick to answer that call for volunteers. Nothing in the previous life of the apostles had prepared them for the calculated discomfort Jesus told them they must prepare to endure.

One of the Twelve was named Levi. A tax collector and thus a member of the moneyed class, he was accustomed to comfort. All tax men were. The other eleven, many of them fishermen, had never wallowed in luxury as Levi had; but Galilean fishermen enjoyed a decent living, well above the poverty line. All must have winced on hearing these marching orders from Jesus. When he first invited them to follow him, they had accepted with joy. Only now did they realize what following him would mean.

They were to travel light. No food, not even a sack to carry food, not a red cent in cash. In short, they were to be beggars. For material possessions they were allowed only a walking stick (all their journeys would be by foot), a pair of sandals, and whatever clothes they had on their backs; they were not even to pack a spare tunic (translated into today's wardrobe, an extra suit). On entering a town, let them accept the first offer of shelter; no matter how meager its furnishings, they should seek no better. If the people in one town refuse them a welcome, let them move on to the next. They had no time for dallying. The task before them was too urgent.

Why did Jesus demand that they live in so Spartan a fashion? Above all, to keep them concentrated on their mission. He was sending them on God's business, not their own. He was God's emissary on earth, but he could not cover all of Palestine by himself. These men he sent as his emissaries, to expel demons and cure the sick in his name, to preach the good news he preached. God's business was too important and time too precious for them to waste their energies on trivial pursuits.

This was also a training mission for the future. The day would come when he would return to his Father and they would be on their own, leading the infant Church in its struggles to secure a foothold in the Roman world. Now, while they still had Jesus with them, they must learn his methods. To bring his message to others, they must live as he lived. Seeing them, future Christians should recognize replicas of himself.

These instructions had an even further purpose. Since it was God's business they were about, God would surely provide their material needs. They must show the world that they trusted God to do so. The people to whom they preached would have a hard time accepting what they said about trusting in God's providence if they were unwilling to put their own lives on the line. In short, they must practice what they preach.

What was to be the substance of their preaching? *Metanoia* is the word Mark uses, rendered in our version as "repentance." The Greek packs a stronger punch than the English. When we say "repent" we get the picture of people beating their breasts and wailing about how much they regret the past. But *metanoia* means actually doing something about the past, changing one's way of living, rooting out whatever sinful habits one has.

What in most of us needs changing is our attitude towards material things, the baggage we carry through life. We cannot survive with no baggage at all, of course, and it would be folly to try. But we can and should take steps to keep their weight down, make sure that material things do not rule our lives.

All of us, whatever our calling, need a dash of the attitude towards material things that the apostles had as they began their first training mission. In the journey through life, those surest to reach the Christian goal are the ones who travel light.

ONLY THE SAMARITAN STOPPED

Fifteenth Sunday in Ordinary Time.
C: Lk. 10: 25-37.

❖❖❖

Although he never attended rabbinical school, his followers addressed Jesus as "Rabbi," meaning teacher. And what a teacher he was! Even the professional Rabbis in Jerusalem could not equal the skills of this vagabond Rabbi from Nazareth. Today's gospel reveals his mastery of two important teaching techniques.

First, instead of replying with a monologue to the lawyer's question, Jesus goads him with a question of his own. He does the same at the close of his story about the Samaritan, bidding the lawyer to judge for himself which of the travelers was a true neighbor. The trick is as old as Socrates. A teacher should not overwhelm students with displays of his own learning, but challenge them to do some thinking for themselves.

Second, when he does hold the floor, Jesus steers clear of arid abstractions, telling a story to make his point. Is there any more appealing way to package an idea? And has any teacher ever told better stories? The tale of the Good Samaritan is one of his best, a favorite even among non-Christians. One would have a hard time finding someone who has not heard it.

In fact, we Christians have heard it so often we are in danger of missing how gravely it must have shocked the Jews who heard it first. Not only does it vilify two guardians of temple worship, a priest and a Levite; it glorifies a member of a group the Jews held in contempt—the Samaritans.

Why do the priest and Levite ignore a fellow human in need? Ironically, they can plead a religious excuse. The victim is "half dead," so inert they cannot tell if he is dead or alive. Now according to ancient Jewish ceremonial law, touching a corpse would render them unclean for a week, unfit to perform the temple service that is their bread and butter. Their safest course is to give the heap of mangled flesh a wide berth.

Of course, the priest and Levite have other reasons for proceeding on their journey without pausing even to examine the victim. To carry him to a nearby inn would be time-consuming, costly, and above all, messy. Furthermore, they may reason, any effort to rescue him would almost certainly prove futile; for if he is not already dead, he will surely be so by nightfall.

Like most good stories, this one contains surprises. The first is the arrival of the Samaritan. The road from Jerusalem to Jericho, a favorite haunt of robbers, was fearsome for all travelers, but for a Samaritan especially so. The Samaritans, heretical descendants of half-breed, renegade Jews, were always unwelcome in the territory of the full-blooded, doctrinally sound Jews of Judea. This Samaritan is probably a trader. At an rate, he is among people who loathe him, and he knows it.

The second surprise is the compassion the Samaritan displays. Every detail must have astounded the first listeners, but the final detail was the clincher. Not only does he settle the current bill, but promises to pay further expenses. A brother could do no more for a brother. What prompts such conduct? Jesus does not say. But surely the Samaritan recognizes in the Jew a common humanity that transcends all inherited prejudices.

Does the kind of prejudice that poisoned the relations between the ancient Jews and Samaritans have any parallels in more recent centuries? Does it infect our contemporary society? For an answer, sit before a globe of the world, blindfold yourself, take a pin in your hand, and stick it on any part of the surface. No land, from Ireland to India, from Brazil to Borneo, has been or is free of prejudice.

The vice is as ancient as pride, as universal as greed.

Jesus saved his biggest surprise to the end, saying "Go and do the same." He does not here say why. But soon he will give his followers a stronger reason for loving all neighbors than the humanity we share. Above all, we share a Redeemer. Jesus died for all the wounded outcasts on every roadside of the world. We cannot love him unless we love whom he loves.

Remember the question he started with: what *must* one do to inherit eternal life? Jesus has not been just entertaining his audience with a duel of wits or thrilling them with an exciting story. He has been answering the most serious question of life. Unless we kill all our prejudices and treat all other humans as the Samaritan did the Jew, we will inherit eternal death.

"Let Them Grow Together Until Harvest"

Sixteenth Sunday in Ordinary Time.
A: Mt. 13: 24-43 (or 24-30).

❖ ❖ ❖

"An enemy has done this." Can you imagine an enemy like the one we meet in this parable? Picture some neighbor with a grudge creeping into your garden at night and pouring poison over your petunias. A deed of such pure spite almost defies imagination. Yet we know that deeds far darker than this actually happen. History records them, the tabloids headline them. People do hurt others just to settle an old score, sometimes just to watch them squirm. The world we live in is no utopia; evil, even Satanic evil, is no fiction. Jesus realized this and wanted his followers to realize it as well. Hence this parable.

The weed in the parable is a kind still found in the East, darnel by name. A perfect weapon of revenge, in its early stages it is a dead ringer for wheat; worse still, by the time it shows its true colors, it is so intertwined with the real wheat that removing it without destroying the entire crop is impossible. Hence the man in the parable is wise to let it grow undisturbed. At harvest time his slaves can do the separating, chuck out the darnel, and prepare the genuine article for market.

The point of the parable? Recall last week's gospel. The sower stood for Jesus himself, who sowed God's word by his preaching. The disciples had listened carefully to that word. Over and over they had heard Jesus proclaim one theme, that the kingdom of heaven was at hand. In what precisely this kingdom would consist, however, as well as exactly when and where it would come, they were not sure. But they had reason to hope that one day they would see it. Then all followers of Jesus would live as he taught them to live, in a community of justice, peace and love. Was this not the kind of kingdom he promised?

If so, then the promise was still unfulfilled. The world looked no better now than on the day they first met Jesus. Their own group was still not free of pride and contention, they still felt stirrings of envy and self-importance. When would the promised kingdom come? How long must they wait?

This parables tell how long. The fullness of the kingdom will not be realized until after the Last Judgment, harvest time in the parable.

Only then will the Church be purged of imperfection and the triumphant reign of Jesus begin. Meanwhile, even among his followers, the bad will live side by side with the good, sinners rub elbows with saints. For all humans this life is a period of trial, and there can be no trial if the possibility of failure is foreclosed. Only where vice is a palpable option can genuine virtue flourish.

The parable is prophetic. Read Church history, especially the lives of the saints. Holiness so heroic it would have been inconceivable in pre-Christian times has marked Church from the earliest days. Certainly God's kingdom has been realized in the lives of individual Christians. The long list of early martyrs who were burnt at the stake or fed to lions is ample proof of this. But not all Christians were willing to be martyrs. As a group, as a world-wide community of the baptized, the Church has always been just like the field Jesus describes in this parable, its wheat intermingled with weeds.

Take the sixteenth century, the high Renaissance. We have all heard tales of its vicious Popes and sybaritic cardinals, of priests so ignorant they hardly understood the Latin of Mass, of convents so relaxed they were little more than dens of vice. Many of these tales are all too true. But the same period also saw some of our greatest saints —Theresa of Avila, John of the Cross, Ignatius Loyola, Francis Xavier, Philip Neri. The list could go on. Hard times beget extraordinary saints. Wheat grows tough in the company of darnel.

Recalling this should help us keep our heads from spinning when we look at the world today. Yes, the Church has had rough sailing of late. Hardly a month seems to pass without another scandalous tidbit about a priest or nun or prominent Catholic making the late news on TV. Vocations are thin, Catholic schools closing down, seminaries half empty, and our churches not nearly as crowded as they used to be. Many Catholics are tempted to despair over the sad state of the Church. They wonder what has happened to the seed Jesus once sowed. Does the word of God have no hearers? Is Peter's bark about to sink?

Good people have always asked questions like this, and always will. That is what today's parable tells us. The fact is that the Church never had the idyllic past people sometimes imagine it had, when its members were at perfect peace among themselves and God's word was held in reverence by all. No, the field has always been infested with weeds. What we need is patience and faith. Faith that God's kingdom *will* come.

A Holiday Wrecked

Sixteenth Sunday in Ordinary Time.
B: Mk. 6: 30-34.

❖❖❖

The apostles, bubbling with excitement, had just arrived back in Capernaum from a missionary journey, the first they had made without Jesus at their side. Two by two, they had trekked through towns and villages in Galilee, preaching to the people and healing their sick. Now Jesus listened as they poured out the story of their adventures on the road.

Unfortunately, he could not listen for long. That he was now at the peak of his popularity was not an unmixed blessing, for the common folk of Capernaum would not allow him a moment of peace. Wherever he went, great numbers sought him out, almost crushed him with their demands. The apostles were soon so busy helping Jesus that they barely had time to eat.

Jesus decided it was time they all took a break. They needed a chance to relax in privacy, to enjoy one another's company again. And so at his bidding they all boarded Peter's bark and sailed for a secluded spot across the lake. Their hopes, however, were soon dashed. Once the people realized where their boat was heading, many made for the same place by foot.

The wind must have been contrary, for the foot travelers arrived at the destination first. By the time Jesus stepped off the boat, a near mob was waiting for him, insisting that he continue to instruct them in the mysteries of God's kingdom. The world has never known a teacher the equal of Jesus. His pupils never had enough. Nor did Jesus. In an instant he was at it again, addressing the crowd from a makeshift outdoor pulpit. He stayed there teaching them all afternoon.

Have you ever heard a speaker whose word seemed directed to you alone? That must have been the impression Jesus made on listeners, and with good reason. He often compared himself to a shepherd, and the Palestinian shepherds of his time were notorious for knowing each sheep in their flock by name, for caring for their individual needs. Jesus, the good shepherd, actually *did* speak to each person in the crowd. He still does.

Mark tells us why Jesus could not resist the entreaties of this crowd. He pitied them. In a comparison that came from the lips of Jesus himself, Mark likens them to "sheep without a shepherd," a rural image so vivid that even city dwellers can grasp its point. Picture scores of sheep wandering aimlessly across the hills, no longer a single flock but a scattering of frightened animals. Each is on its own—hungry, bleating in the cold, with no shepherd to guide it to the sheepfold.

How apt is this picture today? Does it accurately describe the plight of many people in modern society?

Few would deny that it does. Science and technology have worked wonders since the days of Jesus. They have unlocked secrets of the universe that had been hidden from the dawn of history and enriched mankind with thousands of energy-saving gadgets and bodily comforts. If the most learned scholars and opulent monarchs of the past were to return from the grave and discover how much we today know and how luxuriously we live, they would turn green with envy.

Science, however, does not answer the fundamental questions about life, and technology fails to satisfy our deepest cravings. Amid the abundance that surrounds us, many today feel rootless, alone, lost without a compass. That millions of others feel the same way is no help. It only adds to the sense of isolation.

Some sages in the West have labeled our age the post-Christian age, since for many the clear certitudes of the past have given way to the denial of all values. People have lost their direction. To compensate, they search for new and unusual sensations, taking refuge in drink, drugs, unnatural sex, and violence. The image of sheep without a shepherd is perfect. Just reading the daily papers brings it to mind.

At Sunday Mass we are reminded that we do have a shepherd. We do not belong to a leaderless mob, but are all members of a flock that is guided by the same wise and compassionate shepherd that addressed the people of Galilee two thousand years ago. He returns to our altars every time Mass is celebrated and feeds us with bread from heaven just as he fed the crowd that sat listening to him all afternoon by the lakeside.

From Monday to Saturday it is easy to feel lost in a crowd. Whether we live in a teeming city or a bucolic village, modern life can be frighteningly confusing. Sunday Mass gives us a chance to get our bearings, to realize we are not alone but belong to a vast, worldwide flock. In thousands of churches throughout the world we pray for one another and for all lost and wandering sheep. Guided by our Shepherd, we move together to our eternal home.

THE HOSTESS WHO MISSED THE POINT

Sixteenth Sunday in Ordinary Time.
C: Lk. 10: 38-42.

❖❖❖

When they first hear the story of Martha and Mary, many people find themselves rooting for Martha. This has probably been so since the gospels were written. Doers, not dreamers, win the world's loudest applause. In Luke's account Jesus has just told the story of an unforgettable doer, the Good Samaritan, and Martha's conduct seems patterned after his. Jesus is tired and hungry after a day on the road. As the Samaritan aided the wounded Jew, Martha cares for the travel-weary Jesus.

But the situation is very different. Jesus is no victim stretched out half-dead on the roadside. He requires no nursing care. As he approaches the town of Bethany, looking for a place to stop and refresh himself, he realizes that Martha and Mary live there. They have known Jesus for long, and their house beckons him like an oasis. Surely he can rest there in the company of friends. The last thing he wants is to create a fuss.

Sound familiar? Did you ever want to talk to friends, or just be with them, and find the day ruined by the dithering and din of superfluous hospitality? That is what Jesus has to endure. Mary sits at his feet just to listen, for no man ever spoke as this prophet does. But the two are constantly distracted by the fumes of cooking and the clatter of pots and pans. Finally Martha voices her feelings. Why doesn't Jesus get the idle Mary on her feet, make her do her share in preparing meal?

Jesus does not exactly reprove Martha. He does not say that Mary is morally the better of the two. But he implies that Mary is the wiser, for she has chosen "the better part." Martha, for all her good intentions, has wasted the chance of a lifetime. Jesus has not come to her home for an elaborate meal; a simple dish ("only one thing") will do. He mainly wants to talk with the two as a friend to friends. Martha has missed the point.

Missing the point is a common failing. In 1961 a painting by the French artist Matisse, *Le Bateau*, hung in New York's Museum of Modern Art for forty-seven days before someone noticed that it was upside-down. Over 100,000 visitors had viewed it and missed the point. That statistic may say more about the painting than the visitors. But think of how many more thousands attend services in church regularly and still miss the point. They have no such excuse as the viewers of modern art. What is going on in church has certainly been explained often enough.

The Marthas among us are many. Some of them oversee our music. Music is a wonderful way to praise God, a far better aid to group prayer than food to group conversation. Thus the best church music is group music, at least when sung from the heart by the entire congregation. But the Marthas like to take over. Instead of being allowed to belt out a tuneful hymn in God's praise, the congregation must master music they do not enjoy or sit through a recital by aspiring semi-professionals. Someone has missed the point. Musical perfection is no more needed at Mass than at an impromptu songfest. Far more important is that we enjoy what we sing and mean every word of it.

Attendance at a wedding should be a time of wonder, joy, and prayer: wonder at the magnificence of the sacrament, joy in the love of the newlyweds, prayer for their future happiness. The best way to miss the point is to approach it as a display of apparel for brides and bridesmaids, or an occasion to meet old friends and long-unseen cousins. Christian matrimony is a sacrament, not a fashion show or family reunion.

The list could go on: liturgy addicts, with minute directions on how to perform sacred ceremonies, but nary a word on their meaning; parents who fret over their children's ABC's, but who don't bother to teach them their prayers; Sunday worshippers whose main interest is in what their fellow worshippers are wearing; wake-goers appraising the skill of the undertaker rather than praying for the soul of the deceased.

Most people manage to squeeze little enough time for prayer into their week. All the more precious, then, are the few moments they do spend in church. Why be "anxious and worried" about a thousand needless things, when "only one thing" is needed? This is God's house, where all his children are invited to stop and refresh themselves. The Lord is on the altar. Why can't they just sit, like Mary, at his feet? Let them just gaze and listen, with a few words of their own thrown in.

Or with no words at all. A French peasant was once asked by his pastor what he said to God in his frequent visits to church. He answered, "I don't say anything to God. I just sit back and look at him and let him look at me." That kind of prayer is a good deal harder and higher than it sounds. It was Mary's kind of prayer. Everyone should give it a try.

THE TREASURE, THE PEARL, AND THE NET

Seventeenth Sunday in Ordinary Time.
A: Mt. 13: 44-52 (or 44-46).

❖❖❖

The whole world knows the story of Doctor Faust, the medieval scholar who made a midnight deal with the devil, peddling his immortal soul for a lifetime of unlimited power and sensual delight. The reason the legend is so popular is that it rings true. Not just on the stage, but in real life, people face the choice given to Faust all the time, weighing a few years of tangible bliss against an eternity of intangibles. The tragedy is how many of them, like Faust, opt for the former.

The first two parables in this passage tell the story of Faust in reverse. Both the treasure in the field and the pearl of great price stand for the kingdom of heaven. To gain entry to that kingdom, the treasure finder and the pearl merchant sell all they have, meaning they abandon their claim to all that Faust traded his soul to gain. The obvious lesson is that nothing, not even gaining the whole world, profits a person if the kingdom of heaven is lost. Nothing comes near it in value.

The third parable drives home the lesson. The net of human history collects "fish of every kind," from the finest fish to inedible marine rubbish, that is, from the greatest saints to the gravest sinners. Sorting out one from the other is the business of the Last Judgment, when we will either be found among the sound fish or discarded with the flotsam and jetsam.

If this were all these parables said to us, there would be little to say about them. That life is a trial and that eternity hangs in the balance are truths known to Christians from childhood. The trouble is not that we do not *know* them. We do, and so did Doctor Faust.

The trouble is rather that these truths easily fade when the devil—in company with his fellow con men, the world and the flesh,—starts ballyhooing his bargain. His sales pitch can be very convincing, for it makes crude sense: an easy life on earth today beats pie in the sky tomorrow. The fun you have here and now is real; you can see, feel, taste, and touch it. Tomorrow is only a hope, a dream. Perhaps it will never come.

Is there anything in these parables to explode this line of reasoning and expose the devil for the charlatan he is? I think so. It is contained in one tiny detail of the first parable, a detail that suggests one of the most frequently forgotten truths about Christianity. We are told that the treasure finder "out of *joy* goes and sells all he has." Joy? *Before* putting his hands on the treasure? *While* stripping himself of all he owns? Exactly. The frequently forgotten truth is that for those who live by the gospel the joy of the kingdom starts *now.* (A corollary, which those who tell the whole story of Faust usually point out, is that for those who turn their backs on the gospel the bitterness of damnation also starts *now.*)

Only those who have never lived by the gospel think that to do so one must be a sad sack, that sinners have all the fun. The most successful lie of the father of lies is that a Christian is on a joyless journey. The truth is that Christians are not only allowed to be joyful but commanded to be so. Something is heretically wrong when joy is absent. It was a perverted view of the gospel that put the frown on the face of Calvinism.

Proof? Read the lives of the saints. You will not find one who did not radiate joy. Everyone in their presence felt it. Saint Philip Neri said that he would "allow no sadness" in his house; the supposedly grim Saint Ignatius Loyola gave this curt command to his subjects, "Laugh and be strong." The reason for their joy? They knew God loved them; that they were on a journey to where they would possess him fully; and (mark this) that while on this journey they were surrounded with thousands of life's freebies, like sunshine, laughter, friendship, and song.

Read also the gospels. Jesus Christ underwent great suffering in the end, but to the end spread joy wherever he went. Read especially the evangelist John's account of the words he spoke to his apostles on the night before he died, words saturated with joy *(16: 20-24).* Jesus loved life and wanted his followers to love it as well. Where there is love, there is joy.

Selling all we have means being ready to sacrifice whatever it takes to win the joys of the kingdom of heaven. For some saints—Francis of Assisi is the most prominent example—what it took was literally abandoning all earthly possessions. But the same Lord who asked Francis to become a pauper also gave him joy in doing so. No saint was ever happier.

God does not ask all Christians to live as Francis did. But doing whatever God does ask should give all the same joy it gave him. It means entry *now* into the vestibule of his kingdom.

Picnic to Remember

Seventeenth Sunday in Ordinary Time.
B: Jn. 6: 1-15.

People who live in temperate climes usually find spring their favorite season, the most bracing for their spirits as well as the most gracious display of nature. That is certainly what it is in Israel, especially in the region near the Sea of Galilee, one of the garden spots of the nation. Spring is boom time for the tourist industry there, and no wonder. For three glorious months pilgrims breathe the same balmy air and feast their eyes on the same lush scenery that once gave daily joy to Jesus and his fishermen-turned-apostles.

It was springtime ("Passover was near") when the events of this gospel took place. In last week's gospel Mark told how a crowd from Capernaum pursued Jesus to a place by the lake and sat listening to his preaching through the long afternoon. All four evangelists describe what happened next, one of the strangest and most talked-about of the wonders witnessed by the followers of Jesus. Here we have John's version.

The crowd that assembled on the grass was huge. In the dialogue leading up to the miracle, two usually inconspicuous apostles, Philip and Andre, make an appearance. First Jesus asked Philip, who hailed from nearby Bethsaida and therefore should know, where in that region they could buy food for so many mouths. Nowhere, was the gist of Philip's answer. The cost would be far beyond the slender means of Jesus and his band. Then Andrew, also from Bethsaida, spotted a lad hawking five loaves of barley bread and a few dried fish. But what good, he asked, were these among so many? Jesus replied by having the people recline on the grass, as though awaiting a meal.

The details of the meal they were soon served—by what steps so little food turned into so generous a feast—are not clear. Was the boy's basket replenished from on high each time some contents were removed? Did the food just multiply in the hands of Jesus? Did loaves and fish pop into being before the startled eyes of each diner? Such speculation is idle. John says all ate "as much as they wanted" and twelve baskets of leftovers remained. These are the facts. All else is conjecture.

Jesus is divine, the second person of the Trinity. The power that makes barley grow in the fields and fish propagate in the sea can also cause bread and fish to multiply. In this episode the power of Jesus burst forth as never before, in a marvel witnessed by thousands. No wonder a murmur soon passed through the crowd, urging that Jesus be declared a king.

The real puzzler in this episode is not how it happened, but why. Most of the miracles of Jesus were prompted by serious suffering—a man born blind, a leper covered with sores, a widow who had lost an only son. Such hard cases stirred the human compassion of Jesus, and his display of power had a purpose we can grasp. In contrast, the suffering he remedied by feeding these five thousand seems frivolous, the slight twinge of hunger some hikers felt after a few hours without food. Surely this was a strange miracle. So much power for so trivial a purpose!

Yes, it was strange, but its strangeness is all to the good if it starts us thinking. Here are some thoughts that occur.

The feeding of the five thousand can be viewed as a parable in action. As Jesus fed the multitude with material bread, his words to this day feed the world with spiritual bread, nourishment for the soul. Whether they know it or not, all human beings hunger for the wisdom of God. The words of Jesus, who is God incarnate, are more than enough to satisfy this hunger. We hear these words every week. Do we listen?

Even more than a parable in action, this miracle was a prophesy in action. The Church has always viewed the feeding of the five thousand as a preview of an even greater miracle to come, the Eucharist. This notion is not an ingenious theory cooked up by theologians of a later age. Paintings on catacomb walls dating back to the second century show that from earliest times ordinary Christians made the connection.

Jesus was generous in providing material bread for the people who came to him near Bethsaida on that day long ago. He has been even more generous in supplying eucharistic bread for his later followers. See how today he is multiplied in the Eucharist, present as wafers of bread in all the tabernacles of the world, distributed to the faithful at every Mass.

Even the word "Eucharist," which is from a Greek word meaning an act of thanksgiving, is embedded in this story. John tells us that before distributing the bread Jesus "gave thanks." The word he uses in his original Greek is "eucharistein." The Eucharist was the parting gift of Jesus to us, a Passover gift from a man who was soon to die. We can never give thanks enough.

OUR DADDY?

Seventeenth Sunday in Ordinary Time.
C: Lk. 11: 1-13.

❖ ❖ ❖

What lasts less than a minute, is almost two milleniums old, and is known and cherished today throughout the entire world? The Our Father. What is the secret of its enduring popularity? Its composer, as its title suggests, was none other than the Lord Jesus himself. Today's gospel describes its origin.

His disciples had often seen Jesus wrapped in silent union with his Father. The sight made them realize what bumblers they themselves were in the art of prayer. When they asked him how they too could converse intimately with God, this prayer was his answer. They committed it to memory and in later years handed it on to those who heard the word of God from their lips.

When catechumens of the first century prepared for baptism, they all learned the Lord's Prayer, either in the version recorded by Matthew or in the sparser form preserved by Luke in the passage for this gospel. But they were not allowed to join in when Christians recited it in unison, as the Christian community often did, especially during baptism ceremonies and at re-enactments of the Last Supper. That privilege was reserved for the baptized, so much was this prayer regarded as *the* Christian prayer. The Lord's Prayer is still recited at all baptisms and Masses.

It is a begging prayer. All beggings takes courage, but it takes special courage to beg favors from God. Who is a mere human to dare stand before the Almighty and rattle off requests like a child presenting a list to Santa Claus? But we do dare to make this prayer, and the reason we do so is stated in one of the formulas spoken before the Lord's Prayer at Mass. "Jesus taught us to call God our Father, and so we have the courage to say." *Jesus taught us*. That is why we are sure our begging is not an impertinence. We are taught to beg by Jesus himself.

These introductory words of the priest contain two further keys to the Lord's Prayer.

The first is the word "we." This is a group prayer, not a private devotion. Even when we mumble the words in private, we do not ask for merely personal favors; this is the great public prayer of Christians, uttered in the name of all the followers of Christ. Its constituency is even huger than that, for it begs favors, not just for Christians, but for all human beings in the world. We are all children of the same father.

Luke's version contains five world-embracing petitions. *Hallowed be your name*: may all people, by deed as well as word, acknowledge your sovereignty over the entire earth. *Your kingdom come*: may your peace and justice prevail in the affairs of mankind. *Give us each day our daily bread*: give us the wisdom and virtue to stamp out the stupidity and greed that deprive some members of the human family of their share in the bounty of your creation. *Forgive us our sins for we ourselves forgive everyone in debt to us*: give all of us the grace to repent when we offend you, and help us show mercy to all who offend us. *Do not subject us to the final test*: strengthen us all in time of trial, but especially during our final hours.

The second key to this prayer is the word "Father." Of all the truths Jesus revealed, this is one of the least appreciated and most remarkable. The existence of a Supreme Being who caused and sustains the universe has been affirmed by many pagan philosophers, some of them long before the coming of Christ. But as the French philosopher Pascal pointed out, between the God of philosophy and the God that Jesus revealed there is an infinite difference. Jesus, the Word of God who became flesh, has assured us that God is not just an impersonal force of nature that keeps the universe from flying apart. In our experience the closest thing to God is a caring, loving father, in whose image we were formed, who looks after our needs and seeks our happiness.

Furthermore, we know from elsewhere that the word Jesus used to address his heavenly Father at prayer was not the equivalent of our formal "Father," but rather the Aramaic word "Abba," which little Hebrew children used in calling to their father. Our equivalent would be "Papa" or "Daddy." Such was the intimacy Jesus had in addressing his heavenly Father. That he wanted us to have the same trusting intimacy is clear from what he said to his disciples after dictating the Lord's Prayer.

No earthly father, he reminded them, hands out snakes or scorpions to his children. Shouldn't we trust our heavenly Father to be at least as considerate as an earthly father? All we have to do, Jesus tells us, is "ask him." The Lord's Prayer is the Christian community's way of asking our Father for the greatest gift of all: that his Holy Spirit reign in our hearts and breathe peace and justice into the hearts of all mankind.

A VERY BANAL MIRACLE

Eighteesnth Sunday in Ordinary Time.
A: Mt. 14: 13-21.

❖❖❖

If asked to name the most important miracles of Jesus, many would put the one narrated in this gospel high on their list. Everyone is impressed by the spectacle of five thousand families eating their fill on five loaves of bread and a couple of dried fish. Along with the changing of water into wine and the walking on the lake, this episode blends good theater with instant magic, just the formula many look for in a miracle. The word "miracle," after all, means something to marvel What could be more marvelous than turning a famine into a feast?

Examined closely, however, this episode raises a serious question. A huge crowd had traveled several miles on foot to where Jesus was heading by boat with his disciples. With them they brought their sick, and these Jesus healed without fuss, an action seemingly so routine that Matthew covers it in less than a sentence. From other accounts we know it was Passover season, springtime in Galilee. The gathering must have resembled a huge picnic, except for one detail: the people had brought no food. As evening drew on they began to show signs of hunger.

Can we imagine a more banal motive for a miracle? To postpone a meal by half a day is at most a minor bother. Jesus was used to healing the seriously ill and infirm—the blind and lame and leprous. Why did he now waste his Messianic powers merely to allay some stabs of afternoon hunger? Viewed on the scale of suffering alleviated, this miracle rates rather low.

And yet, the multiplication of loaves *was* an important miracle, one of the most important in the New Testament. Of this we can be sure if for no other reason than that it is recorded by all four evangelists, the only miracle of Jesus to receive such coverage. The evangelists must have seen in it some feature that eludes the casual reader. What is it?

We are mistaken if we view the gospel miracles simply as shows of magic, prodigies for the curiosity-seeker to gape at. They were above all powerful signs from heaven. Through them God's finger pointed to some truth he wanted us to think about.

First, they pointed to Jesus himself. In addressing the people of Jerusalem on Pentecost, Peter called Jesus "a man commended to you by God with mighty deeds, wonders, and signs" (*Acts 2:22*). Without miracles Jesus could have been dismissed as just another wandering preacher, without any seal of divine approval. With miracles he was recognizable as God's ambassador.

The miracles of Jesus were also parables in action, visible reminders of the kind of care God has for his weak and wayward children. When he gave sight to the blind, Jesus illustrated the benevolence the Father displays by opening our eyes to divine truths. As the leper was cleansed of his sores by the touch of Jesus, so we are cleansed of our sins by the same divine touch. A miracle would not be a miracle if it did not fill us with wonder. Our wonder, however, should be directed ultimately at the truths the miracle points to, to our loving Father in heaven and to the compassionate Son he sent to redeem us.

The miracle of the loaves had this unique feature, that it pointed to a specific action Jesus planned to perform in the future—the institution of the holy Eucharist. Looking at the crowd receiving bread from the hands of the apostles, we are reminded, first of the apostles receiving the Eucharist from Jesus at the Last Supper, then of ourselves receiving the Eucharist from the hand of the distributor at Mass. The apostles handed bread to thousands who were physically hungry. Every day and all over the world eucharistic ministers distribute the bread of life to millions who are spiritually hungry.

Anyone who questions the connection between this miracle of the loaves and the sacrament of the Eucharist should read the discourse on the Bread of Life in the sixth chapter of Saint John's gospel, which is closely linked to his version of this multiplication of loaves. Even more compelling evidence is in the description the evangelists give of how Jesus performed the miracle. Matthew writes, "Looking up to heaven, he said the blessing, broke the loaves, and gave them to the disciples." Almost identical words are used by the other three evangelists; they are found again in their accounts of the Last Supper; and they are spoken to this day by the celebrant at Mass just prior to his saying the words of consecration.

From earliest times the Church has seen in this miracle a sign pointing to the Eucharist. Out of five loaves came material nourishment for a multitude. Out of a few wafers of sacramental bread comes spiritual nourishment for a church full of worshippers. We are all hungry wayfarers on a journey to heaven. In the Eucharist we devour our pilgrims' food.

THE BREAD OF LIFE

Eighteenth Sunday in Ordinary Time.
B: Jn. 6: 24-35.

This gospel is about bread.

Bread in its everyday sense, the bread we buy in the bakery and that comes in a thousand varieties of shapes and ingredients, is one of life's unsung blessings. Who would be without it? Unless a meal includes bread, many feel it is hardly a meal.

Bread in its wider sense, food in general, is an even greater blessing. Not only does Christianity have nothing against a wholesome diet; it teaches emphatically that we are obliged to eat at least enough to survive. And although moral theologians tell us that gluttony, eating far more than enough, is a sin (one of the seven capital sins), even the most rigorous among them add that in itself it is a trivial sin, not worth mentioning in the same breath as pride, greed, or lust. Gluttony does not in itself make one unworthy of a seat at the heavenly banquet.

As well as feeding ourselves, we have a duty to do what we can to see that our fellow human beings are fed also, both here and in the less bountifully blessed parts of the world. Jesus once said, quoting Scripture, that one does not live "on bread alone" *(Mt. 4: 4)*. He could have added that one cannot live without any bread at all. Too many in our world are only a nibble or two away from starvation. A bread line is always a scandal, a famine usually a disaster. In a world where Jesus once walked, neither should be tolerated.

Bread can also mean food for the mind, a blessing no less precious than food for the body. That is why why no true Christian belittles education. Schoolchildren need nourishing lunches; but their most compelling need is for good mental food in the classroom. Unless their bread of learning is tasty and nutritious, our schools are a waste of money.

"Bread" can have an even higher sense, not food for our bodies or minds, but for our immortal souls. In the journey of life we need nourishment that only God can give. That is the meaning Jesus gives "bread" in this passage, the introductory verses to what has been labeled his "eucharistic discourse." That title can mislead, for it is not until the second section of the discourse that Jesus uses "bread" in the eucharistic sense, the sacramental bread that is served at Mass.

In this first section the word means simply the moral wisdom Jesus imparts through his teaching, the spiritual muscle he bestows on whoever "comes" to him and "believes" in him.

Bread for the body was on the mind of those who first heard this discourse. Jesus delivered it the day after feeding the multitude on five loaves and two fishes. Many who shared that meal went looking for Jesus the next day, finally finding him at Capernaum. Rather than praise them for tracking him down, Jesus rebuked them, saying they sought him only because they "ate the loaves and were filled." Instead of food that "perishes," let them seek food that "endures for eternal life."

One of the great stories in Scripture tells how God showered a bread-like substance called manna on the Jews as they journeyed to the promised land. In the time of Jesus many thought the Messiah's coming was imminent and that when he came manna would again rain down, turning Palestine into a land of plenty. Some of those listening to Jesus now wondered if this man who had multiplied the loaves and fishes could be that Messiah. If so, let there be proof. Let the heavens send manna again.

Jesus replied that God had already sent from heaven the "true bread" that "gives life to the world." When they asked him to give them this bread "always," he stated unequivocally that he was the bread God had sent: "I am the bread of life." No human could make a greater claim. The Jews who gathered in that tiny synagogue by the lake long ago heard Jesus claim to be the most important person in history, the source of spiritual nourishment for mankind throughout all history.

People today are not much different from the people Jesus addressed. Like them, our minds are too much focused on material things, the here and now, food for the body. We fail to see that our own most urgent hunger is for God. Having bread enough for ourselves and supplying bread to those in need are, as we have seen, Christian obligations. The needs of the body should not be neglected. But the bread we mostly crave is Jesus himself. His words contain more genuine wisdom than all the classrooms in the world. This wisdom is more desperately needed in the impoverished parts of the world than a thousand airlifts of food. No one knows this more than the hungry people themselves.

"Give us this bread always," the Israelites pleaded with Jesus. Two thousand years later, still hungry for God and in the presence of the same Jesus, let us make the same plea.

HOW RICH FOOLS DIE

Eighteenth Sunday in Ordinary Time.
C: Lk. 12: 13-21.

❖❖❖

Ne Quid Nimis—"Nothing in excess"—was a wise old Roman proverb. The Duchess of Windsor disagreed. One of her favorite sayings was that we can never be either too thin or too rich. Her first point is mostly ignored, but the second has hordes of adherents. Rare is the person who is satisfied with just enough to get along; most seem in a frenzy for more.

But wisdom has always been on the side of the proverb. All the great religions and moral leaders in history have taught that a surfeit of material possessions can bring death to the human spirit. Soft living has kept more people from greatness than poverty. The Roman philosopher Seneca put it well when he said that "a great fortune is a great slavery."

No one, however, assailed the pursuit of riches more vehemently than Jesus Christ. He never tired of telling his followers that one cannot serve both God and money, that riches are an almost insurmountable barrier to the kingdom of heaven. Today's gospel drives home this lesson. It opens with a man from a crowd imploring Jesus to take his side in a family dispute. The dispute, as is often and sadly the case, is about money. Jesus refuses. He knows what is at the root of the quarrel and puts it bluntly to the crowd: "Avoid greed in all its forms."

Jesus goes on to illustrate this warning with a story that has been labeled the parable of the Rich Fool. One does not have to be a fool to be rich, of course, but there is ample evidence that it helps. Look, for example, at the headlines generated by many of the world's millionaires. It must have been the harebrained high jinks of the upper-crust, moneyed class that the English writer Maurice Baring had in mind when he observed that "If you would know what the Lord God thinks of money, you have only to look at those to whom he gives it."

One doesn't have to be dishonest to be rich, either, although that helps even more than folly. Some people were born with the proverbial silver spoon, others have hit the jackpot with a lucky inheritance, a revolutionary invention, a winning lottery ticket, or even a blockbuster novel. But most fortunes are acquired through greed, and of the "many forms" that greed takes, probably the most common is stealing, which itself has a thousand forms. Few who go through life with a code of absolute honesty ever boost their bankroll to Himalayan heights.

What all greedy people have in common is an exclusive preoccupation with themselves. Money can be put to many good uses, but the greedy often pile it up solely for their own satisfaction. Even if they don't spend it, just having it makes them feel good, secure for the future. Now they can relax, eat heartily, drink well, without a care about how to pay the bills. Notice how the rich fool of the parable employs the first person singular as he schemes what to do with his windfall. "What shall *I* do, for *I* do not have space to store *my* harvest? This is what *I* shall do. *I* shall tear down *my* barns and build larger ones. There *I* shall store all *my* grain...and *I* shall say to *myself*...."

The final test of greed is not in how one has amassed possessions, but in what one does with them once they are stored away. Past greed can still be atoned for by using its gains for a worthy purpose. The Rich Fool, however, is oblivious of any purpose worthier than himself. He never reflects that while he enjoyed a bumper crop, his neighbors may have suffered a blight; that in his own village, at his doorstep perhaps, dwell wretches who do not enjoy three square meals a day. Like many rich people, he resists carefully the stirrings of a socially aware conscience. He suspects how much it can cost.

Even little children can catch the disease of greed. Parents and teachers have a tremendous responsibility. They must show by example that they realize we do not have a lasting city here on earth, that the only balance that counts is the sum of good deeds we can show God at the final judgement.

A college freshman once went for an interview by his academic adviser. "What is your ambition in life?" asked the adviser. "Well, first of all, I want to study hard here in college, get good grades," replied the student. "Good! And after that?" "I think I'll take up law." "And after that?" "I intend to make money, lots of it. Law pays well." "And after that?" "Eventually I guess I'll retire, travel, enjoy life, live well off my earnings." "And after that?" "Eventually, of course, like everyone else, I guess I'll die." "And after that?"

Jesus concludes with a similar question. "The things you have prepared, to whom will they belong?" Death is the final antidote against greed. We will die as penniless as we were born. What, if anything, will we have to show to our Maker?

“TOSSED ABOUT BY THE WAVES”

Nineteenth Sunday in Ordinary Time.
A: Mt. 14: 22-23.

We can easily miss the point of this episode. The temptation is to focus on a few physical details and let our imaginations whirl away. Did Jesus transform himself into a superman who defied the law of physics by swooping down from the mountain to the distressed mariners? At three in the morning the apostles became aware of a figure approaching along the waters. Terrified, they took it for a ghost. What exactly floated before their eyes? Was it Jesus stepping nimbly over the waves as though they were marble? That is what Scripture seems to say and how artists have painted the scene. Is it what really happened?

We can never know for sure. Certainly Jesus “came” to the apostles. But scholars disagree on exactly how to picture his “walking on the sea.” This, however, we do know, that Jesus was no circus performer. His aim was not to dazzle his apostles with the antics of a stuntman, for he never worked miracles frivolously. No, the point of the episode is not *how* Jesus came to the apostles, but *that* he came, and even more important, *why*. The words he spoke as he reached out to the nearly drowning Peter supply the clue. He came *to strengthen their faith.*

Consider the two scenes that open the episode. First, see Jesus “up on the mountain by himself,” wrapped in prayer. After dismissing the crowd and sending his apostles across the waters, he has gone there to converse with his heavenly Father. The apostles would find nothing unusual in that; he often stole away from them to snatch some moments of solitary prayer.

Next, see the apostles in their boat, “tossed about by the waves, for the wind was against it.” One of those sudden squalls for which this lake was famous has caught them by surprise. Seasoned fishermen that they are, the apostles at first sensed no danger. But the waves have kept pounding with no letup, and now they are having a hard time of it.

Put the two scenes together and they form a picture of what is in store for the Church that Jesus will found. In the boat are the apostles, men chosen and trained by Jesus to lead his Church after he is gone. Leading them, as usual, is Peter. But the boat should not be seen as just the physical boat that the twelve apostles sailed in. From the earliest times Peter's bark has been seen as a symbol of the Church itself. In it are not only the original twelve but all members of the Church until the end of time. The waves that engulf it stand for the incessant stormy weather that the Church must endure through the centuries.

We have no way of knowing what scriptural passages have been favorites of the popes throughout history, but this must surely be one of them. No pope has ever enjoyed a reign of totally unruffled calm. This episode would assure them that no matter how severe was the storm of the moment, they were not as endangered as they seemed to be. Jesus, who promised always to remain with his Church, has kept his promise. Although those in Peter's bark may not see him during a storm, he is guarding them from afar, praying for them on the mountain.

When Catholics look at the Church today, they sometimes imagine her woes are unique to our times, that the Church of old could never have been rocked as violently as ours is. Nothing could be further from the fact. Within decades of the Church's birth, severe storms shook some of the most fervent of the early Christians communities. Saint Paul's epistles as well as *Acts* make that abundantly clear. And in no century since then has harmony among Christians ever been perfect. Peter's bark has always held a shipload of sinners as well as saints. And it is afloat in an often vehemently hostile world.

What was the most severe threat the Church has faced in its history? The persecutions launched by Roman emperors? The chaos that came over Europe when this empire fell? The Moslem threat from the east? The heresies and schisms that threatened to shatter and too often did shatter Christian unity? Or are not our own times the stormiest of all, with the decline in vocations, the constant challenges to authority, the growth of secularism and hedonism among our own members?

Perhaps none of the above. Storms are as inevitable in the world where Christians must labor as they were on the waters the apostles once sailed. Our gravest danger today may be rather the same loss of faith that made Peter waver as he moved across the water to Jesus. This gospel should remind us that Jesus is as concerned for his Church today as he was for his apostles when they were in trouble on the lake. He is on the mountain, afar and unseen. But he knows what fearsome storms surround us. He watches us, prays for us. And *he will come* to us.

"STOP MURMURING"

Nineteenth Sunday in Ordinary Time.
B: Jn. 6: 41-51.

"O you of little faith, why did you doubt?"

A popular newspaper feature when I was a boy was Ripley's "Believe it or Not," which tickled millions with its seemingly endless supply of improbable facts and preposterous persons. Sometimes readers chose not to believe. Common sense cautioned that a feat recorded by Ripley simply could not be true.

This gospel tells how Jesus once provoked similar disbelief.

He was in the synagogue at Capernaum, addressing the congregation in words later known as his "Eucharistic Discourse" or, even better, his "Discourse on the Bread of Life." A day or so earlier, many of his listeners had been among the five thousand whom he fed with five loaves and two fishes. One would expect that after sharing that marvelous meal they would give instant credence to anything Jesus had to say, however improbable.

For a while they did. Until he made the assertion that he was some kind of "bread" that had come "down from heaven." At that, many in the congregation balked. Unless Jesus was using the word symbolically, they thought it ridiculous that he should call himself "bread." But what really upset them was his saying he came down from heaven. They knew where he came from; Nazareth was not many miles away. Yes, Jesus had worked wonders among them. But still he was a human being, no more highly born than themselves. How could he claim heaven as his homeland?

Throughout his ministry Jesus had encountered opposition. Almost invariably this came from the political or religious establishment, people like the sin-soaked Herod and the sanctimonious Pharisees. But now the hostility arose from within his natural constituency, the common folk who had always enjoyed his teaching and whose ailing kinfolk he had often cured. These people had looked on Jesus as their champion. But they would not let him insult their intelligence. His claim of a heavenly origin was absurd. Some vociferously chose not to believe.

We should not be too severe in judging those Israelites who did so. Imagine sitting before the TV one night and watching as some oddball preacher tells his audience he has a direct line to the Almighty.

Unlike the rest of us, born in such prosaic places as Cubao or Davao, he claims heaven as his native turf. Don't be fooled, he warns, by his presence on our puny planet. His stay among us lesser mortals is only temporary.

Wouldn't our protest be as loud as those of the congregation that heard Jesus at Capernaum? Especially if we had first-hand knowledge of where the preacher grew up, who his parents were, what schools he attended. Our disbelief would not necessarily be rooted in envy. Common sense tells us that babies, however cherubic, are not delivered direct from heaven.

Where the good people of Capernaum were mistaken was in applying their notions of common sense to Jesus. The whole of his teaching, indeed his very presence on earth, defied "common sense." That God became man, that the eternal Word once walked this earth in human garb, is the central doctrine of our faith. Of course we have trouble believing so improbable a truth. We can never comprehend why God has shown such love for creatures such as ourselves, who so little deserve it. But, common sense or not, it is true. Believe it or cease to be a Christian.

Jesus did not expect immediate acceptance of his words by the congregation at Capernaum. The ultimate evidence for his teaching, the foundation of our faith, was his rising from the dead, and that was still in the future. Even his apostles had a long way to go before fully accepting who he was.

We can be fairly sure, however, that at least some who blinked at what he said in this discourse at Capernaum did eventually join the infant church. And when they did, they could look back and realize that his words had been aimed, not just at those who first heard them, but at those who in future years would mull over them. They were aimed, among others, at us.

And to us he says, as to his first listeners, "Stop murmuring." His words about coming from heaven were no braggart's boast. Their point was not so much about him as about us; not so much about where he came from as why he came, which was to bring "eternal life" to whoever lives by his word. Those who do so he will "raise...on the last day."

Jesus was nearing the climax of his Eucharistic Discourse. What he was about to say would put an even greater strain on his listeners' powers of belief. Soon he would make clear that his words, "I am the living bread," were far from symbolic. He meant them literally, for they referred to the Holy Eucharist, the mystery that this entire discourse was leading up to.

He was soon to unfold this mystery in all its magnificence. That will be next week's gospel. Be sure to tune in.

THE MAN AT THE DOOR

Nineteenth Sunday in Ordinary Time.
C: Lk. 12: 32-48 (or 35-40).

❖❖❖

Visitors to Keble College in Oxford University are struck by a large painting entitled "The Light of the World," the work of the nineteenth century English painter Holman Hunt. In it they see a tall man clothed in the kind of garments people associate with biblical times. Lantern in hand, he is standing before a door during the middle of the night, poised to knock. After examining the painting for a while the visitor may notice a singular feature: the door has no outside latch, making it impossible for the man with the lantern to enter unless someone opens the door from within. This detail of the missing latch is not trivial. In a way it is the whole point of the painting.

This passage from Luke is one of several in the New Testament that Holman Hunt must have had in mind when he conceived this painting. Here Jesus tells a parable about a master of a household who goes away to attend a wedding. Apparently, among the Jews of old, weddings were as late in starting as they often are among us today, and so the master has no way of knowing at what hour he will return. He gives stern orders to his servants (in Christ's time a rich man would have a small army of them) to be ready to open the door as soon as he knocks. He does not want to be kept waiting outside.

"Gird your loins and light your lamps." In those days men wore tunics as outer garments, long loose-fitting robes. These impeded movement and had to be tucked under the belt (what Jesus means by "gird your loins") when action was required. The master does not want his servants to relax by unfastening their belts and letting their robes down; they must be ready to rush to the door at the first knock. The instruction, "light your lamps," has the same purpose. The ancients used oil lamps. For the servants to be ready, their supply of oil had to be plentiful and their wicks kept constantly trimmed.

The point of the parable is easy to grasp: we should stay awake, constantly ready, while we await God's final knock on the door of our lives. That the knock will come is certain. When it will come, the day and the hour, no one can be sure. We have all known people who heard the knock while they were still in their teens and we know others who are now in their eighth or ninth decade and still waiting. No matter when the knock comes for ourselves, however, of this we can be sure: only we can open the door to our souls. The Lord does not force his way into a soul that is not ready to receive him.

The parable goes on to tell what the master will do if he finds the servants awake and awaiting his return. His conduct is so uncharacteristic of masters that it must have struck Christ's original listeners as ludicrous. "He will gird himself, have them recline at table, and proceed to wait on them." Such a reversal of roles seems more fitting for a fairy tale than a biblical parable. No master has ever been known to act in this fashion simply because his servants carried out his orders. Possibly the closest any master ever came to such conduct was when at the Last Supper Jesus washed the feet of his apostles.

The whole point of this part of the parable, however, is its improbability. Jesus wants to startle us into an awareness that the rewards God has prepared for his faithful go beyond anything we deserve or could in our wildest dreams hope for. We cannot form a picture of what eternal bliss will be. Even Saint Paul could not describe it, although once during prayer he was granted a glimpse of it *(2 Cor. 12: 2-4).* Images of men and women sporting halos and strumming on harps as they float blithely through the clouds are worse than useless. This parable does not try to describe heaven, but it does tell us the most important thing about it: if we are prepared when we hear his knock, we will see our Lord and Master. He will be standing at the door of our souls, ready to lead us to an eternity of his company.

The passage concludes with an ominous image: a household that has been invaded by a thief in the middle of the night. "If the master of the house had known the hour when the thief was coming, he would not have let his house be broken into." Here, as in the first part of the parable, the lesson is the necessity of vigilance. Imagine the remorse of someone in our century who returns from a night with friends to find a home that has been ransacked by thieves. Why had no alarm been installed? Think of how much worse will be the groans of those whose souls are ruled by deadly sin when the Lord knocks.

Jesus is the Light of the World. He stands at our doorstep. Some day he will knock. Either we will admit him or the thief will break in and darkness will overcome us. The door, remember, has no outside latch. Only we can admit our Master.

THE WOMAN WHO WOULDN'T TAKE NO

Twentieth Sunday in Ordinary Time.
A: Mt. 15: 21-28.

❖❖❖

Only rarely do the gospels show Jesus moving among Gentiles. In this episode, however, we find him in the district of Tyre and Sidon, pagan territory just north of Palestine. For a Jew in biblical times such an excursion was a rare and unsavory event. The Israelites were a fiercely nationalistic people; non-Jews were disliked, distrusted, and routinely numbered among the damned. The fewer dealings one had with them the better.

Judging from his conduct during his public ministry, one might conclude (wrongly) that in this respect Jesus was no different from his fellow Israelites. His mission, as he tells the Canaanite woman in this gospel, was "only to the lost sheep of the house of Israel." As yet he had given no hint of what he would tell his apostles after his resurrection, that they must bring his salvation to "all nations" *(Mt. 28: 19)*.

When they did receive this commission, it must have seemed as outlandish to their ears as a mandate to evangelize Mars would to ours. Universalism was to be a trademark of the Church that Jesus founded, as novel as the notion of forgiving one's enemies. But this would be made manifest only later, after his apostles had been carefully prepared While Jesus lived, only Israelites heard his gospel. These were the chosen people, in God's plan the first to hear the good news of salvation, the ones from whom it would fan out to the rest of the world.

Why did Jesus violate his custom by entering pagan land on this occasion? The gospels do not say. Commentators speculate that he wanted to be away from the increasingly demanding people of Galilee for a while, to be undisturbed while he prepared his apostles for the final journey to Jerusalem. For whatever reason, there he was, almost as much a stranger in the environs of Tyre and Sidon as we would be in Katmandu. Jesus knew these pagans had as little use for Jews as Jews had for them. But at least they might leave him and his apostles alone.

One Canaanite (pagan) woman, however, refused to leave him alone. She knew his reputation as exorcist and sought help for her daughter, who was troubled by a demon. For the reasons we have just given, Jesus felt constrained to turn her down. But this did not satisfy a mother almost demented with anxiety. She kept coming back, pursued him, hounded him, shouted so loud and long after him that the apostles finally pleaded with Jesus to grant her request. It seemed the only way to get rid of her.

The dialogue that follows seems strange to our ears, hardly intelligible without some help from the commentators. The words of Jesus about food for the dogs seem harsh, even rude. They are softened, however, when we realize that (a) they were proverbial and (b) the word our version renders as "dogs" was closer to our "puppies" in the original. By quoting a familiar piece of homespun wisdom Jesus made his refusal as gentle as possible. His eyes could do the rest.

Entering into the spirit of the proverb, the woman replied that she would be happy to be treated like a puppy if only Jesus would grant her a puppy's reward. A crumb of his power over demons was all she sought for her daughter. This riposte (one scholar calls it a rare instance of humor in Scripture) obviously delighted Jesus. He was e ven more delighted by the faith it revealed, so much so that he gave in and granted her request.

This incident was important to the evangelist Matthew, who wrote for a largely Gentile audience. It proved that, at least on this occasion in his ministry (the gospels record three or four others), Jesus reached out to a non-Jew and thus anticipated the universal mission he would later give to his apostles. This same lesson Matthew had underscored in his infancy narrative, when he gave prominence to the story of the Magi who came from afar to worship at Bethlehem. The good news Jesus preached, the salvation he won, was for all nations.

We might reflect for a moment on how painful it must have been for Jesus to live among people as narrow and self-absorbed as were the Jews of old. But they were far from unique in their age or in human history. The virus of cultural isolationism has never been dormant or left any people untouched. Even among those who today are loudest in calling themselves Christian, some are quick to display hostility towards any race or group that is not their own. Sadly, they often do this in the mistaken belief that it is the way to prove they are loyal Christians.

It is not. Those who divide humanity into "them" and "us," who sprinkle their talk with slurs against those of other religions or races, have little right to the name of Christian. Only ignorance can excuse them. But after hearing the gospels Sunday after Sunday, who among us can honestly plead ignorance?

HE WILL RAISE US ON THE LAST DAY

Twentieth Sunday in Ordinary Time.
B: Jn. 6: 51-58.

❖ ❖ ❖

Our gospel readings in recent weeks have been from John's account of the eucharistic discourse. To grasp today's portion, let us reflect for a moment on the meaning of the Mass.

The Mass goes back to the supper Jesus shared with his apostles the night before he died. At his bidding (*Do this in memory of me*), the Church has for centuries re-enacted what Jesus did and said at that supper. The Mass, then, is a memorial service for Jesus Christ, performed in keeping with instructions he gave a scarce twenty-four hours before his death.

The gospels of Matthew, Mark, and Luke, as well as Paul's first epistle to the Corinthians *(11: 23-27)*, describe in almost identical terms what happened at that supper. Taking bread and wine, Jesus declared the first to be no longer bread but his body, the second no longer wine but his blood. To the Hebrews "body" and "blood" often meant, not the physical substances we mean by the words, but the whole person. That is their meaning here. What had been and still looked like bread and wine, Jesus transformed into himself, his full self, under both appearances.

Next, foreseeing the death he was soon to endure, Jesus offered what had been bread and wine, now himself, to atone for the sins of mankind (*My body will be given up for you; my blood will be shed for you and for all men so that sins may be forgiven*). Thus he turned what would otherwise have been a senseless slaughter into a sacrifice. At Mass Jesus comes to the altar and repeats that sacrificial offering. As well as a memorial service, then, the Mass is a true sacrifice.

John's gospel does not omit the Last Supper. He alone includes the moving words Jesus spoke to the apostles at the close of the meal. But about the words he spoke over the bread and wine during the course of the meal John is silent. Why?

Probably because his gospel has already included this eucharistic discourse. The words, *My flesh is true food*, were prophetic of the Last Supper. And he had just stated, in terms similar to those he was to use at the Last Supper, the connection between the Eucharist and his death: *The bread that I will give is my flesh for the life of the world.*

At these words, John tells us, a quarrel broke out. Since it takes two to make a quarrel, we can presume that some in the congregation tried to give Jesus a fair hearing. But the others drowned them out. "How can this man give us his flesh to eat?" John's language implies that the quarrel was stormy. We can picture the dissenters shouting out from the pews and shaking their fists at the pulpit. Eating human flesh, as Jesus seemed to be urging, has never been a pleasant prospect. The practice was particularly obnoxious to the Jews.

Rather than soften his statement, however, Jesus went on to make it even stronger, urging his listeners not only to eat his flesh but to drink his blood (*My blood is true drink*). Even the best disposed members of the congregation must have found these words hard to swallow. It must have seemed that Jesus was preaching cannibalism, a misunderstanding that persisted through apostolic times. Christians of the first century were sometimes accused by their pagan neighbors of indulging in a cannibalistic cult at their Sunday services.

Everyone finds the words Jesus spoke, first at Capernaum and then at the Last Supper, hard to believe. Without the grace God gave us at baptism, faith in the Eucharist would be beyond reach. To believe that what looks like bread is really Jesus Christ and that by eating this food we prepare our souls for eternity (*Whoever eats this bread will live forever*) is the supreme test of our faith.

The Eucharist is food for our souls, but not magic. Its effects do not flow automatically, no matter how ill we are spiritually. We all know what it is to be so sick in body that we cannot hold food in our stomach. The same can be true of our souls. For the spiritually healthy the Eucharist gives nourishment, restores health. But for the spiritually diseased, whose souls are infected with grave and unrepented sin, the Eucharist is worse than useless. Paul said to the Corinthians: "Whoever eats the bread or drinks the cup of the Lord unworthily will have to answer for the body and blood of the Lord" *(1,11:27)*.

But we need not be so sick. However unsavory our past, God's forgiveness is at hand in the sacrament of Penance (Reconciliation). Armed with his forgiveness, we will devour the Eucharist worthily if, as Paul said, we "discern" Jesus in the bread; that is, if we have faith that the bread we eat is not a mere thing, but the person of Jesus Christ; and that those who feed on him he will *raise on the last day*.

Peace at Any Price?

Twentieth Sunday in Ordinary Time.
C: Lk. 12: 49-53.

❖ ❖ ❖

Do not be surprised if you find this a difficult gospel. Most people do. What Jesus says about fire, baptism, and peace seems at first to make no sense. What kind of fire has he come to set blazing? Why does he speak of baptism as something he has yet to receive when he has already received John's baptism at the Jordan? How can the same Jesus who never ceased preaching peace now say he intends to incite strife within families?

Clearly Jesus is not using the words *fire*, *baptism*, and *peace* in their usual sense. But even when we know their meaning here, what this passage reveals about Jesus may still come as a shock to many, overturning what they thought they knew about the founder of Christianity. He means his words to shock. They are a corrective to half-baked notions many have about the kind of man he was and the kind of mission he came to perform.

Fire has a special meaning in the Old Testament and yet another in the New. Here Jesus seems to have both in mind.

In the Old Testament fire is often purgative. God rids his people of sin by placing them in the crucible of suffering, as a refiner purifies silver or gold *(Zech. 13: 9)*. Jesus came to cleanse us of sin, and he knew that for the process to work it must hurt. If we cannot quit smoking without sweat or shed pounds without discomfort, how can we expect to burn away our attachments to sin without some searing jabs of pain?

Fire in the New Testament often stands for the Holy Spirit, who at Pentecost came to the apostles in the form of fiery tongues, inflaming them with a desire to preach the gospel and send it sweeping like wildfire through the world. That fire is still burning, and we all have the job to keep it alive. If the gospel we have received does not send out sparks to others, then we have allowed its flame to sputter out.

The word "baptism" means literally a dip, an immersion, a plunge into water—rarely, except in holiday season, a pleasant experience. Here Jesus uses the image to represent his plunge into death, now only months away. The prospect of dying a common criminal attracted Jesus no more than it would any other human. He was no masochist, and the religion he founded does not glorify pain. His cry, "how great is my anguish until it is accomplished!" reveals his apprehension, his instinctive recoil from suffering. But this was the kind of death the Father chose for him, and he accepted this baptism willingly. If only he could take the plunge at once and be done with it!

Most of all, however, it is what Jesus says about peace that troubles people when they read this passage. "Do you think that I have come to establish peace on the earth? No, I tell you, but rather division." These hardly sound like words from the man we know as the Prince of Peace. At his birth angels proclaimed an age of peace on earth *(Lk. 2: 14)*. And among his final words to his apostles on the night before he died were "Peace I leave with you; my peace I give to you" *(Jn. 14: 27)*.

The peace Jesus rejects in this passage, however, is peace of a different kind: not the genuine peace of love and reconciliation, but the illusory peace of compromise and surrender. In 1938 Neville Chamberlain, prime minister of England, traveled to Munich for a parley with Adolf Hitler, the upstart bully of Europe. On returning to England Chamberlain announced that he had achieved "peace in our time." But the peace he spoke of was a chimera; all he had done was agree to look the other way while Hitler gobbled up Czechoslovakia. This was a peace cemented, not by mutual respect, but compromise. Such compromises may be necessary evils in the game of politics, but should never be confused with the kind of peace Jesus came to establish. They do not touch the heart. And they rarely work.

Compromise with sin never works. That is what Jesus says here. There are stands we must take that admit no compromise even if the price we must pay is a loss of peace. The examples Jesus gives, disruptions of the most intimate family ties, are extreme, but their very extremity is why he gives them. He wants us never to be in doubt about where our choice should be.

The early Christians often faced such choices. So did some of the most beloved names in the calendar of saints—Thomas Aquinas, Francis of Assisi, and Thomas More come to mind. Read their stories. They all had to choose between Christ and the false promise of "peace" in their own families.

Following the gospel is not all sweetness and light, soft organ music and parish socials. Without a brush with fire, an occasional plunge into suffering, and a personal war or two against the forces of evil, the badge of Christianity is a sham. The peace of Christ is genuine, but it comes with a price.

The Rock

Twenty-first Sunday in Ordinary Time.
A: Mt. 16: 13-20.

Peter was not just another apostle, any more than Everest is just another mountain or the American president just another householder on Pennsylvania Avenue. All the evidence points to Peter as a born leader. In the fishing partnership to which he belonged long before he set eyes on Jesus, he was Number One. Among the twelve chosen companions of Jesus, he was the spokesman for all. In every listing of them his name comes first.

After the Ascension Peter's eminence grew even more evident. If the followers Jesus left behind in Jerusalem were to survive as a community, they needed someone to take charge, someone to hold them together. *Acts* describes how Peter filled this role and became the undisputed leader of the earliest Christians.

Thirty years later Peter was in Rome. What had begun as a tiny gathering of Jews in Jerusalem was now a far-flung Church whose members were Gentiles as well as Jews. Communities of Christians were scattered throughout the Roman world, each with its own leaders. Peter, Bishop of Rome, was leader of them all.

Who elevated Peter to this position? As we learn here, Jesus himself. The words with which he did this are among the most solemn in Scripture, meaty enough for a hundred homilies. In any study of the origins of the Church, they are the central text. Without them we have scant Scriptural evidence for the primacy and powers of the Pope.

On the site where Jesus spoke, Caesarea Philippi, stood a massive temple honoring Tiberius Caesar, the reigning Roman emperor. The words of Jesus were more potent than any emperor's and would do more to alter the course of history than all the decrees of imperial Rome. They had a triple function. They gave Peter a new name, declared him a foundation rock, and empowered him to rule over the Church Jesus would soon inaugurate.

The man we know as Simon Peter was originally plain Simon. For recognizing Jesus as Messiah, he was rewarded with a second name, Peter, meaning rock. For the ancients names were important. They expressed the parents' hopes for what their child would be and do in life. By naming this apostle Peter, Jesus did more than express a hope. The name was his pledge that Peter would in fact be, like a rock, strong, solid, and enduring.

Peter had to be all of these, for on him Jesus declared that he intended to build his Church. This is the first mention of this intention in the New Testament. The word Jesus used for church means a community, a gathering of people for a common purpose. Note that it was Jesus, whom Peter recognized as "Son of the living God," who established this community and gave it its mandate. From Jesus, not Peter or the apostles, the Church took its origin. But the community itself was made of flawed human beings, with the very human Peter as its foundation rock.

Jesus next pledged that his Church would not be overcome by the gates of the "netherworld," a word meaning the abode of the dead. With these words, therefore, Jesus promised that his Church would never perish, but endure as long as the world endured. This was a bold prophecy, that even if the rock of Gibraltar should sink beneath the sea, his Church would remain.

Jesus went on to make clear that what he conferred on Peter was no empty title. Peter was not to be a figurehead with mere precedence of honor over others. His powers were real. His job was to rule. Jesus made this point with two metaphors, both loaded with meaning.

First, he made Peter keeper of "the keys to the kingdom." A key-keeper opens and shuts doors. The Church opens the gates of heaven by proclaiming God's word and dispensing Christ's grace. Thus with this metaphor Jesus gave Peter charge of the preaching of his gospel and the administering of his sacraments.

Second, Jesus gave Peter power to "bind" and "loose," adding that whichever action he chose would be ratified in heaven. This image was used by Rabbinic teachers of Mosaic law to describe their power to interpret this law authoritatively and thus bind or free consciences. Here Peter was given similar power, to interpret with authority the moral teachings of Jesus.

For the Church to endure, the office of Peter had to endure and his powers pass on to his successors, the bishops of Rome, whom we call Popes. "Pope" is from the Italian "Papa," the child's word for father—"Pop" in English.

To some people. "Pop" may seem an overly familiar way to refer to Saint Peter's successor. But the instinct behind it is sound. The Pope, our father, gives commands; we, his children, obey. But we ought not look on him as a cold authority figure. Forget the solemn trappings of the Vatican, the Swiss guards, the grim audiences. Think of the successor of Peter as the father of Christians, our Pop.

"SUCH A SILLY RELIGION!"

Twenty-first Sunday in Ordinary Time.
B: Jn. 6: 60-69.

❖❖❖

In an interview for a national magazine, a celebrated novelist once dismissed twenty centuries of Christianity with a shrug. "It is such a *silly* religion," he confided. He probably meant the quip to shock, but it is too shopworn for that, dating back to when the Church was in infancy. Saint Paul moved among the Gentiles who were as sure as any modern novelist that while paganism begot wisdom, the gospel promoted ignorance. To them Paul's preaching was "foolishness" *(1 Cor. 1: 23).*

Jesus himself, as we learn in this reading, was not immune from the accusation. The occasion was the discourse at Capernaum in which he revealed his intention to institute the Eucharist. At its close his followers split into two camps: those who walked away in disgust at the seeming idiocy of his words and those who, despite misgivings, remained loyal. This rift was the most serious crisis to strike his community of disciples.

The discourse of Jesus had been straightforward and unambiguous. Calling himself "living bread," he said his flesh was "true food" and that those who ate it would "live forever." His meaning was inescapable. Robert Bellarmine, the theologian-saint, once wrote that if the disciples of Jesus were wrong in thinking he meant exactly what he said in this discourse, he had no one to blame but himself. Had he not wanted them to take him at his word, he could have made this clear at the time. Doing so would have prevented a grave shrinkage in their numbers.

How grave it was, close to a mass defection, John makes clear, saying "*many* of his disciples returned to their former way of life." Severing their ties with Jesus in this way could not have been easy. They had abandoned home and livelihood to follow him, witnessed his miracles, been mesmerized by his preaching. But now they would walk with him no longer. The words he had spoken seemed the acme of silliness, mere pietistic gibberish. "Who," they asked, "can accept it?"

Can we? Can an educated person of today, someone bred in our technologically advanced civilization, believe that a wafer that in one instant is plain bread can in the next instant, without changing an iota in appearance, become a human being who died two thousand years ago? All science seems to cry out in protest, denouncing the notion as nonsense. Would not any religion that ask its adherents to believe this doctrine attract only the ignorant, the hopelessly anti-intellectual? Does not this make the Christianity we profess a truly *silly* religion?

No, it does not. At least not for those who take the pains to look at what we Catholics really believe about the Eucharist.

The first thing they will find is that this doctrine does not violate the laws of logic. We do not adore bread or say that bread is the flesh of Jesus or wine his blood. Even God cannot make that true, any more than he can make two and two equal five or a *no* mean a *yes*. What God can do, and does do in the Eucharist, is give one thing the appearance of another.

We call this transubstantiation—a theological mouthful, but its meaning is clear. In trans*form*ation the form or appearance of a thing changes while the substance, the reality, remains (think of a quick-change artist). In tran*substant*iation the appearance remains while the substance, the reality changes. At Mass what was bread and still looks and tastes like bread becomes in reality our Lord Jesus Christ under the appearance of bread. For the scientist it remains bread, since science deals only with appearances, what our senses tell us. But the omnipotent God, who deals with reality, does what he pleases with appearances. Thus the real question is not whether we accept the Eucharist but whether we accept the omnipotence of God.

What the Eucharist reveals about God, however, is not just his omnipotence but, more important, his love. Through the Eucharist, Jesus Christ remains in the world. If we visit one of our churches, we are truly in the house of God, for the same God-man Jesus whom we meet in Scripture is continually present in the tabernacle. And for the minute or so that the communion host retains the appearance of bread after we have received it, Jesus is present in us. As food enters and becomes part of our body, Jesus Christ enters and transforms our souls.

Do we, like "many of his disciples," find this teaching of Jesus impossible to accept? If so, we can no longer walk with him and call ourselves his followers. Faith is not a salad bar from which we can pick and choose. Accepting Jesus means accepting the whole of his teaching, the whole of his love.

By what perversity are the truths we find hardest to accept often those that reveal most about God's love? Jesus *is* God's love. His words *are* eternal life. To whom else shall we go?

THE NARROW GATE

Twenty-first Sunday in Ordinary Time.
C: Lk. 13: 22-30.

❖❖❖

Luke opens by saying that "Jesus went through cities and towns teaching." Today the word "teacher" usually means someone attached to a school or college, with a regular schedule of classes and a fixed roster of students. Jesus was not tied down in this fashion. He was Palestine's most popular roving teacher, stopping at any field or hilltop where people gathered to listen. The course he taught is as important today as it was then. Its description in a catalogue might read: "*Salvation*: How to love God and neighbor, and thus gain entrance to heaven."

Luke adds that in his travels Jesus had a goal—"all the while making his way to Jerusalem." He knew what awaited him there. It was not enough for Jesus to teach us how to find the road to heaven. He had to open the gate for us himself, and that meant paying the price. Ending his days on a cross just outside Jerusalem was the price he chose to pay.

Teachers spend much of their time answering questions, and Jesus was no exception. He knew, as all good teachers do, that the most interesting moments of a class period often come when the students fire questions from the floor. Today's gospel relates how Jesus fielded a question that was sure to awaken interest. In one form or another it has nagged all who take his teaching about salvation seriously: Will only a few be saved? When the final tally is in, will hell be fuller than heaven? Do the bad guys really outnumber the good?

For those listening to Jesus, the question was urgent, since the answer they had from their religious leaders was grim. Many scribes (semi-official guardians of the Mosaic law) taught not only that no Gentile could reach heaven, but that many pure-blooded descendants of Abraham would also fail. Salvation was assured only to those Jews who rigorously observed the hundreds of precepts that these scribes read into the law of Moses. Most Jews found the burden of these precepts intolerable. If the scribes were right, salvation was indeed for the few.

His listeners knew that Jesus often disagreed with the scribes, and so they may have hoped for an undemanding, indulgent answer. If so, they were disappointed. Jesus spent much of his energy toppling the iron edifice of scribal law. Its precepts, he made clear, were inhumane and therefore could not be from God. But he did not erect a cream-puff religion in its place.

His reply was a blunt command: "*Try* to come through the narrow door." Thus Jesus refused to answer the question directly; in his view it missed the point. What should concern us is not how many will get to heaven, but whether we will make it there ourselves. And that, he indicated, will take a heap of trying.

Actually, the English word "try" is too weak; it hardly does justice to what Jesus meant. "Struggle" would be closer, since the Greek word in Luke's text denotes an agonizing effort. He uses the same word for the agony of Jesus in the garden of Gethsemane. Think of the struggle to push one's way through a cramped space. Anyone who has battled to board a Manhattan subway car at rush hour or to squeeze into an African bus at almost any hour will get the picture. Jesus was not alone in paying a price for our salvation. We must pay a price too. To be a Christian one must engage in a lifelong struggle.

After adding the warning that many would "try to enter" heaven and "be unable," Jesus described their plight in a nightmare scene: a frightened, frantic crowd banging in panic at the door of heaven, imploring admittance. But they are greeted by Jesus himself with the icy words, "I do not know where you come from. Away from me, you evildoers!" Who are these door-bangers? Not common riffraff. Not the dope-peddlers, gunslingers, and child-molesters whom all the world brands as evil, but seemingly good people, respectable citizens.

Among them are many contemporaries of Jesus, Israelites who once ate at table with him, heard him preach in their streets. Neither blood ties to Abraham nor strict adherence to scribal law can save them. Had they attended to the teaching of Jesus they would have known that salvation is a matter neither of birth nor of merely external observance. A person's service of God must be sincere, total, internal. If it is, then love of neighbor and all the sacrifices this love entails will follow.

The lesson for our times is clear. Being baptized is not enough. Neither is going to church on Sundays and obeying every rule in the books. It is what happens inside a person at church and how well one guards the light of baptism that counts. Only those who struggle to live by the gospel will be saved.

That is why heaven is sure to spring surprises; why some who are now last will be first and some now first will be last.

PETER PUTS JESUS STRAIGHT

Twenty-second Sunday in Ordinary Time.
A: Mt. 16: 21-27.

Imagine receiving a medal for bravery on one day and being hauled into court for treason on the next. Something like that happened to the apostle Peter. In last week's gospel Jesus named him the foundation rock of his Church and made him keeper of the keys of the kingdom. That was Peter's reward for hailing Jesus as the Messiah, the liberator all Jews awaited. But in today's gospel, the immediate sequel to last week's, Jesus calls Peter a Satan, an obstacle to his Messianic mission.

Where had Peter gone wrong? Simply in this: he rejected the notion of a suffering Messiah. Like most Israelites he envisioned the Messiah as not just a spiritual but a political and military leader, one who would bring prosperity to Israel and free her from bondage to Rome. He saw Jesus maturing into a warrior-king in the mold of king David, leading the nation to victory upon victory. But he forgot two elementary facts about warfare: that to be a war hero one must pay a price; and that the more glorious the victory, the higher the price.

And so, on hearing Jesus predict a violent and ignominious death for himself, Peter was dumfounded. What could Jesus mean by saying he *must* go to Jerusalem and suffer greatly, that he *must* be put to death at the hands of the religious leaders? God forbid! Such a fate was unthinkable. And so, calling Jesus aside, Peter offered some free and friendly counsel: Drop this talk about suffering. That is not the kind of Messiah we all expect. No such disgrace will ever overtake you.

Jesus was probably reminded of the time the Evil One came sidling up to him in the desert to offer similar advice. Win the masses with bread and circuses, Satan whispered; worship me and I will give you such power the whole world will obey you. Jesus banished this desert sneak with, "Get away, Satan!" Now he crushed Peter with similar words, "Get behind me, Satan."

We ought not be harsh on Peter. His heart was in the right place. He just could not bear the thought that his friend Jesus would end his days in pain and shame. How could he conceive that this good man, whose preaching and cures were bringing many Israelites back to God, would one day be rejected by God's own representatives in the holy city of Jerusalem? No, it was not Peter's heart that was at fault, but his head. Jesus accused him of *thinking* as human beings do, not as God does.

What did Jesus mean by "thinking as God does"? Listen to the rest of what he says in this passage, his instructions to his followers on how they are to live. These are all summed up in a favorite paradox of his, sometimes called *the* Christian paradox: "Whoever wishes to save his life will lose it, but whoever loses his life for my sake will find it." Only when we agree with this paradox are we thinking "as God does."

On one level the paradox is a piece of cracker-barrel wisdom anyone can garner from everyday experience. We need no degree in psychology to know that happiness always eludes those who make a career of chasing after it. The most highly touted avenues to bliss—booze, barbiturates, crack, and casual sex come to mind—are among the surest routes to private hells. People who spend their days devising delights only for themselves end with only themselves for company. If asked who are the happiest people in the world, who would point to lonely losers like these?

Thomas Jefferson wrote that the pursuit of happiness is an inalienable human right. What he failed to add is that people who make the pursuit of personal happiness the all-consuming occupation of their life are doomed never to reach it. The prize goes to those who hardly have time to think of their own happiness, so busy are they bringing happiness to others. Happiness is a by-product, an unplanned bonus. Only those who are willing to forego it for the sake of others will actually win it.

On the lips of Jesus this paradox has a much richer meaning. He points to himself as both model and motive for the life of self-sacrifice he wants his followers to embrace. Whoever loses his life *for my sake*, he says, will find it. That means Peter must do more than mind the keys to the kingdom if he wants to gain eternal life. He will have to live and die as Jesus did, suffer and labor long and hard to bring the gospel to the world.

That is what Peter did. After years of laboring for the gospel, he was martyred in Rome. A legend that rings true says he died as he would have wanted, on a cross.

Was this paradox meant only for those who heard it from the lips of Jesus? No, it is for all Christians. We must all learn to think "as God does;" to bear *our* crosses and risk *our* lives for the sake of the one who bore his cross and gave his life for us. That, Jesus said, is the price of eternal life.

LIP SERVICE

Twenty-second Sunday in Ordinary Time.
B: Mk. 7: 1-8; 14-15; 21-23.

❖❖❖

Can religion harm us? Some secularists (often mislabeled as humanists) think so. They say we would all be better off if we had never heard of God—less fretful about what we superstitiously call sin, gentler in judging others, more at home with innocent pleasures. Is this true? Would our lives be fuller, would we be more open to beauty and alert to our social responsibilities if we had never seen the inside of a church or been drilled in the hoary restrictions of religion?

The answer, unfortunately, is a qualified yes—in the sense that *any* religion *can* be rendered harmful to those who profess it. However lofty its original purpose, a religion can be so twisted out of shape that it becomes de-humanizing. And an unbiased reading of history will conclude that this has sometimes been the case. Such counterfeit religions often have two things in common: first, their codes of behavior are cluttered with man-made prohibitions; and second, these prohibitions focus excessively on external conduct.

Look, for example, at the Pharisees. Not all Jews, of course, were Pharisees; and not all Pharisees were the sort that Jesus castigates in this gospel. But these were typical enough to give the whole pack of them a bad name; and the name "Pharisee" has since been fastened on practitioners of any religion at any time in history who have shared their attributes.

What a joyless lot these Pharisees were, with their mindless rituals and tiresome taboos! Even at mealtime they dared not let their guard down, for fear of violating the traditions of their ancestors. Here Jesus denounces their scrupulous washings of hands, their worrisome scourings of kettles and cups (as though Almighty God were on the lookout for a few specks of dirt). Elsewhere we learn of fasts they had to keep, foods they would not eat, people they would not break bread with.

A day in the life of a Pharisee must have been like a day in an airless dungeon. Their service of God was grim. One of the most damning things we can say about them is that they seem never to have had any fun. But virtuous living should be fun. Service of God, like all service, is best rendered with a smile.

How can we make it fun? Eliminate all prohibitions? Throw out all externals? That is what the secular "humanists" would have us do. But the answer is not that simple.

Any religion worth its name has prohibitions. Paying heed to them does not make us into Pharisees. We cannot serve God and at the same time seek unlimited self-gratification. Here Jesus lists the major no-no's found in all genuine religions: *unchastity, theft, murder, adultery, greed, malice, deceit, licentiousness, envy, blasphemy, arrogance, folly.* The point he makes is that these all "come out from within," which is the source of all evil as well as all goodness. They violate, not merely human precepts, but the law God has put in our hearts.

And all genuine religions are concerned with externals, too. All have their share of rituals—songs, vestments, processions, and sacred ceremonies. When Jesus denounced lip service, he did not mean we should not serve God with our lips, but that our lips—our hymns and vocal prayers—should be sincere, express what is actually in our hearts.

Religious rituals need not be empty gestures. Buddhist monks in Nepal hoist prayer flags in the morning to wave in the breeze all day. Who is to say this is not done in a genuine spirit of prayer? In the temples of India Hindus line up to receive a dab of red on their foreheads. Is this merely external show? We have no right to say so. Only those receiving the dab know if it brings them closer to God. Catholics attend Mass on Sunday. Are they honoring God *only* "with their lips"? Perhaps. But Mass can also be the closest we earth-bound creatures come to anticipating the praise we will render to God in eternity.

At worst, religious rituals are hollow routines people go through because tradition and their neighbors demand it. At best they are the most effective means we mortals have to express our delight in God's presence, our total allegiance to his cause.

"But he goes to church on Sunday, so they say that he's an honest man" goes the opening line of a song I heard from my father, who first heard it at Tony Pastor's vaudeville house in Old New York. Unlike most songs of today, this old-timer had a lesson, simple but worth-while: not that we should stop going to church, but that merely going there is never enough.

Pharisaism is not dead, not as long as some Christians treat their religion as a tribal rite, a set of motions they go through just because their ancestors did. Jesus wants to rule our hearts, not our lips. Will we let him?

Dining Out with Pharisees

Twenty-second Sunday in Ordinary Time.
C: Lk. 14: 1; 7-14.

Surrounded as he was by Pharisees at the table of one of the town's leading Pharisees, Jesus must have felt a bit like Daniel in the lion's den. Although far from any danger of being eaten alive, he was on very hostile turf. Not all Pharisees were leagued against him, of course; some few even secretly admired him. But as a group they were deeply suspicious of this strange prophet who had come out of nowhere to challenge their notions of how to please God. They feared that, if ever he succeeded in seducing the people with his lax doctrines, they might be toppled from their pedestals as leaders in Palestine. And so at this banquet they "were observing him carefully." Should he make one false move, they were ready to pounce.

Before they could find an opening, however, Jesus did some pouncing of his own. From what he had observed of their conduct, he was sure the guests needed a lesson in humility, their host a lesson in generosity. These he proceeded to give.

The lesson in humility was a parable, and at first sight it reads like a chapter out of Dale Carnegie's *How to Win Friends and Influence People.* To choose a lower seat with the set purpose of being moved to a higher one is the sort of advice one would expect to come out of Carnegie's bag of tricks. In other words, if you want to succeed, let others be your cheering squad; don't be too obvious in pushing yourself to the top.

There is nothing wrong with this advice. Most of the time it even works. But it is miles from genuine humility. People as proud as Lucifer have plumped themselves down in balcony seats if this seemed a good way to get an invitation to the boxes. Jesus hardly told parables to teach lessons like that.

What, then, *is* the point of this parable? Recall what Jesus saw when the dinner guests arrived—a shoving match among them as each tried to maneuver to a place of honor at table. Why? Because each thought he was more important than the rest, more worthy of respect. This is the attitude Jesus indicted, the pride of the Pharisees. Those who think they deserve better treatment than others are at risk of being judged least by God.

But what if someone is in fact better than others—more intelligent, better educated, more observant of God's law? All this was probably true of most Pharisees. Would it have been virtuous of them to deny it? Should Mozart have told the world he was tone deaf or Cleopatra pretended she was homely?

Not at all. When Jefferson wrote that all men are created equal, he did not mean all are equal in talents or breeding, but that all came equally from the hand of the Creator and therefore have equal rights. The fault of proud people is that they think they are more important *as persons* than others, that they belong to a superior breed of humanity. The old aristocracy was built on this fallacy. People of the upper class honestly believed they were born with an intrinsic excellence that put them above the common herd. They called it better blood.

Well, some may say, happily that notion is dead today. Aristocracy went out of style long before the model T Ford, didn't it? Not exactly. The pride some people take in their nationality or race can be as inane as pride in one's blood. It makes sense to take pleasure in reading the history of one's nation or race, but it is absurd to be personally puffed up because by accident of birth one descends from those who made that history.

Until one behaves towards all humans, however deprived or depraved or unwashed, with the respect that is owed to all God's children, one is not truly a Christian. The point of the parable is that no one is either above or beneath anyone else.

Pride was not the only fault for which the Pharisees were famous. Excessive care in guarding and increasing their material goods was also high on the list. Turning to his host, Jesus pointed out that his hospitality was not a gesture of pure generosity. Greed also played a part. He had invited these dinner guests less out of friendship than in the hope that he would one day be invited to dine at their homes in return.

The counsel Jesus then gave his host has a touch of fantasy. Would anyone really expect this pillar of society to bring "the poor, the crippled, the lame, the blind" into his home and sit them at his table? Scenes like that may occur in a Dickens novel or a Capra movie. One never sees them in real life.

No, one doesn't. But the individual Christian can put this lesson into effect without making a public scene. Everyone is obliged to some works of almsgiving. Even the poor can find people poorer than themselves. The trick of giving anonymously and generously with no hope of return does not require the hand of a Houdini. All one needs is the heart of a Christian.

WHEN CHRISTIAN OFFENDS CHRISTIAN

Twenty-third Sunday in Ordinary Time.
A: Mt. 18: 15-20.

❖❖❖

How our courts deal with wrongdoers against society concerns us as citizens. How we deal personally with those who wrong us individually is a more challenging matter, for it concerns us as Christians. Jesus warned us never to fall into the trap of seeking revenge. We are only make-believe Christians if we are unwilling to forgive, not just in words but from our hearts, all who injure us. But does that mean we must accept every injustice in silence? Never press charges? Never seek redress?

Not at all. In this passage Jesus outlines three steps for his followers to take if they have been wronged by a fellow Christian ("if your brother sins against you"). Clearly the first two steps should guide us whether the offender is Christian or not. Our obligation to behave with justice and charity does not cease even if the other party is a worshipper of the devil. The third step, as we will see, is rarely applicable today.

The first step is to go to the offender and thrash the matter out. At times such an encounter may be physically impossible or predictably futile, but usually it is worth a try. The aim here is to come to terms with the other party informally, to reach a just settlement amicably and without fanfare. Even if this means settling for less than what we think the iron law might require, it is the best approach. Peace and charity are more valuable than mathematically weighed justice. Only Shylocks insist on the last ounce.

How far people today have strayed from this Christian ideal is evident. The first move many of our contemporaries make is to call a lawyer. And lawyers do not earn their living by spreading the sweet fragrance of Christian compassion. Often their advertised aim is to squeeze as much as possible out of the other party or the other party's insurance company. Here is where the victim is in danger of turning into victimizer. Telling half-truths in order to bleed an insurance company may not be a punishable crime. But if our aim is to enrich ourselves beyond what in our heart we know we deserve, doctoring the facts is a sin, possibly a grave sin.

This first step should be private. "Go and tell him his fault between you and him *alone*." Some people broadcast their grievances through the entire neighborhood, thus sinning themselves, for if the other person's sin is not already public, we sin in making it so. In any case, suspected offenders should have a chance to tell their side. Sometimes at the bottom of what seems a monumental injury is a simple misunderstanding.

The next step, if the first gets nowhere, is to ask "one or two" neutral parties to intervene—if we are lucky enough to find go-betweens both willing and able to assume the burden. Here is their chance to be what Jesus wanted all of us to be, peacemakers. With no direct interest in the matter, they should be able to give a fair judgment. Perhaps they can persuade both parties that both are, at least to some degree, in the wrong.

Only if a settlement is still impossible ought a Christian proceed to the third step, a higher tribunal. The tribunal Jesus had in mind when he spoke of telling "the church" was obviously a small, tightly knit community of Christians. Such communities dotted the Roman Empire during the early years of Church history. On occasions these communities had to expel recalcitrant members in the manner Jesus here prescribed, barring them from Christian worship as firmly as tax-collectors and Gentiles were barred from the synagogues of ancient Israel.

Such severe penalties were usually imposed only after every effort to win the offender over had failed. The most important part of that effort, Jesus said, was prayer, with the entire community seeking divine guidance. Such group prayer was sure to be answered, for where even "two or three are gathered together" in his name, Jesus promised to be among them.

That these communities had the authority to mete out such punishment is clear from what Jesus said about binding and loosing. Both their punishments and their pardons were ratified in heaven. The Church in our century still has authority to excommunicate and occasionally exercises it. But such sentences are no longer imposed by the congregations of the local church.

The kind of court Jesus envisioned, therefore, is rarely available today. Our secular courts, although they lack assurance of divine guidance, may provide the only feasible remedy. Having recourse to them if all else fails is permissible for a Christian, provided this is not done in a spirit of revenge. How can we be sure of that? Prayer for guidance is the only answer. Preferably group prayer, where all are gathered in the name of Jesus and share his spirit of compassion.

Why All this Rigmarole?

Twenty-third Sunday in Ordinary Time.
B: Mk. 7: 31-37.

❖❖❖

Dwell for a moment on the setting for this episode. Jesus was in "the district of the Decapolis," that is, pagan territory. Those who brought the deaf-mute to him, begging him to lay on his hand, were Gentiles who had heard reports of the cures Jesus worked among his fellow Jews. To these Gentiles he was not a prophet, not a physician of broken souls, but a magical healer, a fixer of damaged bodies. Now they stood before him, driven there by a simple impulse. The neighbor they brought to him, one of their own, was in distress. Could Jesus help?

Spontaneous compassion for the sufferings of others, like that of these pagans for the deaf-mute, has always marked the serious Christian. Without it we cannot honestly say we have chosen Jesus as our model. Nor can we read about his miracles without being moved by his manner of dealing with the sick and handicapped. His care for them was personal and painstaking. See how he went about curing the deaf-mute in this episode.

He worked slowly, deliberately. First he took the man off by himself, away from the stares of the curious. His aim was to help the poor wretch, not win medals for himself. Next he pressed his fingers on the deaf-mute's ears, touched the impeded tongue with a drop of saliva, looked up with a groan, and said "*Ephphatha*!" meaning "Be opened!" Imagine how we would feel if we were ailing and the leading specialist in town were to drop what he was doing and give us that kind of attention gratis!

Why all this rigmarole? Why prolong the process? Could not Jesus have restored the man's hearing and speech with lightning speed, without moving a finger or uttering a word?

Ask any doctor why, even in this age of wonder drugs and million-dollar diagnostic machines, the medical profession still implores its doctors to cultivate the proper bedside manner. The sick person does not want to be treated as a statistic for hospital records, but as a human being in whose plight the doctor has a personal stake. The good doctor treats all patients as family. That is how Jesus treated this deaf-mute, how he treated all who came begging for his help.

In biblical times little was done, little *could* be done, to bring relief on a large scale to the sick and infirm. Medical science had not even reached infancy. Hospitals as we know them did not exist. Whatever medicine was practiced—both pitifully little and hopelessly ignorant—was done person-to-person.

This is not an appeal for a return to the primitive ways of the past. Modern medical science has performed wonders that the ancients never dreamed of, and only a fool would want to undo them. But few would deny that today's health centers could use a dash more of the person-to-person care that Jesus was so good at. Health workers who take Jesus Christ as their model can supply much of it. They cannot work miracles as he did, but they can supplement the book-knowledge of modern medicine with the kind of personal touch Jesus displays in the gospels.

All of us can do our share. We do not have to be doctors or trained nurses, nor need we send out search parties to uncover opportunities for exercising the corporal works of mercy. Hardly a week passes without someone in need, however slight, crossing our path. If such casual opportunities seem too few, we can explore the possibilities for volunteer service. There is probably not a hospital or institution for the disabled in the country that does not have a welcome mat out for volunteers.

I once knew a blind man who after years of study received a doctorate in literature and was offered a teaching post in a university. Unfortunately, the university was situated in a distant city where the man was a complete stranger. Up to that time he had always had friends to guide him outdoors and fellow students to read aloud for him. How could he manage to maneuver through a strange city and handle the paperwork of teaching without help? With this question still unanswered, he moved to his new city, hoping for the best but fearing the worst.

Within days of his arrival his phone started ringing. Complete strangers offered to read to him and introduce him to his new surroundings. The informal information service of the blind had flashed the emergency message ahead, and a host of volunteers was quickly rounded up. Without them my friend's teaching career would have ended before it began.

We may lack the time or talent to enlist formally as volunteers, but we are all called to perform some kind of service for others. If we are serious about our vocation as Christians we will give freely whatever help we can to those in need. The compassion of Jesus is alive today only if we, his followers, keep it alive. May he open more ears to his call!

A VERY CHRISTIAN KIND OF HATRED

Twenty-third Sunday in Ordinary Time.
C: Lk. 14: 25-33.

❖ ❖ ❖

This is one of those New Testament passages that many prefer to skip. It contains two of the harshest of the "hard sayings" of Jesus, making demands so extreme, so seemingly inhuman, that even good Christians try to look the other way.

How can our preachers shower praises on the family that stays together if Jesus urged his followers to "hate" their nearest kin? How can a father put bread on his table and pay the school fees of his children if he must "renounce all his possessions"? Above all, how could these unfeeling words have come from the same gracious Jesus who supplied wine for a marriage feast and restored life to a widow's son?

Some have suggested that Jesus addressed these words only to a select few. In all ages, starting with those incredible monks of the desert, small numbers of Christians have shown how seriously they took the gospels by embracing lives of awesome austerity. On every continent one can still find comfortless monasteries and convents where monks and nuns spend their spouseless days and nights in prayer and penance. Isn't it likely that Jesus meant the sayings in this passage for these shock troops of his army, not the simple foot soldiers like ourselves? Shouldn't today's average churchgoer just ignore them?

No, they should not. Luke's account is explicit. Jesus addressed these words to "great crowds," inviting all to become his disciples, that is, to learn from him (the word "disciple" means learner) how to live. But before they accepted his invitation, Jesus wanted them to realize where it would lead. Unlike the builder who started a project without funds to finish it, or the king who rushed into battle without weighing the odds against victory, they should consider the cost. Here Jesus warned that the cost would be high.

The cost is as high for Christians today as for those who first listened to Jesus. That is why these hard sayings are read at Sunday Mass. No Christian can hide from them.

Today's churchgoer, however, should understand these sayings as those who first heard them did. Jesus was a Jew, and like all Jews of his time often gave emphasis to his words by what is called Semitic exaggeration. That is what he was doing here. The same Jesus who told his followers not to hate even their enemies could not have meant that they were literally to hate members of their own family. Nor did he mean that no one could follow him unless totally stripped of material resources. After all, neither he nor his apostles were penniless vagrants.

What he did mean, and mean so emphatically that he spoke with the strongest Semitic exaggeration, was both simple and sublime: no love or attachment—not even for the dearest members of our family or for the money we have earned and the property we possess—should interfere with the love and attachment we owe to the God who made us and the Son who redeemed us. In short, *God comes first—no matter what.*

What in the concrete will putting God first mean in the life of a Christian? Certainly that it will be a life of hard decisions. People and things are always trying to crowd God out of our lives. The cross that Jesus told us to bear will never be far if we decide not to let God be the loser.

Think of the martyrs of the early Church who were tossed to lions for refusing to worship idols. Think of Saint Thomas Aquinas, whose decision to join the Dominicans provoked his own kin to kidnap him and hold him captive for over a year. Think of Thomas More, who forfeited his position as chancellor of England and ignored the tears of his wife and daughter rather than acknowledge the king as head of the Church.

Better yet, don't think of these cases. They are too dramatic, too far removed from the everyday. It does no good to daydream about the choice we would make if loyalty to Jesus demanded death, financial ruin, or loss of a loved one. We should think rather of the countless small decisions for or against Christ that confront us daily. These are not the life-or-death choices we see in high drama; but they add up.

Those who are unable to forgo a moment of illicit pleasure, or a gesture of petty revenge, or a chance for a spiteful remark, are not likely to face a firing squad rather than renounce their Faith. The cross Jesus said we must bear is a *daily* cross. Mostly it consists in the many petty sacrifices we must make if we are determined to be agents of God's justice and peace.

Jesus said we must hate even ourselves (our "own life"). That is the heaviest cross. It is hard to say no to a loved one, harder yet to say no to Number One. But it is what Jesus did and the ultimate test of those he has called to follow him.

How Often Forgive?

Twenty-fourth Sunday in Ordinary Time.
A: Mt. 18: 21-35.

The gospel opens with Peter putting a question to Jesus: how often are we obliged to forgive a brother who sins against us? This question was much discussed by the Rabbis of the day. Some claimed biblical authority for limiting the obligation to three times. Enough, they felt, was enough. After a fourth offense no one should be blamed for turning a deaf ear, no matter how shrill the pleas for mercy. Peter proposed a more generous limit: seven times. Where did Jesus draw the line?

The reply of Jesus, seventy-seven times, is a biblical expression. It means forever. A Christian willingness to forgive is not measurable in numbers. No matter how often we have been outraged or how sorely our patience tried, we must never refuse forgiveness.

Why? Jesus explains with a parable. Unlike some of his parables, this presents no knotty problems of interpretation. After a single reading its lesson comes through loud and clear: if we ourselves want to receive mercy from God after we die, we must show mercy to those who offend us while we live. To be forgiven, we must forgive. All Christians are familiar with the equation. We repeat it whenever we recite the Our Father.

One detail, however, may puzzle. The parable seems to suggest that a creature can somehow hurt Almighty God, make a dent in his bliss. bliss. The king, who stands for God, is out by a "huge amount" because of his servant's misconduct. Even if the royal treasury has not been totally emptied, its contents have been gravely reduced. But it cannot be this way with God. He is eternally and serenely happy, incapable of suffering injury. His glory can never fade, no matter how many insults we humans hurl at him. How can this parable suggest otherwise?

As usual, theologians solve the problem with a distinction. True, God's *intrinsic* glory cannot be shrunk by anything we earthly creatures do. But his *extrinsic* glory can be diminished; the praise that should be rendered to him here on earth can be muted, the service we owe him denied. That is what sin does.

An analogy will help. Imagine you are a renowned sculptor and one of your statues, your masterpieces, is on view in an art museum.

One day a frenzied visitor lunges at it with a hammer, pounding much of its marble magnificence into powder. (A lunatic once did exactly that to Michelangelo's *Pieta* in the Vatican). Has this deranged vandal hurt you? No. You remain intact. But he has defaced your creation, lessened the pleasure people take in your works, muffled the applause you merit.

That is what sin does. God is not hurt, but his glory on earth is blurred, for sin disfigures his creation. Above all, it damages the soul of the sinner. As human beings we are God's masterpiece, created in his image; as Christians our souls are stamped with the likeness of his Son. God wants us to reflect his goodness, to re-enact in our dealings with others the compassion of Jesus Christ. Grave sin assaults God's purpose as savagely as the madman assaulted Michelangelo's statue.

What happens when God forgives our sins? He restores us, puts the crushed marble back together, makes the statue whole again. And he does this completely, no half measures. After the madman attacked the *Pieta* in the Vatican, experts spent months restoring it. Today the naked eye detects no trace of damage. God's forgiveness does the same for our souls.

Recall how Jesus treated Peter, the apostle who denied him three times. Peter wept bitterly for his sin, and Jesus forgave him without reserve, restored him to the position he had held. Recall how Jesus treated the penitent thief crucified alongside him. For the thief's one work of compassion and one plea of mercy, he was promised entry into Paradise that day.

That is how we must forgive. Not just often, but always. Not grudgingly, but totally. Not from the lips, but as the final sentence of the parable says, *from the heart.* Words alone will not do. "Forgive your enemies," a wag once quipped, "but keep their names on file." If that is how we forgive, we can expect no forgiveness from God. We will find ourselves on his file.

The parable closes with the king delivering the unforgiving servant to the torturers, thus inviting us to think about our day of judgment. When we stand before God for sentencing, our time of trial will be over. What will God see? Our souls will be utterly bare to him, our most private thoughts and secret desires an open book. Will our hearts reflect the forgiving heart of Jesus? Or will they be frozen with resentment against those who have wronged us, still yearning to get even?

Will our immortal soul, which God carefully fashioned and Jesus often and lovingly restored, be smashed beyond recognition?

THE MEANING OF "MESSIAH"

Twenty-fourth Sunday in Ordinary Time.
B: Mk. 8: 27-35.

❖❖❖

One of the first things we learned as children was that our religion started with a man from Nazareth named Jesus Christ. I doubt that I was the first to suppose that Christ was the family name of this founder and Jesus his given name. We all had first and last names. Why not a Jew of two thousand years ago? What I did not know was that the Jews of old had no family names. What counted for them were a person's given name, village, and ancestry. That Jesus was from Nazareth, the Son of Joseph, from the house of David, was all the identification he needed.

Then where did "Christ" come from? It is not a name, but a title; not, however, a title Jesus grew up with, since at Nazareth no one but his mother and foster father had even an inkling of his real origin and destiny. Thus, although "Christ" was what Jesus was born to be, for most of his life the world took no notice. In time, however, that he deserved this title dawned on his disciples. This gospel tells how Peter was the first to express this conviction and call Jesus the "Christ."

You may wonder where "Christ" appears in the passage, since what Peter calls Jesus is "Messiah." True, but "Christ" is Greek for the Hebrew "Messiah," and since Greek was the language of the early Church, it replaced "Messiah." Both meant "anointed," and since kings were anointed with oil, both came to mean "king." To say "Jesus Christ," then, is to say "Jesus, the king."

When they spoke of *the* Messiah, however, as Peter does here, pious Jews meant, not any king, but a special kind of king, one they were sure would one day come. In popular imagination the Messiah would be a divinely appointed superman whose destiny was to save the nation. Part warrior, part shepherd of God's people, he would first crush their enemies, then ascend the throne David had occupied a thousand years earlier, and finally reign over a land of peace and prosperity. Exactly how the Messiah would accomplish all this was unclear. A few prophets had hinted he would also be a suffering Messiah, but that notion did not take hold. At least not until Jesus came.

In calling Jesus Messiah, Peter spoke for all the apostles. For months they had been with Jesus, listened to his words and witnessed his works. Many people thought Jesus was a reincarnation of one of the great prophets of Israel, another Elias or another John the Baptist. But his apostles knew better. Jesus was not, they were sure, just another holy prophet. He was *the* holy prophet, *the* Messiah, *the* Christ, *the* king.

That is what Peter declared, and if this episode had stopped there, it would have been remarkable enough. But the aftermath was even more remarkable. Jesus went on to answer the question that had stumped Israelites for centuries, telling *how* he would win victory. His words stunned the apostles, especially Peter.

Jesus said nothing about ascending David's throne in glory. Instead, he described how the religious leaders would reject him and put him to death. When, almost as afterthought, he added that he would rise from the dead, Peter was too flabbergasted to notice. A suffering Messiah was to Peter an impossibility. It was unthinkable that the Christ should die in ignominy.

And so Peter called Jesus aside for some friendly advice. His words reveal consummate gall. He actually chided his lord and master, corrected the man he had just declared to be a king, telling him to stop all this gloomy talk about suffering and death. A Messiah cannot suffer. David's successor cannot fail.

The response of Jesus could not have been harsher. Peter's advice, he said at the outset, was worthy of Satan, straight from the handbook of hell. The rest of his rebuke is one of the most important passages in Scripture, revealing, for the first time in Mark, the mystery of the cross. As future leader of the Church, Peter was to be guardian of this mystery.

Peter had been both right and wrong. Yes, Jesus was the Messiah. Ultimate victory was certain. What Peter did not see was that victory is not served on a platter, even to the Messiah. The victorious warrior must first pass through fire. The task of the Messiah was to deliver, not Israel from bondage to Rome, but mankind from bondage to sin. To do this he had to pay the price of our sin. The price was his death on the cross.

Jesus concluded with a personal touch. He knew that Peter and the others wanted to follow him and thus share in his glory. To do this, he now told them, they must first share in his suffering. To save their lives they must risk losing them, to rise with him they must be willing to die for him. His cross must be their cross. That is what we mean by the mystery of the cross, and it is as true for you and me and all Christians who ever lived as it was for Peter, as it was for Jesus himself.

"THIS MAN WELCOMES SINNERS"

Twenty-fourth Sunday in Ordinary Time.
C: Lk. 15: 1-32 (or 1-10)

❖❖❖

What is a sheep worth, one out of a flock of a hundred? To most people, no more than the market price of its carcass. But money is not the only measure of value. To the Palestinian shepherd in biblical times, a lost sheep was worth a long day of searching for it through deep ravines and thorny thickets. How much value he put on a single sheep was written on his face as he carried it home, shouting his joy to his neighbors.

What was a drachma, the silver coin of today's parable, worth in the time of Jesus? To a wealthy landowner, hardly the effort to pick it up. To a casual laborer, a full day of toiling in the fields. And to the woman in the parable, who had only ten drachmas to her name, a day of frenzied peering and poking through every corner of her house until she found it.

What is a human being worth? Physically, not much. The dollar value of the chemicals in the average person's body is little more than a hundred. In 1978 a human skeleton went for $475 (a gorilla's was ten times higher). But a human being is not just a collection of chemicals and bones. The least important person on the face of the earth is worth more than money can buy. How much more? If we measure the value of a sheep and a drachma by what the shepherd and the woman endured to retrieve them, we can measure the value of a human soul by what Jesus endured to redeem it. That is the point of today's parables.

Jesus did not address these parables to the air. Gathered about him were "tax collectors and sinners." The tax collectors were a sorry lot. Scorned as money-grabbers and double-dealers, they had few friends among their fellow Jews. The people Luke here names "sinners" were public sinners, habitual and brazen. They probably felt no shame when they were shunned as sinners, since by their own conduct they had chosen to be outcasts.

Within earshot were some scribes and Pharisees. It was also for them that Jesus told these parables, to show them the true worth of all human beings. About their own worth no doubts assailed them. Strict observers of the law, they felt sure that among Israelites they ranked highest. But for tax collectors and sinners they had only contempt. If Jesus were truly holy, they thought, he would never befriend such trash.

Most people agree that a human being has a unique value, infinitely higher than any animal of the zoo. I say "most" rather than "all" because dissenters exist. Treating other humans as no better than beasts has made many a person rich—professional terrorists, pornographers, sweat-shop owners, slave traders of yesterday, many racists of today. The list goes on.

Why does a human being deserve greater respect than a gorilla? Many people are fuzzy on this issue. Some speak loftily about the "dignity" of the "human family," without saying exactly why our family outranks the laughing hyena's. Even Thomas Jefferson's famous words do not fully satisfy. If it is "self-evident" that we are all "created equal" and endowed with "inalienable rights," how come so many fail to see the evidence?

The Christian tradition affirms that God not only created the human race, but created each member of it in his own image, that is, with a destiny beyond the grave and with the means to shape that destiny. It is above all because we come from God and are made to return to God that we are sacred. To treat a human being as less than sacred is an assault on God himself.

In these parables Jesus makes the case for human value even stronger. If as individuals we lose sight of our destiny and wander from God's path, Jesus Christ seeks us out as the shepherd did his lost sheep and the woman her misplaced drachma. When the Pharisees looked at the sinners and tax-collectors who gathered around Jesus, all they saw were souls that were lost. But no soul is lost if Jesus thought it worth his trouble to try to save it. He suffered and died for *all* sinners.

No Christian wants to be numbered with the scribes and Pharisees. They are the villains of the New Testament, the enemies of Jesus Christ. But this gospel story shows how easily one can fall into Pharisaism. The tax collectors and sinners, after all, *were* thoroughly disreputable. It takes a heap of faith to see beneath the surface, to realize that even the convicted child molester and professional racist were made in God's image and redeemed by Jesus Christ.

We cannot know how guilty these are in God's eye. But of this we can be sure: the invisible grace of Jesus Christ is working to save them. A few seconds of grace can cancel years of depravity. Heaven is bound to have many surprises, not least the many unlikely faces who will gaze on the face of the Lord.

UNFAIR!

Twenty-fifth Sunday in Ordinary Time.
A: Mt. 20: 1-16.

❖❖❖

This parable used to be read in church once every year. I remember how it puzzled me the first time I was old enough to pay it any attention. The landowner's conduct seemed so unfair. Don't those who labor longer deserve higher pay? And not only does his pay scheme seem unfair. By arranging for those who labored all day to see the latecomers get the same wages as themselves, the landowner appears to be rubbing it in.

Even children know life is unfair. But isn't God supposed to be different? Children also know that the rich can do what they please with their money. But isn't heaven supposed to even things out? Yet here is Jesus taking sides with the landowner, saying this is how things are run in the kingdom of God.

The fact that it puzzles is what makes this such a good parable. It starts us thinking, makes us ask questions. The answers are there to find if we look carefully.

Start with the workmen who were hired first. See how their faces light up when the landowner finds them at dawn and offers the usual wages for a day's work in his vineyard. These casual laborers know how lucky they are to find any employment at all. Laboring in a vineyard is no fun, but at least they now know that tonight their children will not go to bed hungry.

Only when they see what the latecomers are paid does their day turn sour. If the parable does nothing else, it shows how pointless is envy. The grumbling of these laborers adds not a tad to their wages. Its only reward is more discontent. That is all envy ever breeds. No vice yields fewer dividends.

Now look at the laborers who are hired late in the day. They are no lazier than those hired at dawn, only less lucky. For long idle hours they have lingered in the market, waiting for their chance, but no one has come to hire them. That these men have waited all day for work makes no difference to most employers. An hour's work should win an hour's pay, not a pittance more. No one should expect payment for good intentions.

That is precisely one of the points of the parable. This landowner stands for God, and God has a keener sense of justice than we do. With him intentions are important, even more so than results. Those who try hardest are in his eyes the best, even if they come in last. And his eyes are all that count.

But the parable is not just about the folly of envy and the value of good intentions. Its main focus is not on the laborers but the landowner, that is, on God. What it tells us about God is that he is generous beyond all expectations. His kingdom is open, not only to those who seem most deserving, but to many who to us seem utterly undeserving. If we think his generosity is blameworthy, that is because we are blind. Jesus came into this world to open our eyes.

Jesus may have had in mind the blindness of the Pharisees when he spoke this parable. They found fault with him for spending time with tax collectors and sinners. But Jesus saw more virtue, at least more potential virtue, in many of these outcasts than in the sanctimonious Pharisees. The parable also had a warning for his disciples. They were the first in time to receive his gospel. Let them not think they are in all ways better than the generations of Christians who will come after them. Finally, the parable speaks to us, lest we think our mere presence in the Church guarantees our salvation or that we are invariably more virtuous than the unbaptized.

When I was a boy one of most vicious gangsters in the United States was gunned down by a rival mobster. Rushed to the hospital, he stayed alive just long enough for a deathbed conversion. A priest gave him the sacraments. When the details hit the papers some Catholics were upset. Why, they grouched, did a priest help that thug into heaven? After his lifetime of sinful fun, will he go to the same place as ourselves? What use were all those years we spent on the straight and narrow?

They could have added another question. Can any of us be sure where we are going after death? God's gift to the world was Jesus Christ, who died for all mankind, not just for those from good homes and protected surroundings. None of us knows what goes on in the heart of a single human being. We cannot assess human guilt or say for sure how any of us will end. Our task is to work out our own salvation in fear and trembling.

We have no claim on God, any more than the laborers had on the landowner. The landowner did not have to hire them, nor did God have to give us existence, still less destine us for heaven. Everything we have is his gift. To some of us he gives more than to others, but to all far more than we merit. For even a day in his vineyard we should be grateful.

WHO IS THE GREATEST?

Twenty-fifth Sunday in Ordinary Time.
B: Mk. 9: 30-37.

❖❖❖

"I'm the greatest!" was the refrain Muhammad Ali loved to chant to cheering fans back in the sixties and seventies. And for a long while he was. For seven years he reigned supreme among the heavyweights of the world. Few took offense at his boasting. His scramble to the top had been skillful, and no one disputed his claim.

Jesus showed no such tolerance towards his apostles, however, when he overheard them quarreling among themselves about who among them was the greatest. He had just returned with them to Galilee and they were on the road to Capernaum. The apostles did not know it, but this was the first leg of what would prove to be their final journey with Jesus to Jerusalem. In contrast to his usual practice, Jesus asked that his presence in Galilee be kept secret. He knew the end was near and wanted as much time as possible alone with the Twelve. They had to be prepared.

As part of that preparation he for a second time described the death that awaited him in Jerusalem, along with his rising from the dead after three days. And for a second time his words just sailed over their heads.

On arriving at Capernaum he asked them what they had been disputing so heatedly on the road. He knew, of course. But good teacher that he was, he wanted to draw the truth from them. Sensing that the truth would displease him, they responded with silence. This gave him the opening he wanted. Rabbi-like, he sat on the ground and had them all sit in a circle around him. Then he patiently explained to them what it took for a follower of his to deserve to be acclaimed the greatest.

The gist of his explanation was simple. He found no fault with their wanting to be first, provided they understood the organizational chart he had in mind for his Church. In the pagan world those at the bottom serve, while those at the top enjoy the perks. But among his followers the order should be reversed. The rulers at the top must serve. Only by becoming servants of others will they make themselves worthy of staying at the top and entering the Christian roster of the great.

Note that Jesus did not say his Church would have no rulers. It would, and in its early years the apostles would fill the ruling posts. His point was rather how they must rule. He must be their model. His entire life had been spent in the service of others. They must learn to do the same.

Soon Jesus spotted a child toddling nearby. Placing it in their midst, he put his arms around it. This scene, one of the best known in the gospels and much beloved by Christian artists, is easily misunderstood. Jesus was not just displaying affection for children, but giving an object lesson. This was his way of driving home the lesson he had just delivered. It showed better than words exactly what he meant by greatness.

To grasp his meaning, we must understand how children were regarded in biblical times. They were loved of course, as children should be. But not sentimentalized, not purred over as patterns of goodness, never made the center of a household's doting attention. Totally dependent on adults, the child had no rights, was neither a "he" nor a "she" but an "it." Its place was at the bottom; its job to wait on its elders and otherwise keep out of their way. In Aramaic, the language Jesus spoke, the word for child and servant was the same. That tells a lot.

That they should not look down on this child or any other helpless person at the bottom of the heap was the message Jesus conveyed by his embrace. The child was only a servant, but so was Jesus. As the child was the servant of the household, Jesus was the servant of mankind. The apostles were not to trample on those whose position was beneath their own. Their rule must be benign. They must be servants to the servants, treat even the lowest person as though that person were Jesus himself.

The lesson was meant not just for the apostles but for all who in future centuries would rule over Christ's flock. Popes, bishops, pastors, all who hold authority in the Church must beware of lording it over their subjects, of treating the people of God as things rather than what they are, immortal souls who have been redeemed by Jesus Christ and whose care has been entrusted to the Church. Whatever they do to these little ones, Jesus will take as done to himself.

The lesson is more for the clergy than the laity. But all can learn from it—parents, teachers, bosses of all kinds. The way for a follower of Jesus to achieve greatness in any field is never by stepping on subordinates. To reach the real top we must treat all others as we would treat Jesus himself. That alone will make us great in God's eyes. No other eyes matter.

SERVING TWO MASTERS

Twenty-fifth Sunday in Ordinary Time.
C: Lk. 16: 1-13 (or 10-13).

❖❖❖

Whoever first said, "Honesty is the Best Policy" would find little to be happy about in today's world. If the daily headlines are any indication, few people take the maxim to heart. Dishonesty is rampant and comes in a thousand forms—financial swindles, kickbacks on government contracts, political bribery, deceptive advertising, insurance fraud, not to mention a slew of such minor league misdeeds as purse-snatching, pickpocketing, and shoplifting. How many of those who commit these crimes are caught? Of those caught, how many are convicted and made to restore their ill-gotten wealth? How many ever see the inside of a jail? We all know the answer: only a tiny minority.

That honesty is the best policy is a slogan drilled into children, but even children must realize that in at least one respect it is a lie. Honesty is no way to make a million. Much of the time dishonesty, crime though it is, pays, and pays big.

Dishonesty is not new in the world. The ancients were as adept at it as we are. Even the Bible is full of it. Although Jesus lived poorly and made his disciples do the same, he was no greenhorn in matters of monetary fraud. He knew how widespread cheating was and how much harm it did to souls. That is why he often attacked the greed that begets dishonesty. Today's gospel is an instance. As usual, he begins with a story.

The main character in the story, the manager of a rich man's estate, is no model of Christian conduct. First of all, he is a slipshod manager, "squandering" his master's property. When finally he is found out and is about to be sacked, he turns also into a crooked manager. At his suggestion and with his connivance, his master's debtors enrich themselves at his master's expense. In this way the manager ensures his future, confident that when he is fired and must make his way in the world outside, these partners in crime will not let him starve. Even his wronged master praises him for his prudent foresight.

A strange narrative, you may think, to come from the lips of Jesus. But tales of chicanery arouse closer attention than tales of virtuous living. And for the three warnings he is about to issue,

Jesus wants all the attention he can get.

First, he warns his listeners that if they want entry into "eternal dwellings" of heaven, they must be as wise in using worldly goods as the crooked manager showed initiative in providing for his future. By his crooked handling of his master's account he has gained friends who will be useful to him later. In an ironic twist, Jesus tells his listeners to display a like initiative: let them so manage the riches entrusted to them during this life that they build credit for themselves in the eternal hereafter.

This is not just a matter of avoiding dishonesty. Our honestly gotten goods, if properly used, will increase our happiness in heaven rather than merely add to our comforts on earth. Here Jesus is making a subtle appeal for almsgiving. The way to win friends in the next world is by imitating the generosity of the saints to the poor in this world. If we love money so much that we can't bear to part with it even to help the needy, we can expect no lavish welcome party in heaven.

The second warning is against even petty acts of dishonesty. "The person who is dishonest in very small matters is also dishonest in great ones." The habit of pocketing money that is not one's own begins with filching small coins, not grand larceny. Once implanted, however, the habit grows. In time even thousands will fail to satisfy. Greed never gets enough.

Here is where parents make the difference. Nothing they can give their children is more precious than the example of total honesty even in the slightest matters. But if they have an itchy palm, their children are sure to notice. And children are great imitators; they are almost sure to follow suit.

The final warning is directed against people who try to have it both ways—remain good Christians while joining the mad chase for money. Jesus says this is impossible. We cannot serve both God and money (which Jesus here calls Mammon). God demands total service: "You shall have no other gods besides me." Money also demands total service. It doesn't fall from the sky; if it is the main thing we want in life, we will soon be stepping on the rights of others and ignoring the laws of God in order to get it. That is a form of idolatry.

Idolatry did not end when the ancient Egyptians stopped their worship of snakes and the Hebrews of the golden calf. To be an idolater all one has to do is decide that making money, not honesty, is the best policy. That kind of idolatry is as up-to-date as the stock returns, as widespread as simple greed.

TWO VERY DIFFERENT SONS

Twenty-sixth Sunday in Ordinary Time.
A: Mt. 21: 28-32.

❖❖❖

Does going to church do a person any good? Are those who never miss Mass on Sunday better human beings than those who routinely skip it—kinder, less greedy, more truthful? Probably all of us have known people who were regularly among the first in the pews on Sunday but spent the rest of the week snapping at neighbors and e xchanging snide gossip. Where is the value in religious observance if it turns out specimens like these?

Some Catholics use this kind of reasoning to justify their own poor observance. As they see it, attendance at church can be a form of hypocrisy. The reason they refuse to join the parade up the aisles on Sunday, they insist, is that they do not want to add to the humbuggery. They acknowledge they are sinners, but open and straightforward sinners, not hypocrites.

This gospel may shed some light on their position.

The parable is among the shortest told by Jesus. It contrasts two sons: the first a loudmouth who promises to obey his father and then proceeds to do as he pleases; the second an insolent brat who brushes aside his father's command but later repents and obeys him. The situation is recognizably true to life and could easily have been stretched into a full-length parable, as it is in the parable of the Prodigal Son. Here, however, Jesus gives the barest outline of events.

The point of the gospel is less in the parable itself than in the people who listened to it and the scolding they received at its close. The encounter took place in the temple; those Jesus addressed were the "chief priests and elders" *(23)*. In Matthew these are code words for the religious leaders who were soon to bring about the death of Jesus. Even after his death they pursued him. *Acts* tells how after Pentecost they did everything in their power to crush the Church he left behind.

Their position as religious leaders of Judaism was a sham. A few years earlier they had heard John the Baptist's call to repentance, but his words failed to move them. They had also heard Jesus, even witnessed some of his miracles. But all they saw in him was a threat to their own entrenched position. His message, like John's, was bitter medicine. By calling on them to repent, both had demanded that they begin by acknowledging their own sinfulness. That, however, they could never bring themselves to do. What had they to repent of? If ever mortals merited the label of hypocrisy, these did. Like the first son in the parable, they were all talk and no performance.

The second son stands for the "tax collectors and prostitutes" whom the priests and elders abhorred. The gospel often pictures Jesus associating with these outcasts of society. But we should keep in mind that neither Jesus nor the gospel writers glorify them. They were the dregs of Jewish society, and those who sentimentalize them distort history. Their modern counterparts are not the sort we would want living near us in a family neighborhood. We should not think they had the approval of Jesus, any more than did the second son before his repentance.

Jesus did, however, reach out to them, as had his cousin John, who baptized hordes of them at the Jordan with his baptism of repentance. Both had some success, for many did repent. Doing so must have been painful, and the process of reform slow and stumbling. Neither John nor Jesus ever promised otherwise.

What does this have to do with the question we started with? What about the people who omit Sunday Mass on the grounds that the church is chock-full of hypocrites? They are wrong. Most churchgoers are like the second son in the parable—not hypocrites, but sinners who repent of their sin. Admittedly, some hypocrites do slip in. I once knew a man who said he went to church because it made him feel good to mingle with respected members of the community. An army chaplain once told me that some officers came to church because they knew their commander would be there and they wanted to impress him. Sunday Mass does no more good for people like that than offering sacrifice in the temple did for the high priests who mocked Jesus on the cross.

But these are surely exceptions. Most people in the pews are there because they want to be closer to God and at peace with their neighbors. For this they need help, and seeking help in church is not hypocrisy. That is what churches are for. The first thing the worshipers do at Mass is "acknowledge" their failures and ask the Lord for "pardon and strength." These are the second son's words. No hypocrite could say them and mean them.

We don't have to pretend we have conquered the devil in order to be churchgoers. All God asks is that we try our best to get the devil out of our system. Holy Mass, the replay of the Sacrifice of Calvary, is surely the best place to do that.

Jesus Speaks Out on Tolerance

Twenty-sixth Sunday in Ordinary Time.
B: Mk. 9: 38-43; 45; 47-48.

❖❖❖

One day John and his companion apostles happened upon a man, a total stranger, who went about expelling demons in the name of Jesus. Now to John this name was a kind of trademark over which the apostles had proprietary rights. After all, Jesus had commissioned only them to invoke it. How dared this outsider, who had possibly never exchanged two words with Jesus, make use of his name? Since he was not one of their company, he was clearly an impostor. And so John asked Jesus what the apostles should do to put and end to the fellow's flagrant malpractice.

Nothing, was the reply. The man did no dishonor to Jesus. Since he was not on Satan's side, he must be on God's side. With so much evil in the world, why hinder one who does good?

This plea for tolerance has not always been heeded. History records persecutions and even wars among Christians over who had the right to fly the banner of Jesus. Happily, such militant "Christianity" is rare today. Although our age has not been conspicuous for tolerance in general, at least the violent feuds that once raged among Christians are mostly things of the past.

The disease of intolerance, however, still infects some Christians, and so that first lesson of this gospel bears repeating. People deserve to be judged more by their actions than by their creeds. When a believer does palpable wrong, we should admit it is wrong. When a loud-mouthed atheist does a good deed, we should all stand up and cheer.

Some Christians are prone to forget, however, that tolerance can be misdirected. While we cannot be too tolerant in dealing with imperfect human beings, towards certain behavior we should be fiercely intolerant. That is the second lesson of this gospel.

Christians ought never condemn those who hold religious error, but they should not shrink from condemning the error itself; they should befriend the sinner, never the sin. God alone knows the human heart. The most egregious error may appear to others as clearest truth, even grave sins may be committed in the conviction that they are acts of virtue.

The danger today is that our indulgence be extended beyond

the violator to God's law to the violation itself. That is what some molders of public opinion are constantly urging us to do. They call this tolerance. Anything else they call bigotry.

If so, Jesus Christ was a bigot. In his eyes nothing excuses sin. No evil comes to it, no suffering so great we should not prefer it. Of course his words about forfeiting hand or foot or eye rather than committing serious sin have a touch of Semitic exaggeration. He does not mean literally that we should cut off a limb or gouge out an eye because we feel they lead us to sin. But he does mean we should be willing to lose a limb, even life itself, if that is the price we have to pay.

Consider homosexuality. Today people say we must not hound or discriminate against homosexuals. True enough. Provided they do not try to propagate their way of life, even active homosexuals s hould be given the respect and love that are owed to all God's children. But when the pleaders for universal tolerance tell us that as good citizens we should condone, even approve, willful homosexuals acts, their advice is Satanic.

Our civil laws may not outlaw homosexual acts between adults. Perhaps they should not. But God's law, the law that binds all mankind, does. Of that there is no room for doubt among Christians. Scripture proclaims it, human reason affirms it, our centuries-long Christian tradition confirms it.

Consider pornography. Few sins are fouler, especially when, as is often the case, it is peddled to children. It can warp for a lifetime their notion of sexual intimacy, blast their chance for a wholesome marriage. Even in those places where it is not an offense punishable by civil law, peddling pornography is a moral pestilence, punishable by the Almighty.

By definition pornography glorifies sin and therefore induces to sin. Its purveyors, if they know what they are doing, are among those condemned by Jesus for enticing "little ones" to sin. Better they be encased in cement and tossed into the nearest river than that they continue to ply their trade.

Pornography is not, as some seem to think, a merely trifling menace. It is a multinational network of filth that rakes in billions annually. To give all the child-corrupting pornographers of the world the punishment that fits an enterprise of this magnitude, the good Lord may need more than a billion pounds of cement—and a thousand rivers of hell to drown them in.

A Lazarus at Our Door?

Twenty-sixth Sunday in Ordinary Time.
C: Lk. 16: 19-31.

This parable opens with a scene of stark realism. Although set in ancient Palestine, its essential feature—the proximity of the desperately poor to the disgustingly rich—has been commonplace through history. In almost any major city today are posh restaurants where the well-clad dine on fine wine and pheasant, while on nearby streets roam the ragged homeless, feeding on scraps. Even poor countries have their quota of fat cats, unaware of the derelicts at their doorstep.

The poor person is rarely unaware of rich people, so ostentatious is their manner of living. Lazarus squatted at the rich man's gate, eager for crumbs from his table. From there he could not help seeing the feasting and hearing the carousing into the night. The rich man, on the other hand, although he must have caught glimpses of the diseased beggar, might as well have been blind to him. The poor can be all but invisible to the well-fed and comfortable.

From realism the parable shifts to fantasy. That there is a hereafter where virtue will be rewarded and sin punished is no fantasy, but many of this story's details about the next life are pure make-believe. As in all good fantasies, however, these details convey truth, in this case a triple truth.

The first is that God will even things out in the end. The rich man writhes in torment while Lazarus bathes in bliss, and they can neither switch places nor exchange visits. Thus the story reminds us that we have only one life to live on earth. How we live here determines where we will dwell for eternity.

But why has the rich man been sentenced to damnation? Only a dyed-in-the wool socialist would say he had no right to spend his own money as he pleased. What then was his sin? If he did anything to deserve being numbered with the wicked, the story should tell us what it was. Is just being rich a sin?

No, but being rich is dangerous, which is the second truth suggested by this story. Jesus never tired of warning against riches. He knew that those who can afford a soft life often buy it and that soft living is the usual prelude to vicious living. The pampered few whose clothes are the latest fashion and whose food the rarest delicacies have little time for God.

But this does not fully explain the rich man's punishment. Wealth is dangerous, yes, but not always fatal. No one was ever damned merely for being a dandy and enjoying fine food. History tells of kings and queens who lived in sumptuous palaces and yet achieved sainthood. Why was it not possible for the rich man in the story to elude the pitfalls of wealth? Which of the evil deeds associated with riches did he actually commit?

Perhaps none. The third lesson is that a sin of omission can be as deserving of punishment as a sin of commission. We are not in this world just to avoid evil, but to do good. The rich man could well have been damned, not for what he did, but for what he did not do, for not lifting a finger to help Lazarus.

If asked why he did not, he could truthfully reply that Lazarus was not his responsibility. He had not created the economic conditions that made such destitution possible, and so he had no obligation to correct them. This attitude is shared by many. The playboys and playgirls of the world are parasites, taking what pleasures they can and giving nothing in return. That others go hungry while they squander their dollars on delicacies is, they admit, unfair; but, they add, not their fault. Life was never meant to be fair, but the survival of the fit. Luckily, they are among the fit.

The rich man had no obligation to solve the economic problems of the time or to lead a crusade against unemployment and homelessness. Had he done either he would doubtless have qualified for a special bonus in the hereafter. But the challenge God gave him was simpler: to recognize the ties that bound him, a child of God, to all other children of God, even the most wretched. Just by giving a gram of help to Lazarus, whom God placed at his gate, the rich man might have qualified for heaven.

The gospel of Jesus Christ offers no sure solution to the problem of world poverty, no political panacea to alleviate the distress of the underclass and clear the homeless from our streets. Any person who can find a cure to these ills should do so, and God's reward will be generous. Meanwhile, like the rich man in the story, we all have more immediate challenges.

People like Lazarus keep crossing our paths. As the rich man in the story had Moses and the prophets to tell him how to treat Lazarus, we have the words and example of Jesus Christ, who died and rose from the dead for us all. If this is not enough to convince us to help any Lazarus we meet, nothing is.

Long Shot

Twenty-seventh Sunday in Ordinary Time.
A: Mt. 21: 33-43.

❖❖❖

We all enjoy it when a long shot wins, especially if the long shot is ourselves. If you think no such good fortune has ever come your way, think again. Just a hundred years ago the odds against any of us even coming into existence were higher than a trillion to one. Just being born makes us all big winners in the lottery of life. God's providence guided the wheel, and we can never thank him enough for having it land on us.

That is not the only windfall we should thank God for. Christianity—its very existence—is another. Humanly speaking, once Jesus was gone, his gospel was doomed to die. God kept it alive. That is one of the truths behind this parable.

Jesus addressed the parable of the vineyard to some high priests and elders, members of the Sanhedrin, the supreme council of Judea. At the close of the parable he cited a passage from the Psalms where David speaks of a stone that is rejected by the builders and against all odds becomes the cornerstone for a new and more glorious edifice. His listeners did not realize it, but Jesus was speaking of himself and the Church he intended to found. He was the stone, his Church the new edifice.

In a short while he would be rejected by the very men he was now addressing, the rulers of Israel, just as the stone was rejected by the builders. He would be treated the same way the landowner's son is treated by the tenants in the parable, the way the prophets were treated by the ancestors of his listeners. As the landowner's son is ejected from the vineyard and killed, Jesus would be crucified on a hill outside Jerusalem.

The point of the parable, however, is that the murder of the son is not the end of the story. Because the rulers of Israel, who were guardians of God's vineyard, had been disloyal, they would be driven from the vineyard and destroyed. But new tenants would replace them and a fruitful harvest follow.

Who among those who heard this parable thought it possible that this would happen? That the leaders of Judaism would be swept away, their temple destroyed, and God's vineyard inherited by Gentiles? That the ancient covenant God had made with Israel would be handed over to a Church that this Galilean carpenter would found and his rag-tag band of followers would lead? Above all, that this Church would endure? All odds were against it.

To his listeners Jesus was an ill-educated preacher from Galilee with a following as ill-educated as himself. What chance did such ignorant zealots have when pitted against the collective wisdom and learning of Israel's high priests and elders?

After the Ascension, when the disciples were on their own, the odds weighed even more heavily against the survival of the gospel. In *Acts* Luke tells us that the loyal followers of Jesus in Jerusalem then numbered only a hundred and twenty. On Pentecost, at the close of Peter's stirring homily to the crowd of pilgrims, three thousand more were added. Did this look like the beginning of a Church that would rock the world? Was this the great edifice for which Jesus was the cornerstone?

Acts goes on to describe an event that proved to be a turning point in the fortunes of the early Church. One day Peter and John passed a cripple begging for alms at the entrance to the temple. Gazing intently at him, Peter told the beggar to rise and walk "in the name of Jesus Christ the Nazarean" *(3: 6)*. At this the beggar leaped up and jumped for joy. Peter then addressed the astonished onlookers, explaining that it was by the power of Jesus, whom they had recently crucified, that the beggar now walked. All were invited to join the growing band of Christians. That night the count mounted to five thousand.

For their effrontery in keeping alive the name of Jesus, however, Peter and John were hauled before the Sanhedrin. There they faced many of the same men who a few months earlier had condemned Jesus to death. Some may even have been among the priests and elders who first heard Jesus narrate this parable. When asked to defend himself, Peter recalled the Psalm Jesus had cited. Now, however, he made explicit what Jesus had only hinted, declaring boldly that Jesus Christ "*is* the stone rejected by *you* the builders, which has become the cornerstone" *(4:11)*.

The members of the Sanhedrin eventually set Peter and John free, but not before charging them never again to preach in the name of Jesus. To which Peter shot back that it was God they must obey, not men; that they could not remain silent about what they themselves had "seen and heard" *(20)*.

Two thousand years later, the Church still proclaims what these two saw and heard. Jesus, the rejected stone, is still the cornerstone. And his Church still defies the odds. "By the Lord has this been done, and it is wonderful in our eyes."

MARRIAGE THE WAY GOD MADE IT

Twenty-seventh Sunday in Ordinary Time.
B: Mk. 10: 2-16 (or 2-12).

❖❖❖

We live in sad times. Consider the mushrooming statistics of divorce. In 1816 the president of Yale University in Connecticut deplored the "alarming and terrible divorce rate" in that state. What alarmed him was news that one of every hundred marriages there ended in divorce. Today divorces across America are more than half as numerous as marriages themselves, and the evil is spreading. Even traditionally Catholic countries, long resistant to divorce, show signs of having caught the virus.

Well, one asks, what is sad about divorce? Aren't husband and wife lucky to be able to split if they find they have made a mistake? Shouldn't marriage breed happiness? When it doesn't, why keep up the pretense? "If at first you don't succeed...."

Even those loudest in plugging for divorce, however, can sense that something is wrong. Every divorce is tragic, an admission of failure. For spouses it always spells heartache; for children, years of confusion and perhaps a lifetime of damage. Only fools are proud to be divorced. Behind their bravado often lurks a nagging doubt. Maybe Yale's president had reason to be alarmed. Maybe, just maybe, Jesus Christ had it right.

No one ever voiced stronger distaste for divorce than Jesus. Imagine his appearing on one of today's TV talk shows to field questions on divorce. Has he softened his opposition, he is asked, since he gave that harsh answer to the Pharisees long ago? Does he still think the good God frowns on divorce?

Yes, he would answer. The reason is that in his eyes the rules of marriage date from "the beginning of creation." They are God's rules, implanted by him in our very nature. Mere humans lack the power to change them, even if they had the wisdom.

Two rules are important. First, marriage is exclusive: one man, one woman. Second, it is permanent. The second rule is what Jesus stresses in this passage, using a bold image to express this permanence. Once married, he says, a man and woman become "one flesh." Neither they nor a divorce-court judge has the right to sever their union, any more than to cut a human being in half. In the old carnival shows magicians entertained audiences by the illusion of sawing through a woman. But divorce is no illusion. It rips apart flesh that God has made one.

Only a hopeless romantic thinks all marriages are made in heaven. But the institution of marriage, the rules that govern it, do come from God, who alone knows what is best for his creatures. Thus marriage is an institution radically unlike, say, a nation's constitution. Wise though it may be, this law was not inspired from on high. It is a product of human ingenuity, as subject to change as the rules for contract bridge. The people made the constitution; therefore the people can amend it, even scrap it if they wish. Marriage, by contrast, is the way, in fact the only way, God planned that humans use their sexual instinct. We can no more amend this plan than reverse the laws of gravity or revise our digestive system.

We are wrong in thinking the partners in a marriage are only two. When a man and a woman enter the true state of matrimony, God is the third and silent partner, present at the exchange of vows. Their union is what from the beginning God intended marriage to be: not simply a way of gratifying passion, but above all a spiritual union. Their most important task and richest reward is in the children God grants them. Through the trials and rewards of life, husband and wife together work out the happiness of their family, both in this world and the next.

What are their chances of succeeding? Excellent, as long as they keep in mind that God is their partner.

What happens if two people go through a marriage ceremony with no intention of entering a permanent union? They are willing to give it a whirl while it works, but are just as ready to part if it sours. In that case they are not getting married at all. They are entering instead into the dual and unstable partnership called concubinage. Unhappily, that is what many marriages today really are. Those who form such unions have no right to take issue with what Jesus here says about marriage. They have not the foggiest notion of what a true marriage is.

Forget all the rubbish about romantic love, so popular with poets and songwriters. When a marriage works, and it does if God is present, its love is sturdier and a thousand times more blissful than the moonshine celebrated in song. Genuine married love is tough love. The spouses know from the outset that trials will come. They don't expect to dwell every day on the giddy peaks of conjugal bliss. But they know where to go for the light and the strength to survive life's inevitable setbacks. God has pledged his help. He is their silent partner.

THE MUSTARD SEED

Twenty-seventh Sunday in Ordinary Time.
C: Lk. 17: 5-10.

❖❖❖

"Increase our faith," pleaded the apostles, and their plea is still echoed by Christians. Faith is a much-abused word. What did it mean to the apostles? What should it mean to us?

Faith is a conviction that something is true, not because we see it is true, but because someone else says so; or that something is bound to happen, not because we can make it happen, but because someone else has undertaken to do it. Faith, then, is the opposite of self-reliance. To have faith is to lean on *someone else.* When that someone else is a fellow human being, theologians call it human faith; when it is God, divine faith.

Relying on someone else is no disgrace. We cannot walk through life alone; to survive, we need other people. Without human faith society would cease to function and progress come to a halt. To go under a surgeon's knife or step onto a jet plane or even enjoy the evening news on television demands faith. When in 1969 Neil Armstrong got out of his spacecraft and took the first midget step on the moon, he was a man of faith. Unless he had relied on thousands of scientists and technicians to get him where he was, he would still have been pacing the earth.

The apostles needed faith, divine faith. Jesus had chosen them to go among the Israelites and preach the same good news he preached, to heal the sick and reclaim sinners as he did. They trembled before this task. How could rough, unlettered men like themselves expect success? They asked Jesus to bolster their faith that God would support their endeavors.

His answer was almost a rebuke—"*If* you have faith the size of a mustard seed," what incredible marvels you would work! (Uprooting a sycamore tree and transplanting it into the sea was a Hebraic expression for seemingly impossible deeds.) The words imply that their faith was still too weak. They must rely more on God. Only God could crown their efforts with success.

Their faith need be no larger than a mustard seed, the tiniest in Palestine. Loud words were not required, only a rock-solid conviction that God was on their side. From this mustard seed of faith would grow a plant beyond their dreams.

The test came later. After the Resurrection Jesus charged them to bring his words and compassion, not just to fellow Jews, but to all nations. Now they needed sturdier faith than ever, the kind that uproots sycamore trees. This ragged band of rustic Hebrews was to persuade the Gentiles of the hostile Roman world that an obscure Hebrew preacher named Jesus, a crucified criminal, was the King and Savior of mankind.

The task seemed all but impossible, especially after Jesus ascended to his Father and the apostles were left on their own. Not entirely on their own, however, since he had promised to remain with them and their successors. His Spirit would guide, enlighten, and sustain them until the end of time. And so they placed their faith in Jesus Christ who, they now realized, was divine, the incarnate Son of God. He had promised to remain among them always, and they relied on his word.

Only this faith can explain the growth of Christianity in the first century. Without it the story of the early martyrs and missionaries would make no sense. And only the continued vigor of this faith explains the later history of the Church.

No Pope could last a day in office without the conviction that he is carrying on the work of Jesus Christ. The men and women who have journeyed to all the corners of the world to spread the gospel would never have set out from home unless they had faith that Jesus Christ was journeying with them. Without faith no parent would ever bring a child for baptism, with the request that the child be allowed to share the same faith. Unless the faith of the apostles had been passed on from generation to generation, the Church would no longer be.

What is opposed to faith? Disbelief, of course. Also discouragement, fear that because our efforts to keep the gospel alive seem unequal to the task, Jesus will renege on his promise. But there is another, more subtle enemy of faith, and Jesus now warned against it. His followers should never forget they are only servants of the Lord, unprofitable servants at that. When success does crown their efforts, let them not take credit to themselves.

Pope, bishops, priests, parents, all members of the Church are not only to live by the gospel but to help spread the gospel. Like the apostles, we are emissaries of Jesus Christ. He works in us, through us. But this gives us no special claim on him. He has promised no special bonus to those who seem to work wonders in his name. However successful our efforts may seem, it is not we who deserve the credit. Our faith should be in God, not ourselves. God owes us nothing. We owe him everything.

Fuss Over a Wedding Garment

Twenty-eighth Sunday in Ordinary Time.
A: Mt. 22: 1-14 (or 1-10).

❖ ❖ ❖

If they had to turn down an invitation to a wedding party, especially one from an important person, most people would make sure they had a good excuse and worded it diplomatically. Anything less would be grave discourtesy. That is why Matthew's version of this parable fails to ring true. The subjects who ignore the king's summons do not even bother to invent excuses.

That is not the only detail in the parable that strains credulity. As the story unfolds, the conduct of the king as well as that of his subjects borders on the fantastic. No king would be so indulgent to his underlings, so ready to give them a second chance; no subjects so insolent towards their king, so abusive towards his messengers. That the king is eventually reduced to filling the seats at his banquet with drifters scooped up from the back alleys of his realm is just one more unbelievable detail in a narrative riddled with the unbelievable.

This does not meant Jesus was a poor inventor or Matthew a poor redactor of parables. Anything but. The purpose of this parable was not to win a prize for realistic fiction, but to drive home two truths: how incredibly generous has been God's treatment of his subjects and how outrageous their response.

Anyone even slightly acquainted with the Old Testament recognizes that those first invited to the wedding party stand for God's chosen people, while the messengers they maltreat stand for his prophets. The high priests and elders to whom Jesus addressed the parable were of course far more than slightly acquainted with their own history. They would have immediately recognized that in describing those who ignore the king's summons, Jesus was pointing a finger at their ancestors. This parable gave them one more reason to see him as an enemy of Judaism. Their resolve to destroy him was only strengthened.

What they could not have realized was that the destruction the king's army ultimately inflicts on his subjects and the invitation he then sends out to strangers are prophetic. In less than forty years their temple would be destroyed and the Old Covenant shattered. Sinners and Gentiles, rounded up from the far corners of the world, would be heirs of the New.

The second part of the parable, where the guest who dares arrive with no wedding garment is cast out into the darkness, bothers some readers. They find it implausible that someone picked up as a last-minute replacement should be blamed for not arriving in formal attire. Since little else the king does in the parable is plausible, their discontent with this section is hard to fathom. At any rate, they theorize that the incident was originally a separate parable about a different wedding feast and that Matthew has artlessly inserted it here.

Perhaps. But we should be wary of efforts to improve on a gospel parable, especially one from so careful a craftsman as Matthew. Examined carefully, the parable makes good sense even when we leave this incident exactly where Matthew put it.

If those first invited represent the Jewish people, those last invited include Gentile members of the Church that Jesus will soon found. At the conclusion of the previous parable Jesus confronted the high priests and elders with the flat assertion that "the kingdom of God will be taken away from you and given to a people that will produce its fruit" *(21: 43)*. In this parable we learn that the people to whom the kingdom is to be given will be gathered hurriedly and at random from wherever they can be found. Among them, Jesus explicitly says, will be "good and bad alike."

The insistence on the wedding garment is a warning to all who will become Christians in future ages, those once numbered among sinners who will be invited to his banquet. They must clothe themselves in the garment of virtuous living. Mere membership in the Church does not guarantee salvation. To share the kingdom in the next life we must all bear fruit in this.

One way of losing our wedding garment is worth mentioning here. Some people are quick to distort what Jesus teaches about the kingdom being taken from the Jews and given to Christians. They imagine the entire Jewish people lie under a curse, that even the Jew next door carries blame for the murder of Jesus.

That lie has been around too long. Anti-Semitism is wrong, doubly so when it masquerades as theology. The Jew of today is no more to blame for the death of Jesus than I am for my uncle Charlie's misconduct last week. To think otherwise is heresy.

If we wish to keep our own wedding garment intact, we must keep the second great commandment by loving all our neighbors. We are in the banquet hall of Christianity by special invitation, we are heirs to the kingdom. But to reach it we must bear fruit. Above all the fruit of Christian charity.

MEET THE MAN WHO HAS EVERYTHING

Twenty-eighth Sunday in Ordinary Time.
B: Mk. 10: 17-30 (or 17-27).

❖ ❖ ❖

The man who ran up to Jesus may remind us of a sign that is said to appear at times in windows of fashionable boutiques, "For the Man who has Everything." This man had everything, but was still ill at ease. After putting his problem to Jesus, he found himself at the most important crossroad of his life. The "one thing" Jesus told him he still lacked was the will to give away everything he had. Hearing this, he slouched away in sorrow. "Everything" is a burden not easy to shed.

In addition to his "many possessions," the man had some enviable personal qualities. First, good breeding. He fell on his knees and addressed Jesus with exquisite politeness. (Jesus even found him a mite too polite and rejected the flattery implicit in "good teacher.") Second, good character. From childhood he had never knowingly violated a commandment. Finally, religious conviction. For him merely obeying God's commandments was not enough. He wanted the surest way to eternal life.

No wonder Jesus looked on him with love. Here was a prospect to gladden the heart of any recruiter. Jesus invited him to join his apostles, to tramp along at his side and help proclaim the good news of salvation. Had the man accepted, he would have been in the vanguard of Christianity, revered as one of the original companions of Jesus. Today we would have churches named in his honor.

Before taking his place with the apostles, however, the man had one more thing to do—sell all his possessions and give every last penny they earned to the poor. Jesus did not want those who walked with him to be loaded down with the excess baggage of wealth. His first followers had to be penniless. On learning this, Mark tells us, the man's "face fell."

Mark continues with one of the strangest lines in Scripture. "He went away sad, for he had many possessions." It turned out that the man who had everything did not have what it took to be an apostle. Life with Jesus, he felt, would have been exciting, even rewarding. But his possessions were too dear. He could not shed them, even for the chance to follow Jesus. They clung too closely to him, so much so they made him sad.

Watching him shuffle away, Jesus turned to his apostles and made his oft-quoted remark about it being harder for a camel to pass through a needle's eye than for "those who have wealth to enter the kingdom of God." These words could not have been intended literally. For a camel to pass through a needle's eye is absolutely impossible. But, as Jesus himself goes on to say, it is not impossible for the rich to be saved.

This saying is what rhetoricians call hyperbole, a willful exaggeration for emphasis. This was a lesson Jesus could not emphasize too much. Riches gravely endanger the soul. It is difficult for the rich to be saved. Terribly difficult. Almost as difficult as to thread a camel through a needle's eye.

The apostles were astounded. This wild notion contradicted what they had always considered a self-evident truth about life. Were not riches a sign that a person has worked hard and thereby earned God's favor? Weren't they God's reward for a life well spent? How could honestly-earned wealth hinder salvation?

Few today are as sure as the apostles were that riches and virtue go together. But our ideas about wealth are just as illusory. Riches are the principal goal for most of our contemporaries, the object of their fondest dreams, the sure sign to the world that they have succeeded in life. It is possible for a Christian today to be just as "amazed" at this teaching of Jesus as the apostles were. It is easy to see that some are called, as this rich man was, to chuck everything and center their lives exclusively on God. But does God ask all of us to do that? To be a true Christian must one be a pauper?

Not exactly. We are not all called to surrender the whole of our possessions, any more than we are all called to endure martyrdom. But for everyone riches are a major peril. In the pursuit of salvation, the odds weigh heavily for the poor. Just yearning for a fortune can lead to the gravest of sins, while its actual possession can make us think we are more important than God, far too important to bother about his commandments.

For whom is the lesson of this gospel intended? Primarily the rich, obviously. But that doesn't let the rest of us off the hook. Riches are relative. For some people the lure of a hundred dollars can be as dangerous as the lure of a million for the rich. If money and material possessions are what we crave, if we treasure them more than we do God, then our chances of salvation are almost on a par with the camel's squeezing through that needle. The man who has every thing can end up missing the one thing that matters, eternal life.

SAYING THANKS TO GOD

Twenty-eighth Sunday in Ordinary Time.
C: Lk. 17: 11-19.

❖❖❖

What does it mean to say "thank you"? The answer should be easy, since the words are so often on our lips. Whenever someone holds a door for us, or makes room in a bus, or even passes the salt at table, to say thanks is as natural as breathing and usually done with as little thought. Because this is so, the words often mean nothing at all, are just a courtesy learned in childhood and rattled off by force of habit.

But sometimes a "thank you" does have meaning. If a doctor pulls us through a risky operation or a stranger helps us change a tire, our words of gratitude come from the heart, meaning at least two things: they acknowledge our debt to the other person, as if to say, "I badly needed this done and could not have done it without you;" and they are words of praise, meaning, "Because you did this for me, I think you are wonderful."

The gospel is about a man who thanked Jesus Christ from the heart. His story has a lesson for us all.

Ten lepers—nine Jews and one Samaritan—approached Jesus. Jews and Samaritans had a centuries-old grudge against one another, but misfortune is a great leveler. Comrades in misery, the ten cried out in chorus, "Jesus, Master, have pity on us." What they wanted Jesus to do, of course, was deliver them from the scourge that afflicted them. Not only were they disfigured and disgraced (leprosy was thought to be a punishment for sin), but worst of all, they were ostracized from normal society, exiled to hovels outside of town, cut off from family and friends.

Word had reached them that Jesus was a holy man with power to heal, and so they sought his help. As the law prescribed, they kept their distance while they tried to raise their voices. The noise they made must have been gruesome, for leprosy invades the vocal chords, reducing the voice to a hoarse croak. The reply of Jesus, that they should go and show themselves to the priests, gave them hope. Priests were the official judges of whether a leper had been cured; only with their say-so could a leper return to society. The ten lepers were confident Jesus would not send them to the priests unless he intended to cure them. They were right. On presenting themselves to the priests, they found that their cures were complete.

But this is not just another miracle story. Its point is in the aftermath of the cures, when only one of the ten returned to give thanks to Jesus. Luke adds, almost in shame, that this lone thankful one was the Samaritan. The other nine must have taken Jesus for granted, feeling that what he had done for them was no more than what his fellow Israelites deserved. But gratitude gushed from the Samaritan, the "foreigner." He could hardly control himself as he rushed back, shouting praise to God for giving the world so wonderful a prophet as Jesus.

The lesson Luke wants the reader to draw is clear. We should stop taking God for granted. The words "Thank God" are probably often on our lips. How often do we mean them? They are present in the prayers at Mass. Do we even attend to them?

Why say "Thank you" to God? He certainly has no need to hear it. No, but we have need to say it. First of all, thanking God sets the record straight. All the good things that have happened to us since birth (including birth itself) we owe to him, even the personal accomplishments we may be proudest of. The grades we got at school, the prizes we won at sports, our success in business—none of these would have been possible without the bodies, brains, and health God gave us. If nothing else, thanking God for his benefits should keep a mere creature from getting stuck-up. It is not we who are wonderful, but God.

Another reason for thanking God, almost as good as the first, is that it is the best antidote to the agony and waste of self-pity. Most people have moments when their lives seem a series of failures—low grades at school, bad luck in sports, busts in business, poor health. How easy at such times to wail internally, and how sure a formula for more misery!

What can such people thank God for? A million things. For starts, they can thank God for sparing them the ugliness and shame of leprosy. They can thank God too (if, please God, it be true) that they don't treat foreigners and people of other races the way the Jews and Samaritans treated one another. That is a moral leprosy, disgracing and disfiguring the soul.

Most of all, however, Christians should thank God for his spiritual gifts—that he made us members of his Church, that he refreshes us with the Sacraments and cleanses us of the leprosy of sin. What would our lives be like, what would the whole world be like, if Jesus had not come into this world? God has been wonderful to us. Why not tell Him so?

DUAL CITIZENSHIP

Twenty-ninth Sunday in Ordinary Time.
A: Mt. 22: 15-21.

Once on a plane ride I sat next to a woman who boasted that she held dual citizenship. She even waved two passports in my face to prove it. Privately I questioned the legality of her having more than one pass-port, but I envied her when she described how handy they were for foreign travel. In crossing borders she simply switched allegiance to whichever country was more convenient. Still, I wondered. To which country did she pay income tax? Which team did she root for in the Olympics? What would she do if one of her countries made war on the other? Convenience aside, dual citizenship poses problems.

All Christians enjoy dual citizenship. By baptism we owe loyalty to Jesus Christ, for we are citizens of his kingdom. We also owe allegiance to the country where we were born or naturalized. Does this dual citizenship, *should* it, pose problems? This reading from Matthew provides an answer.

For many Jews of the first century, payment of taxes was a nagging issue. Throughout their history the people of Israel had never distinguished, as we do, between religious and secular authorities. All their affairs belonged to God. On the other hand, Palestine was now part of the vast Roman empire, whose troops had taken control of their land a century earlier. Since then the Israelites had both endured the drawbacks and enjoyed the benefits of Roman rule. Should God's chosen people now pay the financial tribute that Caesar demanded of his subjects?

The celebrated *Pax Romana* had its price. Each adult was obliged to pay an annual head tax of a denarius, the average daily wage of a manual laborer. On this coin was the image of the reigning Caesar. Pious Jews worried that payment of this tax would indicate loyalty to someone other than God.

The question put to Jesus, then, was genuine. But the motive of the questioners was not. Their aim was not to learn from Jesus, but to "entrap" him. If he spoke for the tax he would alienate the pious; if against it, he would challenge the authority of Caesar. The trap, they thought, was inescapable.

Although aware of their hypocrisy, Jesus seized the chance to enunciate a principle that is as timely for people today as it was for his contemporaries. "Repay to Caesar what belongs to Caesar and to God what belongs to God."

What belongs to Caesar? A good deal. Human beings cannot live together without the benefits they receive from Caesar, that is, without a government of some sort. To survive, we need firefighters, roads, water, hospitals, and a thousand other services only Caesar can supply. God does not directly put out fires or build roads. These are Caesar's business.

To do his job Caesar needs money, and money cannot be had without taxes. As citizens we are obliged in conscience to pay taxes. Without these revenues our nation would have no police or parks or roads. Cheating on taxes is cheating one's neighbors, who depend on Caesar. It is little different from outright theft.

Besides paying Caesar's taxes, we must obey Caesar's laws, unless they are manifestly immoral. Even traffic laws can oblige seriously. Speeding kills. So does driving after drinking. Neither is outright murder, but the effect can be the same.

Caesar has claims on more than our tax money and our respect for his laws. It is our Christian duty to cast as informed a vote as we can on election day and to participate according to our abilities in the political process. Ambition and greed are not the only motives for entering politics. Why should not Christians enter politics with the aim of serving their neighbor?

To God, however, and not to Caesar, belong the most precious parts of us, our deepest loyalty. If a conflict occurs in these areas we must always choose God over Caesar. When the early Christians were commanded by Caesar to offer incense to pagan gods, they refused. That was God's territory. When Thomas More was told to acknowledge the supremacy of the king in Church affairs, he went to his death rather than obey. Caesar was usurping the authority of God. When in our century soldiers are ordered to bomb innocent civilians, do they refuse? They should. Caesar's command cannot justify murder.

For most of us such extreme situations never arise. But we should never doubt where our loyalty should go if they ever do. No amount of propaganda from Caesar can make it right to perform an action that our conscience says is unjust. A thousand court decisions should not make the Christian waver in the conviction that abortion is just another name for infanticide. And that human life belongs, not to Caesar, but to God.

We hold two passports. Let us never forget which is the more precious. We owe much to Caesar, but everything to God.

WHO'S ON FIRST?

Twenty-ninth Sunday in Ordinary Time.
B: Mk. 10: 35-45 (or (42-45).

❖❖❖

When I was young, biographers of saints rarely gave much space to escapades that might sully the good name of their subject. Their aim was to edify their readers, make them want to emulate the spiritual giants of the past. Items that put a saint in a bad light they soft-pedaled or left unmentioned.

In time this pietistic pussy-footing went out of fashion. The older works remained on library shelves, of course, but a new breed of saint-watchers emerged. These portrayed saints, not as icons of improbable rectitude, but as the flawed pilgrims to eternity they truly were, often fumbling as clumsily as ourselves as they inched their way toward salvation. I was among those who cheered this new style, happy to be rid of the old.

Only later did it dawn on me that the "new" style was, in fact, as old as Scripture. Telling the often unedifying truth about the patriarchs and kings of Israel was never an embarrassment for the authors of the Old Testament. Not surprisingly, a similar candor was routine for writers of the New, who were closer than we to the events they recorded and thus closer to the ever-candid Jesus. Anyone who doubts this should spend a few moments paging through the four gospels. What they reveal about the apostles is often far from uplifting.

Eager to please their Master though they were, the apostles were capable of shameful conduct. The gospels portray them acting in ways that are cowardly, quarrelsome, mendacious, pugnacious, even treacherous. We have no need for a snooping journalist to produce a "tell all" book about the apostles. The sainted authors of the gospels have already poked through the closets.

This passage is a good example. The brothers James and John already enjoyed seniority over most of the Twelve, for they had been among the first to leave their fishing nets and follow Jesus. Along with Peter they had even received favored treatment at his hands. But this was not enough. Convinced that Jesus, whom they now recognized as the Messiah, would soon found his kingdom, they had their hearts set on securing top positions. In the kingdom to come they hoped to lord it over the others.

Incredibly, they went to Jesus with this request, so little had they absorbed of his teaching about humility and service. In his cabinet, they told him, they wanted to be appointed Number One and Number Two (that is what sitting at the right and left of a ruler meant). Ambition could hardly aspire for more.

Beneath their ambition, however, Jesus detected generosity. And so, instead of rebuking them, he told them they had no idea what they were in for if their request should be granted. He had already predicted the torments he would have to endure in winning his kingdom. Were they ready to drink the same cup of suffering as he did, bathe in the same waves of anguish? When they insisted they were, he told them that although their places in his kingdom could not yet be disclosed, their offer to follow him would be accepted. In their labors to preach the gospel both were destined to suffer far more than they bargained for.

When the other apostles got wind that James and John were cozying up to Jesus in hope of preferment, they were incensed. Jesus now had not just two power-hungry apostles on his hands, but ten others who were seething with the envy that springs from endangered ambition. For these others were every bit as ambitious as James and John. Their envy grew from fear of being outflanked.

They all needed to listen again to the lesson Jesus had given them not long ago, when he overheard them squabbling about who among them was the greatest. For men who were to lead his Church, that lesson could not be repeated too often. And so he gathered them all together again and went through the points.

In his Church, he said, there must be no grabbing for power nor abuse of power by those who have it. Those appointed as leaders must serve their subjects as selflessly as Jesus served even the lowliest among his followers. Thus greatness among them must be measured by a norm totally different from that of the Gentiles. Those on top must be slaves to those below.

The lesson is valid, not only for ecclesiastics, but for all Christians in all walks of life. The ideal of service and humility should guide us everywhere—in the workplace, the schoolroom, the home. The urge to "lord it over" others and make one's "authority over them felt" is universal. That is why the world has an oversupply of browbeating bosses, martinet educators, domineering spouses, and overdemanding parents. We must pray always and earnestly not to be numbered among them.

The apostles, like all saints, had to grope their way to the ideal of service, slowly and painfully. They did not learn the lesson in a day. Neither will we. But at least let us grope.

"Pray Always"

Twenty-ninth Sunday in Ordinary Time.
C: Lk. 18: 1-8.

❖❖❖

Most Catholics have heard of Lourdes, the town in southern France where in 1858 a girl named Bernadette told of meeting and speaking with a woman who called herself the Immaculate Conception. Bernadette is a canonized saint now, and Lourdes a place of pilgrimage. Every year thousands crowd into the tiny town to pray at the grotto where they believe the mother of God once stood. Among them are many sick and disabled who have heard that the water beneath the grotto has power to heal.

Doctors are in constant attendance. As well as caring for the immediate needs of the sick, they scrutinize any claim of a cure. A claim is verified only if members of the medical team are convinced that science has no possible explanation for a pilgrim's recovery. They are not easily convinced.

How many confirmed cures have occurred at the shrine? In its first hundred years, only fifty-eight, and the rate has remained about the same. That seems a trickle, yet the sick keep coming, hordes of them. Many are repeaters. They know the odds for a cure are less than for first prize in a state lottery, but still they come back, and year after year remain unhealed.

How reconcile this with today's gospel? Luke introduces the parable by stating its point flatly: we should pray continually "without becoming weary." And Jesus closes by saying that if the crusty and crooked judge finally relented and answered the widow's plea, how much more will the good God listen to the pleas of those who "call out to him day and night."

Does he? What about those pilgrims who leave Lourdes as unwell as the day they arrived? And the millions of afflicted people around the world whose prayers go unanswered? They have persevered day and night. What good has it done them?

Most people are familiar with the standard answer, that God does not grant what we ask in prayer if he knows it is not for our good. But isn't that a dishonest answer? What would we think of a father promising his daughter anything she wants for Christmas, and then reneging when she asks for some medicine to ease her pain? Would not a cure be good for those suffering pilgrims at Lourdes? Are they better off as they are? If by her perseverance in prayer the woman in the parable received justice from the judge, why should not prayer give to the lame the power to walk? Will they have to persevere in prayer until the day they die? What good will a cure do them then?

Clearly the parable means something else. Jesus does not pledge a favorable answer to anyone who repeats a prayer often and loudly enough. Prayer is not magic. If it were, our hospitals would soon empty out and all our sick hurry off to churches.

What did he promise? One answer is on the faces of those who return from Lourdes, still on stretchers, still not cured. They are not bitter. Rarely do they think their time or money was wasted. Physically they may have gained nothing, but spiritually they are refreshed and at peace. Their days at Lourdes have brought them closer to God, readier to accept his will. Spiritual healing is a higher good than physical healing, just as pain is a lesser evil than sin. The greatest gift pilgrims receive at Lourdes may be to realize that this is true.

Jesus did not come into the world to end all suffering. When he declared that the poor and the hungry are blessed and promised relief from their distress, he did not guarantee that this relief would be material or would be granted in this life.

What kind of favors should we pray for? Look at the petitions in the prayer Jesus composed for us, the "Our Father"—that God rule over our hearts, that we always do his will, that past sins be forgiven and future temptations overcome. If like the widow in the parable we keep praying for these gifts, pestering God with our repeated appeals, we can be sure of a favorable answer. That is the lesson of this parable.

This does not mean we should never ask for material favors. Jesus instructed us to pray for our daily bread. Nor is it wrong to pray for miraculous favors. Miracles do take place, and not just at Lourdes. But spectacular cures are rare, occurring mostly when God wants to send a special message to earth. Jesus had to work wonders to establish his credentials as Son of God. Mary had an important message for the world at Lourdes. And Saints sometimes heal the sick with a touch; so close is their union with Jesus that their hands share his power to heal.

Most Christians will never see a physical miracle. Jesus has promised something far better. When he comes for judgment, those who have prayed always without becoming weary will have their most fervent prayer answered. As pilgrims at the close of a journey, they will be welcomed to their eternal home.

The Love of God Comes First

Thirtieth Sunday in Ordinary Time.
A: Mt. 22: 34-40.

❖❖❖

Many of us feel uneasy with the first great commandment. We aren't sure what the words mean. How can petty creatures like ourselves have love for the all-powerful deity that fashioned the universe and keeps it running? Awe, yes. Obedience too. But love? Just trying to think about God is hard enough. We all feel more comfortable with the second great commandment. At least we think we know what Jesus meant by love of neighbor.

Do we? Start with the word "neighbor." Here, fortunately Jesus left no room for doubt. Remember the Good Samaritan? He earned his title and proved himself a true neighbor by helping a wounded stranger. More remarkably, the stranger he helped was a Jew, and therefore a person we would expect him to avoid. Samaritans and Jews disliked one another intensely. They had no good reason. That was just the way they were brought up.

Why did he help the Jew? We are not told. Perhaps on seeing his wounds the Samaritan's pity just welled up spontaneously. Whatever the reason, his action tells us what Jesus meant by neighbor. Not just friends, but strangers. Not just people we like, but people we loathe. Not just those who help us, but those who harm us. Our neighbors, quite simply, are all the people in the world, regardless of race or nationality or status.

This is a clue to what Jesus did *not* mean by love. The word has many meanings, so many it often seems to have lost all meaning. It may merely denote a strong liking for a person or thing, as when a secretary says she loves her boss and only means she enjoys the extra time off he just gave her; or when a child says, "Mom, I love your apple pie" in hopes of a second helping. More frequently the word refers either to the physical union between a man and woman or the tender affection our songwriters exalt in romantic ballads.

Obviously the Samaritan had none of these loves for the Jew. Nor can we have any of them for people on the other side of the globe, although all of them are our neighbors. The Samaritan's love consisted in action, doing good for someone. That is the kind of love Jesus meant when he told us to love our neighbors. We must *want* good for them, *do* good for them.

What did he mean by adding "as ourselves"? Certainly not that we should try to love the shoemakers in Tibet *as much as* we love ourselves, spend as much time on their concerns as on our own. Rather, he was indicating the *kind* of love we should have for our neighbors. Whatever we want for ourselves, we should want and as far as possible do for all others.

When I have injured someone, I want forgiveness; therefore I should forgive those who injure me. When I am hungry I want food; therefore I must try to feed the hungry. When I am sick I want care; when in the dumps, cheering up. Therefore I should give care and cheer to others. I do not like to be snubbed or patronized; therefore I should never snub or patronize others.

Why should we love *all* our neighbors? Jesus does not tell us here. But the question must be faced. Loving one's neighbor does not come naturally. It is easy to love some of the people some of the time, but not all of the people all of the time. Without a good motive, Christian love of neighbor is impossible.

To find the motive we must return to the first commandment. As with the second, start with what the love of God does *not* mean. You may have seen artistic renditions of saints caught up in ecstatic prayer, aflame with the love of God. Forget them. The love we owe God is more prosaic; not in feelings, but actions. We love God the way a child loves a parent, by doing what the parent wants. And we do it for much the same reason. As the child came from parents, we came from God. As the child is nurtured and protected by parents, showered with gifts from them, so are we by God. Therefore, whatever our loving father wants us to do, we do. There is no other way to love God.

But our finite minds cannot comprehend the infinite. How can we know God enough to love him? Think of a father who has gone to war and the child who has never seen him. The only way the child can know him is through his gifts and letters. That is how we know God. We are surrounded by his gifts; our very existence is his gift. And the letter he has sent us is Jesus Christ, through whom alone we glimpse what God is like.

Jesus is the measure of how much God loves mankind, for he came to earth to redeem us. We cannot say we love God unless we love every person God loves and for whom Jesus Christ lived and died. Jesus made the equation plain. To mistreat a neighbor is to mistreat him. To help a neighbor, to help him.

Our love for God is the motive for our love of our neighbor. Our love of our neighbor is the test of our love for God.

HE CALLED HIM "RABBONI"

Thirtieth Sunday in Ordinary Time.
B: Mk. 10: 46-52.

❖❖❖

Jericho in New Testament times was a garden spot. Situated in the fertile valley of the Jordan, it boasted abundant streams and an almost tropical luxuriance of trees and flowers. Cleopatra once had a villa in Jericho (a gift from Marc Anthony), and Herod the Great built a pleasure palace there. Our age is not the first to provide lavish watering places for the idle rich.

For all its splendor, however, Jericho had its share of the lame and leprous and otherwise disabled. Among these was the blind beggar Bartimaeus, who spent his days by the roadside begging for bread. This gospel finds him near the gate where the road led southwest to Jerusalem, a half-day's journey away.

It was a good spot, much frequented, since Jericho was a stopping-off place for people en route to the holy city. The reason for the "sizable crowd" in this gospel was that it would soon be Passover. Jesus and his apostles were among the pilgrims traveling to the festival in Jerusalem. This was his final journey there with the Twelve. Calvary was just weeks away.

To most people in Jericho Jesus was not totally unknown. For years stories about his healing power had been making the rounds of towns and villages in Palestine. And since this was not his first journey as an adult to Jerusalem, he had to have passed through Jericho before. At any rate, Bartimaeus knew enough about this holy man from Nazareth to have made up his mind who he was. And so, as soon as he learned Jesus was within earshot, he cried out, "Jesus, son of David, have pity on me."

It is important to grasp exactly what these words meant to the crowd that first heard them. Through his foster father Joseph, Jesus certainly belonged to the house of David. So did thousands of other Israelites. For the Jews of that time, however, "Son of David" meant more than legal descent; it was a title reserved for the long-awaited Messiah. Thus in Mark's gospel Bartimaeus became the second person (the first was Peter) openly to address Jesus as Messiah. Learned scribes were still unable to agree on who he was, but the blind Bartimaeus knew.

Some bystanders, anxious to shield Jesus from nuisance, tried to hush Bartimaeus. Probably they did not think the plight of a blind beggar, one of hundreds of Israelites as blind as himself, important enough to take the time of this busy preacher from Galilee. But their meddling only made Bartimaeus strain his lungs harder as he shouted again his plea to Jesus.

To their surprise, Jesus stopped in his tracks and summoned the shouter to his side. Hearing this, Bartimaeus bounced up, flung aside the cloak that impeded his movement, and fairly leaped to the feet of Jesus, who asked what he sought.

According to the version read at Mass, the reply of Bartimaeus was "Master, I want to see." Actually, he said more than this tame translation suggests. Mark reports his words as, "Rabboni, I want to see." Now the word "Rabboni" is certainly a variant of "Rabbi," and "Rabbi" means master or teacher; but it is a variant with an important difference. "Rabboni" is what grammarians call a caritative or term of endearment, as different from "Rabbi" as "dad" from "father" or "mommy" from "mother." It means "dear" or "beloved" master. Members of a Rabbi's family, intimate friends, and devoted students might address him with this intimacy, but not strangers, certainly not roadside beggars.

Which proves that Bartimaeus did not consider that Jesus and he were strangers to one another, but friends. It never occurred to him that he was too lowly for Jesus to bother with, or Jesus too busy for him. Our prayers should be like that.

Jesus replied, "Go your way; your faith has saved you." In an instant the eyes of Bartimaeus were opened. At last he could feast his eyes on the fabled beauties of Jericho.

But in fact his attention went elsewhere. Mark tell us that after Jesus exited through the gate and started up the road to Jerusalem, Bartimaeus "followed him on the way." The words contain a clear hint that Bartimaeus became, instantly but not surprisingly, a devoted follower of Jesus.

Later Bartimaeus seems to have become a member of the early Christian church. So well known was he to his fellow Christians that Mark identifies him by name, the only person cured by Jesus who is so identified in his gospel. He must have told his story over and over to fellow Christians. The reason Mark's account is so vivid is that his source was either Bartimaeus himself or someone who had heard the story from his very lips.

What made his story worth repeating was not so much that he gained physical sight as that he ended by following Jesus. His Rabboni, his dear master, became his Lord and dear leader. May he always be Rabboni to us, too, our dear master and leader.

A Flawed Prayer

Thirtieth Sunday in Ordinary Time.
C: Lk. 18: 9-14.

❖❖❖

Rascals can be charmers, at least in fiction. In novels and on the stage the glamorous roué and the genial idler often win the hearts of the most principled people. But one fault never charms, resists all whitewashing: self-righteousness. It is the most irritating species of pride, itself the ugliest of vices. Few are seriously offended by the woman who purrs over her hairdo or the man who brags about his golf-swing. But a smug certitude that one excels in virtue always repels. Let God hand out the medals for moral excellence, not oneself.

That is why today's parable is so popular. It features a villain we all love to hate. The portrait Luke here paints is what pops into many people's mind when they hear the word "Pharisee." Merely contemplating his own moral excellence in the privacy of his home does not satisfy this Pharisee. He must go to the temple and tally up his good deeds for God to hear. While doing so he spies at prayer a tax collector, whose sins he proceeds to contrast with his own virtues. Whoever invented the phrase "holier than thou" must have had this scene in mind.

A wise man once remarked that when the world is unanimous in condemning someone, watch out. No living person can be totally bad, without even a spark of potential goodness.

Can we find that spark in this Pharisee? Imagine we are lawyers for his defense. Is there anything to say in his favor?

I think so. Since he addresses God within the hallowed temple, we can assume that the Pharisee is telling the truth. The first point in his defense, then, is that he performs his religious duties, fasting even more than the law requires and giving generously to support the temple. So far, not bad. Add that he is not avaricious, nor double-dealing, nor a libertine, and the Pharisee appears to be a fairly upright citizen.

But, the prosecution will urge, he should not be telling all this to the world. His boasting cancels out his good deeds.

Not so. He is speaking to God, not the world. And he is not boasting, but thanking God. An honest self-examination has laid bare his good deeds, and now he gives credit where it belongs. This is something all Christians should learn to do. Without God's help all of us would be hopelessly mired in sin. To praise God that we are not is a prayer that must please him.

Even the most skillful defense lawyer, however, cannot clear the Pharisee of all charges. After all, the person telling the story is Jesus, and he ends by condemning him. But it is important to see why. Where exactly has the Pharisee gone wrong?

Jesus introduces the story by defining self-righteousness. It does not consist in just feeling good about the laudable deeds one has performed; that is a harmless vanity. Rather, its essence is in scorning others, "holding everyone else in contempt." The pride of the self-righteous is always competitive. It does not merely say, "Oh, what a good boy am I," but also "Oh, what a bad boy are you." Thus the Pharisee thanks God that he is not "like other men," especially the tax collector praying beside him. No one has the right to pass such judgment on others. Virtue and vice reside inside a person. Only God sees what goes on there. All we can see is the outside.

Self-righteousness is the one fault people never accuse themselves of. Ask a man if he has any vices, and he will laughingly assure you he has, then possibly point to some drinking and swearing. Ask a woman, and she may admit to gossiping or petty vanity. One might even detect a whiff of pride in these admissions, a devilish delight in wrongdoing, a preening "unholier than thou" pose. But no one owns up to being self-righteous. Pharisaism has no constituency. It is something we judge our neighbors guilty of, never ourselves.

That is why this sin is so insidious. People quick to spot self-righteousness in their neighbor may thereby be guilty of it themselves. The Pharisee of today need not appear at all like the puffed-up Pharisee of this parable, looking down his nose at the tax collector while rattling off a list of his own virtues. This sin is rarely so obvious. Anyone who rashly judges and looks down on a neighbor has the makings of a Pharisee. And all judgements of what goes on inside another are rash.

"Stop judging, that you may not be judged," warned Jesus in his Sermon on the Mount *(Mt. 7: 1)*. The words refer to judging the interior of another's heart. The Pharisee may have witnessed the tax collector in a thousand sins. But he did not, could not, know that at the very instant he was passing judgement on him, the tax collector was making peace with God.

"O God, be merciful to me, a sinner," words we can all say with truth, are the only sure cure for self-righteousness.

"BUT DO NOT FOLLOW THEIR EXAMPLE"

Thirty-first Sunday in Ordinary Time.
A: Mt. 23: 1-12.

❖ ❖ ❖

Controlled anger aimed at corruption in high places is no sin. Jesus himself indulged in it, as this passage from Matthew proves. It is the opening salvo of a barrage that goes on for an entire chapter, mounting in fury with every verse. In all literature it would be hard to find a tongue-lashing more scathing. Anyone who thinks it a Christian duty always to make excuses for the misdeeds of people supposedly dedicated to God should read the entire discourse. Jesus made no excuses.

His target was the nearest thing the Israelites had to a religious establishment, the unholy alliance of scribes and Pharisees. These occupied "the chair of Moses," posing as the authentic voices and living examples of the Jewish religion. Even before Jesus spoke out, some Jews must have suspected what humbugs many of these scribes and Pharisees truly were. Out of respect, however, most kept their misgivings to themselves.

Jesus did not. As God's spokesman, he was empowered to expose corruption. Note that he did not say all scribes and Pharisees without exception fitted his bill of indictment. Many, both then and later, were blameless. Some even embraced his gospel with enthusiasm. But the vices he mentioned were sufficiently widespread among them to be regarded as typical.

What were these vices?

Outrageous lack of charity was one. As religious leaders, the scribes and Pharisees should have helped their fellow Israelites serve God better. Instead, they put obstacles in their path and laid heavy burdens on their shoulders. Their interpretations of the Mosaic law were so narrow and rigorous that ordinary people could not possibly live up to their standards. But they had little concern for ordinary people.

Pride was another, along with the ostentatious religiosity it generated. They paraded their piety in public, demanding that others seat them in places of honor and address them with ornate titles. Such pomposity is often the stuff of high comedy; on the stage it can be uproariously funny. In real life, however, where souls are at stake, it comes closer to tragedy.

Their gravest offense and trademark vice was hypocrisy. They did not even try to live up to the true principles of Judaism. The virtue of charity is said to cover a multitude of sins. The vice of hypocrisy, contrariwise, cancels a multitude of virtues. The otherwise good works of the scribes and Pharisees were poisoned by this vice, for they performed them "to be seen." Jesus likened this to cleansing the outside of the cup while neglecting the inside. "Whitewashed tombs," he called them.

What could the ordinary Israelites do about this moral degeneracy in their spiritual leaders? Jesus did not ask his listeners to join him in publicly unmasking hypocrisy in high places. As God's emissary to Israel, he had an authority not given to them. Their task was more modest, but by no means easy. "Do and observe all things whatsoever they tell you, but do not follow their example." This, the most important sentence in this passage, is as timely now as when Jesus spoke it.

Our age happily has no exact equivalent of the scribes and Pharisees. Most of those who officially proclaim God's word do their best to stay on the path they trace for others. Those who do not, who preach one thing and practice another, are rarely in the same league as the Pharisees of old. When clerical offenses make news today, they are usually sexual or financial, the kind that sells papers. For all their gravity, such offenses do not strike at the foundations of religion as seriously as pharisaical hypocrisy does. But they still do incalculable harm, whether they occur among Catholic or Protestant clergy.

That such offenses do occur should surprise no one. Jesus predicted they were bound to erupt *(Mt. 18: 7)*. What is new about today's scandals is that they have the disconcerting habit of being featured on the evening newscast or in the morning's tabloids. That is a pity, since this public airing of offenses takes a high toll, and not just from those already ill-disposed to religion. Watching such stories unfold can tempt even seasoned Christians to abandon the struggle. If commissioned officers cannot repulse the enemy, what hope for the lowly foot soldiers?

Young people are the most gravely harmed by scandals. But for adults too, even the most worldly, the damage can be grave. To keep them from damaging us, we must remember what Jesus here told his listeners. If the guide knows the way, obey him. But do not follow him when he strays from the path.

We have many companions on the road to salvation, but only one leader, Jesus Christ. His ministers may fail us, but he never will. We should listen to them, but follow only him.

Love God and Do as You Please

Thirty-first Sunday in Ordinary Time.
B: Mk. 12: 28-34.

❖❖❖

The Israelites of old had their faults, but religious indifference was not among them. No Jew questioned the existence of God or our obligation to obey him. Their advantage over the Gentiles, in fact, for which they thanked God daily, was that they knew exactly what God wanted of them. He had given his law, the Torah, to his people, a law recorded in Scripture. The Torah made Judaism unique, a religion built on law.

The problem, however, was that this law contained 613 distinct commandments. Ordinary Jews not only found it difficult to remember all of them all of the time, but next to impossible to keep from violating at least some of them some of the time. Rightly sensing that the 613 precepts could not all be of equal weight, they often begged learned Rabbis to point to some one commandment that captured the essence of them all, a "first commandment." In this gospel a scribe puts this request to Jesus.

Most Rabbis answered by quoting the *Shema*, a prayer Jews recite twice daily, itself based on a passage Jesus here quotes from *Deuteronomy (6: 4-5)* about loving God above all things. Others pointed to a passage of *Leviticus (19: 18),* also quoted by Jesus,which the famous Rabbi Hillel once paraphrased in these words: "What you hate for yourself, do not do to your neighbor. This is the whole law, the rest is commentary." The importance of both commandments, therefore, had long been recognized. Jesus was not the first to do so.

He seems, however, to have been the first to join the two, thus giving the key to *his* law, the new law of Christianity, which for his followers replaced the law of Judaism. Love for one's neighbor is the best known item in this new law, the one that should most visibly set Christians apart from pagan. But such love is impossible unless motivated by love of God. To love God above all is therefore the first law of all.

Many people today deny its primacy. Among them, of course, are those who call themselves secular humanists and do not believe in God at all. Although these are only a minority of the world's population, their influence is enormous. If asked which of the two commandments cited by Jesus is more important, probably a whopping majority, even of our fellow Christians, would reverse the order. Caring for the poor and oppressed, they blandly assert, does more good for the world than going to church on Sundays or mumbling prayers at bedtime.

Consider the position of the secular humanists. The motive they propose for loving our neighbor is seductively simple: our common humanity. Since we all belong to one human family, the reasoning goes, we must care for one another, promote our common welfare. Who needs to bring God into the picture?

The main problem with this formula is that it doesn't work. A moment's reflection will show that it is built on the sands of sentimentality. Any strong wind will blow it down.

If there is no God to set the rules, why not make whatever rules we please? Why prefer the welfare of others to our own convenience? Why, in the name of "common humanity," show kindness to people whose manners disgust us and morals repel us? Why must we love *all* our neighbors? Why not just the nice ones?

The Christian reason, the one built on rock, is in the first commandment. The only conceivable reason for loving every one of our neighbors is that our love of God compels us.

Be clear on what love of God means. The words Jesus quotes from Scripture about putting heart and soul and mind and strength into this love can mislead. He was not saying that love of God is a matter of sweet emotion. Like all genuine love, it consists in deeds, often very unpleasant deeds. Loving God above all things means our allegiance to God is total. In any decision we make, God's will, however displeasing to us, comes first.

Why? Because we owe him everything—the air we breathe, the earth we tread. He has given us life here and prepared for us an eternity with him hereafter. We came from God, we go to God.

The same holds for other members of our race. God also made them in his image. If we love God, we must love them too, all of them. We have no need of 613 commandments. Just two will do: love God and love the millions of neighbors he gives us.

Thus Jesus boiled the commandments of God down to two. Saint Augustine went even further, boiling them down to one. "Love God," he told his flock, "and do as you please."

Sound like heresy? Yes, but it is not. If we truly love God, the only thing that will please us is what we know will please him. That means loving the people he loves, whoever they are, wherever they are, whatever their faults. He became man for them, died for them. He alone has authority to reject them.

JESUS INVITES HIMSELF TO THE HOUSE OF A SINNER

Thirty-first Sunday in Ordinary Time.
C: Lk. 19: 1-10.

❖❖❖

In this passage Luke introduces us to Zacchaeus, the bantam-size tax collector of Jericho. We see him perched atop a sycamore tree, as keyed-up as a child waiting for a parade to begin. He is peering down the road, straining for a glimpse of Jesus passing through. The last thing he expects is that the prophet from Nazareth will take any notice of him.

When a president halts a motorcade or a pope a procession to say a word to a bystander, cameras start clicking. How we would love to have some shots of Jesus summoning Zacchaeus down from his treetop bleacher, of the two walking away arm-in-arm to the tax collector's house! The meeting between Jesus and Zacchaeus is one of the most charming episodes in Scripture.

Zacchaeus himself, however, was not—at least not at first—a very charming person. Luke says he was the chief tax man in Jericho "and also a wealthy man." The addition is a tautology. In biblical times anyone in charge of collecting taxes in a large commercial town like Jericho was bound to be wealthy, for he was bound to be a crook. Zacchaeus was possibly the most unpopular man in town. Everybody knew he worked for the Romans, everybody knew he was crooked, everybody called him a sinner. And for once, everybody was right.

Word had come that Jesus was about to pass through Jericho. His reputation preceded him, and a mingling of the curious and the pious thronged the roadside. Some hoped he would rally the Israelites to rebel against Rome, others that he would lead them back to a purer service of God. All were anxious to see what he looked like, perhaps hear him preach, perhaps witness a miracle. The crowd was impatient, buzzing with excitement.

Why did Zacchaeus join this crowd? Rogue though he was, he must have felt in his heart some pangs of remorse. Perhaps, uneasy with the way he had made his fortune, he was anxious to change his ways and be welcomed into the homes of respectable Jews. Just catching sight of Jesus, the compassionate prophet from Nazareth, might help him find his way back to God.

So many others had turned out to see Jesus, however, and they towered so high above his head, that at first Zacchaeus feared he would see nothing. In frustration he ran along behind them, looking for an opening. Finally, as a last resort, he shimmied up a sycamore and squatted among its branches.

Soon came the moment that would change his life. Jesus stopped and looked up. From the spark in his eyes one might think he had known the tax collector all his life. He bade Zacchaeus down, saying he wanted to visit his house.

Once alone with Jesus, Zacchaeus proved to be a model for repentant sinners. Too often sinners try to get the best of both worlds. They say they want to leave their sins behind, but at the same time they want to hold onto the rewards of sin. Those who have enriched themselves by dishonest means say, "Lord, I cheated that customer, that insurance company, that merchant, but now I am sorry. Just let me keep what I've got my hands on, and I promise never to be dishonest again."

Zacchaeus used no such evasions. He made a clean break, ridding himself entirely of his ill-gotten wealth. He planned to go even further than Jewish law required, giving half his fortune to the poor and restoring fourfold to those he had defrauded. Being rich did not make this surrender any easier. The richer one is, the harder it often is to part with money. Zacchaeus learned that genuine repentance for an injustice can hurt at least as much as the hurt one has inflicted on another.

Meanwhile an ugly crowd was milling outside. The people who had come out to see Jesus were not pleased. They had been astonished when Jesus stopped to talk with so notorious a thief, perplexed when the two of them greeted one another like old friends, shocked when Jesus crossed the threshold of Zacchaeus's house. Soon tongues started wagging, fingers pointing. This was a scandal. "He has gone to stay at the house of a sinner."

This was not the first time Jesus gave scandal. The kind of scandal he gave is technically known as pharisaical, since only someone with the spirit of a Pharisee could be shocked at a show of friendship or a grant of forgiveness to a sinner. By now Jesus must have been weary of explaining why he offered to people like Zacchaeus the same promise of salvation that he offered to all Israelites and under the same conditions.

At no small cost to himself, Zacchaeus accepted this offer. Not to understand why it was made, why Jesus invited himself into Zacchaeus's house, is to miss the whole point of why he came into this world. Jesus summed up this point beautifully: "The Son of Man has come to seek and to save what was lost."

WAITING FOR THE GROOM

Thirty-second Sunday in Ordinary Time.
A: Mt. 25: 1-13.

To appreciate this parable it helps to know something about wedding customs in biblical times. They differ considerably from what we are used to in our part of the world today, although in parts of the Orient many of them still survive in some form. Here is how, according to cultural historians, a typical wedding took place among the neighbors of Jesus Christ.

The festivities began when the groom, along with a band of young male companions, arrived at the bride's house. There he was greeted by the bridesmaids who then led him and his bride on a noisy, torchlit procession through the town. Eventually they came to the threshold of the groom's house. Then and there the nuptial ceremony took place, consisting in nothing more than the groom's formal reception of the bride into his home. This was followed by the wedding feast, a gala affair attended by half the village. The merrymaking could go on for days.

The parable begins at the doorstep of the bride's house, where the ten waiting bridesmaids have fallen asleep. At midnight they are awakened by the arrival of the groom with his band of revelers. He is late of course, but this was foreseeable. Punctuality has never been a major concern for grooms.

Only half the bridesmaids are prepared. Anticipating that the groom might be delayed, five of them have brought along an extra supply of oil for their torches. The other five, who have made no such provision, discover that their torches have flickered out during their sleep, and now they have no oil to relight them. Unable to talk their cautious companions into sharing some, they hurry off to the nearest oil dealer.

By the time they have purchased oil and dashed back to the groom's home, they have missed both procession and ceremony. Finding the doors barred against them, they knock frantically, hoping not to miss the wedding feast as well. But the groom is so miffed by their absence from the ceremony that he refuses to open and allow them to be seated with his guests. In the end the unlucky five are left standing outside in the cold.

But they are not exactly unlucky. The parable rightly brands them "foolish," and fools are not usually mere victims of an unlucky roll of the dice. The other five, by contrast, are "wise." "Wise" and "foolish" are the key words of the parable.

The lesson is clear. Through our own folly we can go through life as unprepared for the coming of the Lord as the five foolish bridesmaids are for the groom. We may even find ourselves locked out in the cold when the heavenly banquet begins. Being prepared does not demand superhuman wisdom. Just an ounce of sense is what we need, as much sense as the five wise bridesmaids had.

Thus the parable is not really about a wedding, but death. The bridegroom stands for Jesus Christ. His sudden arrival stands for the moment when, ready or not, each of us will face our Redeemer for judgment. The parable reminds us, not only that the moment of his coming is unpredictable, but that if he finds us unready there will be no remedy. Death comes only once.

We have a lifetime to be sensible and keep our flasks filled. If we spend our days foolishly, our flasks will be empty when death comes. Unable to borrow from others, we will have to meet death alone. The parable closes with the terse lesson, "Stay awake, for you know neither the day nor the hour."

An old-fashioned lesson, so old it almost sounds trite. But it becomes less trite as the years go by and we tick off the names of friends and dear ones who have been snatched away, some without a moment's notice. November is the month we remember these dead in our prayers. This parable invites us to remember also ourselves, warning that death may come when we least expect it. With each November the warning grows more urgent. Death does not always announce its coming, which can be as stealthy as a thief in the night, as unpredictable as a tardy bridegroom.

We need not, however, restrict our understanding of this parable to the lesson that Jesus explicitly drew from it. If we focus on the sensible rather than the foolish bridesmaids, the parable suggests the total Christian view of death, the view that alone gives meaning to life. Dag Hammarskjold implied this view when he wrote, "Do not seek death. Death will find you. But seek the road that makes death a fulfillment."

Death should mean fulfillment, not standing outside in the cold, envying the revelry of the guests within. Fortunately, we do not have to "seek" the road that makes it a fulfillment. We already know the road; at baptism our feet were set on it. Our task is to stay on that road. Then at the moment of death we will, like the sensible bridesmaids, join the eternal banquet of the Lord and "enjoy forever the vision" of Christ's glory.

Woe for the Scribes, Praise for the Widow

Thirty-second Sunday in Ordinary Time.
B: Mk. 12: 38-44 (or 41-44).

❖❖❖

This passage contains two seemingly unrelated scenes. First Jesus tells his disciples what he thinks of the high and mighty scribes; then he observes and comments on a pious widow. The contrast is stark: fierce denunciation of ostentation and greed followed by unstinting praise of a poor person's generosity.

The scribes receive a lot of attention in the New Testament, most of it unflattering. In Israel a scribe was originally someone who could both read and write (rare accomplishments in those times) and who sold these skills to others. By the time of Jesus, however, the term was limited to those who in addition to literacy had training in Jewish law. Sometimes Scripture calls them lawyers, a designation that fits as long as we remember that the law they dealt with was the only law the Jews had, the religious law they had received from Moses.

For centuries these scribes, most of them Rabbis, had construed that law in so pettifogging a fashion that they actually added layers of new obligations to the original Mosaic text. To the uninitiated this scribal law was an impenetrable jungle that seems to have made even less sense than our tax law does to the average citizen today. Yet, as lawyers will, the scribes succeeded in making themselves indispensable. For the Israelites the law of Moses was the basis of religion. They needed these experts to instruct them in it, to settle disputes, even to handle such mundane matters as the estates of widows.

One might expect a group whose business was religious law to have a more than average share of virtue. Unfortunately, these did not. They did, however, try to appear virtuous to others. Here Jesus mentions some details of their masquerade—the stately robes they wore, the deference they demanded and received, the seats of honor they filled, the long prayers they recited in public. But it was all pretext, for their hearts were ruled by vainglory and avarice. One way of satisfying their avarice was by defrauding widows. When entrusted with their estates, the scribes often succeeded in pocketing the revenue.

Mention of widows prompts Mark to follow this denunciation of the scribes with the story of the poor widow's offering. Jesus and his disciples were now in the section of the temple called the treasury, where passing pilgrims plunked coins into one of thirteen chests that were placed there to collect funds for the upkeep of the temple. This was all done quite publicly. The big givers, often undoubtedly scribes, made their donations with appropriate flourish, to the approving murmurs of onlookers. Those less generous, on the other hand, had to expose their parsimony to the derision of all. The genuinely poor, like the widow in this gospel, had to endure the same shame as the pikers.

This episode used to be called "The Widow's Mite," the word "mite" being a fairly forgotten term for a very small amount of money. Our translation, "two small coins worth a few cents," is closer to the original, which speaks of two Greek coins called *lepta*, each worth a fraction of a cent. This widow was one of the poorest. These coins were the last to her name.

What lesson can we draw from this study in contrast, the outwardly glittering but inwardly counterfeit scribes alongside the outwardly drab but inwardly golden widow? Certainly not that we should draw up a list of people we know who are present day equivalents of the scribes. Such people certainly still exist, but it is not our place to pass judgment. Jesus, who reads people's hearts and will one day pass judgment on us all, has authority to do so. But not his apostles, and certainly not ourselves. We see only the surface, not the heart.

Fortunately few of us will ever deserve the condemnation Jesus passed on the scribes. That is because few of us will ever be raised to such positions of eminence. But for the apostles who first heard this instruction and for all the leaders of the Church in the centuries since, the lesson could hardly be more pertinent. We should pray that our leaders never forget that the most important benefactors of the Church are the little people who have no surplus to be generous with but still give what they can, often more than they reasonably can. God sees more value in these hard-earned pennies of the poor than in all the lavish benefactions of the rich.

Jesus looks for utter sincerity in his followers. Although tolerant of all sorts of human failures, he has no patience for pious humbugs. Big shot or small fry, rich or poor—these make no difference in his eyes. What counts is that we be what we profess to be and never rest satisfied with appearances. And when we give, let us try to give as this poor widow gave—generously and from the heart.

ALL ARE ALIVE TO GOD

Thirty-second Sunday in Ordinary Time.
C: Lk. 20: 27-38 (or 27; 34-38).

❖❖❖

Heaven is a bedrock truth of our faith. Without it the whole structure of Christianity would come tumbling down. As children we learned that baptism made us "heirs of heaven." A favorite image in Christian literature pictures life as a pilgrimage that ends only when those who have obeyed God's law enter the heavenly city to dwell there forever. If there were no heaven, all our struggles to stay on the narrow road would be wasted. Saint Paul told the Corinthians (some of whom had doubts about the next life), "If for this life only we had hoped in Christ, we are the most pitiable people of all" *(I, 15: 19).*

Has it ever struck you that, important though everyone says heaven is, no one says much about it? And that what little they do say hardly leaves you panting to get there? Recently I read what some of the saints wrote on the subject. Saint Robert Bellarmine, for example, called heaven "a great sea of divine and eternal joy, which will fill us within and without, and surround us on all sides." Not much to whet our appetites there!

What did Jesus say about heaven? The *fact* of heaven is implicit in all his teaching. But did he ever try to describe it? No, but possibly the closest he came to doing so was in this passage from Luke. Some background is necessary.

The Sadducees, a tiny sect of priests in Jerusalem, were well-heeled, polished, powerful, and in unholy cahoots with Rome. Needless to say, they had few followers among the masses. Although they were guardians of the temple, their style of life was not what one looks for in a church person. Jesus, the new prophet from Galilee, they considered a threat, fearing he might spark an uprising and thus upset their delicate alliance with Rome. And so, although usually at loggerheads with the Pharisees, they joined forces with them in opposing Jesus.

In the eyes of most fellow Jews, the Sadducees were also heretics. Among their heresies was the belief that for humans death is the absolutely final curtain. Life beyond the grave, so certain to the Pharisees and so central to the teaching of Jesus, had in their view no foundation in authentic Scripture.

Here we see them approach Jesus, not as honest inquirers, but scoffers whose aim was to ridicule the notion of a hereafter. Picture them putting their question to him, probably with much nudging of elbows and smug winking of eyes. How, they asked, could a Jew believe the dead will rise again? It would mean, in the case they posed, that in heaven a woman would have seven husbands—an impossible household, doomed to dissolve in chaos. Polyandry was unthinkable to the Jews.

The question betrayed a childish picture of heaven. Instead of brushing it aside as a half-baked sophistry, however, Jesus dealt with it seriously. The Sadducees were not the only ones with such notions about heaven, nor would they be the last. By answering their question Jesus could set the record straight.

Note that in his answer Jesus does not describe what life in heaven *is*. That would be impossible. Heaven by its nature is indescribable. On admission there, one enters a wholly new sphere of existence. Even the saints who now enjoy heaven could no more describe it to us than explain the game of chess to a frog or teach a cat to read Shakespeare. Saint Paul says that our minds simply lack the power to grasp the notion of heaven *(I Cor. 2: 9)*. It is a realm beyond space and time and therefore beyond the comprehension of earth-bound intellects.

Instead of attempting the impossible, Jesus says something about what heaven is *not*. No one will marry in heaven, and no one will die. As Saint Paul told the Corinthians, the bodies of the blessed in heaven, unlike the bodies we have on earth, will be "spiritual" bodies, neither engaged in procreation nor subject to corruption *(I, 15: 42-44)*. Here on earth people live on in time through their offspring. There time as we know it does not exist and procreation is unnecessary. The saints are eternally present to God, in a state of unending bliss.

All this sounds hopelessly abstract. Perhaps the best way to think of heaven, after all, is through earthly images, inadequate though they are. We can recall whatever has given us deepest joy—the most dazzling displays of nature, the finest works of art, the heights of human friendship and love. In heaven will be all these and far more, for God is the source of them all. There happiness will be total. Here we have fractured moments of joy. There we will enjoy forever lasting beauty, unalloyed friendship, the love of the author of love. In the pilgrimage of life, heaven is our journey's end.

The Sadducees were wrong. There is an afterlife of total and enduring bliss. It is worth all our energies to reach it.

God Wants a Return on His Investment

Thirty-third Sunday in Ordinary Time.
A: Mt. 25: 14-30 (or 14-15; 19-20).

❖❖❖

"To everyone who has, more will be given and he will grow rich; but from the one who has not, even what he has will be taken away." Although this saying was a favorite of Jesus, even good Christians often wince when they hear it. That life is unfair, that the rich grow richer and the poor poorer, has sadly been true throughout history. Revolutionaries and reformers never let us forget it. But who would have expected this grim statistic to be cited approvingly by the founder of Christianity?

An African Christian once told me how troubling he found the passage. Was the message of Jesus to the impoverished people of the world that they will never catch up, their lot will only grow worse, and they had better just grin and bear it? Not exactly, I told him. Jesus had no direct interest in economic theory or politics. To understand this saying, we must take a good look at what occasioned it, the parable of the talents.

In ancient times a talent was a unit of weight; and when the object weighed was a precious metal, it became a unit of money. A talent-weight of silver, for example, was worth more than a thousand dollars in today's currency. The meaning we now give to the word "talent"—an innate aptitude—derives from the way Christian preachers have interpreted this parable.

What happens when people with an aptitude for music lavish time and energy in developing it? Like the good and faithful servants in the parable, they grow richer in that talent, for their skills are sharpened with practice. But if, like the lazy servant, they bury their talent, they may lose what small skill they started with. That is the gist of this parable. God wants us to cultivate our talents, not let them rot with neglect.

Theologians remind us that our most precious talents are the supernatural virtues of faith, hope, and charity that God infused in our souls at baptism. True, but the parable applies as well to our natural talents, which also come from God.

The physical world that surrounds us will not last forever; but while it does last, it is in our custody, and God wants us to use it lovingly. That is what we do when we apply our talents to such endeavors as science, art, medicine—even sports and entertainment. These enhance the visible universe and thereby give glory to its Maker. Neglecting such talents is not as sinful as neglecting faith, hope, and charity, but it is certainly sinful and deserving of punishment.

The *World Almanac* has an alphabetical list of the world's great inventions, everything from Pascal's adding machine to Judson's zipper. There one can also find lists of history's greatest works of art, music, literature. We would be wrong to dismiss these achievements as unimportant in the eyes of God. They are the products of human talents, which are God's gifts; and they have enhanced the world, which is God's garden.

Like the king in the parable, God has been far from evenhanded in distributing talents. But we need no parable to tell us what is obvious to a six-year-old, that we were not all endowed equally at birth. For those at the lower end of the line the parable has a warning. Let them not think their disability gives them an excuse to drop out of God's talent show. They will be held as accountable for their use of God's gifts, however small, as will those more generously endowed.

Paging through the names of great inventors and artists in the almanac, one wonders what our world would be like if they had frittered away their days, whining that others were more talented than themselves. Would not that be a sin? When they hear the word "sin," many people think exclusively of the *evil* deeds people *commit*, such as murder, theft, adultery. Too seldom do they think of the *good* deeds people *omit*. These include not just acts of compassion for their neighbor, but also the right use of their talents.

On judgment day God will call us to account for such sins of omission. And his wrath will fall, not only on the bountifully endowed who abuse their talents, but also on those to whom he has given slender talents. From these, of course, God expects only slender returns. But from all he demands some return.

He has every reason to do so. Our talents belong to him as surely as the talents in the parable belong to the king. We have them only on trust. This is an area where the Christian outlook differs totally from the pagan. Christians know, or should know, how foolish it is to take credit for their talents. The voices one hears in a choir are no more the property of the choristers than the hearts they were born with or the hairs on their head. God owns everything. He loaned us what talents we have. And he looks for a return on his investment.

The Christian View of History

Thirty-third Sunday in Ordinary Time.
B: Mk. 13: 24-32.

❖❖❖

The snippet of Scripture chosen for a Sunday gospel sometimes says little to us after a first reading. Even a trained theologian may be unable to decipher it without being familiar with the context in which it occurs. This passage, from Mark's thirteenth chapter, is a good example. Its very first sentence presents a puzzle: "But in those days after that tribulation..." The Sunday worshipper rightly wonders. What days was Jesus talking about? What kind of tribulation?

To find the answers we must read through the whole of Mark's chapter thirteen, itself the most difficult in his gospel. There we find that the time Jesus spoke of is *now*—not the exact hour on our watches or the date on today's newspapers, but the entire span of time between the moment Jesus spoke and the moment when human history will come to a close. Today is part of that "now." We are living in those "days of tribulation."

During those days, Jesus has explained, his followers can expect false Messiahs, earthquakes, famine, and war; and they themselves will suffer persecutions. We need not be historians to know how accurate that prophecy has proved to be. Such tribulations have plagued mankind from the first century to the present and will continue until our planet stops spinning.

Jesus made this prediction during a discourse to his disciples shortly before his death. Theologians call this his "eschatological" discourse, a word meaning "pertaining to the last things." When they hear the term "last things" people usually think of their own last things, their death and whatever reward or punishment will follow. Here Jesus takes a more sweeping view, the death of the entire universe as well as the "new heaven and new earth" *(Rev. 21: 1)* that will replace it.

The disciples prompted this eschatological discourse by asking Jesus when the world would come to an end, an event they wrongly took as simultaneous with the destruction of the temple. The answer of Jesus was deliberately evasive. Saying the end would be preceded by false Messiahs, earthquakes, famine, war and persecution is the same as saying it can come at any time, for these events occur throughout history. Effectively Jesus was telling all of us that the exact time of the end is none of our business. What is our business is getting ready for the end that will certainly come. We must always be ready.

Jesus went on, in the passage used for today's gospel, to describe how the end will take place, but the picture he paints is as unfocused as the time when it will happen. The darkened sun and moon, the crashing stars and shaken heavens, the coming of the Son of Man in the clouds—these are not supposed to be a literal picture of that last day. The images are poetic, mostly borrowed from Old Testament prophets. Their point is simply that the cosmos as we know it will cease. Once that happens, all who have lived by God's law will be gathered together and Christ's eternal reign will begin.

This picture of his final coming and the inauguration of his eternal realm is the climax of the entire chapter and what the Church wants us to dwell on. About the days of tribulation we already know more than enough. But the Christian view of history does not end there. It looks forward to the last of all "last things," when Jesus will return "with great power and glory" to gather his faithful and lead them to eternal bliss.

As we look at the world today and see the tribulations it still endures, we should not lose sight of where history is heading. What this gospel wants us to see is that, as sure as spring follows winter, the everlasting kingdom of Jesus will follow these days of tribulation. Eternity may seem far away, but even now, at this moment, Jesus "is near, at the gates."

The passage contains a final puzzle: What did Jesus mean by the words, "This generation will not pass away until all these things have taken place"? Some commentators think "all these things" refers to the destruction of the temple, the event that Jesus had predicted at the beginning of his discourse. More likely, I think, the "generation" Jesus spoke of was the Christian era. What Jesus was saying is that Christianity, his Church, will last until the end of history. His followers will be there to greet him at his second coming.

One of the acclamations used at Mass goes "Christ has died, Christ has risen, Christ will come again." Those three sentences sum up the most important events in both human history and our personal history. When Christ comes again, we will be there. Between now and then is not just a time of tribulation. Above all, it is a time of expectation and preparation; a time to look up and see Jesus at the gates, a time to get ready.

"THEY WILL PERSECUTE YOU"

Thirty-third Sunday in Ordinary Time.
C: Lk. 21: 5-19.

When will the world end? People have been wondering for centuries. For centuries, too, half-crazed Christians have claimed to know the answer. From its beginnings Christianity has been plagued by rumors that doomsday is about to dawn. Our own century has had its share of false prophets who have marched their followers to some mountainside or cavern where together they could all watch for the Second Coming of the Lord.

In 1975 I visited such a group in a remote section of the African bush (this delusion has no nationality). Their leader was sure the final cataclysm would strike by 1976, and they awaited it with as much terror as prayer. Only when it missed its schedule did they disband and return to a saner life.

Not just saner, but more Christian. The error of these misguided souls is not that they expect the Second Coming and try to be ready. That Jesus will come to judge the living and the dead is the creed of every Christian. Their error is rather that they think they can pinpoint the date, blithely disregarding what Jesus himself said on the topic. Several times he was asked to reveal when the world would end, and each time he refused. Clearly he considered the curiosity that prompted the query to be unhealthy. A Christian needs no timetable divulging the hour of Christ's coming. We should strive always to be ready.

Today's gospel describes how the apostles once put the question to Jesus and how, as usual, it went unanswered. Their curiosity was prompted by his prophecy about the razing of the temple. This prophecy was fulfilled about forty years later, on 9 August 70 A.D., when Roman soldiers, outraged at the stubborn resistance of the Jews, set the temple ablaze. Its ruin was complete. Today only the wailing wall remains.

The temple was the pride of the Jews, one of the wonders of the ancient world. A massive structure with towering pillars of gleaming marble, it seemed indestructible, a sign of God's abiding presence. They thought it would not cease to exist until time itself ceased. Thus when Jesus spoke of the day when not a stone would be left of it, his apostles took him to be referring to the last day of human history.

Their question about when this would happen is really about when the world will end.

Jesus responded with a clear warning against paying heed to false prophets. The signs they point to as omens that the final reckoning is near cannot be trusted. Wars, famines, insurrections, and the like will always be part of human history.

Idle as he considered the question, however, Jesus took the opportunity to repeat a favorite lesson. Another thing, he said, that is bound to happen between now and the last day, as certain as wars and insurrections, is the persecution of his followers. If they intend to remain faithful to his teaching, then, they must expect harassment, ostracism, imprisonment, even death. These are part of the ordinary price one must pay to be a Christian. No one should be surprised when they happen.

What is truly surprising is that this lesson, so often repeated, is so often forgotten. Recently the newspapers carried the story of the six priests in a distant land who were murdered simply because they preached the biblical doctrine of justice and strove to lessen the sufferings of the poor. Their murder was by no means unique. Similar atrocities have bloodied almost every page of Church history. How should a Christian react when they occur? Surely we should grieve for the dead and lament the loss of their labors for Christ. But we should not be surprised, not even gloomy. Pride would be a fitter response, and joy that Christians are still willing to die for the gospel.

How do we react when public figures talk about abortion and pornography as though only Victorian crackpots oppose them? When people in the media treat unlimited sexual license as though it were an inherent right of all mankind? When our objections to the dispensing of condoms among schoolchildren are dismissed as pietistic prudery? Of all the anti-Christians loose in the world, these propagandists for pagan modernity are the most irritating. They do not persecute with a sword; ridicule is their weapon. And while ridicule cannot kill, it sure can sting. No wonder Jesus told us we need "patient endurance."

But it is not enough just to endure these false prophets. We must defy both them and their dogmas. In doing so, we should not be upset to find we are in the minority. For a Christian, being in the minority is par for the course. The Sermon on the Mount will never score high in opinion polls. The true gospel will always be unfashionable, scorned by the spirit of the age. When Jesus said "All will hate you because of me," he used a Semitic exaggeration. He meant all those who *think* they count.

The Last Surprise

Last Ordinary Sunday: Christ the King.
A: Mt. 25: 31-46.

❖❖❖

An American priest stationed in India once received a visit from his sister. Young and impressionable, she was ecstatic during her first few days in the exotic Orient. But then her brother blundered badly. He took her for a stroll through the slums of Bombay. So traumatic was the experience for her that the next day he had to bundle her onto a jet bound for home.

Can we blame her? Up to then she had barely set foot outside her snug and antiseptic hometown in the American heartland. Nothing had prepared her for the filth and famine that are everyday sights in some parts of the world—rat-infested warrens, squalid hovels, open sewers, diseased and spindly children. She was a prayerful Catholic, but it never occurred to her that the Jesus she prayed to could have much in common with the people who lived in such sub-human surroundings.

I am not suggesting that we all go traipsing through slums (every country has some that might rival Bombay's) to get a whiff of real poverty. Human distress should not be treated as a curiosity for sightseers. An American politician on the campaign trail, when urged to add an inner city ghetto to his scheduled stops, is said to have remarked, "If you've seen one slum, you've seen them all." The quip sounds callous, but it makes a valid point. Merely gaping at suffering solves nothing. Doing something about it is what counts. And no one has a stronger motive for doing something than the Christian.

This gospel tells us why. It opens with a magnificent panorama: the world has come to an end and all the nations are gathered before the throne of Jesus Christ. The onetime itinerant preacher from Galilee is at last revealed for what he is, the Son of God, redeemer and king of all mankind. As king he is about to pass judgment on the whole of history, and the assembly is hushed in expectation. The eternal destiny of every human being who ever lived is about to be revealed.

Jesus was fond of surprises. Now he springs his last and possibly greatest surprise. One might expect this final reckoning to make mention of the stirring events that have shaped history—the rise and fall of nations, the booms and busts on Wall Street, the high points in art, literature, science. Instead, Jesus evokes images of the little people, the nameless masses who have borne a more than fair share of life's misfortunes—the hungry children, the wandering refugees, the homeless men and women, the gravely sick, the wretches who languish behind bars. To each man and woman who ever lived Jesus says either "Because you helped these unfortunates, welcome to my kingdom" or "Because you passed them by, were too busy to be concerned with their fate, depart into eternal darkness."

The lesson could not be clearer. We make our deepest impression on God not so much by singing his praises as by helping the lowliest of his human creatures. The needier those we help, the more favor we find in heaven. That is why the Church has always made it her business to do more than build places of worship and conduct sacred service. She works also for the physical and emotional needs of people, opposing not only sin but the conditions that are often created by sin and are in turn conducive to more sin—poverty, disease, ignorance, apathy, injustice. Those who refuse to lift a finger to ease these conditions or who turn their backs on the forces mobilized against them hardly deserve the name of Christian.

In the fourth century a pagan Roman soldier was approached in the snow by a thinly clad stranger begging for alms. The soldier took off his cloak, cut it in two, and gave half to the beggar. That night he had a vision of the heavenly court, where Jesus sat enthroned amidst his angels and saints. From the shoulders of Jesus hung the half-cloak the soldier had given the beggar. The soldier was soon baptized and became one of the greatest saints of the early Church, Martin of Tours. A similar story is told of the young Francis of Assisi. While tending to the sores of a leper he had met on the road, Francis saw the leper's face transformed into the face of Jesus.

Legends? Perhaps, but the truth these tales embody is no legend. It comes straight from this passage of Matthew. Whatever we do for the sick and the suffering, Jesus takes as done for himself. Why? Because he sees, with a clarity we can only strive for, that we are all children of his Father, all redeemed by his own blood. He died for us all, is brother to us all.

Jesus is now enthroned as king of the universe. But he once lived among us as a commoner, and he still identifies with common people, including slum people. He wants us to ease their suffering. Those who will not help them do not love him.

IN PILATE'S CHAMBERS

Last Ordinary Sunday: Christ the King.
B: Jn. 18: 33-37.

❖❖❖

Pontius Pilate was a little known colonial bureaucrat who for ten years ruled over a relatively insignificant outpost of the Roman empire. No one familiar with his career as governor of Judea would have expected his tenure there to make more than a ripple on the stream of history. A single incident, trivial though it seemed at the time, made the difference: his encounter with Jesus. That is the scene John describes in this gospel.

On one side sits Pilate, politician to his fingertips, proud embodiment of the imperial power of Rome. His manner is smooth, efficient, no-nonsense. On the other stands Jesus, the itinerant preacher from Galilee. With his attire rumpled and his features haggard after a harrowing night, he seems a misfit in Pilate's trim chamber. But his eyes are steady, his presence commanding. He does not flinch before Pilate.

Normally an alleged criminal like Jesus would not merit a hearing before the governor. Pilate had weightier matters to attend to than what appeared to be the delusions of a fanatic. What made this case unusual was the main charge against Jesus.

On the previous night the supreme council of the Jews had found Jesus guilty of blasphemy and declared him worthy of death. To their regret, however, they could not carry out their sentence, for their Roman conquerors reserved capital punishment to themselves. And so at daybreak the high priests of the council hustled Jesus over to the governor's residence. They could not accuse Jesus of blasphemy (a matter of no concern to Pilate), so they trumped up some charges that painted him as a revolutionary. Chief among them was that he had claimed he was a king.

Pilate probably had the same lofty disdain for his Jewish subjects that is said to have marked British officials in their dealings with Africans. Convinced that everything they did was for the good of these "backward" subjects, they wondered why so many resented their colonial masters. Shouldn't they be grateful for the benefits of a superior civilization?

Was Jesus, Pilate wondered, one of those unruly ingrates? Was he aiming to put the clock back and restore the barbaric kingdom of Israel?

As the man responsible for law and order in Judea, Pilate had to find out. Recently several would-be Messiahs (the word, Pilate knew, meant king) had rallied their followers and put parts of Palestine in turmoil. Rome was not pleased. If Jesus were another of these, he had to be stopped.

And so, Pilate summoned the prisoner to his chamber. One look at Jesus prompted his scathing query, "Are *you* the king of the Jews?" How can a nobody like yourself, a mere preacher with no armed followers behind you, claim to be a king?

To make Pilate realize he was treading on matters outside his competence, Jesus answered with a question of his own. Was Pilate, he asked, using "king" in its Roman, political sense, or its Jewish, religious sense? Pilate fired back in scorn, "*I* am not a Jew, am I?" How could anyone imagine that *I*, a Roman governor, would use a word in its Jewish sense?

That should have ended the matter, for Jesus then assured Pilate that the kingdom he ruled was not of this world and therefore no threat to Rome. But Pilate's curiosity had been whetted and he would not let the matter drop. Jesus had, after all, spoken of possessing a "kingdom." So Pilate tried once again, "Then you *are* a king?" To this Jesus answered calmly, "You say that I am," a Jewish expression meaning, "Yes, as a matter of fact, I am." He then went on to explain that his mission as king, his whole purpose in life, was to reveal truth to mankind. The only realm that concerned him was truth.

We all say we want truth. Few things frustrate us more than realizing we have been cheated by falsehood. We look (often in vain) for truth in news reporting and advertising, truth from our doctors and politicians. But above all we want (or should want) truth about the fundamental issues of life—where we came from, why we are here, what lies beyond the grave.

That is the kind of truth Jesus was talking about. To reveal it to those who live in darkness (that is, to all mankind) was why he "was born" and "came into the world." He is lord of truth. His subjects are those who listen to his voice.

Pilate eventually handed Jesus over for crucifixion. Doing so quieted the mob, and sending one more Jew to the grave did no violence to Pilate's conscience. As a final gesture of contempt for the whole lot of them, however, he had this headsign posted on the cross: "Jesus of Nazareth, King of the Jews."

Change it to read, "Jesus of Nazareth, King of all Mankind, Lord of Truth." He revealed eternal truths to the world. These truths are what we celebrate on this feast of Christ the King.

ACTING LIKE A KING

Last Ordinary Sunday: Christ the King.
C: Lk. 23: 35-43.

❖❖❖

"Nothing of importance happened today," noted George III of England in his diary before going to bed on 4 July 1776. How could he know that on that day in Philadelphia he had lost the allegiance of his American colonies and would never regain it? Events that later generations consider world-shaking can appear humdrum when they take place, even to close participants.

If Pontius Pilate had kept a diary, would he have made a similar entry for the day Jesus Christ redeemed the human race? Probably. Sentencing a criminal to crucifixion was routine for Roman governors. A Roman citizen, however grave his offense, could not be reduced to such shame, but it was standard for slaves and members of conquered nations. The nearly mute Galilean whose case he had heard that morning did not strike Pilate as a man who could change the course of history.

What about the soldiers who carried out his sentence? Nailing hoodlums to crosses and standing guard while they twisted for a day or two in torment were ho-hum affairs for them. Habit had made them immune to such horrors. Did they find anything at all notable about the last hours of Jesus?

Almost certainly yes, unless they were hard of hearing. A crucifixion was usually a raucous business, with the victim hooted by the lowest trash in town. What made the mob that turned out for this crucifixion different was that the loudest jeers came, not from the usual rabble, but from the most prestigious people in Jerusalem, the religious rulers. And the target of their venom, the convict on the middle cross, was himself a religious leader, venerated by some Jews as the Messiah.

The taunts aimed at Jesus were not the only sounds that made this crucifixion unique. Historians record that one of the most revolting features of a crucifixion was the stream of obscenities that gushed from the victim, blasting his fate, his slayers, his beholders. One of the thieves on Calvary spat out his wrath in this manner, even joining the chorus of profanities hurled at Jesus. But the other thief and Jesus were mostly silent. The few words they did speak were so out of place the soldiers must have thought they were madmen.

The good thief began by reproving his fellow thief. We deserve our fate, he admitted, but this man has done no wrong. Then, turning to Jesus, he addressed him as a king about to take possession of his throne, begging his good favor. In reply Jesus spoke mysteriously of welcoming the thief to paradise.

The sign on his cross identified Jesus as king of the Jews, but that was just Pilate's petty revenge against those who had pressured him into passing the death sentence. This lunatic carpenter, the sign said to them, is the closest any of your race will ever come to being king. The good thief, on the other hand, was in dead earnest when he spoke of Jesus entering his "reign." The word shows he believed Jesus really was a king.

A king? The mangled flesh hanging alongside the thief did not have the look of royalty. Like the good thief himself, Jesus at that moment was one of the world's colossal losers. Why then address him as king? What did the good thief mean?

The same thing we mean today as we honor Christ the King. Some people dislike the title, not just because kings have gone out of style, but because those whom we read about are rarely worth our respect. Most were little more than prancing martinets, puffed-up hooligans in fancy dress. To show how different a kind of king Jesus was, the Church chooses this scene on Calvary for today's gospel. No one reading it can miss the point.

The good thief must have realized what Jesus had tried to make Pilate realize when he told him his kingdom did not belong to this world. The kings who have reigned in this world wielded material power. Ruling by physical force, they received the obedience one expects from slaves. The supremacy of Jesus, however, is spiritual. He rules the hearts of his followers by his love and example, and the service they give him is free.

How did Jesus display his spiritual power on Calvary? By words, both those he did not speak and those he did. If ever a man had the right to howl out to heaven with rage at the savagery of his fellow men, it was Jesus. Instead, the only words the thief heard from him were prayers, especially prayers that God forgive his mockers and murderers. To remain silent under a shower of such catcalls as Jesus received, to pray for his enemies rather than revile them, was a spiritual triumph.

The good thief realized that the self-mastery, the holy forbearance, the fortitude that Jesus displayed could belong only to God's chosen one, the Messiah—a word that means king.

No person ever deserved the title more than Jesus.

A LIGHT TO THE GENTILES

February 2: Presentation of the Lord.
Lk. 1: 22-40 (or 22-32).

❖❖❖

The Church considers the feast of the Presentation so important that when it falls on a Sunday its Mass usually replaces the regular Sunday Mass. Moreover, the first Mass of the day is traditionally preceded by a candlelight procession. Several questions occur. What makes this feast so meaningful that it merits special treatment? Why is it associated with light? Above all, what message does it have for Christians today?

Forty days after the birth of Jesus, Joseph and Mary brought him to the temple in Jerusalem. There, as Jewish law required, they presented their "first-born male" to God. The law did not oblige parents to travel all the way to Jerusalem for this ceremony. But from Bethlehem to Jerusalem was only a day's journey, and so it was no trouble for this couple to consecrate their infant to God in the magnificent setting of the temple.

There the threesome was greeted by Simeon, who here makes his solo appearance in Scripture. About Simeon we know absolutely nothing except that, being "righteous and devout," he looked forward to "the consolation of Israel," that is, the coming of the Messiah. Artists have traditionally made him into an elderly priest of the temple, but that is guesswork. His words of blessing as he beheld the infant Jesus are Simeon's only claim to fame. These words are now known as the *"Nunc Dimittis"* ("Now...let your servant go") canticle, which is recited daily during the night prayer of the "Liturgy of the Hours." In this canticle, rather than the actual presentation of Jesus, is the main message the Church wants us to attend to today.

The holy Spirit had revealed to Simeon that one day he would lay eyes on the "Messiah of the Lord." Now he astounded the bystanders in the temple by declaring that the Messiah had finally arrived. This ordinary-looking infant in the company of this unpretentious couple was none other than the Saviour of Israel. The source of Simeon's certitude, according to Luke, was again the holy Spirit. Now that his eyes had at last feasted on the Messiah, he was prepared to die in peace.

Simeon did more, however, than identify Jesus as the Messiah. His canticle contained a surprise. He did not just point to Jesus as the

Messiah, but called him "a light for revelation to the Gentiles." With these words he revealed that the scope of the Messiah's mission was far vaster than the Israelites had always imagined. It is the broad extent of Christ's mission and the role each of us should play in it that make this feast of the Presentation important.

The term "Gentiles" is from the Latin *gentes*, meaning nations. It denoted the nations of non-Jews, the *goyim*. For these pagan hordes, unenlightened worshipers of false gods, pious Israelites in biblical times had little more than contempt.

That is why these words of Simeon were so surprising. He said Jesus was both the Messiah and a light to the Gentiles. How, those listening must have wondered, could the Savior of Israel have anything to do with Gentiles? For us, however, Simeon's words are prophetic, one of Scripture's earliest hints of the universality of Christ's mission. Jesus was not only the consolation of Israel, but God's messenger to all mankind.

Consider this: what Gentiles were to ancient Jews, non-Christians (many of whom call themselves Christians) are to us. And it is the task of all Christians to try to make the light of the gospel penetrate to them. The opening sentence of *Lumen Gentium* (Light of the Gentiles), the Second Vatican's document on the Church, reads, "Christ is the light of all nations." True, but he no longer lights the world by his visible presence on earth. If his light is to shine at all in the world today, it must do so through his reflected light in the lives of individual Christians. *We* must be bearers of his light.

Ours is not an inward-looking religion. The Church is not a private club that caters exclusively to the well-being of its members. Its task is to make Christ's light shine as far as possible in the most improbable corners of our still predominantly pagan world. Failing that, it fails as the Church.

By the word "Church," we mean more than the Pope and his network of bishops. The Church is ourselves. We are all part of the century-long candlelight procession of Christians, by baptism enlisted in its chorus. This does not mean we are all called to be foreign missionaries. And God forbid that we all have a try at preaching. But if all of us were to live by the light of the gospel, we would make things brighter and morally better by far in whatever part of the world we work and play.

If the light of the gospel is alive in us, others will be drawn to its warmth. Our task is to keep the light burning.

The Guardian

March 19: Saint Joseph, Husband of Mary.
Mt. 1: 16; 18-21; 24 (or Lk. 2: 41-51).

❖❖❖

Joseph is a popular saint, or at least his name is popular. Look at the many churches, schools, and hospitals named after him, not to speak of the individuals. He is also a powerful saint. Among the men and women whose help we invoke during the eucharistic prayer at Mass, Joseph is second only to Mary. And Mary, as everyone knows, is the most powerful of all.

Joseph was a carpenter. Apart from that, what the evangelists tell us about him is barely enough to fill a postcard. But in the first of the two readings the Church offers for today's gospel, Matthew provides the one essential fact from which flows all of Joseph's popularity and power. He was the father of Jesus; not, the passage makes clear, the biological father, but the legal father, with all the rights and responsibilities that belonged to the head of a Jewish household.

While Jesus was growing up at Nazareth and during the years of his ministry at Capernaum, his neighbors and friends referred to him as "the son of Joseph" *(Lk. 4: 22; Jn. 6: 42)*. It did not dawn on them that for Joseph he was only an adopted son. They had no reason to suspect anything unusual about his origin.

How unusual it really was we learn from the first chapter of Matthew. He starts his account of "how the birth of Jesus came about" with Joseph betrothed to Mary. From what we know about the marriage customs of the time we can be sure that both of them were young, by today's standards far too young for marriage. Imagine the anguish and disbelief that gripped the young Joseph on discovering that his even younger fiancee, whose virtue he had never had reason to doubt, was with child.

In such a plight another might have exposed Mary to the punishment of the law. Joseph, a "righteous man," decided instead on a quiet separation. He could neither explain Mary's condition nor accept what to almost anyone else would have been clear evidence of guilt. His distress must have been enormous.

Fortunately, this distress did not last long. God's messenger brought word that Mary was as innocent as Joseph had thought. The child she bore had been conceived by the holy Spirit and was destined to "save his people from their sins." Hearing this, Joseph went peacefully ahead with the marriage ceremony. By becoming Mary's husband he became legal father to her child.

We should not think that after hearing the angel's words, Joseph grasped the full truth about the identity of Jesus. Years later the apostles, who had witnessed Jesus in the full exercise of his powers, needed months before they even suspected he was the Messiah. And it was not until after his resurrection that their eyes began to open to his divinity. Joseph's knowledge was probably even more limited. But the angel's words made at least two things clear: that a great prophet was soon to be born to Mary; and that it was his own duty to become both guardian and guide to her and her child.

It is first of all for his role as guardian, to whom God, in the words of the opening prayer, "entrusted our Savior," that the Church honors Joseph today. He was present at the birth of Jesus, having guarded Mary on the journey to Bethlehem. When an angel warned of Herod's designs, he brought Mary and Jesus to the safety of exile in Egypt. And on Herod's death he led them back to Nazareth, where he supported them by his carpentry.

All of us are sometimes called on to guard others—as parents, teachers, doctors, nurses, civil servants, even bus conductors and traffic wardens. Joseph is a good model to follow in such tasks. He guarded the child Jesus as a treasure held in trust for God. All human beings under our care are treasures redeemed by Jesus Christ. We should guard them as his property.

Joseph not only guarded Jesus; he guided him with his fatherly authority. This we learn in Luke's account of how Jesus was lost and found in the temple. Many readers are so engrossed with wondering why Jesus lingered in the temple that they miss the importance of the final clause, one of the most remarkable in Scripture: "He (Jesus) was obedient to them."

Think of what these words mean. If Jesus obeyed Joseph, then Joseph must have given commands to Jesus, for without commands no obedience is possible. Joseph, for all his sanctity, was a creature, a speck of next-to-nothingness when compared with the infinite majesty of God. Yet at Nazareth, as head of the holy family, he gave orders to the Son of God.

We are all called at times to issue commands, even though we may know, as Joseph did, that those over whom we have authority are better in God's eyes than ourselves. The orders Joseph gave to Jesus must have been wise and gentle. Pray that with his help, any orders we give may be wise and gentle too.

SHE STARTED IT ALL

March 25: Annunciation.
Lk. 1: 26-38.

❖❖❖

At the age of eight Shirley Temple, the movie star moppet of the thirties, was said to be the most photographed woman in the world. The Virgin Mary was about twice that age at the time Luke talks about in this gospel, her first starring role in Scripture; and while photography was yet to be invented, no woman in history has been featured more often on canvas. The episode described in this reading is one of the all-time favorite subjects for artists. Typically their works capture a look of astonished reverence on Mary's eyes as she learns she has been chosen to give birth to the Savior of the world.

Treasured though these paintings are, they rarely convey the reality of the scene. Ignoring the backwardness of village life in biblical times, their makers have embellished with luxurious trappings the drab simplicity that marked everyday life at Nazareth. Their works often show Mary kneeling at prayer in a chamber almost fit for royalty, while nearby a radiant creature with wings announces the glad tidings from on high. What really happened was more prosaic. It was also, for those who probe beneath the surface, more marvelous.

Scripture does not say Mary was at prayer when the angel came to her. It is just as likely that she heard the message of the angel while she was walking through the fields near Nazareth or drawing water from the village well. Even if we prefer to imagine the encounter taking place in the privacy of Mary's home, we should realize how far from posh a typical home at Nazareth was. Housing for a poor family there might be only a cave dug out of the side of a hill. Mary lived in no mansion. She was an unpolished peasant, not a princess.

Moreover, the angel may not have appeared to her in bodily form at all. An angel (the word means messenger) of heaven is by definition a spirit and can communicate with earth-bound creatures by gently invading their imaginations. It could well have been such as unseen messenger who whispered God's words into Mary's soul.

To realize what was truly marvelous at the moment of the Annunciation we must forget about how the event would have appeared to the eyes of any prying intruder and concentrate instead on what it meant in the eyes of God.

On an otherwise unremarkable day at Nazareth God sent a message to Mary, a young maiden who seemed destined never to leave a print on the sands of history. But she had already stirred attention in heaven. Her virtue was such that the messenger began by saluting her as God's "favored one," adding that the Lord was "with" her. Nowhere in Scripture does God shower higher praise on any of his earthly creatures.

Mary was not only mystified by these compliments; in her humility she was confounded, deeply troubled. Only the truly holy are truly humble, for only they realize how far from God all humans are. Mary was only an unschooled peasant from the hills of Galilee, but she knew better than the wise of this world the place of a creature before God. She wondered how the all-powerful Yahweh could take notice of a nobody like herself.

But the angel went on, explaining what God planned to do to her and through her to all mankind. She was to "conceive...and bear a son" who would succeed to David's throne and whose rule would last forever. The execution of this plan, however, had not yet taken place. It awaited Mary's consent.

She did consent, and because she did the march of history changed course. At her words, "I am the handmaid of the Lord. May it be done to me according to your word," the second Person of the Trinity stepped directly into our world. Few events could be less impressive to human eyes, but none more important for human souls. At these words of Mary, God entered her womb and clothed himself in human flesh. Thus he joined our human race and launched his career as redeemer to us all.

Has anyone ever asked you, or have you ever asked yourself, why Catholics are so devoted to Mary? Or where in Scripture we find grounds for our devotion? The best way to answer both questions is by pointing to this passage from Luke.

In today's Mass the Annunciation is called "the beginning of the Church." Strange words, when we consider that Pentecost has always been celebrated as the Church's birthday. But before the Church was born, Jesus had to be born. And before he was born, a willing mother had to be found. Without Mary's agreement to fill that role, Pentecost could never have happened.

Mary started it all. Her reply to the angel, consenting to give birth to the Lord, affected our lives as profoundly as her own. The Mother of Jesus is also our mother, mother of all Christians, mother of our Church.

"JOHN IS HIS NAME"

June 24: Birth of St. John the Baptist.
Vigil: Lk. 1: 5-17. Day: Lk. 1: 57-66; 80.

❖❖❖

Although these Masses honor the birth of John the Baptist, the Scripture readings say little about his actual birth. Instead we learn how his father Zechariah was told he was to have a son and a why he gave him the name that he did. At the naming ceremony, eight days after John's birth, this name caused an uproar among his kinfolk. In biblical times naming a newborn was serious business, and all the relatives felt involved.

People today are easily puzzled by the importance scriptural characters attached to names. Would the son of Zechariah and Elizabeth have followed a different path if he had answered to a different name? Surely calling him Jason or Jupiter would not have made John any less holy or more controversial than he was. Why does Scripture make such a fuss over a name?

Because Scripture is dealing with older times, when ways of thinking were different. People then knew the meanings of names and were at pains to choose one that expressed their hopes for a child's future. In special cases, as we see here, God himself decided on the name. When he did so, it expressed more than a hope; it was God's promise for the child's future. Thus the name "John," meaning "God has shown mercy," sums up John's career. His very presence among the Israelites, preparing "a people fit for the Lord," was an expression of God's mercy.

In the gospel reading for the vigil Mass, Luke tells how John's name came about. One day while the Hebrew priest, the childless Zechariah, was offering incense in the sanctuary of the temple, he received a message from on high. An angel told him that his prayer had been answered and his wife Elizabeth would give birth to a son who was destined to be "great in the sight of the Lord." This son was to be called John.

For Zechariah the prospect of a son was good news, so good he doubted it could be true. In punishment he was struck dumb. And so when the relatives gathered for the naming ceremony nine months later, Zechariah had to leave the talking to his wife. When, obviously under instruction from her husband, she declared the boy's name should be John, the assembled kinfolk protested. No ancestor of theirs answered to that name. They yielded only after Zechariah confirmed in writing the choice of this name.

Soon the whole neighborhood was alive with rumors about the child. The Lord's hand, everyone said, must be on him. People like Zechariah and Elizabeth would not go our of their way to choose so unexpected a name without instruction from on high.

These neighbors were right. John, who "was filled with the holy Spirit even from his mother's womb," grew to such greatness that Jesus later declared that "among those born of women, no one is greater then John" *(Lk. 7: 28)*. While still a boy he went to live in the wilderness, feeding and clothing himself with the careless abandon of a savage. Not until he reached manhood did he make his first appearance as a preacher.

Then, for a few blazing years, John more than made up for his father's nine months of silence. His voice, calling on his countrymen to repent, made tremors across the land of Israel. Sinners came crowding to his hermitage in the desert and heard him thunder against the ills of the age. Those who repented, he baptized in the Jordan, fulfilling the prophecy that he would "turn many of the children of Israel to the Lord their God."

Then, as suddenly as he had appeared, John vanished from sight. Shamed by his words of reproach, Herod first imprisoned and then beheaded him. By this time, however, John's work was complete. Jesus, to whom all his preaching had been prelude, was deep in his own mission of launching the kingdom of God.

John's career reminds us of the obvious but often neglected truth that to show compassion for sinners we need not keep mum about our opposition to sin. Although none of us is called to roar against the sins of our day as loudly as John did against those of his, neither should we be mute. Silence is golden, but not when it can be construed as consent to sin.

Too many Christians today are cringing souls, Milquetoasts too timid to let out a peep against the moral atrocities of our age. Some sins (abortion is one) are not only condoned by many outspoken contemporaries; they are considered sign of an advanced civilization. If we remain silent others may think we agree with the moral lunacy that rages around us. It takes courage to speak out for the moral code of the Sermon on the Mount.

Today let us ask God for a mite of the courage he gave to John. When words denouncing sin are called for, let us make ourselves heard. Even the feeble words of untrained Christians, if spoken with conviction, can find their mark. We can all, like John, be instruments of God's mercy.

An Odd Couple

June 29: Saint Peter and Paul, Apostles.
Vigil: Jn. 21: 15-19; Day: Mt. 16: 13-19.

Most people picture Nero as a bloated Roman emperor who played his fiddle while flames consumed his city. The fiddle is probably legend, but the fire was all too real and reduced half of Rome to ashes. Needing a scapegoat, Nero blamed the Christians, devotees of a new religion named after an obscure Jewish prophet. One ancient historian says that in the persecution Nero then mounted, a "huge multitude" perished.

Among them were the two men we honor today: Peter, the first bishop of Rome; and Paul, the apostle of the Gentiles. Little did Nero dream that the spiritual conquests notched by this pair of seemingly madcap preachers would one day make a deeper mark on history than all the military conquests of Rome.

As the risen Jesus had foretold, Peter met his end by stretching out his hands on a cross, just as his Master had done. He was buried under what is now the main altar of the Vatican basilica that bears his name. Excavations have uncovered his tomb, and a line of tourists files past it daily.

Paul was dispatched by beheading on the Via Ostia, just outside Rome. Tradition places his burial place on the site of what we know as the church of Saint Paul's-outside-the Walls.

Forty years earlier these two were unknown to one another and unlikely ever to meet. They had little but their race and religion in common. Both would probably have stared in disbelief if told where and in what company they would end their days.

Peter was a fisherman with little or no schooling, almost totally ignorant of the great world outside Palestine. Paul had a broader background. An educated Jew of the Diaspora and by birth a Roman citizen, he moved while a youth from his native Tarsus (in what is now Turkey) to Jerusalem, where he studied under Gamaliel, the noted teacher of Pharisaism. A Pharisee himself, Paul was a champion of the old religious traditions and therefore a foe of the newfangled ways of the Christians.

The Lord burst into the lives of these two, summoning both to live by his gospel and to teach it to others. Among his early followers Peter was the first to name Jesus the Messiah. Jesus replied by dubbing Peter "The Rock," on whom he promised to build a church that would outlast the centuries.

Jesus called his first disciples "fishers of men." In the bark of the Church, Peter was to be chief fisherman, in charge of the others and responsible for the entire catch. But although Jesus gave him authority over his fellow Christians, Peter was not to be a despot. Rather, he was to rule over his subjects in the manner of a shepherd feeding and tending his lambs and sheep. Like his Master, Peter must be a *good* shepherd.

On the first Christian Pentecost the world learned how good he was. It was then that he revealed his gift of eloquence, a tongue with power to inflame his listeners with the same love of God and neighbor that Jesus had ignited in himself. After his Pentecostal discourse, about three thousand Jews, the first of many notable catches, entered Peter's bark. From that day the numbers caught in his net continued to swell.

By the mid-sixties Peter had settled at Rome, then the administrative center of the civilized world and therefore ideal as headquarters for a Church that aspired to reach out to all mankind. This was not an idle dream. Already communities of Christians dotted the Gentile land between Jerusalem and Rome.

The person most responsible for this growth was Paul. Jesus had entered his life with the suddenness of lightning. Only a blinding flash could move this lover of Judaism to look kindly on the prophet from Nazareth, the man he held responsible for undermining Jewish traditions. The bolt from on high came while Paul was traveling to Damascus, intent on crushing the tiny community of Jewish Christians there. Along the road he received his "revelation of Jesus Christ." To persecute Christians, he now realized, was to persecute the Messiah, for Jesus was the Messiah, who somehow lived in the members of his Church.

The aim of Paul's preaching was that "all the Gentiles" might hear the gospel *(2 Tim. 4: 17)*. Only a person with Paul's cosmopolitan background would dare such a mission, and only a preacher with his eloquence was equipped to succeed. Before Paul, Christianity was confined almost exclusively to Jews and in danger of settling into the same narrow nationalism that marked other religions. By the time of his death it belonged, as Jesus insisted it must belong, to all nations.

After Jesus himself, Peter and Paul were most responsible for making the Church what it has been through the ages and still is today. With good reason the Church honors them with this feast. All of us are still in their debt.

We Are All Called to Share Her Glory

August 15: Assumption.
Vigil: Lk. 11: 27-28; Day: Lk. 1: 39-56.

❖❖❖

"Behold, from now on will all ages call me blessed." Thus sang Mary in her "Magnificat," the song of joy she composed after learning she was to be the mother of the Messiah. Today, two thousand summers later, we can testify to the accuracy of that prophesy. The Church has many feasts to pour blessings on Mary, but none greater than the one we celebrate today.

The Assumption was declared a teaching of the Catholic Church by Pius XII in 1950. In so doing the Pope did not invent a new doctrine, requiring us to believe something that Christians in previous ages had never heard of. Popes and General Councils have power to define doctrines, not create them. Defining a doctrine no more makes it true than issuing a birth certificate brings a child into the world. It simply puts an official stamp on something that was known to be true all along.

In declaring the centuries-old belief in the Assumption a matter of faith, the Pope invited all Catholics to do some hard thinking about it. What exactly does it say about Mary? What does it tell us about ourselves?

Christians have always seen Mary as the holiest of God's creatures, one who outdid all others in both hearing the word of God and keeping it. The angel who called on her at Nazareth addressed her as "God's favored one," chosen to give birth to the Messiah. The faithful understood these words to mean Mary was not only totally without sin; she was moreover untouched by the consequences of our race's ancient fall from grace. Thus, when her days on earth were over, she passed instantly to eternal bliss. In *The Book of Revelation* the author sees in heaven "a woman clothed with the sun" *(12: 1)*. From earliest times Christians have seen in this woman a likeness to Mary.

That she was worthy of heaven and now dwells there is not, however, what we honor Mary for today. The same could be said of any of the saints. Rather, this feast honors the manner of her entrance to heaven, different from that of any other creature.

Saint Paul tells us that on Judgment Day all those who fall asleep in Christ will rise from the dead *(1 Cor. 15)*. Their risen bodies, however, will not be the same as on earth, for they will no longer be subject to decay and death. "The trumpet will sound, the dead will be raised, and we will be changed. For that which is incorruptible must clothe itself with incorruptibility" *(52-53)*. We should not think of heaven, then, as a place where disembodied spirits will swirl around in an eternal vacuum. The bodies of those who will be judged worthy of heaven are destined to pass from what Paul calls an "earthly" into a "heavenly" state *(36-47)*, but will remain bodies nonetheless. As bodies they will enjoy eternal bliss.

Mary has already attained that heavenly state. That is what we mean by the doctrine of the Assumption. Since she was immune from original sin, her body did not suffer the corruption that is the consequence of that sin. God did not, in the words of the Papal definition, allow "decay to touch her body." Instead, when her time on earth was over, she passed (was assumed) instantly, body and soul, to final beatitude.

What we celebrate today, then, is not a purely spiritual gift that God has bestowed on Mary, but one inherent in her flesh. She is not the only saint who enjoys heavenly bliss today, but she is the only one already endowed with a glorified body. Her body was not allowed to rot, as ours will, in the grave. All others must await the final judgment for their bodies and souls to be reunited and together clothed with immortality. Even now, however, Mary is in final glory.

What lesson can we draw from Mary's Assumption? This much, at least, that our own bodies, which are destined for the same glorious state as hers, are worthy of reverence. We know only too well how subject they are to disease and decay; worse still, that the flesh they are made of is weak and easily falls prey to sin. We know too, or should know, how misdirected and perilous is the modern fondness for pampering the flesh. But we should also realize how downright unchristian is the notion that our bodies are inherently unholy objects, fit only for sin. This cannot be so, for God has destined them to dwell with him and our Blessed Mother in eternal glory.

The flesh is not evil. The eternal Word became flesh and dwelt in Mary's womb. Genuine Christianity has never taught contempt for the body. Paul calls our bodies temples of the Holy Spirit *(1 Cor. 3: 16-17)*. Today's feast reminds us that this temple is made for eternity and should be treated with appropriate respect. Mary, body and soul, has gone ahead of us to everlasting bliss, where she awaits our joining her.

A TRIUMPH?

September 14: Triumph of the Cross.
Jn. 3: 13-17.

❖❖❖

The cross is *the* symbol of Christianity. Crosses mark our churches and adorn our altars; we begin and end our prayers with the sign of the cross; at the close of Mass the priest blesses the people by moving his right hand in the form of a cross. So familiar is this symbol that we are in danger of forgetting that in the beginning it was not a mere ornament or gesture but a most efficient form of capital punishment. That is why the title of today's feast contains a glaring oxymoron, an enormous paradox—the "triumph" of the cross.

Triumph means victory, something we glory in. Where is the triumph in capital punishment? Try switching the image to a gas chamber or an electric chair. No one would employ those as symbols of victory. But death by poison gas or electrocution is downright benign when compared with death by crucifixion.

Mankind has possibly never devised a more exquisitely painful means of execution, certainly none more degrading. Crucifixion first appeared in Persia about five centuries before Christ. Eventually the rulers of the Roman empire adopted it, but only for the most atrocious crimes and even then only if the criminal were a slave or member of a conquered nation. To crucify a fellow Roman citizen would be unthinkable.

A crucifixion got under way with a procession. The criminal, flanked by soldiers and prodded by whips, lugged a cross beam on his shoulders as he staggered and stumbled through crowded lanes. On reaching the place of execution the soldiers stripped the victim, then stretched him out on the ground while they nailed his hands to the horizontal beam. Finally, this beam was hoisted and fixed to the vertical pole already in place. The criminal's feet, about five feet from the ground, were then nailed to the wood. Death usually came within hours, although some wretches survived for days, howling and screeching with pain and thirst. They shouted obscenities at their executioners and cursed the fate that had brought them to this end.

We find it hard to believe today, but crucifixion was a popular spectator sport. Its usual location was a hill, giving the whole town a good view. The hill where Jesus died was just outside the city wall;

his last hours were plainly visible to all in Jerusalem, and all were mesmerized by the sight. What they saw was a man whose days had ended in disgrace. None saw the scene as a triumph. The prophet of Nazareth had failed.

Through the years many more have also have been mesmerized by this scene, but with a difference. Where those in Jerusalem saw defeat, generations of Christians have seen victory. Why?

First, as Paul wrote to the Philippians, because Jesus accepted his cross willingly. He did not curse his fate, as did the other two in the hill, but "humbled himself, becoming obedient to death, even death on a cross" *(2: 8)*. Jesus was not on Calvary because he had been compelled to yield to superior force. True, Judas had set a trap for him, but he had walked into it with eyes open, fully aware that he was walking to a death fit for criminals and slaves. But he also knew that by this kind of death he accomplished the task his Father had set for him. Accepting the cross was a triumph of will over instinct.

Second and more important, consider the motive Jesus had for his willing acceptance of the cross. Among those present on Calvary was one man who knew exactly what his motive was. This was Nicodemus, a Pharisee who secretly sided with Jesus. He knew that Jesus was dying for love. Jesus had told him so.

Months earlier Nicodemus had visited Jesus by night to ask about his teaching, and in a single sentence Jesus had summed up both the meaning of his life and the motive for his death: "God so loved the world that he gave his only Son, so that everyone who believes in him might not perish but might have eternal life...that the world might be saved through him." God gave Jesus to the world out of love for us, and Jesus gave his life on the cross out of that same love. He wanted to save us.

Young folk, who take the lyrics of romantic songs seriously, think of love as a pleasing emotion, and they are right. To love and to be loved give the warmest pleasure. But most soon discover that love has a price, that its very pleasure demands that one be willing to sacrifice for the sake of the beloved. Most parents know this, and their children soon learn it too. The deepest loves and the staunchest friendships thrive only because genuine lovers and true friends are skilled in the art of sacrifice. For them giving counts more than getting.

The Christian cross is a symbol of triumph because on it took place the greatest sacrifice in history. Jesus not only died, he died *this* way, and he did so out of love for us.

THE WHOLE CROWD OF THEM

November 1: All Saints.
Mt. 5: 1-12.

We can begin by dismissing the notion that the feast of All Saints is a kind of celestial Academy Award ceremony, with trophies going only to those who have graced the world with smashing performances of Christian virtue. Actually, we should think of it rather as a kind of God-sponsored Amateur Hour. Today the Church asks us to join in a cheer, not just for a few superstars of sanctity, but also for the army of obscure, unheralded winners of eternal life, heaven's silent majority. No books tell their story, no Christian calendars feature their names. All we know is this simple fact: *they made it.*

They lived, died, did time in Purgatory, and now enjoy eternal bliss. How many are they? We hear so much about how hard it is to live by the gospel that some may imagine only a handful stagger across the finish line. But Scripture, our only authority on the subject, paints a different picture.

In *The Book of Revelation* the writer beholds a mob scene in heaven "a great multitude, which no one could count, from every nation, race, people, and tongue," and soon learns that this crowd consists of those "who have survived the time of great distress" *(7: 9-14)*. The survivors, then, are many.

At the Last Supper Jesus sounded a similar note, assuring his apostles of "many dwelling places" in his Father's house *(Jn. 14:2)*. Is it conceivable that God will allow those dwelling places to remain forever untenanted?

But did not Jesus also warn that the road to eternal life is narrow, rugged, and hard to find? Yes, but it was precisely to help us find and hold on to this road that he came to earth. He did not live and die in vain. No one is guaranteed salvation, but we can be certain that many who now have homes in heaven wandered far and often from the narrow path while still on earth. Those sinners of yesterday have become blessed saints in heaven today. God's grace did the trick.

One reason the Church gives us this feast is to remind us that with the same grace we too can be saints. We should all look forward to the day when we will be part of the throng that the author of *Revelation* saw before God's throne, joining their celestial celebration on this feast of All Saints.

What, me a saint? Of course. Not canonized, to be sure, but a saint nonetheless. Sainthood is the ambition of every serious Christian. We all want to go to heaven, and to be in heaven is, in the truest sense of the word, to be a saint.

Jesus made no secret of how we can become saints, how we must strive to live if we wish to join his company in heaven. His directions are on every page of the gospels, but nowhere more luminously so than in the Sermon on the Mount. Today's gospel, from the opening of that sermon, contains the beatitudes, thumbnail instructions from Jesus Christ on how to be a saint.

The American historian, James Truslow Adams, wrote that it would be "a good idea...to muffle every telephone, stop every motor and halt all activity for an hour some day, to give people a chance to ponder for a few minutes on what it is all about, why they are living, and what they really want." He probably thought this "good idea" was also an startlingly original idea, but actually it has been around for ages. One reason the Church tells Catholics to attend Mass every Sunday is precisely to give us all a chance to consider "what it is all about."

If the most important "why" of living is to serve God and help others do the same, if "what we really want" is to live with God forever in heaven, then we should welcome the moments the Mass gives us to ponder the words of Jesus Christ. And our pondering should not stop as soon as the priest gives the final blessing at the close of Mass. The Scripture readings usually give enough food for thought to last through the week.

Try it out with today's gospel. Go over it privately, slowly, personally. Make it fresh by re-wording each beatitude. Instead of "Blessed are...." say, "I will reach heaven if I am...."

Think of how different the world would be if each of us made a conscious effort to be "poor in spirit," that is, not to allow material possessions be the preoccupation of our lives but instead to be generous with all we own; to "mourn," that is, to sympathize with all who are in need; to show mercy and forgiveness to those who injure us; to make God the object of deepest longings, put him first in all our decisions; to be instruments of peace rather discord; to accept cheerfully whatever sufferings we must endure as followers of Christ.

Try ticking off the beatitudes one by one. Spending a minute mulling over each of them could change our lives. It could even give us top billing in the Amateur Hour of uncanonized saints.

WHERE "FOUL CRIMES...ARE BURNT AND PURGED AWAY"

November 1: All Souls.

1. Jn. 6: 37-40; 2. Jn. 11: 17-27 or 21-27; 3. Jn. 14: 1-6.

❖❖❖

Years ago a well-known magazine editor and health faddist boasted that he expected to live forever. His sensible diet and program of exercises would prove that far from being inevitable, death is just another preventable disease. Most people dismissed him as a fool, of course, and were not surprised when one morning they found his name in the obituaries, one more proof that the fool-killer comes for us all in the end.

Has it ever occurred to you that the Christian notion of death *sounds* much like that of this loony editor? Of course we realize we will all die in the sense that one day we will take our last breath on earth. But for a Christian, death does not mean total cessation of life. In the Creed we proclaim that we believe in "life everlasting." We too expect to live forever.

Sacred Scripture makes this point over and over. To the congregation at Capernaum Jesus promised that those entrusted to him by his Father would have "eternal life," that he would "raise" them "on the last day." To the mourning Martha he declared that whoever believes in him "shall never die." And at the close of the Last Supper he gladdened the hearts of his apostles with the assurance that in heaven there is no housing shortage, but rather "many dwelling places."

All Souls is a day for recalling these promises. Our thoughts turn to family members and friends who have departed, but with hope rather than in sorrow. The prayer in today's first Mass asks God to "strengthen our hope that all our departed brothers and sisters share in his (Christ's) resurrection."

This is also a day of prayer that the sufferings of these departed be lessened. While we believe that heaven has many dwelling places, we also believe that Purgatory, heaven's vestibule, has many sufferings. Praying for the relief of these sufferings is a practice we have inherited from the earliest Christians. Without a belief in Purgatory some of the writings they left on the walls of catacombs would make no sense. Souls in heaven need no prayers; souls eternally damned can use none. Our prayers are for those in the middle area of Purgatory.

Why Purgatory? In the first act of *Hamlet,* Shakespeare shows his awareness of traditional Catholic doctrine. There the ghost of Hamlet's father moans that he expects his torments to last *"Till the foul crimes done in my days of nature / Are burnt and purged away."* Shakespeare wrote poetry, not theology. But behind these words is the traditional doctrine of Purgatory.

A theologian might point out that the "foul crimes" the ghost speaks of must have been either venial sins or grave sins that have been forgiven but not wholly made up for. Otherwise the ghost would not be in Purgatory at all. In Purgatory not only do such sins receive the punishment they deserve, but their after-effects are wiped clean. We all know from experience that even after we have repented of our sins and received God's pardon, our hearts can remain cluttered with the debris that sin leads behind—pride, sensuality, and the selfish cravings our "foul crimes" have fostered. That we have made our peace with God does not automatically mean we are ready to dwell in his presence. Purgatory is where God gets us ready.

Purgatory is a consoling doctrine. Few of us can face death as smugly as the American writer Thoreau who, when a kindly aunt leaned over his deathbed to inquire, "Henry, have you made your peace with God?" is said to have replied, "I was not aware that we had quarreled." Most of us are only too aware that we have quarreled with God, or at least slighted him. If death were to strike us this instant, our instinct would be to cringe with shame from his gaze and like the apostle Peter blurt out, "Depart from me, Lord, for I am a sinful man" *(Lk. 5: 8).*

The ghost of Hamlet's father describes the pains of Purgatory in terms so harrowing that I will not repeat them here. Even though these are healing pains rather than pains of festering infection, even though the souls that suffer them know they are deserved and that with each moment of suffering the bliss of heaven is closer, the pains of Purgatory are real.

During this month of November we do our part to relieve those sufferings, praying especially for those close to us who have left this world. Their souls, we know, have not been annihilated. Some may have already entered the domain of "light, happiness, and peace" and begun to "share forever the vision of God's glory." But many must still be in the antechamber of Paradise, where the blemishes that their souls accumulated during life are purged away. These want our help.

For them and for all the faithful departed we pray today, as we trust that someday others will do the same for us.

GOD'S HOUSE IS OUR HOUSE

November 9: Dedication of St. John Lateran.
Lk. 19: 1-10.

❖❖❖

Most liturgical feasts celebrate a person, either one of the Persons of the Trinity or some great saint. Today is an exception. This feast celebrates a physical church, the oldest and most venerable in Christendom, the Roman basilica (we would call it a cathedral) of St. John Lateran. Today this church is one of the principal tourist attractions in Rome. The "John" in its title is for the basilica's patron, John the Baptist, the fiery forerunner of Jesus Christ. "Lateran" derives from the ground on which the basilica stands, which in ancient times belonged to the wealthy Laterani family of Rome.

The first Lateran church was built by the emperor Constantine in the fourth century. After several fires and renovations, this was transformed during the fourteenth century into the basilica that still stands. Since for centuries the Pope, the bishop of Rome, resided on Lateran territory, this became his parish church. Although he now lives in Vatican City, the Holy Father remains pastor of St. John Lateran to this day.

Even after we have learned this piece of history, however, the reason for today's celebration can be puzzling. Only rarely does any feast replace the regular Sunday Mass. Today, however, in all churches the Latin rite Mass will probably be offered in honor of this basilica in Rome, an edifice relatively few Catholics have seen and most have never even heard of.

John Lateran is certainly a splendid piece of architecture, but by no means the finest in the world. Even if it were, of what interest is this to Catholics in far-off places like Manhattan or Manila? It is also an important church, but not the most important, hardly in the same class as the basilica of Saint Peter in the Vatican. Even if it were, doesn't it seem strange to make such a fuss over a merely physical edifice?

Does any structure of stone deserve the same kind of veneration we give to a saint? The importance of a church is that it is God's house, where the Eucharist is present and the people of God gather to pray and receive the sacraments. In these respects all churches are equal, a tumble-down chapel as worthy of awe and respect as the greatest cathedral of Europe.

We do have good reason to pay special honor to the basilica of John Lateran, however, and it is simply this: because of her history she has won the title, "mother and chief of all the churches of Rome and of the world." In honoring John Lateran, then, we honor churches everywhere, our own parish church included. They are all, like their mother, houses of God.

Scripture recounts the labor the Jewish people put into building their temple, and today's first reading shows the delight they took in flooding it with their prayers and hymns. The temple was the greatest source of self-esteem for the Jews of old, the center of their worship. There they offered sacrifice to the true God, seeking his protection in their struggles. Our parish churches deserve no less pride and care.

Any place where Mass is celebrated is God's local temple. Wherever people worship—whether it be a nipa hut in Mindanao, a village school in Nigeria, of the lounge of a ship on the high seas—God is there. He needs no artistic trappings to receive our worship or to meet us in the sacraments.

Some churches, especially in Europe, are famous for their architecture and artistic treasures. Gaping tourists as well as serious students stroll through their aisles with the same mixture of nonchalance and intensity they display in the richest art museums. As long as they are well-behaved and do not disturb those who are in church to pray, these visitors are welcome. But they miss the meaning of the art they are admiring if they ignore the faith that motivated it, the urge their ancestors felt to build a dwelling fit for the Almighty. The plainest parish church is no less a work of such faith than the most lavish cathedral. The time spent planning for it and the money donated to pay for it had the same purpose, to honor God.

The gospel is not about a church. The house it deals with belonged to Zacchaeus, who until his encounter with Jesus had been one of the least godly men in Jericho, a tax-collector and notorious sinner who had grown rich on money extorted from fellow townsmen. But Jesus entered this house and with him salvation. His presence transformed it into a kind of church and its owner into a follower of the gospel.

We meet Jesus in our parish church as surely as Zacchaeus did in his home. The Lord does not come to this house only on rare occasions, but is present every day. Encountering him there—worshiping him at Mass and meeting him in the sacraments—can change our lives as completely as it did that of Zacchaeus.

OUR SOLITARY BOAST

December 8: Immaculate Concepcion.
Lk. 1: 26-38.

❖ ❖ ❖

"Well, nobody is perfect." How often have we used a cop-out like that to explain away our failures! Its beauty is that it does not twist the facts. No one will challenge our claim to be less than A-One. Perhaps somewhere the world harbors a genius with a perfect IQ score, but none who can repeat the feat every day of the year. Occasionally a baseball pitcher enters the record book with a perfect game, but no pitcher has flawless control every time he ascends the mound. Being human, we are all imperfect. We stumble, we fail, sometimes miserably.

If this is true for IQ scores and athletic achievements, it is even more true in the sphere of morality. We want our own way, even when aware that our way is not the right way, that it hurts our neighbor or violates God's law. And this moral malady is not something we caught from our neighbors or can blame wholly on early environment. Human beings are factory-flawed. At birth, fresh from the assembly line, we were already damaged goods. This we all know from experience. No proof is necessary.

People sometimes ask what is meant by original sin. Theologians may debate how to interpret the biblical account of our first parents' disobedience in the garden of Eden; anthropologists may dismiss the whole of *Genesis* as fable. But no one can reasonably maintain that the truth embodied in the story of the Fall is a fable. We need not be Solomons in wisdom to perceive that some terrible calamity has ravaged our race. We pledge lasting fidelity to God, yet turn tail at the first rumblings of temptation. We reach for the stars, then find pleasure rolling in the muck. That is our human condition.

When Saint Paul lamented, "I do not do the good I want, but I do the evil I do not want," *(Rom. 7: 19)* he was speaking for us all. To be human is to inherit the consequences of the primal act of defiance against our Maker. We are still reeling in the aftershock. That is our experience of original sin.

The consequences of this sin are everywhere. We see them blazoned on daily headlines, they provide material for our most treasured literature, they infest the recesses of our own hearts. Since the dawn of history all members of the human family have hankered after and dallied with forbidden fruit.

All except two: Jesus and his mother. Both were human, but both were exceptions who escaped the common fate of our race. Mary is the exception we celebrate today. Some people imagine the doctrine of the Immaculate Conception involves some impenetrable mystery. Actually, it is one of the least difficult doctrines of our faith to grasp. It means simply that Mary is what we all wish we were, free from the shackles of self-love and perverse longings. She was "full of grace," never disfigured by the pockmarks of sin or even teased by a hunger for sin. God made her that way, to be fit to give birth to his Son.

Today we take time out to honor Mary for this privilege. Doing so is an old tradition. From the earliest centuries the Church has sung songs to Mary, hailing her as the holiest child of Adam to walk the earth. How could she be otherwise? God chose her to be the mother of the Incarnate Word. She was, in the words of the angel who brought her the news of her glorious destiny, God's "favored one." The Lord was always "with her."

After centuries of mulling over the sinlessness of Mary, the Church formally declared the doctrine of the Immaculate Conception. Here are the words of the papal definition in 1854: "From the first instance of her conception, by the grace and privilege of Almighty God, and in consideration of the merits of Jesus Christ, the Savior of the human race, the Virgin Mary was preserved and exempted from the strain of original sin."

These words are understandably cold, the product of emotionless theological analysis. But on this feast we want more than an intellectual grasp of the Immaculate Conception. Today let us sing the praise of Mary from our hearts.

We do not hesitate to feel pride when a fellow countryman captures a gold medal in the Olympics; a brother has the right to lead the applause for a sister who gets top honors at graduation; crowds of admirers greet astronauts returning home from a journey through outer space. Today the Church asks us to celebrate Mary's unparalleled goodness in a similar spirit.

Throughout the world today Catholics cheer Mary, who now reigns as Queen of Heaven. Except for her divine Son, she is the only member of our race whose soul was never blemished by acts of sin or even ruffled by the urge to sin. In the words of the English poet Wordsworth, she is "Our tainted Nature's solitary boast." Today is our day for boasting.

About the Author

Joseph V. Landy, S.J. was born in 1924 in New York State, where he joined the Jesuits at the age of seventeen. In addition to degrees in philosophy and theology (Woodstock College), he has degrees in English from Fordham University in New York and Oxford University in England. His career as a priest has been spent mostly teaching, and wherever he taught he also preached.

Father Landy spent five years at the Ateneo de Manila (Philippines), where he taught courses in English from 1966 to 1971. He also spent five years each at Fordham University (New York) and Saint Peter's College (New Jersey), thirteen years at the University of Nigeria, and a year each as visiting professor at LeMoyne College (Syracuse) and Loyola University (New Orleans).

The author lives at Murray-Weigel Hall, a Jesuit residence adjoining Fordham University campus in The Bronx, New York, where he spends his days in three pleasant and rewarding activities—reading, writing, and praying.

